SOURCES FOR FORGING THE MODERN WORLD

Edited by James Carter and Richard Warren

NEW YORK   OXFORD
OXFORD UNIVERSITY PRESS

Oxford University Press is a department of the University of Oxford.
It furthers the University's objective of excellence in research, scholarship,
and education by publishing worldwide. Oxford is a registered trade mark
of Oxford University Press in the UK and certain other countries.

Published in the United States of America by Oxford University Press
198 Madison Avenue, New York, NY 10016, United States of America.

For titles covered by Section 112 of the US Higher Education
Opportunity Act, please visit www.oup.com/us/he for the
latest information about pricing and alternate formats.

Library of Congress Cataloging-in-Publication Data

Names: Carter, James Hugh, editor. | Warren, Richard A., 1961- editor.
Title: Sources for forging the modern world / edited by James Carter and
   Richard Warren.
Description: New York, NY : Oxford University Press, [2019]
Identifiers: LCCN 2018011607 | ISBN 9780190901936 (pbk.)
Subjects: LCSH: History, Modern. | History, Modern–Sources.
Classification: LCC D208 .S575 2019 | DDC 909.08–dc23
LC record available at https://lccn.loc.gov/2018011607

9 8 7 6 5 4 3 2 1

Printed by Sheridan Books, Inc., United States of America

CONTENTS

INTRODUCTION

HOW TO USE THIS SOURCEBOOK

In *Sources for Forging the Modern World*, we try to convey the excitement and challenge of doing history: working with sources to construct credible explanations of life in the past and change over time. In this sourcebook, we have selected a group of documents we think useful for helping students practice the craft of historical analysis. Here, we offer some suggestions for how to make the most of this sourcebook.

It is important to emphasize at the outset that historical research is broader and, frankly, more chaotic than a reader of this sort suggests. For one thing, as we noted in the *Forging* text, there are many kinds of primary sources, not only written documents, but also photographs, paintings, music, even buildings, and other objects. In the pages that follow, you will find a wide variety of written primary sources—speeches, letters, memoirs, government documents, and so on—but no other kinds of primary sources. The illustrations in the *Forging* text provide examples and descriptions of other kinds of primary sources. Your instructors may provide you with even more sources with which to work and guidance about how to work with them.

Most of the documents in this sourcebook are translations of primary sources into English. In cases where the documents were produced originally in languages other than English, there were often multiple translations, accompanied by controversies over the best way to translate key ideas from the original languages into English. We have tried to provide you with translations that are accepted by scholars as conveying the authors' original intent. You will see in many documents text that appears within brackets. These are notes that were added by the translators to improve the readers' comprehension of the document. In addition, for some documents we have embedded within the texts additional translation, context or information that we think is useful. Those notes appear in brackets and italics and bear the attribution "—*Ed.*", which means that the additional text comes "from the editors" of this sourcebook.

We have chosen these sources specifically because we believe that analyzing and discussing them will help you understand major themes in modern world history. To help you in this undertaking, we have provided questions at the end of each document to help you reflect on the historical insights that might be gained. These aren't easy questions with simple answers; they are intended to help you think about how primary sources connect to bigger research questions. Bear in mind that most of the sources you will read in these pages are short excerpts of much longer documents. If you were doing historical research on your own, you would have to develop your own questions and make your own decisions about what parts of individual documents were most important for your research, and why.

CONTEXT ANALYSIS

Much of the challenge and reward of working with primary sources involves deciding what kinds of primary sources best serve your research needs. Just finding sources is itself an enormous challenge. In many cases, historians may have in mind an ideal set of primary sources to help them answer their research questions, but that perfect source may never be found, or it may never even have existed. Once a primary source document is located, further mysteries must be solved: Who produced it? When? Was it meant to be a public or a private document? Who saw it? Do similar documents exist? Where might I find them?

Answering these questions is a big part of the research process, but in this sourcebook, we have chosen to provide you with important background information for each document, so that you can practice other research skills. As you engage with each source, take some time to consider how answers to the following questions can help you understand and analyze it:

- Document Type: what kind of document are you reading? For example, is it a speech, a law, or a private letter?
- Author/Producer of Source: who produced the document? Is it an individual or a group? What rank, status, gender, and/or social role do the authors/producers have in their society?
- Motivation, Means, and Audience: Why was the document produced? How was it produced and distributed? Who was the intended audience?
- Context: What was happening in the authors' lives and in the country/region/kingdom/world, at the time the document was being produced?
- Comparison: Is this source unique or rare? Alternatively, is this source just one example of something that is produced regularly by the author or other people like the author, related to the same events or time period?

In sum, as you read the sources themselves, keep asking:

- How do the answers to these contextual questions affect the way you need to read and interpret this document?

CONTENT ANALYSIS

Understanding the context within which a primary source was generated is an important step in historical analysis. Next, as you analyze the content of each primary source, ask questions in the following categories:

- Assertion: What is the document trying to prove/achieve?
- Evidence: What evidence is presented to support the assertions?
- Internal Logic and Truth Claims: How does the document connect assertions with evidence? What does this reveal about the authors' assumptions about how the world works?
- Precision and Limits: Do the authors impose any limits on what is claimed in the source? Are there assertions of universal truths or only very specific observations related to time, place, or other circumstances?
- Verification: What contents of the document could be subject to verification with reference to other sources? What contents cannot be proved or disproved by any measure?

Putting together the answers to all of these contextual and content questions, you will be ready to draw some more general conclusions about how the source can help to build a better understanding of world history as you address the broader questions for consideration that accompany each source.

ABOUT THE EDITORS

James Carter is Professor of History at Saint Joseph's University, Philadelphia, and holds a PhD in Modern Chinese History from Yale University. He is the author of *Creating a Chinese Harbin: Nationalism in an International City, 1916–1932* (Cornell University Press, 2002) and *Heart of Buddha, Heart of China* (Oxford University Press, 2010), among other publications. When not teaching Forging the Modern World, he writes about the history of cultural interactions between China and the West.

Richard Warren is Professor of History at Saint Joseph's University, where he has served on the faculty since 1995. He is the author of numerous works on the political culture of modern Mexico, including *Vagrants and Citizens: Politics and the Masses in Mexico City from Colony to Republic* (Scholarly Resources, 2001).

CHAPTER 1

THE MANY WORLDS OF THE FIFTEENTH CENTURY, 1405–1510

1.1 "THE STAGING POST FOR COMPANIES OF PILGRIMS FROM THE SUDAN AND CARAVANS OF MERCHANTS GOING TO CAIRO." IBN KHALDUN, *MUQQADIMAH*, CA. 1378

Ibn Khaldun (1332–1406), born in the city of Tunis, was an important scholar of history and philosophy in the Arab world. He is often considered a forerunner of the disciplines of anthropology and sociology. He is best known for writing *Kitab al-Ibar (The Book of Lessons)*, and especially for its al-Muqqadimah (Introduction), from which the following selections are drawn. Ibn Khaldun's writing stands out from that of his contemporaries because it demonstrates a sense of contingency and emphasizes change over time, observing that places exhibit different characteristics at different periods. Some scholars attribute this sensitivity to change to Ibn Khaldun's experience with the Black Death, which killed many of his family members, including his parents. The following selections do not present Ibn Khaldun's theories of history or politics. Instead, these are descriptive passages about the commercial, social, and cultural conditions of North Africa in the middle of the fourteenth century.

In these desert lands beyond the erg *[dune fields–Ed.]* they have a strange method of digging for running water which is not found in the Tell *[a mountain range in northern Algeria–Ed.]*. A well is dug very deep and its sides are lined until the excavation reaches hard rock. This is cut away with pickaxes until it is thin; then the workmen come up and throw a mass of iron on to it. This breaks the layer of rock over the water, which gushes upwards, fills the well, and overflows on to the surface of the ground as a river. They assert that the water is sometimes so swift that nothing can get out of its way. . . .

[Hilal, chamberlain of Abu Tashfin, ruler of Tlemcen *[a province in northwestern Algeria–Ed.]*, went on the pilgrimage to Mecca.] He set sail in (7)24/1324 and disembarked at Alexandria. He went with the

Source: Ibn Khaldun, *Muqqadimah*, (Paris: Quatremère, 1858–1868), Vol. 3. In Nehemia Levtzion and J. F. P. Hopkins, eds., *Corpus of Early Arabic Sources for West African History* (Princeton, NJ: Markus Wiener, 2001), 340–342.

pilgrims from Egypt in the party of the Commander [of the Caravan]. On the way he met the sultan of the Sudan from Mali, Mansa Musa, and a firm friendship grew up between them.

It [Ghadamis] *[an oasis town in northwestern Libya–Ed.]* has become very populous and extensively urbanized because it has become the staging post for companies of pilgrims from the Sudan and caravans of merchants going to Cairo and Alexandria as they recover from the fatigue of crossing the sandy waste which lies across their path before they reach the Rif *[a mountainous region in present-day Morocco–Ed.]* and the Tell, and a gateway for the pilgrims and merchants to penetrate that waste on their return.

THE SULTAN'S GIFT TO THE KING OF MALI OF THE SUDAN BORDERING ON THE MAGHRIB

Sultan Abu al-Hasan was well known for his ostentatious ways and his presumption to vie with the mightiest monarchs and adopt their customs in exchanging gifts with their peers and counterparts and despatching emissaries to distant kings and far frontiers. In his time the king of Mali was the greatest of the kings of the Sudan and the nearest to his kingdom in the Maghrib *[the region of north Africa that borders the Mediterranean Sea–Ed.]*. Mali was 100 stages distant over desert from the southern frontiers of his realms.

When Abu al-Hasan took Tlemcen from the B. 'Abd al-Wad in 737/1337, seized their authority, and conquered the realms of the Central Maghrib, people talked of the affair of the beleaguering and death of Abu Tashfin [ruler of Tlemcen] and of the aggressiveness of the sultan and his contempt of the enemy and the news spread through all lands. So Sultan Mansa Musa of Mali (who has been mentioned above in the appropriate section) aspired to correspond with him. Accordingly, he deputed some of his subjects to go as emissaries with an interpreter drawn from the veiled men of Sanhaja who are the neighbours of his kingdom. They presented themselves before the sultan and congratulated him on his victory over his enemies. Abu al-Hasan received them with honour, lodged them well, and sent them

away fittingly. Desirous of displaying his customary opulence, he chose, from his household treasury, the rarest and most magnificent objects of Maghribi manufacture and appointed several of his courtiers, including the secretary of chancellery *(katib al diwan)* Abu Talib b. Muhammad b. Abu Madyan and his freedman 'Anbar the eunuch to convey them to the king of Mali (who was by then) Mansa Sulayman, son [sic] of Mansa Musa, because his father had died before the return of his deputation. He also ordered certain of the desert Arabs of the Ma'qil *[a nomadic people of northern Africa–Ed.]* to travel with them in both directions, and this duty was undertaken by 'Ali b. Ghanim, emir of the Awlad Jar Allah of the Ma'qil, who accompanied them on their way in obedience to the sultan's command. This cortege set off across the desert and reached Mali after much effort and long privation. He received them with honour and cordiality and dismissed them honourably. They returned to the one who had sent them accompanied by a deputation of Mali grandees who lauded his authority, acknowledged his rights, and conveyed to him that with which their master had charged them, namely [the expression of] humble submission and readiness to pay the sultan his due and act in accordance with his wishes. Their mission being carried out, the sultan had achieved his aim of vaunting himself over other kings and exacting their submission to his authority and so he fulfilled God's due thanks for His favour.

[In 749/1348–1349, following the conquest of Ifriqiya *[an area comprising what is today Tunisia, eastern Algeria, and western Libya–Ed.]* by Abu al-Hasan, several deputations converged on Constantine.] Among them also was a delegation from the people of Mali, kings of the Sudan in the Maghrib, who had been sent by their king Mansa Sulayman to offer congratulations on the dominion over Ifriqiya.

THE DEPUTATION OF THE SUDAN, THEIR GIFT, AND THE AMAZEMENT WHICH THEY PROVOKED WITH A GIRAFFE

When Sultan Abu al-Hasan sent to the king of the Sudan, Mansa Sulayman, son of Mansa Musa, the gift which has been mentioned in its place, Mansa

Sulayman occupied himself in preparing a comparable gift. For this purpose he collected wonderful and strange objects of his country. Meanwhile Abu al-Hasan died [in 752/1351], and by the time the gift had reached the furthest outpost of Mali at Walatan, Mansa Sulayman had died [also about 760/1358–1359].

Dissension now broke out among the people of Mali. Authority over them became divided and their [rival] kings tried to seize power. They killed each other and were preoccupied with civil war until finally Mansa Jata emerged and consolidated power in his hands. Examining the regions of his empire, he was told of the circumstances of this gift and was informed that it was at Walatan. He ordered it to be sent on to the king of the Maghrib and added to it a giraffe, a strangely shaped and large-framed creature resembling various other animals.

They departed from their country and reached Fez in Safar [in] [7]62/December 1360-January 1361. The day of their arrival was a memorable one. The sultan sat to receive them in the Golden Tower as he would for a review, and criers summoned the people to go out to the open space outside the city. They came out, "hastening out of every mound" until the space was too small for them and they climbed upon each other in the press [a]round the giraffe in amazement at its form. The poets recited poems of eulogy and congratulation and description of the scene.

The deputation presented themselves before the sultan and delivered their messages affirming the affection and sincere friendship [of their king], apologizing for the slow arrival of the gift because of the dissension among the people of Mali and their struggle for power, praising their sultan and the state of their realm. During all this, the interpreter was translating for them and they were twanging their bowstrings in approbation according to their approved custom. They greeted the sultan by scattering dust on their heads in conformity with the custom of non-Arab kings….

Then the king remounted and the assembly dispersed. Talk of it became widespread. The deputation continued to be entertained by the sultan, who died before their departure. His successor, however, continued to give them hospitality until they departed for Marrakesh and from there passed on to the territory of the Dhawi Hassan, Ma'qil Arabs who inhabit the [desert to the south of the] Sus and whose territory marches with that of the Sudan. And from there they rejoined their sultan.

QUESTIONS TO CONSIDER

1. How does this passage describe commerce and trade? What role does long-distance trade or travel play? How is it accomplished? How might this compare with other parts of the world in the same time period?
2. What evidence is available to assess the role of religion in the societies described? Do religious figures or rituals play important roles? What place, if any, do different religions have?

1.2 "ZHENG HE, WHO HAD BEEN SENT TO THE VARIOUS COUNTRIES OF THE WESTERN OCEAN, RETURNED." *MING VERITABLE RECORDS*, 1405–1431

The study and recording of past events has been a central mission of the Chinese government going back to at least the third century BCE. Each ruling dynasty was expected to write the official history of the preceding dynasty. To assist their successors in this task, each dynasty recorded the daily events at court in great detail, which became the raw materials for the dynasty's official history. The "Veritable Records" (like the "Annals" or "Chronicles" of European governments or dynasties) are extensive and invaluable as primary sources.

The *Ming Dynasty Veritable Records (Ming Shilu)* run to 40,000 pages. They describe events of relevance to the imperial court and at times actions of the emperor himself. The selections presented here concern the voyages led by Ming Admiral Zheng He (1371–1433?) on behalf of the Ming court. The seven voyages of Zheng He took place between 1405 and 1433. The following selections date from the first, third, and fourth voyages, conducted between 1405 and 1416. They help illustrate the nature of the voyages, including insights into their itineraries, activities, and goals.

Not all place and personal names recorded in the *shilu* have clear modern referents. In these cases, transliterations of the original Chinese are repeated here.

11 JUL 1405

The eunuch Zheng He and others were sent to take Imperial orders of instruction to the various countries in the Western *[Indian–Ed.]* Ocean, and to confer upon the kings of those countries patterned fine silks and variegated thin silks interwoven with gold thread, as appropriate. (Yong-le reign: Year 3, Month 6, Day 15)

18 JUL 1405

The Zhe-jiang and other regional military commissions were ordered to build 1,180 ocean-going ships. (Yong-le reign: Year 3, Month 6, Day 22)

8 OCT 1407

The new Empress of Heaven temple at Long-jiang was completed. Zhu Zhuo, a vice minister in the Court of Imperial Sacrifice was sent to offer sacrifices and dedicate the temple. At this time, the eunuch Zheng He had returned from his mission to Calicut, Melaka and other *fan [a generic term used to refer to non-Chinese peoples–Ed.]* countries and he said that the spirits had been greatly responsive and helpful. It was for this reason that the temple was erected. (Yong-le reign: Year 5, Month 9, Day 8)

6 JUL 1411

The eunuch Zheng He and others, who had been sent as envoys to the various countries in the Western Ocean, returned and presented Ya-lie Ku-nai-er, the captured king of the country of Sri Lanka, and his family members. Previously, He and the others had been sent as envoys to the various *fan* countries. However, when they reached Sri Lanka, Ya-lie Ku-nai-er was insulting

Source: Geoff Wade, translator, *Southeast Asia in the Ming Shi-lu: An Open Access Resource* (Singapore: Asia Research Institute and the Singapore E-Press, National University of Singapore, 2005). Accessed from epress.nus.edu.sg/msl.

and disrespectful. He wished to harm He, but He came to know of this and left. Ya-lie Ku-nai-er also acted in an unfriendly way to neighbouring countries and repeatedly intercepted and robbed their envoys. All the *fan* countries suffered from his actions. When He returned, he again passed Sri Lanka and the king enticed him to the country. The king then had his son Na-yan demand gold, silver and precious objects, but He would not give these to him. The king then secretly despatched over 50,000 *fan* troops to rob He's ships. They also felled trees to create obstructions and impede He's route of return, so that he could not render assistance. He and the others found out about this and they gathered their force and set off back to their ships. However, the route had already been blocked. He thus spoke to his subordinates, saying: "The majority of the troops have already been despatched. The middle of the country will be empty." He also said: "Our merchants and troops are isolated and nervous and will be unable to act. If they are attacked by surprise, the attackers will achieve their purpose." Thus, he secretly ordered persons to go to the ships by another route with orders that the government troops were to fight to the death in opposing the attackers. He then personally led 2,000 of his troops through a by-path and attacked the royal city by surprise. They took the city and captured alive Ya-lie Ku-nai-er, his family members and chieftains. The *fan* army returned and surrounded the city and several battles were fought, but He greatly defeated them. He and the others subsequently returned to the Court. The assembled ministers requested that the king be executed. The Emperor pitied the king for his stupidity and ignorance and leniently ordered that he and the others be released and given food and clothing. The Ministry of Rites was ordered to deliberate on and select a worthy member of the family to be established as the country's king in order to handle the country's sacrifices. (Yong-le reign: Year 9, Month 6, Day 16)

18 DEC 1412

The eunuch director Zheng He and others were sent to take Imperial orders to the kings of the countries of Melaka, Java, Champa, Samudera, Aru, Cochin, Calicut, Nan-bo-li, Pahang, Kelantan, Jia-yi-le, Hormuz, Bi-la, Liu-shan and Sun-la, and to confer upon them brocaded fine silks, silk gauzes, variegated thin silks and other goods as appropriate. (Yong-le reign: Year 10, Month 11, Day 15)

10 OCT 1415

La-zha Jia-na-yin who had been sent with others by his father Zai-nu-li A-bi-ding, king of the country of Samudera, offered tribute of local products. The eunuch director Zheng He presented the captured leader of the Samuderan bandits Su-gan-la (Alt: Su-wo-la). Previously, He had received orders to go as an envoy to Samudera and to confer upon the king Zai-nu-li A-bi-ding variegated silks and other goods. Su-gan-la (Alt: As above) was the younger brother of the former king and was plotting to kill Zai-nu-li A-bi-ding and seize the throne. He was angered that the envoys did not confer presents upon him and thus led his soldiers, numbering tens of thousands, to intercept and kill the government troops. Thus, He led his forces and the troops of that country in doing battle, with the result that Su-gan-la (Alt: As above) was defeated and fled. He was pursued to the country of Nan-bo-li. There, he was captured together with his wife and children and they were subsequently brought back. At this time, they were presented at the Auxiliary Ministry of War. The Minister Fang Bin said: "Su-gan-la (Alt: As above) has been greatly rebellious and unprincipled. He should be handed over to the judicial offices so that his offences can be punished." Accordingly, it was ordered that the Ministry of Justice mete out punishment in accordance with the law. The Ministry of War was ordered to record the achievements realized by the Imperial troops in the fighting. Thus, Tang Jing, a circulating-official guard commander and Wang Heng, a circulating-official assistant commander, both of the Naval Right Guard; Lin Zi-xuan, a circulating-official commander of the Jin-wu Left (Alt: Right) Guard; Hu Hou (Alt: Hu Jun), a circulating-official assistant commander of the Long-jiang Left Guard, and Ha-zhi, a circulating-official vice commander of the Kuan-he Guard were all given hereditary posts. The Embroidered-Uniform Guard Full Battalion Commanders Lu Tong, Ma Gui, Zhang Tong and Liu Hai were all promoted to circulating-official assistant guard commanders. The other battalion, company and platoon commanders, a total of 140-plus persons, including Wang Fu-heng (Alt: Wang Fu-xiang), were employed in appropriate posts. (Yong-le reign: Year 13, Month 9, Day 8)

28 DEC 1416

As the envoys from the various countries of Calicut, Java, Melaka, Champa, Sri Lanka, Mogadishu, Liu-shan, Nan-bo-li, Bu-la-wa, Aden, Samudera, Ma-lin, La-sa, Hormuz, Cochin, Nan-wu-li, Sha-li-wan-ni and Pahang, as well as from the Old Port Pacification Superintendency, were departing to return home, suits of clothing made from patterned fine silks were conferred upon all of them. The eunuch Zheng He and others were sent with Imperial orders as well as embroidered fine silks, silk gauzes, variegated thin silks and other goods to confer upon the kings of these countries, to confer a seal upon Ke-yi-li, the king of the country of Cochin, and to enfeoff a mountain in his country as the "Mountain Which Protects the Country."

The Emperor personally composed and conferred an inscription for the tablet, as follows:

"The civilizing influences and Heaven and Earth intermingle. Everything which is covered and contained has been placed in the charge of the Moulder, who manifests the benevolence of the Creator. The world does not have two ultimate principles and people do not have two hearts. They are sorrowful or happy in the same way and have the same feelings and desires. How can they be divided into the near and the distant!

One who is outstanding in ruling the people should do his best to treat the people as his children. The Book of Odes says: 'The Imperial domain stretches for thousands of li, and there the people have settled, while the borders reach to the four seas.' The Book of Documents says: 'To the East, extending to the sea, to the West reaching to the shifting sands and stretching to the limits of North and South, culture and civilizing influences reach to the four seas.' I rule all under Heaven and soothe and govern the Chinese and the *yi [non-Chinese peoples–Ed.]*. I look on all equally and do not differentiate between one and the other. I promote the ways of the ancient Sagely Emperors and Perspicacious Kings, so as to accord with the will of Heaven and Earth. I wish all of the distant lands and foreign regions to have their proper places.

Those who respond to the influences and move towards culture are not singular. The country of Cochin is far away in the South-west, on the shore of the vast ocean, further distant than the other *fan* countries. It has long inclined towards Chinese culture and been accepting of civilizing influences. When the Imperial orders arrived, the people there went down on their hands and knees and were greatly excited. They loyally came to allegiance and then, looking to Heaven, they bowed and all said: 'How fortunate we are that the civilizing influences of the Chinese sages should reach us. For the last several years, the country has had fertile soil, and the people have had houses in which to live, enough fish and turtles to eat, and enough cloth and silk to make clothes. Parents have looked after their children and the young have respected their elders. Everything has been prosperous and pleasing. There has been no oppression or contention. In the mountains no savage beasts have appeared and in the streams no noxious fishes have been seen. The sea has brought forth treasures and the forests have produced excellent woods. Everything has been in bountiful supply, several times more bountiful than in ordinary times. There have been no destructive winds, and damaging rains have not occurred. Confusion has been eliminated and there is no evil to be found. This is all indeed the result of the civilizing influences of the Sage.' I possess but slight virtuous power. How could I have been capable of this! Is it not the elders and people who brought this about? I am now enfeoffing Ke-yi-li as king of the country and conferring upon him a seal so that he can govern the people. I am also enfeoffing the mountain in the country as 'Mountain Which Protects the Country.' An engraved tablet is to be erected on this mountain to record these facts forever. It will also be engraved as follows: The high peak which rules the land, guards this ocean state, It spits fire and fumes, bringing great prosperity to the country below, It brings rain and sunshine in a timely way, and soothes away troubles, It brings fertile soil and drives off evil vapours, It shelters the people, and eliminates calamities and disharmony, Families are joyful together, and people have plenty throughout the year, The mountain's height is as the ocean's depths! This poem is inscribed to record all for prosperity." (Yong-le reign: Year 14, Month 12, Day 10)

QUESTIONS TO CONSIDER

1. From the perspective of the Chinese imperial court, what explicit goals for the voyages can you derive from the texts? Beyond these, can additional intentions be inferred?
2. What conclusions can be drawn about the reception of the Chinese in the different ports they visited? How did Chinese travelers engage with the social and political systems of the regions they visited?

1.3 "THERE ALSO CAME ENVOYS FROM RIGA, IUR'EV, KOLYVAN, AND LÜBECK." *TREATY OF NOVGOROD WITH THE HANSEATIC TOWNS*, 1436

The Hanseatic League was a federation of merchant guilds in northern European cities that lasted from the fourteenth to the seventeenth centuries. The League defies many assumptions about modern political organization. It was neither a single territorial state nor a federation of states, though it maintained military forces and signed treaties. As a result, the League's relationship to other political powers and territorial rulers was often a subject of contention and eventually contributed to the League's demise.

The passage presented here describes a treaty between representatives of the League and the city of Novgorod, so-called in modern-day Russia. Novgorod was a republic from the twelfth century until its absorption by the Grand Duchy of Moscow (Moscovy) in the 1470s. Novgorod was one of the original port cities with a Hanseatic League *kontor* (trading post).

The German envoys came to Novgorod the Great. . . . There also came envoys from Riga, Iur'ev (Dorpat), Kolyvan (Reval), and Lübeck, from seventy-three towns on this seacoast and beyond the sea, and from all the merchantry. And the German enjoys . . . concluded an agreement with the Novgorod *posadnik* [mayor–Ed.] Boris Iur'evich, and with the Novgorod *tysiatskii* [local military commander–Ed.] Fedor Iakovlevich, and with the merchant elders, for all of Novgorod, to the effect that German merchants shall have free passage to come to Novgorod the Great and to leave, by water and by land, in accordance with the old oaths sworn upon the cross, and in accordance with this treaty and by this agreement, without any deceit. Likewise did the German envoys . . . conclude an agreement with the Novgorod *posadnik* Boris Iur'evich, and with the Novgorod *tysiatskii* Fedor Iakovlevich, and with the merchant elders Aleksandr and Efrem, and all the merchants' sons, and all of Novgorod the Great, for all the seventy-three towns and for all the merchantry, to the effect that the people of Novgorod should have free passage to travel to the German land and to the German towns, by land and by water, to come and go with their goods,

Source: George Vernadsky, ed., *A Sourcebook for Russian History from Early Times to 1917*, Vol. 1, *Early Times to the Late 17th Century* (New Haven, CT: Yale University Press, 1972), 76–77. Online at www.furthark.com/hanseaticleague/src_pri_1436novgorodhanses.html.

in accordance with the old treaties and in accordance with the old oaths sworn upon the cross, and in accordance with this treaty and by this agreement, without any deceit. And the German merchants shall trade with the merchants of Novgorod in Novgorod the Great or on the Neva [River–Ed.], in accordance with the old oaths sworn upon the cross and in accordance with this treaty and by this agreement, without any deceit. The people of Novgorod shall give legal protection to the Germans as to their brother Novgorodians, and the Germans shall give legal protection to the people of Novgorod as to their brother Germans. And Novgorod the Great shall render justice to Germans who make complaint, in accordance with the old treaties, and in accordance with the old oaths sworn upon the cross, and in accordance with this treaty and by this agreement, without deceit. Likewise shall the Germans render justice to the people of Novgorod who

make complaint, in accordance with the old treaties and in accordance with the old oaths sworn upon the cross, and in accordance with this treaty and by this agreement, without any deceit, on either side. . . . And if any Russian is on the German blacklist, he shall be taken off the blacklist and traded with as before. And as for the people of Novgorod who were under arrest in the German settlement, or who were themselves detaining Germans, the Germans shall not sue the people of Novgorod for this but shall trade with them as before. To all of this the Novgorod *posadnik* Boris Iur'evich, and the Novgorod *tysiatskii* Fedor Iakovlevich, and the merchant elders Aleksandr Matveevich and Efrem Iakovlevich have agreed, for all their towns and for their entire land, and have affixed their seals. Likewise have the German envoys . . . agreed for the seventy-three towns and for their entire land, and affixed their seals to this treaty.

QUESTIONS TO CONSIDER

1. Who are the parties to this treaty? What appear to be the goals of the treaty being negotiated here? What concerns are the negotiators trying to address?
2. How are groups of people in this document identified? What important distinctions separate one group from another, and how are those distinctions determined or enforced?

1.4 "THEY EXCHANGED GOLD UNTIL THEY DEPRESSED ITS VALUE IN EGYPT AND CAUSED ITS PRICE TO FALL." AL-UMARI, *MANSA MUSA'S VISIT TO CAIRO*, 1324

This selection is from the historian al-Umari (1300–1349), describing the visit of the Emperor of Mali, Musa Keita I (ca. 1280–ca. 1337), to Cairo as part of his pilgrimage to Mecca in 1324. Known in many chronicles, including the *Muqqadimah* (Source 1.1) as Mansa Musa, the Emperor ruled over territory in West Africa that includes what today are parts of Mali and Mauritania.

Source: Nehemiah Levtzion and J. F. P. Hopkins, eds., *Corpus of Early Arabic Sources for West African History* (Cambridge, UK: Cambridge University Press, 1981), 269–273. Excerpt online at www.digitalhistory.uh.edu/active_learning/explorations/1492/mansa_musa_visit.cfm.

During Mansa Musa's reign, Mali may have been the world's largest producer of gold. A thriving trade connected West Africa with the Mediterranean and from there with the rest of Europe and the Indian Ocean. Demand for gold made Mali immensely wealthy. Mansa Musa is often described as the wealthiest man ever to have lived, though measuring this sort of claim is very difficult. Images from the time often depicted Mansa Musa on a gold throne holding a giant gold coin and wearing a golden crown.

From the beginning of my coming to stay in Egypt I heard talk of the arrival of this sultan Musa on his Pilgrimage and found the Cairenes eager to recount what they had see[n] of the Africans' prodigal spending. I asked the emir Abu . . . and he told me of the opulence, manly virtues, and piety of his sultan. "When I went out to meet him [he said] that is, on behalf of the mighty sultan al-Malik al-Nasir, he did me extreme honour and treated me with the greatest courtesy. He addressed me, however, only through an interpreter despite his perfect ability to speak in the Arabic tongue. Then he forwarded to the royal treasury many loads of unworked native gold and other valuables. I tried to persuade him to go up to the Citadel to meet the sultan, but he refused persistently saying: "I came for the Pilgrimage and nothing else. I do not wish to mix anything else with my Pilgrimage." He had begun to use this argument, but I realized that the audience was repugnant to him because he would be obliged to kiss the ground and the sultan's hand. I continue[d] to cajole him and he continued to make excuses, but the sultan's protocol demanded that I should bring him into the royal presence, so I kept on at him till he agreed.

When we came in the sultan's presence, we said to him: "Kiss the ground!" but he refused outright saying: "How may this be?" Then an intelligent man who was with him whispered to him something we could not understand and he said: "I make obeisance to God who created me!" then he prostrated himself and went forward to the sultan. The sultan half rose to greet him and sat him by his side. They conversed together for a long time, [and] then Sultan Musa went out. The sultan sent to him several complete suits of honour for himself, his courtiers, and all those who had come with him, and saddled and bridled horses for himself and his chief courtiers. . . .

This man [Mansa Musa] flooded Cairo with his benefactions. He left no court emir nor holder of a royal office without the gift of a load of gold. The Cairenes made incalculable profits out of him and his suite in buying and selling and giving and taking. They exchanged gold until they depressed its value in Egypt and caused its price to fall. . . .

Gold was at a high price in Egypt until they came in that year. The mithqal [about 4.25 grams–Ed.] did not go below 25 dirhams [a unit of currency–Ed.] and was generally above, but from that time its value fell and it cheapened in price and has remained cheap till now. The mithqal does not exceed 22 dirhams or less. This has been the state of affairs for about twelve years until this day by reason of the large amount of gold which they brought into Egypt and spent there. . . .

QUESTIONS TO CONSIDER

1. What was Mansa Musa's impact on Cairo when he traveled through it? What was his relationship with the city? What factors affected that relationship?
2. What does Mansa Musa's pilgrimage suggest about long-distance travel and exchange during this era? What implications does this passage's depiction of the distribution of wealth and power have for your understanding of long-term trends in world history?

1.5 "IF WE WERE WILLING TO BARTER FOR SO MANY RUBIES, HE WOULD AMPLY SATISFY US." *THE ITINERARY OF LUDOVICO DI VARTHEMA OF BOLOGNA*, 1510

Ludovico di Varthema (ca. 1470–1517) was born in Bologna, Italy. Little is known about his life beyond what he describes in an account of his travels between 1502 and 1508, published in Rome in 1510. The book, *The Itinerary of Ludovico di Varthema of Bologna*, recounts Varthema's travels as a soldier of fortune and merchant across the Arabian Peninsula, Persia, East Africa, South Asia, and Southeast Asia, including his service as a guard for a caravan on the *hajj*—the mandatory pilgrimage of the Islamic faithful to the holy city of Mecca mentioned in Source 1.4.

During his travels, Varthema joined a Persian merchant. Together they traveled through South Asia, meeting two (most likely) ethnic Chinese Christian merchants interested in doing business in "Pego" (Pegu, or contemporary Bago), a major port city in southern Burma (Myanmar), and capital of the kingdom often referred to by the same name. The following excerpt is Varthema's description of Pegu and the merchants' transactions with Pegu's ruler.

The city of Pego is on the mainland and is near to the sea. On the left hand of this, that is, towards the east, there is a very beautiful river, by which many ships go and come. The king of this city is a pagan. Their faith, customs, manner of living and dress, are after the manner of Tarnassari; but with respect to their colour, they are somewhat more white. And here, also, the air is somewhat more cold. Their seasons are like ours. This city is walled, and has good houses and palaces built of stone, with lime. The king is extremely powerful in men, both foot and horse, and has with him more than a thousand Christians of the country which has been above mentioned to you. And he gives to each, for pay, six golden pardai per month and his expenses. In this country there is a great abundance of grain, of flesh of every kind, and of fruits of the same as at Calicut. These people have not many elephants, but they possess great numbers of all other animals; they also have all the kinds of birds which are found at Calicut. But there are here the most beautiful and the best parrots I had ever seen. Timber grows here in great quantities, long, and I think the thickest that can possibly be found. In like manner I do not know if there can be found in the world such thick canes as I found here, of which I saw some which were really as thick as a barrel. Civet-cats are found in this country in great numbers, three or four of which are sold for a ducat. The sole merchandise of these people is jewels, that is, rubies, which come from another city called Capellan, which is distant from this thirty days' journey; not that I have seen it, but by what I have heard from merchants. You must know that in the said city, a large pearl and diamond are worth more here than with us, and also an emerald. . . .

On the second day after the return of the king, our Christian companions took us to speak with him. Do not imagine that the King of Pego enjoys as great a reputation as the King of Calicut, although he is so humane and domestic that an infant might speak to him, and he wears more rubies on him than the value of a very large city, and he wears them on all his toes.

Source: *SOAS Bulletin of Burma Research* (Autumn 2004), 2(2): 126–129, ISSN 1479-8484.

And on his legs he wears certain great rings of gold, all full of the most beautiful rubies; also his arms and his fingers [are] all full. His ears hang down half a palm, through the great weight of the many jewels he wears there, so that seeing the person of the king by a light at night, he shines so much that he appears to be a sun. The said Christians spoke with him and told him of our merchandise. The king replied: "That we should return to him the day after the next, because on the next day he had to sacrifice to the devil for the victory which he had gained." When the time mentioned was past, the king, as soon as he had eaten, sent for the said Christians, and for my companion, in order that he might carry to him his merchandise. When the king saw such beautiful corals, he was quite astonished and greatly pleased; for, in truth, among the other corals there were two branches, the like of which had never before entered India. This king asked what people we were. The Christians answered: "Sir, these are Persians." Said the king to the interpreter: "Ask them if they are willing to sell these things." My companions answered: "That the articles were at the service of his highness." Then the king began to say: "That he had been at war with the King of Ava for two years, and on that account he had no money; but that if we were willing to barter for so many rubies, he would amply satisfy us." We caused him to be told by these Christians that we desired nothing further from him than his friendship,—that he should take the commodities and do whatever he pleased. The Christians repeated to him what my companion had charged them to say, by telling the king that he might take the corals without money or jewels. He hearing this liberality answered: "I know

that the Persians are very liberal, but I never saw one so liberal as this man;" and he swore by God and by the devil that he would see which would be the more liberal, he or a Persian. And then he desired one of his confidential servants to bring him a certain little box which was two palms in length, worked all round in gold, and was full of rubies, within and without. And when he had opened it, there were six separate divisions, all full of different rubies; and he placed it before us, telling us we should take what we wished. My companion answered: "O, sir, you show me so much kindness, that by the faith which I bear to Mahomet [*Muhammad, the prophet of Islam–Ed.*] I make you a present of all these things. And know, sir, that I do not travel about the world to collect property, but only to see different people and different customs." The king answered: "I cannot conquer you in liberality, but take this which I give you." And so he took a good handful of rubies from each of the divisions of the said casket, and gave them to him. These rubies might be about two hundred, and in giving them he said: "Take these for the liberality you have exercised towards me." And in like manner he gave to the said Christians two rubies each, which were estimated at a thousand ducats, and those of my companions were estimated at about one hundred thousand ducats. Wherefore by this he may be considered to be the most liberal king in the world, and every year he has an income of about one million in gold. And this because in his country there is found much lacca [*the source of lacquer–Ed.*], a good deal of sandal-wood, very much brazil-wood, cotton and silk in great quantities, and he gives all his income to his soldiers.

QUESTIONS TO CONSIDER

1. How can this excerpt help us to understand the relationship among religion, ethnicity, and economic activity in Asia during the early sixteenth century?
2. What appear to be the most important factors that determine the value of the goods being exchanged? Why?

1.6 "THEY BRING THEIR PALE GOLD AND GIVE IT IN EXCHANGE." MA HUAN, *OVERALL SURVEY OF THE OCEAN'S SHORES*, 1433

Ma Huan (ca. 1380–1460) was a Chinese translator and scholar who traveled on several of Zheng He's voyages. He was a Muslim, which aided in his ability to observe Muslim holy sites and cities such as Mecca. His understanding of Arabic enabled him to interpret during Zheng He's voyages in the Middle East. He began writing a book in 1416, after his first voyage, and modified it after subsequent voyages in 1421 and 1431. The book, titled *Yingya Shenglan (The Overall Survey of the Ocean's Shores)*, was first published in 1433 (a revised edition appeared in 1451).

This text can be compared with the official reports contained in the *Veritable Records* (see Source 1.2). The two passages address different dates and locations, but even so, you can see the ways that the same or similar experiences can yield different historical information depending on the nature of the observer and what the observer is trying to learn. The selection presented here records Ma Huan's impressions of Hormuz, an important port city on the strait of the same name, in modern Iran. Hormuz will also play a role in Source 3.2.

HORMUZ

Setting sail from the country of Ku-li *[Calicut–Ed.]*, you go towards the north-west; [and] you can reach [this place] after travelling with a fair wind for twenty five days. The capital lies beside the sea and up against the mountains.

Foreign ships from every place and foreign merchants travelling by land all come to this country to attend the market and trade; hence the people of the country are all rich.

The king of the country and the people of the country all profess the Muslim religion; they are reverent, meticulous, and sincere believers; every day they pray five times, [and] they bathe and practise abstinence. The customs are pure and honest. There are no poor families; if a family meets with misfortune resulting in poverty, everyone gives them clothes and food and capital, and relieves their distress.

The limbs and faces of the people are refined and fair, and they are stalwart and fine-looking. Their clothing and hats are handsome, distinctive, and elegant.

In their marriage- and funeral-rites they all obey the regulations of the Muslim religion. . . . .

In their diet the people must use butter; it is mixed and cooked in with their food. In the market roast mutton, roast chicken, roast meat, wafercakes, *ha-la-sa* [most likely a meat and grain dish] and all kinds of cereal foods—all these are for sale. Many families of two or three persons do not make up a fire to prepare a meal—they merely buy cooked food to eat.

The king uses silver to cast a coin named a *ti-na-erh*; the diameter, [in terms of] our official *ts'un*, is six *fen*; [0.7 inch] on the reverse side it has lines; the weight is four *fen* on our official steelyard [0.0479 troy ounces]; it is in universal use.

Their writing is all in Muslim characters.

Source: Ma Huan, *Overall Survey of the Ocean's Shores* [1433], Trans. and ed. J.V.G. Mills. Hakluyt Society Extra Series, No. XLII (Cambridge, UK: Cambridge University Press, 1971), 136–146, 165–172.

Their market-places have all kinds of shops, with articles of every description; only they have no wine-shops; [for] according to the law of the country wine-drinkers are executed.

Civil and military officials, physicians, and diviners are decidedly superior to those of other places. Experts in every kind of art and craft—all these they have.

Their juggling and acrobatic performances are none of them unusual; but there is one kind [of unusual performance] [in which] a goat mounts a high pole;[this] is most amusing; for this trick they use a wooden pole about one *chang* long *[a little more than ten feet–Ed.]*; on the top of this wooden pole, it is only just possible to set the four hooves of the goat on the wood; they take the pole, set it firmly on the ground, and hold it steady; [then] the man leads up a small white billy-goat; he claps his hands and does a sing-song; the goat capers about to the beat of the drum, and comes up close to the pole.

First, it takes its two fore-feet and places them firmly on the pole; next, it takes its two hind-feet and with one jerk sets them on the pole; next, a man takes a wooden pole and leans it over in front of the goat's legs; the goat again takes its two fore-feet and places them on the top of the pole; afterwards it takes its two hind-legs and raises them up with a jerk, whereupon the man holds the pole steady; while standing on the tops of the two poles, the goat makes posturing movements like dancing gestures; [a man] brings another pole and joins it on, adding five or six lengths in succession to the tops and increasing the height by about a [foot] after the [goat] has stopped dancing, it stands upon the middle pole; whereupon the man pushes away the pole and catches the goat in his hands.

Then again, he will order [the goat] to lie on the ground and appear to be dead; when he orders it to stretch out its fore-legs, it stretches out its fore [legs]; [and] when he orders it to stretch out its hind-legs, it stretches out its hind-[legs].

Then again, there is [a man who] takes along a large black monkey about [three feet] tall; after it has performed all manner of clever tricks, [the man] directs a bystander to take a kerchief, fold it up several times, and tie it tightly [a]round both eyes of the monkey; he directs a different person to give

the monkey a surreptitious hit on the head and hide himself in the thick of the crowd; after this [the man] releases the kerchief and directs [the monkey] to seek out the person who struck him on the head; however vast the crowd, the monkey goes straight to the man who originally [struck him] and picks him out; it is most strange.

The climate of the country [includes] cold weather and hot weather; in the spring the flowers bloom, and in the autumn the leaves fall; they have frost, [but] no snow; rain is rare, [but] the dew heavy.

They have one large mountain, the four faces of which produce four kinds of articles. One face produces salt, like that of the sea-side-red in colour; the people chisel out a lump with an iron hoe-like quarrying stone; some lumps weigh thirty or forty *chin* [40 50 pounds]; moreover, it is not damp, and when they want to eat it, they pound it into powder for use. One face produces red earth—like the red colour of vermilion. One face produces white earth—like lime; it can be used for white-washing walls. One face produces yellow earth—like the yellow colour of turmeric.

In all cases chiefs are ordered to superintend [the quarrying]. Of course they have travelling merchants who come from every place to purchase [these products] and sell them to be used.

The land produces rice and wheat, [but] not much; it is all bought in different places and comes here to be sold; the price is extremely cheap.

For fruits they have walnuts, [almond fruit], pine-nuts, pomegranates, raisins, dried peaches, apples, Persian dates, water-melons, cucumbers, onions, leeks, shallots, garlic, carrots, melons, and other such things. The carrots—red, and as large as a lotus-root—are very plentiful. The melons are very large; some [stand two feet] high. The walnuts have a thin white shell, which breaks when you squeeze it in the hand. The pine-nuts are about [two inches] long.

The raisins are of three or four kinds; one kind resembles a dried date and is purple; one kind is as large as a lotus-seed, has no pips, and is candied; [and] one kind is round, as large as a white bean, and rather white in colour. The almond fruit resembles a walnut; it is pointed, long, and white; [and] inside there is a kernel which in flavour surpasses the flesh of the walnut. The pomegranates are as large as tea-cups. The apples are as big as [one's] fist–very fragrant and delicious. . . .

In this place they have all the precious merchandise from every foreign country. Further, there are [sapphires, rubies, topaz, emeralds, diamonds, . . . coral-tree beads, branches, and stems, and golden amber, amber beads, rosary beads, wax amber, black amber . . . all kinds of beautiful jade utensils, crystal utensils, and ten kinds of flowered pieces of brocaded velvet . . . woolens of every kind, . . . felt, *mo* crepe, *mo* gauze, all kinds of foreign kerchiefs with blue and red silk embroidery, and other such kinds of things—all these are for sale. Camels, horses, mules, oxen, and goats are plentiful. . . .

Again, [the place] produces a kind of animal called "fly-o'er-the-grass"; the foreign name is *hsi-ya-kuo-shih*

[most likely a Eurasian lynx] it is as big as a large cat; all over its body [it has markings] exactly like tortoise-shell or cantharides; the two ears are pointed and black; its nature is mild, not vicious; if lions, leopards, or other such fierce beasts see it, they prostrate themselves on the ground; indeed it is king among the beasts.

The king of this country, too, took a ship and loaded it with lions, [giraffes], horses, pearls, precious stones, and other such things, also a memorial to the throne [written on] a golden leaf; [and] he sent his chiefs and other men, who accompanied the treasure-ships despatched by the Emperor, which were returning from the Western Ocean; [and] they went to the capital and presented tribute.

QUESTIONS TO CONSIDER

1. What is your overall impression of the place Ma Huan is describing? What seems to be its relationship to other parts of the world?
2. How do Ma Huan's observations compare with those made in the *Ming Veritable Records* (Source 1.2)? In which way is each source more or less useful than the other in helping us understand the voyages of Zheng He?

CHAPTER 2

THE NEW GLOBAL INTERFACE, 1486–1639

2.1 "WE SHALL POWERFULLY ENTER INTO YOUR COUNTRY." *THE SPANISH REQUIREMENT*, 1510

During the first years after Columbus and his crew landed in the Western Hemisphere, Spaniards functioned with little oversight of their activities and interactions with the indigenous populations. In the early sixteenth century, some Catholic clergy denounced the actions of Spaniards in the Americas as contrary to Catholic teaching and called on the monarchy to act. This condemnation, coupled with crown concerns about their material interests in the Americas, led the Council of Castile, the chief administrative and judicial body of the Spanish realms, to issue orders that an ultimatum should be recited any time Spaniards encountered a new population of indigenous peoples in the Americas. This speech, called the *Requerimiento (Requirement)*, is reproduced here. It was probably first delivered in the Americas in 1514 and most likely read in either Latin or Spanish.

On the part of the King, Don Fernando, and of Doña Juana, his daughter, Queen of Castile and León, subduers of the barbarous nations, we their servants notify and make known to you, as best we can, that the Lord our God, Living and Eternal, created the Heaven and the Earth, and one man and one woman, of whom you and we, all the men of the world, were and are descendants, and all those who came after us. But, on account of the multitude which has sprung from this man and woman in the five thousand years since the world was created, it was necessary that some men should go one way and some another, and that they should be divided into many kingdoms and provinces, for in one alone they could not be sustained.

Of all these nations God our Lord gave charge to one man, called St. Peter, that he should be Lord and Superior of all the men in the world, that all should obey him, and that he should be the head of the whole human race, wherever men should live, and under whatever law, sect, or belief they should be; and he gave him the world for his kingdom and jurisdiction.

And he commanded him to place his seat in Rome as the spot most fitting to rule the world from;

Source: National Humanities Center Toolbox Library, *Primary Sources in U.S. History and Literature*, nationalhumanitiescenter.org/pds/amerbegin/contact/text7/requirement.pdf.

but also he permitted him to have his seat in any other part of the world, and to judge and govern all Christians, Moors [Muslims–Ed.], Jews, Gentiles, and all other sects. This man was called Pope, as if to say, Admirable Great Father and Governor of men. The men who lived in that time obeyed that St. Peter and took him for Lord, King, and Superior of the universe; so also they have regarded the others who after him have been elected to the pontificate, and so has it been continued even till now and will continue till the end of the world.

One of these Pontiffs [popes–Ed.] who succeeded that St. Peter as Lord of the world, in the dignity and seat which I have before mentioned, made donation of these [lands–Ed.] to the aforesaid King and Queen and to their successors, our lords, with all that there are in these territories, as is contained in certain writings which passed upon the subject as aforesaid, which you can see if you wish.

So their Highnesses are kings and lords of these [lands–Ed.] by virtue of this donation: and some islands, and indeed almost all those to whom this has been notified, have received and served their Highnesses, as lords and kings, in the way that subjects ought to do, with good will, without any resistance, immediately, without delay, when they were informed of the aforesaid facts. And also they received and obeyed the priests whom their Highnesses sent to preach to them and to teach them our Holy Faith; and all these, of their own free will, without any reward or condition, have become Christians, and are so, and their Highnesses have joyfully and benignantly received them, and also have commanded them to be treated as their subjects and vassals; and you too are held and obliged to do the same. Wherefore, as best we can, we ask and require you that you consider what we have said to you, and that you take the time that shall be necessary to understand and deliberate upon it, and that you acknowledge the Church as the Ruler and Superior of the whole world, and the high priest called Pope, and in his name the King and Queen . . . in his place, as superiors and lords and kings of these [lands–Ed.] by virtue of the said donation, and that you consent and give place that these religious fathers should declare and preach to you the aforesaid.

If you do so, you will do well, and that which you are obliged to do to their Highnesses, and we in their name shall receive you in all love and charity, and shall leave you, your wives, and your children, and your lands, free without servitude, that you may do with them and with yourselves freely that which you like and think best, and they shall not compel you to turn Christians, unless you yourselves, when informed of the truth, should wish to be converted to our Holy Catholic Faith, as almost all the inhabitants of the rest of the islands have done. And, besides this, their Highnesses award you many privileges and exemptions and will grant you many benefits.

But, if you do not do this, and maliciously make delay in it, I certify to you that, with the help of God, we shall powerfully enter into your country, and shall make war against you in all ways and manners that we can, and shall subject you to the yoke and obedience of the Church and of their Highnesses; we shall take you and your wives and your children, and shall make slaves of them, and as such shall sell and dispose of them as their Highnesses may command; and we shall take away your goods, and shall do you all the mischief and damage that we can, as to vassals who do not obey, and refuse to receive their lord, and resist and contradict him; and we protest that the deaths and losses which shall accrue from this are your fault, and not that of their Highnesses, or ours, nor of these cavaliers who come with us. And that we have said this to you and made this Requisition, we request the notary here present to give us his testimony in writing, and we ask the rest who are present that they should be witnesses of this Requisition.

QUESTIONS TO CONSIDER

1. In this document, what is the Spanish crown asking the indigenous peoples of the Americas to do? Based on their responses, what will they receive in return?
2. According to the document, how does sovereignty (the right to rule over people and places) work? What gives Spanish explorers the authority to act in the Americas?

2.2 "WHENEVER THEY CHOSE TO COME, THEY WOULD SEE WHO WE WERE." *LETTER OF HERNÁN CORTÉS TO KING CHARLES V, 1520*

Hernán Cortés (1485–1547) was born in Spain to a family of some social and economic status. Through family connections, he was able to travel to the island of Hispaniola in 1504, where he acquired a land grant and an *encomienda* (a grant of indigenous laborers). From there, he participated in the conquest of Cuba, from which he acquired more resources and a political position. In 1518, Cortés was commissioned by the Governor of Cuba to organize an expedition of conquest to the mainland of Central America. The governor changed his mind, but Cortés ignored the order to stand down. He departed with his crew in February 1519. Thus began the Conquest of Mexico and a lifetime of legal wrangling for Cortés.

Between 1519 and 1526, Cortés wrote a series of letters directly to the King of Spain to explain and justify his actions. In the following excerpt, from a letter written in 1520, Cortés describes several types of encounters with indigenous populations as he made his way from the coast inland to the Aztec capital of Tenochtitlan. Some of those he met along the way became allies of the Spaniards, while others resisted Cortés and his troops.

Most Excellent Prince, in the other report I told Your Majesty of the cities and towns which at that time had offered themselves to the service of Your Highness and which I held subject. I also spoke of a great lord called Mutezuma [*Moctezuma II, the Aztec Emperor–Ed.*], whom the natives of these lands had spoken to me about, and who, according to the number of days they said we would have to march, lived about ninety or a hundred leagues from the harbor where I disembarked. And, trusting in God's greatness and in the might of Your Highness's Royal name, I decided to go and see him wherever he might be. Indeed I remember that, with respect to the quest of this lord, I undertook more than I was able, for I assured Your Highness that I would take him alive in chains or make him subject to Your Majesty's Royal Crown. . . .

On leaving this valley I found a great barrier built of dry stone and as much as nine feet high, which ran right across the valley from one mountain range to the other. It was some twenty paces wide, and all along the top was a battlement a foot and a half thick to provide an advantageous position for battle; it had only one entrance, some ten paces wide. At this entrance one wall doubled over the other, in the manner of a ravelin [*a type of fortification–Ed.*], within a space of forty paces, so that the entrance was not direct but had turns in it. When I asked the reason for this wall, they replied that that was the frontier of the province of Tascalteca, whose inhabitants were Mutezuma's enemies and were always at war with him. The natives of the valley, because I was going to see Mutezuma their lord, begged me not to go through the territory of his enemies, for they might be hostile to me and do me some harm; they themselves would lead me to Mutezuma without leaving his territory, in which I would always be well received.

But those of Cempoal told me not to do this, but to go through Tascalteca, for what the others had said

Source: Hernán Cortés, *Letters from Mexico*, translated, edited and with new introduction by Anthony Pagden; With an Introductory essay by J. H. Elliott (New Haven, CT: Yale University Press, 1986), 48, 57–61.

was only to prevent me from forming an alliance with that province. They said that all Mutezuma's people were wicked traitors and would lead me to a place whence I could not escape. As I held those of Cempoal in greater esteem than the others, I took their advice, leading my men with as much caution as possible. And I, with some six horsemen, rode half a league ahead, not in anticipation of what later befell me, but to explore the land, so that if anything should happen I might have time to gather and instruct my men.

After proceeding four leagues, we reached the brow of a hill, and the two horsemen who went in front of me saw some Indians dressed in the feathers they wear in battle, and bearing swords and bucklers, who when they saw the horses began to run away. I arrived soon after and I called out to them to return and not to be afraid; as we approached them (there must have been about fifteen Indians) they banded together and began to throw spears and to call to others of their people who were in a valley. They fought so fiercely with us that they killed two horses and wounded three others and two horsemen. At this point the others appeared who must have been four or five thousand. Some eight horsemen were now with me, not counting the dead, and we fought them making several charges while we waited for the other soldiers whom I had sent a horseman to fetch; and in the fighting we did them some damage, in that we killed fifty or sixty of them and ourselves suffered no harm, although they fought with great courage and ferocity. But as we were all mounted we attacked in safety and retreated likewise.

When they saw our men approaching, they withdrew, for they were few, and left us the field. After they had gone, several messengers arrived, who said they came from the chieftains of that province and with them two of the messengers I had sent, who said that the lords of the province knew nothing of what those others had done; for they were of an independent community and had done it without his permission. They regretted what had happened and would pay me for the horses which had been killed; they wanted to be my friends, wished me good

fortune and said I would be welcomed by them. I replied that I was grateful to them and that I held them as friends and would go where they said. That night I was forced to sleep in a river bed one league beyond where this happened, for it was late and the men were tired.

There I took all the precautions I could, with watchmen and scouts both on foot and on horseback. When it was light I departed, keeping my vanguard and baggage in close formation and my scouts in front. When, at sunrise, I arrived at a very small village I found the other two messengers weeping, saying that they had been tied up to be killed, but had escaped that night. Only a stone's throw from them there appeared a large number of Indians, heavily armed, who with a great shout began to attack us with many javelins and arrows. I began to deliver the formal requerimiento [Requirement– Ed.] through the interpreters who were with me and before a notary, but the longer I spent in admonishing them and requesting peace, the more they pressed us and did us as much harm as they could. Seeing therefore that nothing was to be gained by the requerimiento or protestations, we began to defend ourselves as best we could, and so drew us fighting into the midst of more than 100,000 warriors who surrounded us on all sides. We fought all day long until an hour before sunset, when they withdrew; with half a dozen guns and five or six harquebuses and forty crossbowmen and with the thirteen horsemen who remained, I had done them much harm without receiving any except from exhaustion and hunger. And it truly seemed that God was fighting for us, because from such a multitude, such fierce and able warriors and with so many kinds of weapons to harm us, we escaped so lightly.

That night I fortified a small tower on top of a hill, where they kept their idols. When it was day I left two hundred men and all the artillery behind and rode out to attack them with the horsemen, one hundred foot soldiers and four hundred Indians of those I brought from Cempoal, and three hundred from Yztaemestitan. Before they had time to rally, I burnt five or six small places of about a hundred inhabitants, and took prisoner about four hundred persons, both men and women; and returned to the camp having suffered no loss whatever. The following day at dawn, more than 49,000 men, who covered the entire ground, attacked the camp with such force that some of them broke in and fought the Spaniards hand to hand. We then went out and charged them, and so much did Our Lord help us that in four hours' fighting we had advanced so far that they could no longer harm us in the camp, although they still made some attacks. And so we fought until late, when they retired.

The following day I left before dawn by a different route, without being observed, with the horsemen, a hundred foot soldiers and my Indian allies. I burnt more than ten villages, in one of which there were more than three thousand houses, where the inhabitants fought with us, although there was no one there to help them. As we were carrying the banner of the Cross and were fighting for our Faith and in the service of Your Sacred Majesty in this Your Royal enterprise, God gave us such a victory that we killed many of them without ourselves receiving any hurt. Having gained our victory, we returned to camp a little after midday, for the enemy was gathering from all directions.

The following day messengers arrived from the chieftains saying that they wished to be vassals of Your Highness and my friends; and they begged me to forgive them for what they had done. I replied that they had done wrong, but that I was content to be their friend and to forgive what they had done. The next day some fifty Indians who, it seemed, were people of importance among them, came to the camp saying they were bringing food, and began to inspect the entrances and exits and some huts where we were living. The men from Cempoal came to me and said I should take notice of the fact that the newcomers were bad men and had come to spy and see how we could be harmed, and I could be certain that that was their only purpose in coming. I ordered one of them to be captured discreetly so that the others did not see, and I took him aside and through the interpreters threatened him so that he should tell me the truth. He confessed that Sintengal, who is captain general of this province, was waiting with many men behind some hills opposite the camp to fall on us that night, because, they said, they had fought with us by day and gained nothing and now wished to try by night, so that their people should fear neither the horses nor the guns nor the swords. They had been sent to spy out our camp and to see where it could be entered, and how they might burn the straw huts. Then I had another Indian seized and questioned him likewise, and he repeated what the other had said and in the same words. Then I took five or six and they all confirmed what I had heard, so I took all fifty and cut off their hands and sent them to tell their chief that by day or by night, or whenever they chose to come, they would see who we were. I had the camp fortified as best I could, and deployed my men where I thought most advantageous, and so remained on the alert until the sun set.

QUESTIONS TO CONSIDER

1. What themes (or tropes) does Cortés repeat in his writing to the King? Why do you think he chose to emphasize these themes?
2. What roles, motivations, and personal attributes does Cortés ascribe to the indigenous peoples?

2.3 "THEY WERE LIKE ONE WHO SPEAKS A BARBAROUS TONGUE." *INDIGENOUS ACCOUNTS OF THE CONFLICT WITH CORTÉS, MID-SIXTEENTH CENTURY*

In 1545, Bernardino de Sahagún (1499–1590), a Franciscan missionary in New Spain, began to conduct interviews with indigenous elders in central Mexico. Using Nahuatl, the language of the Aztec Empire, Sahagún continued this project for four decades, compiling 2,400 pages of text and illustrations regarding the culture, society, religious beliefs, political organization, and environment that existed prior to the arrival of Europeans. As part of this project, Sahagún also collected testimony about the era of the conquest and the collapse of indigenous autonomy.

The original manuscript was discovered in a library built in Florence by Pope Clement VII and is generally referred to as the Florentine Codex. Following are excerpts from the manuscript that describe early encounters between indigenous peoples and Cortés's expedition.

EXCERPT 1

At last they came. At last they began to march toward us. A man from Cempoala [*referred to as Cempoal in Source 2.2–Ed.*], who was known as the Tlacochcalcatl [Chief of the House of Arrows], was the first official to welcome them as they entered our lands and cities. This man spoke Nahuatl. He showed them the best routes and the shortest ways; he guided and advised them, traveling at the head of the party.

When they came to Tecoac, in the land of the Tlaxcaltecas [*inhabitants of the province called Tascalteca in Source 2.2–Ed.*], they found it was inhabited by Otomies [*a distinct indigenous ethnic group–Ed.*]. The Otomies came out to meet them in battle array; they greeted the strangers with their shields.

But the strangers conquered the Otomies of Tecoac; they utterly destroyed them. They divided their ranks, fired the cannons at them, attacked them with their swords and shot them with their crossbows. Not just a few, but all of them, perished in the battle.

And when Tecoac had been defeated, the Tlaxcaltecas soon heard the news; they learned what had taken place there. They felt premonitions of death: terror overwhelmed them, and they were filled with foreboding.

Therefore the chiefs assembled; the captains met together in a council. They talked about what had happened, and said: "What shall we do? Shall we go out to meet them? The Otomi is a brave warrior, but he was helpless against them: they scorned him as a mere nothing! They destroyed the poor *macehual* [*commoner–Ed.*] with a look, with a glance of their eyes! We should go over to their side: we should make friends with them and be their allies. If not, they will destroy us too. . . ."

Therefore the lords of Tlaxcala went out to meet them, bringing many things to eat: hens and hens' eggs and the finest tortillas. They said to the strangers: "Our lords, you are weary." The strangers replied: "Where do you live? Where are you from?"

They said: "We are from Tlaxcala. You have come here, you have entered our land. We are from Tlaxcala; our city is the City of the Eagle, Tlaxcala." (For in ancient times it was called Texcala, and its people were known as Texcaltecas.)

Source: Miguel León-Portilla, ed., *The Broken Spears: The Aztec Account of the Conquest of Mexico*, with an Introduction by Miguel León-Portilla (Boston: Beacon Press, 1922), 38–39, 51–52.

Then they guided them to the city; they brought them there and invited them to enter. They paid them great honors, attended to their every want, joined with them as allies and even gave them their daughters.

The Spaniards asked: "Where is the City of Mexico? Is it far from here?"

They said: "No, it is not far, it is only a three-day march. And it is a great city. The Aztecs are very brave. They are great warriors and conquerors and have defeated their neighbors on every side."

At this time the Tlaxcaltecas were enemies of Cholula. They feared the Cholultecas; they envied and cursed them; their souls burned with hatred for the people of Cholula. This is why they brought certain rumors to Cortés, so that he would destroy them. They said to him: "Cholula is our enemy. It is an evil city. The people are as brave as the Aztecs and they are the Aztecs' friends."

When the Spaniards heard this, they marched against Cholula. They were guided and accompanied by the Tlaxcaltecas and the chiefs from Cempoala, and they all marched in battle array.

When they arrived, the Tlaxcaltecas and the men of Cholula called to each other and shouted greetings. An assembly was held in the courtyard of the god, but when they had all gathered together, the entrances were closed, so that there was no way of escaping. Then the sudden slaughter began: knife strokes, and sword strokes, and death. The people of Cholula had not foreseen it, had not suspected it. They faced the Spaniards without weapons, without their swords or their shields. The cause of the slaughter was treachery. They died blindly, without knowing why, because of the lies of the Tlaxcaltecas.

And when this had taken place, word of it was brought to Motecuhzoma [*Moctezuma II, the Aztec Emperor–Ed.*]. The messengers came and departed, journeying back and forth between Tenochtitlan and Cholula. The common people were terrified by the news; they could do nothing but tremble with fright. It was as if the earth trembled beneath them, or as if the world were spinning before their eyes, as it spins during a fit of vertigo. . . .

When the massacre at Cholula was complete, the strangers set out again toward the City of Mexico. They came in battle array, as conquerors, and the dust rose in whirlwinds on the roads. Their spears glinted in the sun, and their pennons [*pennants; battle flags– Ed.*] fluttered like bats. They made a loud clamor as they marched, for their coats of mail and their weapons clashed and rattled. Some of them were dressed in glistening iron from head to foot; they terrified everyone who saw them. Their dogs came with them, running ahead of the column. They raised their muzzles high; they lifted their muzzles to the wind. They raced on before with saliva dripping from their jaws.

EXCERPT 2

Then Motecuhzoma dispatched various chiefs. Tzihuacpopocatzin was at their head, and he took with him a great many of his representatives. They went out to meet the Spaniards in the vicinity of Popocatepetl and Iztactepetl [*two volcanoes at the edge of the Valley of Mexico–Ed.*], there in the Eagle Pass. They gave the gods ensigns of gold, and ensigns of quetzal feathers, and golden necklaces. And when they were given these presents, the Spaniards burst into smiles; their eyes shone with pleasure; they were delighted by them. They picked up the gold and fingered it like monkeys; they seemed to be transported by joy, as if their hearts were illumined and made new. The truth is that they longed and lusted for gold. Their bodies swelled with greed, and their hunger was ravenous; they hungered like pigs for that gold. They snatched at the golden ensigns, waved them from side to side and examined every inch of them. They were like one who speaks a barbarous tongue: everything they said was in a barbarous tongue.

QUESTIONS TO CONSIDER

1. How do these descriptions compare to the way Cortés describes early encounters between indigenous peoples and Spaniards in Source 2.2?
2. The events described in this document occurred decades prior to these interviews, which were conducted by a Catholic priest. How do you think those facts influenced the way information was presented? Can you find any evidence to support your hypothesis?

2.4 "THE SPANISH COMMONWEALTH WILL BE GRAVELY RISKED." *LETTER OF VICEROY OF NEW SPAIN LUIS DE VELASCO TO EMPEROR CHARLES V, 1553*

Luis de Velasco (1511–1565) was born into a noble family and served the Spanish crown in both military and government positions in the Navarre region of Spain. In 1550, he was appointed as the Viceroy of New Spain, only the second man to hold this office. The viceroy resided in Mexico City, which was built upon the ruins of the Aztec capital of Tenochtitlan. As Viceroy, Velasco was tasked with implementation of the New Laws (1542), the Spanish crown's plan to assert greater control over events, resources, and outcomes in the Americas. In the letter excerpted here, Viceroy Velasco describes for the crown the challenges he faces in imposing royal authority in New Spain and laments the toll that his service to the crown has taken on him.

Carrying out the new laws and provisions that were given me and that have been sent since has put the land in great trouble and necessity, which every day grows greater because their execution came all at once. Among the Spaniards there is great discontent and much poverty, and among the Indians more laxity and ease than their little constancy will suffer. I am afraid that troubles very hard to remedy are going to come from one side or the other, because the country is so full of blacks and mestizos, who greatly outnumber the Spaniards, and all of whom wish to purchase their liberty with the lives of their masters; this bad breed will join anyone who rebels, whether Spaniards or Indians. In order to preserve this land in the service of our Lord and obedience to your majesty, there are some measures I will mention here that are necessary and almost forced upon us if this land is not to be lost. May your majesty order these things to be considered and make what provision you see fit; in advising you what I feel and serving faithfully to death I will do my duty. What I would regret more than death would be that the land should be lost while it was my responsibility.

The principal thing your majesty should order to be proclaimed is the distribution that has been suggested by the conquerors and settlers. . . . Those who inform your majesty that the land can be held by friars alone, without being defended by Spaniards who have the means with which to serve and something to lose if they don't do their duty, in my view deceive themselves and do not know the natives well, because they are not so firm in our holy faith, nor have they so forgotten the evil beliefs they had in the time of their infidelity, that such great matters should be trusted to their virtue. . . .

Next, your majesty should order that part of the Spanish people, mestizos, and blacks be culled out and sent on some conquest, since there are too many in the land; and if this is not to be done, then order the door shut to Spaniards of any kind, so they will not enter New Spain, and deport the mestizos who could be sent in the ships that go back to Spain, because they are very harmful to the Indians. . . .

Next, whoever governs here should have fuller powers than your majesty has given to me, because every time I give orders in matters of general

Source: James Lockhart and Enrique Otte, eds., *Letters and People of the Spanish Indies: Sixteenth Century* (New York: Cambridge University Press, 1976), 185–194.

administration, they appeal to the Audiencia *[royal court–Ed.]*, and most times the order never takes effect, which is very harmful and gives rise to effrontery from which serious trouble could result. The greatest service I have done your majesty in this office has been to put up with some of these Audiencia judges, who have certainly exceeded the bounds in some things, claiming that they are superior, and if I had not used great moderation and patience, there could not have failed to be great division and confusion in the land. . . .

Your majesty would do me great favor in giving me license, after I am reviewed, to return to die in Spain, where, in order to come and serve as your majesty ordered me, I left my wife and children in much necessity, because I have no enterprises or revenues in this land; truly the salary lacks 3,000 ducats and more of covering what I am forced to spend each year, and so the little property I have is mortgaged and I am in debt; I hope not to have to pay it off posthumously. I beg your majesty to deign grant me a sufficient salary or the license that I ask, before I reach utter ruin, since your majesty always does favors to those who have served and now serve you, and I think I am one of the deserving ones, for the fidelity and care with which I have served for more than thirty years. I find myself old and poor and two thousand leagues from my home and relatives and friends, where I cannot assert myself except through favors your majesty should do me; and since I ask it in order better to serve, it does not seem insolent to ask. . . .

The mines and all the properties of value here in New Spain are diminishing greatly on account of the abolition of personal services and Indian porters, because without that it is impossible to work mines or supply them with provisions. What horses and other beasts of burden can transport is little, and let no one depend on the Spaniards and blacks and mestizos to make up for the Indians, because they can neither dig ore nor smelt. Let no one make your majesty believe that the mines can be worked without Indians; rather the moment they raise their hands from labor the mines will be finished, unless the Spaniard work them personally, and I doubt that they would do that though they die of hunger. . . .

The regent in conjunction with the Council of the Indies has sent to order me to carry out everything decreed and ordered in the many laws and other new provisions, which is being done, with great resentment among the Spaniards, since it touches all of them in general. Among other things, the Council has declared that it is personal service to have Indians carry tributes belonging to the royal treasury to this city; since the greater part of this tribute is provisions, and carrying them has been forbidden, there is great need in this city, and we can find no means to remedy it. If the Indians do not supply it, no industry or effort of mine nor of the Spaniards will suffice to supply the city even with bread, water, firewood, and fodder for horses, which are our strength in this land. Counting the number of people who generally reside in the city, I find that between Spaniards and Indians, mestizos, blacks and strangers who come on business, there are usually two hundred thousand mouths to feed. . . .

I do my best to see to the supply, but even so, if the law is to be kept, the Spanish commonwealth will be gravely risked.

QUESTIONS TO CONSIDER

1. What can this letter tell us about the changes that have occurred in central Mexico since the fall of the Aztecs in 1521?
2. According to Velasco, what major new initiatives should the Spanish crown undertake if it wishes to achieve its goals in the Americas? What evidence does Velasco provide to support his assertions?

2.5 "THE DUTCH MUST MAINTAIN THEIR RIGHT OF TRADE." HUGO GROTIUS, *THE FREEDOM OF THE SEAS*, 1609

Hugo Grotius (1583–1645) was born in Delft, studied at the University of Leiden, traveled abroad with Dutch diplomats, and acquired a law degree at the University of Orleans (France). During his career, he provided legal advice to powerful Dutch individuals and organizations, including the Dutch East Indies Company (VOC), and served for a time as Holland's Attorney General. His career and, at times, his freedom were tied up with the political and religious upheaval of northern and central Europe during the seventeenth century. He died in the city of Rostock (present-day Germany). Grotius's treatise on maritime trade, excerpted here, had an enduring impact on debates over global trade and competing rights claims.

CHAPTER X: TRADE WITH THE EAST INDIES DOES NOT BELONG TO THE PORTUGUESE BY VIRTUE OF A TITLE BASED ON THE PAPAL DONATION.

No one has granted it except perhaps the Pope, and he did not have the power. For no one can give away what he does not himself possess. But the Pope, unless he were the temporal master of the whole world, which sensible men deny, cannot say that the universal right in respect of trade belongs to him. Especially is this true since trade has to do only with material gains, and has no concern at all with spiritual matters, outside of which, as all admit, Papal power ceases. Besides, if the Pope wished to give that right to the Portuguese alone, and to deprive all other men of the same right, he would be doing a double injustice. In the first place, he would do an injustice to the people of the East Indies who, placed as we have said outside the Church, are in no way subjects of the Pope. Therefore, since the Pope cannot take away from them anything that is theirs, he could not take away their right of trading with whomsoever they please. In the second

place, he would do an injustice to all other men both Christian and non-Christian, from whom he could not take that same right without a hearing. Besides, what are we to say of the fact that not even temporal lords in their own dominions are competent to prohibit the freedom of trade, as has been demonstrated above by reasonable and authoritative statements?

Therefore it must be acknowledged, that the authority of the Pope has absolutely no force against the eternal law of nature and of nations, from whence came that liberty which is destined to endure for ever and ever. . . .

CHAPTER XIII: THE DUTCH MUST MAINTAIN THEIR RIGHT OF TRADE WITH THE EAST INDIES BY PEACE, BY TREATY, OR BY WAR.

Wherefore since both law and equity demand that trade with the East Indies be as free to us as to anyone else, it follows that we are to maintain at all hazards that freedom which is ours by nature, either by coming to a peace agreement with the Spaniards, or by concluding a treaty, or by continuing the war. So far as peace is

Source: Hugo Grotius, *The Freedom of the Seas, or the Right Which Belongs to the Dutch to Take Part in the East Indian Trade*, trans. Ralph Van Deman Magoffin, Introduction by James Brown Scott (New York: Oxford University Press, 1916), 66, 72–76.

concerned, it is well known that there are two kinds of peace, one made on terms of equality, the other on unequal terms. The Greeks call the former kind a compact between equals, the latter an enjoined truce; the former is meant for high souled men, the latter for servile spirits. Demosthenes *[an Athenian statesman (384-322 BCE)–Ed.]* in his speech on the liberty of the Rhodians says that it was necessary for those who wished to be free to keep away from treaties which were imposed upon them, because such treaties were almost the same as slavery. Such conditions are all those by which one party is lessened in its own right, according to the definition of Isocrates *[an Athenian scholar (436-338 BCE)–Ed.]*. For if, as Cicero *[a Roman politician (106-43 BCE)–Ed.]* says, wars must be undertaken in order that people may live in peace unharmed, it follows that peace must be called not a pact which entails slavery but which brings undisturbed liberty, especially as peace and justice according to the opinion of many philosophers and theologians differ more in name than in fact, and as peace is a harmonious agreement based not on individual whim, but on well-ordered regulations.

[In the following paragraph of the original text, Grotius makes many additional references to philosophical and historical texts. We have chosen only several to highlight.–Ed.]

But if we are driven into war by the injustice of our enemies, the justice of our cause ought to bring hope and confidence in a happy outcome. "For," as Demosthenes has said, "everyone fights his hardest to recover what he has lost; but when men endeavor to gain at the expense of others it is not so." The Emperor Alexander *[Alexander III of Macedon (356-323 BCE)–Ed.]* has expressed his idea in this way: "Those who begin unjust deeds, must bear the greatest blame; but those who repel aggressors are twice armed, both with courage because of their just cause,

and with the highest hope because they are not doing a wrong, but are warding off a wrong." Therefore, if it be necessary, arise, O nation unconquered on the sea, and fight boldly, not only for your own liberty, but for that of the human race. . . .

Following these principles, a good judge would award to the Dutch the freedom of trade and would forbid the Portuguese and others from using force to hinder that freedom, and would order the payment of just damages. But when a judgment which would be rendered in a court cannot be obtained, it should with justice be demanded in a war. Augustine *[of Hippo, a Catholic saint (354-430 CE)–Ed.]* acknowledges this when he says: "The injustice of an adversary brings a just war." Cicero also says: "There are two ways of settling a dispute: first, by discussion; second, by physical force; we must resort to force only in case we may not avail ourselves of discussion." And King Theodoric *[454-526 CE–Ed.]* says: "Recourse must then be had to arms when justice can find no lodgment in an adversary's heart." Pomponius *[a Roman jurist from the 2nd century CE–Ed.]*, however, has handed down a decision which has more bearing on our argument than any of the citations already made. He declared that the man who seized a thing common to all to the prejudice of everyone else must be forcibly prevented from so doing. The theologians also say that just as war is righteously undertaken in defense of individual property, so no less righteously is it undertaken in behalf of the use of those things which by natural law ought to be common property. Therefore, he who closes up roads and hinders the export of merchandise ought to be prevented from so doing . . . , even without waiting for any public authority. Since these things are so, there need not be the slightest fear that God will prosper the efforts of those who violate that most stable law of nature which He himself has instituted, or that even men will allow those to go unpunished who for the sake alone of private gain oppose a common benefit of the human race.

QUESTIONS TO CONSIDER

1. What are the major ideas and actors that Grotius considers in making his assertions about the way things should be? Why were these ideas so important to the Dutch at this time?
2. How do you think different individuals and groups around the world responded to Grotius's assertions? What counterarguments might they have proposed to Grotius's assertions?

2.6 "JAPANESE SHIPS ARE STRICTLY FORBIDDEN TO LEAVE FOR FOREIGN COUNTRIES." *SAKOKU EDICT, 1635*

In 1600, the Battle of Sekigahara established the victorious Tokugawa family as the ruling power in Japan. Tokugawa Ieyasu and his descendants claimed the title "Shogun," the highest military officer in the islands, which also gave them control over most governmental decisions. Although the Emperor remained in place as the ceremonial ruler of Japan, real power resided with the Tokugawa, who resided in Edo (Tokyo today). As the Tokugawa tried to unify Japan after several centuries of often violent decentralization, they had also to contend with the increasing presence of Europeans, who first arrived in Japanese waters in the 1500s with military, commercial, religious, and political ambitions.

One response to both internal and international circumstances was the so-called Closed Country Edicts, a series of documents issued in the early 1600s. These proclamations did not completely isolate Japan, but they did tightly control access to the islands. This last edict dates from 1635 and defined Japanese policies in this regard for more than 200 years.

CLOSED COUNTRY EDICT OF 1635

1. Japanese ships are strictly forbidden to leave for foreign countries.
2. No Japanese is permitted to go abroad. If there is anyone who attempts to do so secretly, he must be executed. The ship so involved must be impounded and its owner arrested, and the matter must be reported to the higher authority.
3. If any Japanese returns from overseas after residing there, he must be put to death.
4. If there is any place where the teachings of padres (Christianity) is practiced, the two of you must order a thorough investigation.
5. Any informer revealing the whereabouts of the followers of padres (Christians) must be rewarded accordingly. If anyone reveals the whereabouts of a high ranking padre, he must be given one hundred pieces of silver. For those of lower ranks, depending on the deed, the reward must be set accordingly.
6. If a foreign ship has an objection [to the measures adopted] and it becomes necessary to report the matter to Edo [*Modern Tokyo, the seat of the Tokugawa government–Ed.*], you may ask the Omura domain [*the area around the city of Nagasaki–Ed.*] to provide ships to guard the foreign ship, as was done previously.
7. If there are any Southern Barbarians (Westerners) who propagate the teachings of padres, or otherwise commit crimes, they may be incarcerated in the prison. . . .
8. All incoming ships must be carefully searched for the followers of padres.
9. No single trading city shall be permitted to purchase all the merchandise brought by foreign ships.
10. Samurai [*members of Japan's military elite–Ed.*] are not permitted to purchase any goods originating from foreign ships directly from Chinese merchants in Nagasaki.

Source: David J. Lu, ed., *Japan: A Documentary History: The Dawn of History to the Late Tokugawa Period* (Armonk, NY: M. E. Sharpe, 1997), 196–197.

11. After a list of merchandise brought by foreign ships is sent to Edo, as before you may order that commercial dealings may take place without waiting for a reply from Edo.
12. After settling the price, all white yarns (raw silk) brought by foreign ships shall be allocated to the five trading cities *[Kyoto, Edo, Osaka, Sakai, and Nagasaki–Ed.]* and other quarters as stipulated.
13. After settling the price of white yarns (raw silk), other merchandise [brought by foreign ships] may be traded freely between the [licensed] dealers. However, in view of the fact that Chinese ships are small and cannot bring large consignments, you may issue orders of sale at your discretion. Additionally, payment for goods purchased must be made within twenty days after the price is set.
14. The date of departure homeward of foreign ships shall not be later than the twentieth day of the ninth month. Any ships arriving in Japan later than usual shall depart within fifty days of their arrival. As to the departure of Chinese ships, you may use your discretion to order their departure after the departure of the Portuguese *galeota* (galleon) *[the Portuguese fleet–Ed.]*.
15. The goods brought by foreign ships which remained unsold may not be deposited or accepted for deposit.
16. The arrival in Nagasaki of representatives of the five trading cities shall not be later than the fifth day of the seventh month. Anyone arriving later than that date shall lose the quota assigned to his city.
17. Ships arriving in Hirado *[a small island in southwest Japan, not far from Nagasaki–Ed.]* must sell their raw silk at the price set in Nagasaki, and are not permitted to engage in business transactions until after the price is established in Nagasaki.

You are hereby required to act in accordance with the Provisions set above. It is so ordered.

QUESTIONS TO CONSIDER

1. What concerns seem to motivate the rules put forth in this edict? How do they reflect the changing global interconnections of the seventeenth century?
2. To what extent does this edict actually "close" Japan? How do these acts compare to the strategies used by other powers at this time to manage political and economic relations? What might account for similarities and differences?

CHAPTER 3

THE PARADOXES OF EARLY MODERN EMPIRE, 1501–1661

3.1 "HOW THINGS ARE IN REAL LIFE." NICCOLÒ MACHIAVELLI, *THE PRINCE*, 1513

Niccolò Machiavelli (1469–1527) was born in the city-state of Florence (Italy). He served the rulers of Florence as a diplomat, military strategist, and political adviser but was removed from office, jailed, and tortured as a suspected plotter against the ruling Medici family in 1513. Machiavelli's most famous work, *The Prince*, is excerpted here. Machiavelli prepared this text, a primer on how to rule, at the time he was out of favor with the Medici family. He noted in his dedication of the book that he hoped to show the Medici family that "the fifteen years I have spent studying statecraft have not been wasted," and that they would "start putting me to use." Machiavelli never returned to significant state service. He devoted the last years of his life to writing on a wide range of subjects, including biography, military strategy, and political philosophy.

A ruler, then, should have no other concern, no other thought, should pay attention to nothing aside from war, military institutions, and the training of his soldiers. For this is the only field in which a ruler has to excel. It is of such importance that military prowess not only keeps those who have been born rulers in power, but also often enables men who have been born private citizens to come to power. On the other hand, one sees that when rulers think more about luxuries than about weapons, they fall from power. . . .

So, a ruler must think only of military matters, and in time of peace he should be even more occupied with them than in time of war. . . .

My hope is to write a book that will be useful, at least to those who read it intelligently, and so I thought it sensible to go straight to a discussion of how things are in real life and not waste time with a discussion of an imaginary world. For many authors have constructed imaginary republics and principalities that have never existed in practice and never could; for the gap between how people actually behave and how they ought to behave is so great that anyone who ignores everyday reality in order to live up to an ideal will soon discover he has been taught how to destroy himself, not how to preserve himself. For anyone who wants to act the part of a good man in all circumstances will

Source: Niccolò Machiavelli, *The Prince*, edited and translated by David Wootton (New York: Hackett, 1995), 45–55.

bring about his own ruin, for those he has to deal with will not all be good. So it is necessary for a ruler, if he wants to hold on to power, to learn how not to be good, and to know when it is and when it is not necessary to use this knowledge. . . .

Going further down our list of qualities, I recognize every ruler should want to be thought of as compassionate and not cruel. Nevertheless, I have to warn you to be careful about being compassionate. . . . A ruler ought not to mind the disgrace of being called cruel, if he keeps his subjects peaceful and law-abiding, for it is more compassionate to impose harsh punishments on a few than, out of excessive compassion, to allow disorder to spread, which leads to murders or looting. The whole community suffers if there are riots, while to maintain order the ruler only has to execute one or two individuals. Of all rulers, he who is new to power cannot escape a reputation for cruelty, for he is surrounded by dangers. . . .

This leads us to a question that is in dispute: Is it better to be loved than feared, or vice versa? My reply is one ought to be both loved [and] feared; but since it is difficult to accomplish both at the same time, I maintain it is much safer to be feared than loved, if you have to do without one of the two. For men one can, in general, say this: They are ungrateful, fickle, deceptive and deceiving, avoiders of danger, eager to gain. As long as you serve their interests, they are devoted to you. They promise you their blood, their possessions, their lives, and their children, as I said before, so long as you seem to have no need of them. But as soon as you need help, they turn against you. Any ruler who relies simply on their promises and makes no other preparations, will be destroyed. . . .

For love attaches men by ties of obligation, which, since men are wicked, they break whenever their interests are at stake. But fear restrains men because they are afraid of punishment, and this fear never leaves them. Still, a ruler should make himself feared in such a way that, if he does not inspire love, at least he does not provoke hatred. For it is perfectly possible to be feared and not hated. . . .

I conclude, then, that, as far as being feared and loved is concerned, since men decide for themselves whom they love, and rulers decide whom they fear, a wise ruler should rely on the emotion he can control, not on the one he cannot. But he must take care to avoid being hated, as I have said. . . .

You should therefore know there are two ways to fight: one while respecting the rules, the other with no holds barred. Men alone fight in the first fashion, and animals fight in the second. But because you cannot always win if you respect the rules, you must be prepared to break them. A ruler, in particular, needs to know how to be both an animal and a man. . . .

Since a ruler, then, needs to know how to make good use of beastly qualities, he should take as his models among the animals both the fox and the lion, for the lion does not know how to avoid traps, and the fox is easily overpowered by wolves. So you must be a fox when it comes to suspecting a trap, and a lion when it comes to making the wolves turn tail. . . .

So a ruler need not have all the positive qualities I listed earlier, but he must seem to have them. Indeed, I would go so far as to say that if you have them and never make any exceptions, then you will suffer for it; while if you merely appear to have them, they will benefit you. So you should seem to be compassionate, trustworthy, sympathetic, honest, religious, and, indeed, be all these things; but at the same time you should be constantly prepared, so that, if these become liabilities, you are trained and ready to become their opposites. You need to understand this: A ruler, and particularly a ruler who is new to power, cannot conform to all those rules that men who are thought good are expected to respect, for he is often obliged, in order to hold on to power, to break his word, to be uncharitable, inhumane, and irreligious. So he must be mentally prepared to act as circumstances and changes in fortune require. As I have said, he should do what is right if he can; but he must be prepared to do wrong if necessary.

QUESTIONS TO CONSIDER

1. According to Machiavelli, what are the most important characteristics that a successful ruler must have? Why?
2. What does Machiavelli's advice to "The Prince" reveal about his views of political power in general?

3.2 "WITH GOD'S HELP WE SANK AND UTTERLY DESTROYED ONE OF THE ENEMY'S GALLEONS." SEYDI ALI REIS, *THE MIRROR OF COUNTRIES*, 1557

Seydi Ali Reis (1498–1563) was the son and grandson of naval officers. He, too, became a naval commander in the Ottoman Empire. A skilled navigator, Seydi Ali Reis served in the Mediterranean Sea before Sultan Suleiman I (1494–1566) appointed him Commander of the Ottoman fleet in the Indian Ocean. In this post, his attempt to return fifteen galleys (oceangoing vessels propelled primarily by oars) from the Persian Gulf to their home port on the Red Sea resulted in a series of disasters, including costly encounters at sea with the Portuguese, hostile local rulers, and bad weather. The Commander finally returned to Istanbul two years after receiving his assignment, by land, without any of his ships.

The Mirror of Countries, Seydi Ali Reis's account of his adventure, appeared in Turkish in 1557. It was not published in English until the end of the nineteenth century. The following excerpt, published in 1917, describes the part of the journey that took the fleet down the Persian Gulf and out into the Arabian Sea, ending with an encounter with the ruler of Gwadar (today a city in Pakistan). In several places in the text, Seydi Ali Reis makes important references to the "Padishah." This is an honorific title, meaning "master of kings" in Persian. It is a reference to Sultan Suleiman I.

On the first of Shawal *[the tenth month of the Muslim year–Ed.]* we left the harbor of Basrah, accompanied, as far as Ormuz *[Hormuz–Ed.],* by the frigate of *Sherifi Pasha.* We visited on the way from Mehzari the grave of Khidr, and proceeding along the coast of Duspul (Dizful), and Shushter in Charik, I made pilgrimages to the graves of Imam Moham-med, Hanifi, and other saints *[early leaders of the Islamic faith–Ed.].*

From the harbor in the province of Shiraz we visited Rishehr (Bushir) and after reconnoitering the coasts and unable to get any clue as to the whereabouts of the enemy by means of the Tshekleva *[a small boat–Ed.]* I proceeded to Katif, situated near Lahsa and Hadjar on the Arabian coast. Unable to learn anything there, I went on to Bahrein, where I interviewed the commander of the place, Reis Murad. But neither could he give me any information about the fleet of the infidels. . . .

Next we came to Kis, i.e., old Ormuz, and Barhata, and several other small islands in the Green Sea, i.e., the waters of Ormuz, but nowhere could we get any news of the *[Portuguese–Ed.]* fleet. So we dismissed the vessel, which Mustafa Pasha had sent as an escort, with the message that Ormuz was safely passed. We proceeded by the coasts of Djilgar and Djadi, past the towns of Keimzar or Leime, and forty days after our departure, i.e., on the tenth of Rama-zan, in the forenoon, we suddenly saw coming toward us the Christian fleet, consisting of four large ships, three galleons, six Portuguese guard ships, and twelve galleys, 25 vessels in all. I immediately ordered the

Source: Charles F. Horne, ed., *The Sacred Books and Early Literature of the East* (New York: Parke, Austin, and Lipscomb, 1917), Vol. IV: *Medieval Arabic, Moorish, and Turkish,* 337–341.

canopy to be taken down, the anchor weighed, the guns put in readiness, and then, trusting to the help of the Almighty, we fastened the filandra *[a flag identifying the ship's origin–Ed.]* to the mainmast, the flags were unfurled, and, full of courage and calling upon Allah *[an Arabic word meaning God–Ed.]*, we commenced to fight. The volley from the guns and cannon was tremendous, and with God's help we sank and utterly destroyed one of the enemy's galleons. Never before within the annals of history has such a battle been fought, and words fail me to describe it. The battle continued til sunset, and only then the Admiral of the infidel fleet began to show some signs of fear. He ordered the signal-gun to fire a retreat, and the fleet turned in the direction of Ormuz.

With the help of Allah, and under the lucky star of the Padishah, the enemies of Islam had been defeated. . . .

On the day after we passed Khorfakan, where we took in water, and soon after reached Oman, or rather Sohar *[a port city on the northeast coast of Oman–Ed.]*. Thus we cruised about for nearly 17 days. When on the sixth of Ramazan, . . . we saw in the morning, issuing from the harbor of Maskat, . . . 32 vessels in all, commanded by . . . the son of the Governor *[probably of the Portuguese settlement at Goa–Ed.]*. They carried a large number of troops. The boats and galleons obscured the horizon with their *[sails–Ed.]* all set; . . . . Full of confidence in God's protection we awaited them. Their boats attacked our galleys; the battle raged, cannon and guns, arrows and swords made terrible slaughter on both sides. The *[attack from our boat–Ed.]* tore large holes in their hulls, while our galleys were riddled through by the javelins thrown down upon us from the enemy's turrets, which gave them the appearance of bristling porcupines; . . . . One of our galleys was set on fire by a bomb, but strange to say the boat from which it issued shared the like fate. God is merciful! Five of our galleys and as many of the enemy's boats were sunk and utterly wrecked, one of theirs went to the bottom with all sails set. In a word, there was great loss on both sides; our rowers were now insufficient in number to manage the oars, while running against the current, and to fire the cannon. We were compelled to drop anchor (at the stern) and to continue to fight as

best we might. The boats had also to be abandoned. *[Captains–Ed.]* of some of the foundered ships, and *[the officer in charge–Ed.]* of the volunteers, with the remainder of the Egyptian soldiers and 200 carpenters, had landed on the Arabian shore, and as the rowers were Arabs they had been hospitably treated by the Arabs of Nedjd.

The ships of the infidel fleet had likewise taken on board the crews of their sunken vessels, and as there were Arabs amongst them, they also had found shelter on the Arabian coast. God is our witness. Even in the war between Khaiveddin Pasha and Andreas Doria no such naval action as this has ever taken place. When night came, and we were approaching the bay of Ormuz, the wind began to rise. . . .

However, we were not allowed to touch the shore, and had to set sail again. During that night we drifted away from the Arabian coast into the open sea, and finally reached the coasts of Djash, in the province of Kerman. This is a long coast, but we could find no harbor, and we roamed about for two days. . . . In the morning a dry wind carried off many of the crew, and at last, after unheard-of troubles and difficulties, we approached the harbor of Sheba.

Here we came upon a *[pirate ship–Ed.]*, laden with spoils, and when the watchman sighted us they hailed us. We told them that we were Mussulmans *[Muslims–Ed.]*, whereupon their captain came on board our vessel; he kindly supplied us with water, for we had not a drop left, and thus our exhausted soldiers were invigorated. This was on Bairam day, and for us, as we had now got water, a double feast-day. Escorted by the said captain we entered the harbor of Guador *[Gwadar–Ed.]*. The people there were Beluchistanis and their chief was Malik Djelaleddin, the son of Malik Dinar. The Governor of Guador came on board our ship and assured us of his unalterable devotion to our glorious Padishah. He promised that henceforth, if at any time our fleet should come to Ormuz, he would undertake to send 50 or 60 boats to supply us with provisions, and in every possible way to be of service to us. We wrote a letter to the native Prince Djelaleddin to ask for a pilot, upon which a first-class pilot was sent us, with the assurance that he was thoroughly trustworthy and entirely devoted to the interests of our Padishah.

QUESTIONS TO CONSIDER

1. What does this passage reveal about the balance of political and military power in the Persian Gulf region in the middle of the sixteenth century?
2. Compare the ways in which Babur (Source 3.5) and Seydi Ali Reis describe warfare. To what do they attribute successes and failures? How can we account for similarities and differences in the way they choose to communicate about events and their outcomes?

3.3 "HAVE MERCY ON THESE POOR PEOPLE! LET WHOEVER CAN STAB, SMITE, SLAY." THE TWELVE ARTICLES OF THE UPPER SWABIAN PEASANTS AND MARTIN LUTHER, AGAINST THE MURDERING AND ROBBING BANDS OF PEASANTS, 1525

The German Peasants' War of the mid-1520s consisted of a series of violent conflicts involving peasants, village dwellers, and even some elites, in an area including much of what is now Germany, as well as parts of eastern France, Switzerland, and Austria. The movement had religious, political, and economic dimensions. Hundreds of thousands of individuals were involved at different stages of the confrontation, making it the largest popular uprising in Europe prior to the French Revolution, which began almost 250 years later. The rebels were met with harsh responses across central Europe.

During the uprising, rebel groups and their opponents used print technology to pursue their interests. Two examples are excerpted here. The first document is a list of demands from a group of peasants from Upper Swabia, located in today's south-central Germany. The participants in these uprisings justified their acts with reference to the teachings of Martin Luther (1483–1546), the priest who sparked the Protestant Reformation with his thoughts and actions. Luther, who began his challenge to the Catholic Church and the authority of the Papacy with publication of the 95 Theses in 1517, issued multiple responses to the protesters, one of which is Excerpt 2.

EXCERPT 1: THE TWELVE ARTICLES OF THE UPPER SWABIAN PEASANTS (1525)

Because the peasants are assembled, there are many antichristians who now find reason to disparage the gospel, saying, "These are the fruits of the new gospel: to be obedient to no one, to rise up and rebel everywhere, to form infantry units with great violence, to band together to reform spiritual and

Source: Excerpt 1: *The Twelve Articles of the Upper Swabian Peasants* in Michael G. Baylor, ed., *The Radical Reformation* (Cambridge, UK: Cambridge University Press, 1991), 231–238. Excerpt 2: Martin Luther, *Against the Murdering and Robbing Bands of Peasants*, in J. M. Porter, *Luther: Selected Political Writings* (Philadelphia: Fortress Press, 1974), 85–88.

temporal authorities, to expel them, perhaps even to kill them." The following articles reply to all these godless, superficial critics, first, to stop them from disparaging the word of God, and second, to justify on Christian grounds the disobedience, indeed the rebellion, of all the peasants (Romans 1).

First, the gospel is not a cause of rebellions or insurrections, because it speaks of Christ the promised Messiah, whose words and life teach nothing but love, peace, patience, and unity, so that all who believe in Christ become loving, peaceful, patient and united. If the basis of all the peasants' articles (as will be clearly seen) is directed toward hearing the gospel and living according to it, how can antichristians call the gospel a cause of rebellion and disobedience? Although certain antichristians and enemies of the gospel oppose such demands, and want to flare up and revolt against them, the gospel is not the cause of this, but the devil, that most pernicious enemy of the gospel, who inspires such behavior in his followers through lack of faith, so that the word of God (which teaches love, peace, and unity) is suppressed and robbed. . . .

Therefore, Christian reader, zealously read the following articles, and then judge them. Here are the articles.

ARTICLE ONE

First, it is our humble desire and request, and the intention and conviction of us all, that henceforth we want to have the full power for a whole congregation to select and elect its own pastor; and also the power to remove him, if he acts improperly. (I Timothy 3, Titus 1, Acts 14, Deuteronomy 17, Exodus 31, Deuteronomy 10, John 6, and Galatians 2.). . . .

ARTICLE TWO

Second, since a just tithe has been established in the Old Testament, and fulfilled in the New (as the whole Epistle to the Hebrews says), we will gladly pay the just grain tithe to the full—but in the proper way. . . . From it they shall give the parson, who has been elected by the whole congregation, enough to maintain himself and his family modestly, according to the determination of the whole congregation. And whatever is left over should be distributed to the destitute people of the village, according to their circumstances and the determination of the congregation (Deuteronomy 26). What is left over after this should be retained, in case travel is necessary for the sake of the territory. . . .

ARTICLE THREE

Third, until now it has been the custom for us to be regarded as a lord's personal property, which is deplorable since Christ redeemed us all with the shedding of his precious blood—the shepherd as well as the most highly placed, without exception. Thus, Scripture establishes that we are and will be free. (Isaiah 53, I Peter 1, I Corinthians 7.). . . . Without a doubt, as true and just Christians, you will also gladly release us from serfdom, or show us from the gospel that we should be serfs.

ARTICLE FOUR

Fourth, until now it has been the custom that no poor man has been allowed the right to hunt game or fowl or to catch fish in flowing water. We think that this is completely improper and unbrotherly; rather, it is selfish and not compatible with the word of God. (Genesis 1, Acts 10, I Timothy 4, I Corinthians 10, Colossians 2.). . . .

ARTICLE FIVE

Fifth, we also have grievances concerning the use of woodlands. For our lordships alone have appropriated all the woods, and when the poor man needs wood, he must buy it at double the price. It is our conviction that, regardless of the kind of woods involved—whether possessed by spiritual or by temporal authorities who have not bought it—it should revert to the whole community. (As is shown in the first chapter of Genesis.). . . .

ARTICLE SIX

Sixth, we have a serious grievance concerning labor services, which increase from day to day. We want to be granted some understanding, and accordingly not to be so severely burdened. Rather, we should be shown gracious understanding, for our forefathers served only according to the word of God. (Romans 10.)

ARTICLE SEVEN

Seventh, henceforth we no longer want to be burdened by a lordship; rather, if a lordship has been bestowed on someone correctly, he should receive his lordship through an agreement between lords and peasants. Lords should not force or compel their peasants, seeking to get more services or other dues from them without payment. The peasant should be able to use and enjoy his property in peace, without being burdened. (Luke 3, I Thessalonians 4.). . . .

ARTICLE NINE

Ninth, we are burdened by the great outrage that new laws are constantly being made, so that we are punished not according to the facts of a case, but sometimes out of envy and sometimes out of favoritism. It is our conviction that we should be punished according to ancient written law, and that cases be treated that way and not on the basis of favoritism. (Isaiah 19, Ephesians 6, Luke 3, and Jeremiah 26.). . . .

IN CONCLUSION

Twelfth, it is our conclusion and final conviction that if one or more of the articles we have composed here is not in accordance with the word of God, we will retract these articles, if they can be shown to be improper according to the word of God.

EXCERPT 2: MARTIN LUTHER, *AGAINST THE ROBBING AND MURDERING HORDES OF PEASANTS* (1525)

The peasants have taken upon themselves the burden of three terrible sins against God and man; by this they have abundantly merited death in body and soul. In the first place, they have sworn to be true and faithful, submissive and obedient, to their rulers, as Christ commands when he says, "Render to Caesar the things that are Caesar's" [Luke 20:25]. And Romans 13[:1] says, "Let every person be subject to the governing authorities." Since they are now deliberately and violently breaking this oath of obedience and setting themselves in opposition to their masters, they have forfeited body and soul, as faithless, perjured, lying, disobedient rascals and

scoundrels usually do. St. Paul passed this judgment on them in Romans 13[:2] when he said that those who resist the authorities will bring a judgment upon themselves. This saying will smite the peasants sooner or later, for God wants people to be loyal and to do their duty.

In the second place, they are starting a rebellion, and are violently robbing and plundering monasteries and castles which are not theirs; by this they have doubly deserved death in body and soul as highwaymen and murderers. Furthermore, anyone who can be proved to be a seditious person is an outlaw before God and the emperor; and whoever is the first to put him to death does right and well. For if a man is in open rebellion, everyone is both his judge and his executioner; just as when a fire starts, the first man who can put it out is the best man to do the job. For rebellion is not just simple murder; it is like a great fire, which attacks and devastates a whole land. Thus rebellion brings with it a land filled with murder and bloodshed; it makes widows and orphans, and turns everything upside down, like the worst disaster. Therefore let everyone who can, smite, slay, and stab, secretly or openly, remembering that nothing can be more poisonous, hurtful, or devilish than a rebel. It is just as when one must kill a mad dog; if you do not strike him, he will strike you, and a whole land with you.

In the third place, they cloak this terrible and horrible sin with the gospel, call themselves "Christian brethren," take oaths and submit to them, and compel people to go along with them in these abominations. Thus they become the worst blasphemers of God and slanderers of his holy name. Under the outward appearance of the gospel, they honor and serve the devil, thus deserving death in body and soul ten times over. I have never heard of a more hideous sin. I suspect that the devil feels that the Last Day is coming and therefore he undertakes such an unheard-of act, as though saying to himself, "This is the end, therefore it shall be the worst; I will stir up the dregs and knock out the bottom." God will guard us against him! See what a mighty prince the devil is, how he has the world in his hands and can throw everything into confusion, when he can so quickly catch so many thousands of peasants, deceive them, blind them, harden them, and throw them into revolt, and do with them whatever his raging fury under takes. . . .

Now since the peasants have brought [the wrath of] both God and man down upon themselves and are already many times guilty of death in body and soul, and since they submit to no court and wait for no verdict, but only rage on, I must instruct the temporal authorities on how they may act with a clear conscience in this matter. . . .

First he must take the matter to God, confessing that we have deserved these things, and remembering that God may, perhaps, have thus aroused the devil as a punishment upon all Germany. Then he should humbly pray for help against the devil, for we are contending not only "against flesh and blood," but "against the spiritual hosts of wickedness in the air" [Eph. 6:12; 2:2], which must be attacked with prayer. Then, when our hearts are so turned to God that we are ready to let his divine will be done, whether he will or will not have us to be princes and lords, we must go beyond our duty, and offer the mad peasants an opportunity to come to terms, even though they are not worthy of it. Finally, if that does not help, then swiftly take to the sword.

For in this case a prince and lord must remember that according to Romans 13[:4] he is God's minister and the servant of his wrath and that the sword has been given him to use against such people. If he does not fulfil the duties of his office by punishing some and protecting others, he commits as great a sin before God as when someone who has not been given the sword commits murder. . . .

Therefore, dear lords, here is a place where you can release, rescue, help. Have mercy on these poor people! Let whoever can stab, smite, slay. If you die in doing it, good for you! A more blessed death can never be yours, for you die while obeying the divine word and commandment in Romans 13[:1, 2], and in loving service of your neighbor, whom you are rescuing from the bonds of hell and of the devil. And so I beg everyone who can to flee from the peasants as from the devil himself; those who do not flee, I pray that God will enlighten and convert. As for those who are not to be converted, God grant that they may have neither fortune nor success. To this let every pious Christian say, "Amen!" For this prayer is right and good, and pleases God; this I know. If anyone thinks this too harsh, let him remember that rebellion is intolerable and that the destruction of the world is to be expected every hour.

QUESTIONS TO CONSIDER

1. What wrongs are the participants in the Peasants' War trying to correct? What are the terms under which they justify their actions and their proposed solutions?
2. What is the tone of Martin Luther's response to the protesters? Why does Luther respond this way?

3.4 "ONLY THOSE WHO JUSTLY DESERVE TO BE PUNISHED SHOULD BE PUNISHED." ROBERT BELLARMINE, *THE OFFICE OF A CHRISTIAN PRINCE*, 1618

Robert Bellarmine (1542–1621) was a member of the Society of Jesus, an order of Catholic priests also known as the Jesuits. The Jesuit order was founded by Ignatius of Loyola (1491–1556), a Spanish nobleman and military officer who turned toward the priesthood while convalescing from a serious battlefield injury. The Society of Jesus saw its goal as spreading and defending the Catholic faith and the Pope against the rising tide of Protestantism. In this contest, Robert Bellarmine played a major role. Educated in Italy and Belgium, Bellarmine became one of the most influential theologians defending Catholic beliefs against Protestant criticisms as a professor of "controversial theology." While most of Bellarmine's writings focused on theology, he did produce a work on politics in 1618, *The Office of a Christian Prince*. This work was prepared for Crown Prince Ladislaus (1595–1648) of Poland, who would rule as King of Poland and Grand Duke of Lithuania from 1632 to 1648. Like Machiavelli's *The Prince* (see Source 3.1), *The Office of a Christian Prince* is another example from the vast genre of "princely advice literature" produced across the Eurasian world in the early modern era.

Next, St. John condemns false accusations made by soldiers saying, "Do not make false accusations." This is another vice that soldiers generally fall into. It often happens that they level false accusations against anybody they encounter: they are spies, or enemies, or deserters. And without any basis in justice, the soldiers robbed or wounded such people or took them captive. Unhappy are those who have nobody to testify to their innocence; they are forced to either buy their way out of trouble by a large sum of money or to endure cruel sufferings. Would that such things were not commonplace in Christian military camps! Good princes ought to devote their full strength to driving these things from our midst. In the end, the blessed Precursor of our Lord teaches all soldiers to be content with their wages and not pillage the property of others. We do not know whether the soldiers who heard what St. John said carried it out. We do know this: that in our times not only is this salutary teaching observed rarely, and by few [soldiers], but also no small trouble is inflicted on the citizens of the cities where the soldiers need to have winter quarters or stay for a time. But perhaps city folk are forced to provide the things the soldiers lack because the soldiers are not paid their salaries on time.

This can happen because the soldiers do not receive their salaries on time, but in the interval justice is disregarded. God, who sees and weighs everything on an accurately balanced scale, will severely punish those who do evil. Princes therefore ought to work so that the salaries owed the soldiers are paid on time. Then, if the soldiers do not follow the commands of St. John, it should be brought to the princes' attention in such a way that the soldiers learn to be content with their pay and not inflict harm on the city folk with whom they are living.

These things that have been said about soldiers can be applied to all the court officials: they too

Source: John Patrick Donnelly, S.J., ed. and trans., *Jesuit Writings of the Early Modern Period, 1540–1640* (Indianapolis: Hackett Publishing, 2006), 225–230.

should be content with their salaries. If they receive anything beyond their salary they should recognize the generosity of the prince and not take it as retribution owed them. Besides that, they should set an example of modesty, kindness, and justice to all other people who serve private inheritors and reside in private homes. It frequently happens that while the prince is modest and kindly, his court officials are arrogant and harsh. The prince insists on justice and does no injury to anybody, but his officials are not content with their own salaries; they lust after gifts and practically sell access to the prince or to other things that are part of their office. But vices of this sort, which can affect the prince's good reputation, can be easily headed off if the prince earnestly and frequently recommends household discipline to the chief steward of the palace and orders him to take care, either personally or through others, that nothing happen in the palace that might result in injury to God or to the prince's reputation. . . .

There remains one crime that is common to soldiers and court officials: that they easily flatter their prince. They praise to the skies anything he says or does, as if it were a statement of the highest wisdom or a most splendid deed. Like a sweet poison, this flattery slips easily into [the prince's] mind, unless he has a mind truly humble and fully submissive to God. It is beyond telling how numerous and serious are the troubles that arise when the poison of flattery takes over the prince's mind. For the person who gives ear to flatterers first reeks with pride and walks, as the Scriptures say, into great and marvelous things that are above him and thinks that everything is easy for him [Ps. 131:1]. He then scorns the advice of the wise or spurns them as timid, or if they happen to steer him away from deeds that are more dangerous than advantageous, he thinks they are envious of his glory. . . .

It now follows for us to reflect on how princes should deal with their equals. By "equals" we refer to those men who are not superior to or subject to one another, such as are all those who are called independent princes. . . .

So that we may warn princes a bit more carefully about such an important matter, they should take it for granted that it is not in any way permitted to oppress by war a neighboring prince or any other person unless the conditions for a just war are present. The four conditions [for a just war] usually listed are: legitimate authority, a just cause, a good intention, and reasonable conduct. . . .

But we have to give very close attention to this: the injury that is being redressed by war should not be dubious or minor but certain and serious. Otherwise there is danger that a war may cause more harm instead of the good that was hoped for from the war. . . .

A good intention, which is the third condition, is extremely necessary for a just war. . . . Not only does the absence of this third condition make the war unjust, it makes it a bad war even if it is just. In this respect, the third condition differs greatly from the two previous ones. If they are not present, the war is not only bad but also unjust since it would clearly be contrary to justice. But when a war is undertaken for a just cause and by the authority of a prince but without a good intention, it is against charity but not against justice.

This factor also deserves careful consideration here: when a war is going to be started as a means for peace, the means are still very important and dangerous. It should not be started immediately; rather other, easier and better, means should be tried first, as that Moses pointed out in Deuteronomy, "When you approach a city to attack it, offer terms of peace to it" [Dt. 20:10].

There remains the last condition: how [the war is waged]. War should be fought in such a way that only those who justly deserve to be punished should be punished. First those who are not from the number of the enemies should be set aside—for instance those who are not citizens of the enemy state. Those soldiers who have mistreated, pillaged, persecuted, or captured people through whose land they were marching or those who when barracked among people often repaid their kind hospitality with evil deeds, should not be treated mercifully. Such soldiers cannot be excused because their salaries are not paid them on time, for soldiers have no right to the goods of people who have done them no harm. Neither should civilians and friendly peasants be made to pay up because the prince has not paid his soldiers their salaries. Next, young children, women, old men, and others who cannot bear arms are out of bounds. Still, these people who cannot fight can be captured and stripped if they belong to the hostile state. But they certainly cannot be rightly killed, unless somebody of this sort is killed by an unintentional accident, for instance when a soldier accidentally shoots an arrow into an enemy formation and by chance kills a boy or weak old man. God Himself ordered this of the Hebrews when they were waging war, that they were to spare children and women. Natural reason teaches the same thing. What purpose is served by killing many people who cannot fight, unless it be to show off one's beastly cruelty? Those passages in Scripture in which God Himself commands that neither children nor women nor cattle are to be spared should not be mentioned.

God's command should be obeyed completely since nobody can ask Him, "Why are you doing this?" Finally, according to the law of the Church the following kinds of people are not to be harmed: priests, monks, converts, pilgrims, merchants, and peasants who are coming or going or living by agriculture and the animals used in plowing or in transporting seed to the fields—for they have a right to enjoy a proper security. These are then the conditions of a just war. Without [these conditions] no prince should harass any other prince. Still less should a powerful prince harass a weaker one. Otherwise he should fear the judgments of God, who often brings it about that the weaker prince easily defeats the stronger one.

QUESTIONS TO CONSIDER

1. According to Bellarmine, what role do force, violence, and/or coercion play in rulership? Under what conditions can or should these alternatives be used?
2. What are the primary differences between Bellarmine's "rules for rulers" and those of Machiavelli (Source 3.1)? Are there any ideas about rulership on which they seem to agree or overlap at all?

3.5 "CONQUEST TOLERATES NOT INACTION." *MEMOIRS OF BABUR,* CA. 1526

Babur (1483–1530) was the founder of the Mughal Empire, a hereditary Islamic dynasty on the Asian subcontinent from 1526 to the middle of the eighteenth century. From the age of 12 until his death, Babur kept a journal to record his exploits and to provide advice to his successors. Over time, the memoir, known as the *Baburnama (The Book of Babur)*, was translated into different languages and distributed widely. The memoir provides observations on culture, vivid descriptions of landscapes and animal life, accounts of personal triumphs and challenges, and general thoughts on political and military strategy.

Following are two excerpts from the *Baburnama*. The first is from Babur's account of the Battle of Panipat in 1526, during which Babur defeated the army of Ibrahim Lodhi, who ruled the Sultanate of Delhi, which covered much of the Asian subcontinent. Sultan Ibrahim died during the battle. The second excerpt is from correspondence between Babur and his son, Humayun, who became Emperor in 1530. Kamran is another of Babur's children, and Kwaja Kalan is a trusted general and confidant.

Source: *The Baburnama: Memoirs of Babur, Prince and Emperor,* trans. Wheeler M. Thackson (New York: Modern Library, 2002), 320–330, 422–435.

EXCERPT 1: THE MARCH TOWARD DELHI

After sending a party out in pursuit of Ghazi Khan, we placed our feet in the stirrup of resolve, grabbed the reins of trust in God, and directed ourselves against Sultan Ibrahim, son of Sultan Sikandar son of Bahlul Lodi the Afghan, who controlled the capital Delhi and the realm of Hindustan at that time. He was said to have a standing army of one hundred thousand, and he and his *begs [a high-ranking officer–Ed.]* had nearly a thousand elephants. After one march Baqi Shiqavul was given Dipalpur and dispatched as reinforcement to Balkh. Much money was sent to the aid of Balkh, and presents of the booty that fell to us during the conquest of Malot were sent to the families and children in Kabul. . . .

We marched from there, arrayed the right and left wings and center, and had a *dim [an assessment of military preparedness–Ed.]*. We had fewer men than we had estimated. I ordered the whole army, in accordance with rank, to bring carts, which numbered about seven hundred altogether. Master Ali-Quli was told to tie them together with ox-harness ropes instead of chains, after the Anatolian manner, keeping a distance of six to seven large shields between every two carts. The matchlockmen could then stand behind the fortification to fire their guns. Five or six days were spent arranging it, and when it was ready I summoned to general council all the begs and great warriors who knew what they were talking about. We discussed the following: Panipat was a town with lots of suburbs and houses. The suburbs and houses would protect one side, but it was necessary to fortify our other sides with the carts and shields and to station matchlockmen and foot soldiers behind them. This having been decided, we marched, bivouacked, and then came to Panipat on [April 12].

To our right were the town and suburbs. Directly before us were the arranged shields. To the left and elsewhere were trenches and pylons. At every distance of an arrow shot, space was left for one hundred to 150 cavalrymen to emerge. Some of the soldiers were hesitant, but their trepidation was baseless, for only what God has decreed from all eternity will happen. They cannot be blamed, however, for being afraid, even if God was on their side.

They had traveled for two or three months from their homeland, and had had to deal with an unfamiliar people whose language we did not know and who did not know ours. A group confused, peace of mind shattered. A people preoccupied, a very strange people.

Sultan Ibrahim's army was estimated at one hundred thousand. He and his commanders were said to have nearly a thousand elephants. Moreover, he possessed the treasury left over from two generations of his fathers. The custom in Hindustan is to hire liege men for money before major battles. Such people are called *badhandi*. If Sultan Ibrahim had had a mind to, he could have hired one hundred thousand to two hundred thousand troops. Thank God he was able neither to satisfy his warriors nor to part with his treasury. How was he to please his men when his nature was so overwhelmingly dominated by miserliness? He himself was an inexperienced young man who craved beyond all things the acquisition of money—neither his oncoming nor his stand was calculated to have a good end, and neither his march nor his fighting was energetic.

EXCERPT 2: FROM A LETTER TO HUMAYUN

To Humayun. Thinking of you with much longing, I greet you. . . .

Item: Kamran and the Kabul *begs* were ordered to go join you, and you all will proceed to Hissar or Samarkand or whichever direction is in our best interests. Through God's grace you will defeat your enemies, take their territory, and make your friends happy by overthrowing the foe. God willing, this is your time to risk your life and wield your sword. Do not fail to make the most of an opportunity that presents itself. Indolence and luxury do not suit kingship.

Conquest tolerates not inaction; the world is his who hastens most. When one is master, one may rest from everything—except being king.

If by God's grace and favor, Balkh and Hissar are won and subdued, let one of your men stay in Hissar and one of Kamran's in Balkh. If by God's grace and favor, Samarkand is also subdued, you stay there yourself and, God willing, I will make Hissar royal demesne *[properties of the ruler himself–Ed.]*. If Kamran thinks Balkh is small, write me. God willing, I will make up the deficiency to him out of those other territories.

Item: You know that this rule has always been observed: six parts to you and five to Kamran. Always observe this rule yourself and do not break it.

Item: Conduct yourself well with your younger brother. Elder brothers need to have restraint. It is my hope that you will get along well with him, for he has grown up to be a religiously observant and fine young man. Let him also display no deficiency in homage and respect for you.

Item: I have a few complaints of you. For two or three years now none of your men has come. The man I sent returned exactly a year later. Is this proper?

Item: In your letters you keep talking about being alone. Solitude is a flaw in kingship, as has been said, "If you are fettered, resign yourself; but if you are a lone rider, your reins are free." *[This is a quote from the work of the 13th-century Persian poet Sa'di–Ed.]* There is no bondage like the bondage of kingship. In kingship it is improper to seek solitude.

Item: As I asked, you have written your letters, but you didn't read them over, for if you had had a mind to read them, you would have found that you could not. After reading them you certainly would have changed them. Although your writing can be read with difficulty, it is excessively obscure. Who has ever heard of prose designed to be an enigma? Your spelling is not bad, although it is not entirely correct either. . . . Your handwriting can be made out somehow or other, but with all these obscure words of yours the meaning is not entirely clear. Probably your laziness in writing letters is due to the fact that you try to make it too fancy. From now on write with uncomplicated, clear, and plain words. This will cause less difficulty both for you and for your reader. . . .

Item: There were such conquests and victories while we were in Kabul that I consider Kabul my lucky piece and have made it royal demesne. Let none of you covet it.

Item: Conduct yourself well. Make friends with Sultan Ways. Bring him in and act upon his opinion, for he is an experienced man. Keep the army disciplined and in training. Buyan Shaykh has had verbal instructions from me that he will communicate to you. With longing, peace.

Written on [November 26].

In my own hand I wrote Kamran and Khwaja Kalan letters of similar content and sent them off.

QUESTIONS TO CONSIDER

1. To what does Babur attribute his successes on and off the battlefield? What evidence does he provide to support his assertions about success?
2. How would you compare Babur's observations about rulership and authority, as one who has held power and commanded armies, with the advice to rulers from Machiavelli and Bellarmine?

3.6 "EVERYTHING FROM YOUR OWN PERSON UP TO THE WHOLE NATION SHOULD BE A MATTER OF STUDY." GU YANWU, *TRUE LEARNING* AND *ON BUREAUCRATIC LOCAL ADMINISTRATION*, CA. 1660

Gu Yanwu (1613–1682) was born just thirty years before the fall of China's Ming Dynasty. The Ming was weakened by numerous economic, administrative, and political challenges, including problems facing local government. Government in China was based on principles of Neo-Confucianism, a set of ideas developed in the Song Dynasty (960–1279) that supposedly interpreted the teachings of Confucius (551–479 BCE). Civil service examinations, a tool for staffing the Ming government, were based on Neo-Confucian ideas and emphasized principle over practice, book learning over experience, and application of Confucian ideals to situations that took place 2,000 years after Confucius's death.

Gu Yanwu railed against the shortcomings of Neo-Confucian thought and strove to strengthen Ming administration in the dynasty's last years, gaining a reputation as a reformer. When the Ming fell to invading Manchus in 1644, Gu refused to serve the new Qing Dynasty, but continued to study local conditions and suggest more effective principles not only for government administration, but also for economic activity, military tactics, and other endeavors. The passages selected here focus mainly on his concerns with government.

EXCERPT 1: ON THE CONCENTRATION OF AUTHORITY AT COURT

He who is called the Son of Heaven holds supreme authority in the world. What is the nature of this supreme authority? It is authority over all the world, which is vested in the men of the world but which derives ultimately from the Son of Heaven. From the highest ministers and officials down to the regional magistrates and petty officers, each holds a share of this authority of the Son of Heaven and directs the affairs of his charge, and the authority of the Son of Heaven is thereby magnified in dignity. In later ages, there appeared inept rulers who gathered all authority into their own hands. But the countless exigencies of government are so broad that it is quite impossible for one man to handle them all, so that authority then shifted to the laws. With this a great many laws were promulgated to prevent crimes and violations, so that even the greatest criminals could not get around them, nor the cleverest officials accomplish anything by evading them. People thereupon expended all their efforts in merely following the laws and trying to stay out of difficulty. Thus, the authority of the Son of Heaven came to reside not in the officials appointed by the government but in their clerks and assistants [who were familiar with the laws]. *Now* what the world needs most urgently are local officials who will personally look after the people, and yet today the men who possess least authority are precisely these local officials. If local officials are

Source: W. T. de Bary and R. Lufrano, comps., *Sources of the Chinese Tradition*, 2nd ed., Vol. 2 (New York: Columbia University Press, 2000), 36–41.

not made known to the higher authorities, how can we hope to achieve peace and prosperity and prolong the life of the nation?

EXCERPT 2: ON BUREAUCRATIC LOCAL ADMINISTRATION

If one understands why the enfeoffment system (*fengjian*) [*roughly the equivalent of feudalism in medieval Europe, a system in which people are given land in exchange for the promise of service–Ed.*] was transformed into the system of centralized bureaucratic local administration (*junxian*) one can understand why the evils of the bureaucratic system must be transformed in turn. But can the bureaucratic system be transformed back into the enfeoffment system? I say not. If, however, a sage were to arise who could infuse the spirit of the enfeoffment system into the body of the bureaucratic system, all-underHeaven would be well governed. . . .

By elevating the rank of senior local officials, giving them authority over the means of production and the regulation of the people, abolishing the posts that oversee them, making their positions hereditary, and allowing them to select subordinates by their own methods, what I have called "infusing the spirit of the enfeoffment system into the bureaucratic system" might be accomplished and order fashioned out of the evils of the past two thousand years. . . .

My proposal is to transform the county magistrate into an official of the fifth rank and change his title to "district magistrate." Those who fill this position should be natives of the area within a thousand *li* [*approximately one-third of an English mile–Ed.*] of the county in which they serve and be familiar with local customs. At first, they are to be called "probationary magistrates." If after three years they show themselves to be equal to the post, their appointments are to be regularized [and if they succeed in three more three-year terms] they are to be appointed for life. Those magistrates who retire because of age or illness are to be succeeded by their sons or younger brothers. If they have no descendants, they should select their own successors.

. . . . Thereafter the same procedure shall be followed for the successors. . . . Now, caring for the people is like the work of a family in raising domestic animals. One family member is assigned the task of tending the horses and oxen, and another grows the fodder. If, however, the master's hired foreman is sent to oversee them, he will not even be able to calculate the amount of fodder without consulting the master, and the horses and oxen will waste away. With my program, it would not be this way. I would select as groom one who is diligent and skillful, give him full charge of the horses and oxen, and grant him land, the produce of which would always exceed the fodder needs of the animals. If the animals grow fat and reproduce, I would reward the groom; if not, I would flog him.

The reason the empire's troubles have become so numerous is that the master, not trusting his grooms, has sent servants to oversee them. Not trusting even these, the master has become confused as to what his own eyes and ears tell him. But if one truly loves his horses and oxen, he will not calculate the cost of the fodder. If a horse is tended by a single groom, it will grow fat. If the people are governed by a single official, they will be content. . . .

Some will object: "If there are no supervisory officials, won't the magistrates serve only their own interests?" Or: "Isn't it improper that their power be passed down to their lineal descendants?" Or: "Won't men who come from within a thousand *li* of the county in which they serve tend to favor their own relatives and friends?" I say, however, that the reason so many magistrates today abuse their office for their own private gain is precisely because they come from so far away. If they were required to be residents of the same place, then even if they wanted to abuse their office for private gain, they would be unable to do so. . . .

It is every man's normal disposition to cherish his own family and to favor his own children. His feelings toward the ruler and toward all other men are inevitably not as strong as his feelings toward his own kin. It has been this way as far back as the Three Dynasties. The ancient sages availed themselves of this spirit and made use of it. Out of the self-interest of everyone throughout the empire they formed a public spirit of one accord in the ruler, and thus the empire was in good order.

Accordingly, if we let the county magistrate take a personal interest in his hundred *li* of territory, then all the people in the county will become in effect his children and kin, all the lands of the county in effect his lands, all its walls his defenses, and all its granaries his storehouses. His own children and kin he will of course cherish rather than harm; his own fields he will manage well rather than abandon; his own defenses and storehouses he will mend rather than neglect. Thus, what is viewed by the magistrate as "looking out for my own" will be viewed by the ruler as "acting responsibly," will it not? The proper governance of the empire lies in this and nothing else.

QUESTIONS TO CONSIDER

1. At certain points, Gu Yanwu seems to be advocating for a more centralized government. In other places, he calls for more local autonomy. How can we reconcile these two views? What principles are guiding Gu's ideas?
2. How do Gu Yanwu's ideas about government compare to the other advice literature in this chapter or other theories developed around this time with which you are familiar? What similarities and differences in goals or values can you detect?

CHAPTER 4

PRODUCTION AND CONSUMPTION IN THE FIRST GLOBAL ECONOMY, 1571–1700

4.1 "SOME MAKING A PROFIT, OTHERS LEFT BANKRUPT." EVLIYA ÇELEBÍ, *THE BOOK OF TRAVELS*, CA. 1630–1672

Evliya Çelebí (1610–1683) was the son of the Ottoman sultan's chief goldsmith. As he tells his own life story, at the age of 20, the Prophet Muhammad came to him in a dream to announce that God's plan was for Evliya to travel the world and write about what he encountered. Over the coming decades, he traveled through much of the Ottoman Empire, as well as parts of the Safavid Empire and into Europe as well. The literary product of these travels was *Seyahatname (The Book of Travels)*, a ten-volume tome covering events between 1630 and the early 1670s. The volumes are filled with rich details, strong opinions, some exaggerated accounts of events and places, and even some fabrications. In the following excerpts, Evliya describes two market towns in the Ottoman Empire: Diyarbekir, east of Istanbul on the west bank of the Tigris River, and Doryan, west of Istanbul.

EXCERPT ON THE ROYAL COVERED BAZAAR AT DIYARBEKIR

Altogether 2,008 shops constitute the wellbuilt area of the bazaar, the Market of Beauty. Firstly, there is the bazaar of Hasan Pasha, then the army bazaar, the druggists' bazaar—the brains of those who pass through it are scented with perfumes—and the goldsmiths' bazaar. All these bazaars are constructed with vaults of fitted stone, huge as the Vault of Chosroes [*Built sometime between the 3rd and 6th centuries CE in today's Iraq, this arched palace wall remained the largest free-standing architectural feature of its kind for a millennium or more. Here, Çelebí is clearly exaggerating about the structures in Diyarbekir–Ed.*].

Further, there is the market of the blacksmiths, the bazaar of the locksmiths, the bazaar of jewellers

Source: *An Ottoman Traveller: Selections from the Book of Travels of Evliya Çelebí*, trans. and commentary by Robert Dankoff and Sooyong Kim (London: Eland Publishing, 2001), 113–114, 298–300.

and goldsmiths, the bazaar of the boot makers, the saddlers' bazaar, the bazaar of the silk manufacturers and the bazaar of the traders in cloth. In short, there are shops of 366 different trades and crafts. But the market hall in the army bazaar is a well-kept, beautifully ornamented solid building of fitted stone, with iron gates on both ends. It is crowded with the richest merchants, and one finds here valuable goods of the highest quality and the most expensive sorts of jewellery from all countries. Swords, scimitars, maces, axes, arrows, daggers, spear-blades and arrowheads such as those forged hereabouts are made nowhere else, except perhaps by the weapon-smiths of Isfahan.

The Armenian blacksmiths, while beating their hammers and pumping their bellows, sing songs with their fine voices. . . . And their servants strike their hammers in twenty-four different rhythmic patterns. . . .

When the cotton carders beat the cotton, the strings of their carding bows produce sounds in various musical modes. . . .

They cultivate here a special type of basil that everyone plants along the borders of his plot. In a month's time it becomes thick as a forest and tall as a spear, impenetrable to the glance. All their humble houses along the bank of the Tigris have their doors and walls and roofs made out of basil. The basil stems remain rooted in the earth and the leaves remain green and continue to grow finding moisture in the soil. It is impossible to see from one house to the next through these walls of basil. The huts are so overgrown that the brains of the men and women living in them are perfumed night and day with the fragrance of basil and the other flowers in these gardens, such as roses, Judas trees and hyacinth. The women's quarters of each garden pavilion are also such pleasure-huts of basil. . . .

The melons that grow in these gardens have no match, except perhaps the melons of Bohtan in the province of Van. The Diyarbekir melons are huge, very juicy and sweet, and with a delicious aroma as of musk and ambergris. If you eat one of them the fragrance of melon will not leave your brain for an entire week. There is even a tradition among the ulema *[specialists in Islamic law–Ed.]* of Kurdistan and the scholars of Soranistan that Abu Bakr the Faithful

[573–634 CE; the Prophet Mohammed's rightful successor as Caliph in the Sunni Islamic tradition–Ed.] exuded a fragrance like that of melon; and the ulema of Diyarbekir claim that this can only be their Tigris melon. The aroma is such that the brain of one who eats it or just smells it is imbued with ambergris.

Some of these melons attain a weight of 40 or 50 okkas *[The okka would be the equivalent of almost 3 lbs., though it was not standardized as a measure at the time Çelebí was writing. However, it is clear that Çelebí was describing these melons as truly gigantic–Ed.].* They all have a green colour. People take them as presents to various countries, as far as they remain fresh. Some people use them to prepare zerde (a yellow-rice dish), flavoured with cinnamon and cloves, according to the recipe of the Caliph Mu'awiya. Not even Athens honey could make a zerde so fragrant as this dish is with Diyarbekir melons.

The watermelons, however, do not deserve much praise. The basil on the other hand grows into such huge trees that in seven or eight months they can be used as tent-poles or stakes, and when one burns them in a fire they smell like Chinese hyacinth.

In short, the people of Diyarbekir are the envy of the world for the delights they enjoy for seven or eight months of the year along the bank of the Tigris; when their nights are like the Night of Power, and their days like the holiday of the Festival of Sacrifice; holding concerts worthy of *[Sultan]* Husayn Bayqara *[1438–1506–Ed.]*; and thinking to snatch a bit of pleasure from this transitory world.

DESCRIPTION OF THE FAIR AT DOYRAN

[A]t the border of the kadi-district of Usturumça (Strurnitsa) there is a delightful wooded meadow and a broad plain. The fairgrounds are laid out like a chessboard, with several one- and two-storey stone buildings … resembling a fortress. Lining the thoroughfares are over 1,000 shops roofed with tiles that comprise the fair. . . .

Once a year, during the cherry season, 100,000 people gather in this plain. They come from Turkey and Arabia and Persia, Hind and Sind, Samarkand and Balkh and Bukhara, Egypt and Syria and Iraq and Western Europe—in short from the seven climes. All the merchants of land and sea arrive here with their merchandise and set up their tents and pavilions and huts-of-sorrow and booths of reed and straw in the surrounding valleys. It is like an army-camp bazaar for the troops of Alexander the Great [Alexander III (356–323 BCE), ruler of Macedon–Ed.] or Darius [ruler of Persia (550–486 BCE)–Ed.] or Kay Khusraw [a legendary Persian warrior and also the name of several sultans of the 13th and 14th centuries–Ed.]. This valley becomes a sea of men. Myriads of bales of goods are brought out and bought and sold, including bird's-milk and man's-milk and lion's-milk—bird's-milk is eggs, man's-milk is mother's milk, and lion's-milk is wine—you can find all of these. Indeed, of eggs, I have seen ostrich eggs. I have even see men sell their own children!

On the days of the fair, thousands of shopkeepers—purveyors of food and drink, bakers and cooks and tanners—from all the nearby towns and villages set up their tent stalls. The jostling crowds are like a rabble army, and the market is brisk for forty days and forty nights. Even women openly sell their secret wears [wares?]. Thousands of people become wealthy as Korah, [an ancient Near East ruler of legendary wealth mentioned in both the Quran and the Hebrew Bible–Ed.] while other thousands dissipate their wealth in revelry and end up poor as mice.

Also there is a separate market for sheep and goats, another for horses and mules, and one for oxen and water-buffaloes. Only there is no camel market since there are no camels in Rumelia. But there is a market in human beings where thousands of lovely boys and girls are bought and sold; and a separate slave market for black Arabs with 40,000 or 50,000 customers, since blacks are highly prized as servants in these regions.

In the main fairgrounds the various shopkeepers are installed, including the great merchants, worth hundreds of thousands of guruş [a unit of currency–Ed.] who set up shop in the tiled stone buildings mentioned above. They lay out their wares—precious stuffs such as silks and satins and velvets; or jewels such as rubies, emeralds, chrysolite, turquoise, agate, etc.—turning their countertops into decked-out brides or idol temples of China. For this han [a large stone building–Ed.] bazaar is as secure as a fortress and everyone openly displays his most expensive goods.

Meanwhile the business in the outer fairgrounds is equally brisk. The vast plain is filled with row on row of tents, pavilions, covered stalls, booths made from kilims or from pilgrim-garbs—it resembles a tulip garden—and goods are being exchanged in every corner.

Also there are the cookshops of Kay Kavus; maybe 1,000 places where whole lambs and sheep are being turned on spits; and over 1,000 coffee houses and boza [a fermented grain beverage–Ed.] shops and wine taverns. Invariably some people get drunk and brawls break out. Then the officer stationed here—the chief kadi [judge–Ed.] of Serres, the colonel of the janissary [Sultan's guard–Ed.] troop, the tax-agent's voyvoda [lord (official)–Ed.] and comptroller—step in and mete out fines and punishments, so the place is actually very safe.

And whatever entertainers there are on the face of the earth can be found here in the public squares and in the tents—jugglers, tightrope walkers, gamblers; players with bottles or bowls or glasses; mace-wielders, strong-men, rope-dancers, puppeteers, shadow puppet players, tumblers, sword-swallowers; trainers of dancing bears, monkeys, goats and donkeys; cudgel-wielders, lassoers, snake charmers, bird fanciers; tricksters with straps or paper or mirrors or jars or heads—in short, all the world's conjurers and alchemists and illegitimates come here in swarms and display their skills. Then there are the singers and dancers and instrumentalists; clowns and comics; reciters of ghazals and kasides (i.e., shorter lyrics and longer odes); wrestlers and archers; pretty boys and lovers and singing girls and women.

Whoever has not seen this spectacle . . . should not say that he has seen very much. . . .

After all the bustle and commotion and buying and selling—some making a profit, others left bankrupt—everyone returns home and the fairgrounds turn into a water mill whose stream has run dry, so a passerby would wonder if there were ever people here at all. The wise will take a lesson from this and withdraw from the pomp and show of this perishable world. But it is a wonderful spectacle!

QUESTIONS TO CONSIDER

1. What sense of the relationships between urban and rural, local and long-distance economic activity emerges from Evliya's descriptions?
2. What kinds of different jobs/professions are described in this excerpt? How are different races, ethnicities, and genders mapped on to different kinds of work?

4.2 "A GREAT HARM NOT ONLY TO THE SERVICE OF GOD, BUT TO THE SECURITY AND PEACE OF OUR KINGDOMS." *AFONSO OF CONGO TO THE KING OF PORTUGAL, 1526* AND *ADVICE TO THE KING OF SPAIN AND PORTUGAL ON SLAVERY,* CA. 1612

Nzinga Mbemba (ca. 1460–1543), prince of the kingdom of Congo in west-central Africa, took the name Afonso when he was baptized a Catholic in 1491. He became King Afonso I in 1506, succeeding his father on the throne. During his reign, Afonso I established close relations with Portugal and the Portuguese crown. His own son, Henrique, was educated in Portugal and became a Catholic priest. The letter excerpted here is one Afonso sent in 1526 to King João III of Portugal, as Afonso grew increasingly impatient with, and desperate about, the conduct of the Portuguese in Congo.

The second document excerpted here was written almost a century later. References to events in the document suggest it was written in 1612. The author is unknown, but it was discovered in a government archive, which leads researchers to conclude that it was an advisory message produced for King Philip II of Portugal, who was also King of Spain at the time the note was written. The document provides the King with a review of the growth of slavery and the conduct of subjects involved in the slave trade within the King's dominions.

EXCERPT 1: AFONSO OF CONGO TO THE KING OF PORTUGAL, 1526

Sir, Your Highness [of Portugal] should know how our Kingdom is being lost in so many ways that it is convenient to provide for the necessary remedy, since this is caused by the excessive freedom given by your factors and officials to the men and merchants who are allowed to come to this Kingdom to set up shops with goods and many things which have been prohibited by us, and which they spread throughout our Kingdoms and Domains in such an abundance that many of our vassals, whom we had in obedience, do

Source: Excerpt 1: Basil Davidson, ed., *The African Past. Chronicles from Antiquity to Modern Times* (Boston: Little, Brown, 1964), 191–194. Excerpt 2: "Proposta a Sua Magestade sobre a escravaria das terras da Conquista de Portugal," Document 7, 3, 1, No. 8, Seção de Manuscritos, Biblioteca Nacional Rio de Janeiro. In Robert Edgar Conrad, ed., *Children of God's Fire: A Documentary History of Black Slavery in Brazil* (Princeton, NJ: Princeton University Press, 1983), 11–15.

not comply because they have the things in greater abundance than we ourselves; and it was with these things that we had them content and subjected under our vassalage and jurisdiction, so it is doing a great harm not only to the service of God, but the security and peace of our Kingdoms and State as well.

And we cannot reckon how great the damage is, since the mentioned merchants are taking every day our natives, sons of the land and the sons of our noblemen and vassals and our relatives, because the thieves and men of bad conscience grab them wishing to have the things and wares of this Kingdom which they are ambitious of; they grab them and get them to be sold; and so great, Sir, is the corruption and licentiousness that our country is being completely depopulated, and Your Highness should not agree with this nor accept it as in your service. And to avoid it we need from those [your] Kingdoms no more than some priests and a few people to teach in schools, and no other goods except wine and flour for the holy sacrament. That is why we beg of Your Highness to help and assist us in this matter, commanding your factors that they should not send here either merchants or wares, because it is our will that in these Kingdoms there should not be any trade of slaves nor outlet for them.

EXCERPT 2: ADVICE TO THE KING OF SPAIN AND PORTUGAL ON SLAVERY, CA. 1612

Modern theologians in published books commonly report on, and condemn as unjust, the acts of enslavement which take place in the Provinces of this Royal Empire, employing for this purpose the same principles by which the ancient theologians, doctors of canon law, and jurists have regulated legitimate and just acts of enslavement. According to these principles, only infidels who are captured in just wars, or who because of serious crimes have been condemned by their Rulers may be held as legitimate slaves, or if they sell themselves, or if they are sold by their own fathers who have legitimate need. And because, by the use of these four principles, great injustices are committed in the buying and selling of slaves in our Empire, as will later be seen, it is also certain that most of the slaves of this Empire are made so upon other pretexts,

of which some are notoriously unjust, and others with great likelihood may be presumed to be so as well. . . .

Not even the merchants themselves deny that they collect these slaves in the ways described, but they defend themselves saying that they transport them so that they may become Christians, and so that they may wear clothes and have more to eat, failing to recognize that none of this is sufficient to justify so much theft and tyranny, because, as St. Paul says, those who perform evil acts in order to bring about some good are justly condemned before God. How much more is this true in a matter as serious as the freedom of human beings. . . .

Concerning the principle of just war, it is known that, since they are infidels and barbarians, the Kings and private Lords of the entire Conquest are not normally motivated by reason when they make war, but rather by passion, nor do they examine or consult others about their right to do so. Therefore most of their wars are unjust wars carried on merely for greed, ambition, and other unjust causes. Often the same may be presumed about the wars carried on by individual Portuguese captains, because, greedy as they are to capture slaves and other prizes, they often do so without any concern for their consciences. . . .

Concerning the two other principles: the need to sell oneself to seek release from an unjust death or some other great misery; or being sold by one's father who is in dire need—these are the causes of many unjust acts of enslavement in those places. Because in some places, as has been said, some persons make a pretense of wanting to eat others, or of wishing to slaughter them, so that they can be sold. Many fathers sell their sons for almost nothing, without being in any dire need which might justify such a sale, which is invalid and without any force in law, because the power is not given to a father to sell his minor son, except in dire need, according to common scholarly doctrine. And also in place of their children they sell other relatives who are close at hand, and other strangers using tricks which they invent for the purpose, saying, or making them say, that they are their sons. And in Brazil before the abovementioned law of King Sebastian, the Portuguese persuaded the Indians to sell themselves, and since, because of their ignorance, they didn't understand how important this was, they sold themselves for a cotton jacket and some breeches, which later they wore out in the service of their own masters. And when they later understood the trick, if it was not possible for them to run away, some died from their misery and others lived in a state of perpetual grief. And one may suspect that in all likelihood the same thing happens in other places, such as Guinea, the land of the Kaffirs, etc.

And this ill-treatment and enslavement is scandalous to everybody, and especially to those same heathens, because they abandon our religion, seeing that those who are supposed to convert them are the same persons who enslave them in such unjust ways, as is witnessed every day. And this is felt especially by those of greater understanding, such as the Japanese. So much is this so that this comprised the principal chapter of the Decree with which twenty-five years ago the tyrant Cambucodono, Universal Lord of all Japan, ordered the exile of all those who accepted that conversion, claiming that they went about buying and making slaves in those ports, on the pretext of Religion, because little by little they were plotting to subjugate all those States and to make them tributary to Portugal. . . .

All the other provinces of Europe are also shocked by us, saying that the Portuguese, who look upon themselves as pious and devoted, commit such extraordinary acts of injustice and inhumanity.

QUESTIONS TO CONSIDER

1. What advice does each author give the King of Portugal? What are the similarities and differences in their explanations for why the King should follow their advice?
2. Based on your reading of the two documents, what appear to be the fundamental long-term dynamics of slavery and the slave trade in the Portuguese Empire during this era? Why?

4.3 "HE POURS OUT THE TREASURES OF THE INDIES." JOSÉ DE ACOSTA, *NATURAL AND MORAL HISTORY OF THE INDIES*, 1590

Like Robert Bellarmine (see Source 3.4), José de Acosta (1540–1600) was a Jesuit priest. Born in Spain, Acosta lived in Peru from 1571 to 1587. He published *A Natural and Moral History of the Indies* in Spain in 1590. The book is a massive compendium of information about every aspect of the Western Hemisphere known to the Spanish at that time. Acosta summarizes the European understanding of the natural world, pre-Columbian religions, and political organizations, as well as the state of affairs in Spanish America in the late sixteenth century. Acosta's work was translated into numerous European languages and read widely by elites around the Atlantic world. In the following excerpt, Acosta describes the silver mining economy of Potosí in the Viceroyalty of Peru.

Source: José de Acosta, *Natural and Moral History of the Indies*, ed. Jane Mangan (Durham, NC: Duke University Press, 2002), 177–183.

For, as appears from the royal books of the House of Trade of that place and is affirmed by old men worthy of belief, at the time when the Licenciado Polo was in charge, which was a good many years after the discovery of the mountain, every Saturday they set aside 150,000 or 200,000 pesos, and the royal fifths [*a tax of 20 percent on silver production due to the Spanish crown–Ed.*] were worth 30,000 and 40,000 pesos weekly and half a million pesos yearly, more or less. So according to this calculation a matter of 30,000 pesos was extracted daily, and the king's fifth was worth 6,000 pesos a day. One more thing must be stated about the wealth of Potosí, and this is that the calculation I have made is only the silver that was stamped and set aside for the royal fifth. It is very well known in Peru that for a long time the silver called "ordinary" was used, which was not stamped or set aside, and the conclusion of those who know a great deal about the mines is that at that time a very large proportion of the silver that was taken out of Potosí never had the royal fifth set aside. This was the silver that circulated among the Indians and much of the Spaniards' silver, a practice that, as I saw, lasted until my time. Thus we may well believe that a third, if not half, of the wealth of Potosí was not recognized or set aside for the royal fifth. . . .

Finally, today his Catholic Majesty receives, year after year, a million pesos simply from the royal fifths of silver that come from the mountain of Potosí, not counting further wealth from quicksilver and other prerogatives of the Royal Treasury, which constitutes another great treasure. Experts make the calculation and say that everything that (sic) has been subjected to the royal fifth in the customs house of Potosí, even though the books of the first separations are not presented as accurately as they are today, for in the early years the weighing was done with a steelyard [*a type of balance–Ed.*], such was the abundance of silver. But, by means of the instructions and calculations made by the viceroy Don Francisco de Toledo in the year fifteen hundred and seventy-four, it was found that up to that year there were 76 million pesos, and, from that year to fifteen hundred and eighty-five inclusive, it appears from the royal registers that 35 million pesos were registered. So, adding what was registered up to the year fifteen hundred and eighty-five, 111 million pesos were assayed, and each peso was worth 13 reales and 1 cuartillo. And this is not counting the silver that remained unregistered, or was registered in other royal customs houses, and not counting what has been spent in ordinary silver and the silver still not registered, which is an incalculable amount. This accounting was sent from Potosí to the viceroy in the year that I mentioned, when I was in Peru, and from that time to this the wealth that has come from Peru in the fleets has been still greater. For in the fleet in which I traveled in fifteen hundred and eighty-seven, 11 million pesos came from Peru and Mexico in the two fleets; almost half was the king's share, and two-thirds of that was from Peru.

I have made this calculation especially so that my readers may understand how great is the power that Divine Majesty has graciously placed in the hands of the kings of Spain, heaping so many crowns and realms upon them that through Heaven's special favor the East and West Indies have been joined, circling the world with their power. We must believe that this has occurred through the special providence of our God, for the good of those people who live so far distant from their head, who is the pope of Rome, vicar of Christ Our Lord, and also for the defense of the Catholic Faith itself and the Roman Church in these parts, where the truth is so much resisted and persecuted by heretics. And, since this is ordained by the Lord on high, who both gives and takes away kingdoms to whomever he wishes and as he wishes, we must humbly petition him to graciously favor the pious zeal of the Catholic king, granting him good fortune and victory over the enemies of the Holy Faith, for it is in this cause that he pours out the treasure of the Indies that God has given him and requires even more. . . .

The richest ore is refined in those little wind ovens called *guairas*; this is the ore that contains the most lead, and the lead causes it to melt. To make it melt better the Indians throw in what they call *soroche*, which is an ore resembling lead. When subjected to fire the dross falls below, the lead and silver melt, and the silver floats on top of the lead until it is skimmed off; then they refine the silver many more times.

From one hundredweight of ore, 30 or 40 or even 50 pesos' worth of silver can be extracted by smelting. As a sample, they showed me ores that had produced by smelting more than 200 or even 250 pesos per hundredweight, a very rare degree of richness and almost unbelievable if I had not seen the proof of it by fire. A poor grade of ore gives 2 or 3 pesos, or 5 or 6, or not much more; ordinarily this ore does not contain lead but is dry and thus cannot be smelted by the use of fire. Hence for a long time a very large amount of these poor ores existed in Potosí, which were cast aside and considered to be the dross of the good ores until the method of extracting silver with quicksilver came into use. This meant that those piles of slag, as they were called, turned out to be immensely rich, for it is the strange and wonderful property of quicksilver to refine the silver and serve for these poor, dry ores; and less quicksilver is expended and consumed in them than with rich ores, for the richer they are the more quicksilver they ordinarily consume.

Today most refining of silver, and nearly all of it in Potosí, is done with quicksilver, as is also true of the mines of Zacatecas and others in New Spain. There used to be more than six thousand guairas on the slopes of Potosí and on the peaks and hills; these are the little wind ovens where the ore is smelted. They were placed like illuminations, and it was a pretty sight to see them burning at night and casting their light so far, each of them like a red coal of fire. Now I doubt whether there are more than one or two thousand of them, for as I have said they give little result and smelting by quicksilver is much more profitable.

QUESTIONS TO CONSIDER

1. What are the key things one can learn about the silver mining economy in the late sixteenth century from reading this passage?
2. Acosta practices a sixteenth-century version of historical research and writing. How does he describe cause–effect relationships and explain why things happen the way they do?

4.4 "SHALL YOU GROW TO BE A GREAT TREE." A LETTER FROM THE ADMINISTRATOR OF NAGASAKI TO THE GOVERNOR GENERAL OF THE DUTCH EAST INDIA COMPANY, 1642

Starting in the early seventeenth century, Japan's Tokugawa rulers implemented a policy of *sakoku* (see Source 2.6). Usually translated as a "closed country" policy, these directives did not cut Japan off from all foreign interactions but did tightly control them. All trade with European states was limited to an annual Dutch mission based on an island in Nagasaki harbor for a limited period of time. Because the Dutch were the only Europeans in regular contact with Japan, European ideas or technologies in general became known as "Dutch learning" in Japan, a label that persisted into the nineteenth century.

The document presented here is a 1642 Japanese description of their relationship with the Dutch trading mission sent at the request of Dutch officials who wished to gain a fuller understanding of the situation.

Source: François Caron and Joost Schouten, *A True Description of the Mighty Kingdoms of Japan and Siam*. Reprinted from the English Edition of 1663 with Introduction, Notes, and Appendixes by C. R. Boxer (London: Argonaut Press, 1935), 89–91.

Last year the Hollanders' ships for the first time came to Nangasacqui [Nagasaki–Ed.], where they live on an island, free from danger of fire, and drive their trade unmolested; furthermore our Superiors have ordained that we should lodge the Captain in our own house, and not withstanding that the same is not very commodious, yet the Captain is satisfied therewith, and has lodged there in person, whereby the house and we were honored, for which we are duly grateful.

The Captain has handed to us the present which was bestowed upon us, to wit a piece of Serge, a piece of Russet, and three Catties of red silk, wherefore we are thankful. Last year I have likewise given the merchant Augustyn a letter, and instructed him about Japanese affairs, but subsequently heard that he was wrecked with the ship off Quinangh, and drowned, to our grief.

I have observed that Your Honour has [not?] well understood the Japanese Government['s intentions], and sent a Letter with divers requests thereto. At present the Governor of Nangasacqui [Nagasaki–Ed.] is Bassa Sabrosey Mondonne, who has governed there since many years, so that matters are not now as formerly; he is an intelligent and kind-hearted Gentleman, who has received the Hollanders kindly; he has known from of old that they have traded in Japan, and he does not allow anyone to lend money to them, but will do them much good, more than can be described with the pen.

All men say that the time when the Hollanders came in Nangasacqui [Nagasaki–Ed.], will prove to have been a lucky time for them.

Your Letter is not right in some particulars, and therefore we have deemed it advisable not to forward it to our Government, but to keep it in Nangasacqui [Nagasaki–Ed.], and advise you of this fact; there are more than thirty points in the same [which are wrong?], which we will not recount here, hoping that if you read this through carefully, you will certainly understand the same. But as yet you do not understand fully these Japanese customs, which is the reason why you have drawn up such a Missive. Should you wish to write to the Government in Japan, you must have some patience first, and trade 4 or 5 years in Nangasacqui [Nagasaki–Ed.], when you will be able to see how you are treated here, and how everything is regulated for the good of the Company.

The Laws of Japan are upright, though somewhat harsh and severe, especially against the Christians; but seeing that the Hollanders have traded long years in Japan and have never tried to propagate Christianity, or troubled themselves about such matters, but have always behaved themselves peaceably, the Government has in view of this allowed them to come and traffic in Nangasacqui [Nagasaki–Ed.], being a place of no private Lord, but of the Emperor himself, where all foreign nations may drive their trade; if you also should wish to do so, all will be well. But be pleased to order your Subordinates, whom you send to Japan, or instruct to remain there, to guard themselves from the outward observance of religion, so that they may keep their Christianity secret and concealed; should they thoroughly understand the Japanese Laws and punctually obey the same, then you may obtain all you wish, even unasked; but should you write again to the Japanese government, and make some request about Christianity therein, matters will go ill; similarly so long as the Hollanders do anything which savors of Christianity, then shall they obtain nothing, whatsoever they may ask.

If it should be found out that we connived at Christianity to some extent, we should all, Siroye Mondonne, the Interpreters, and all who are on the island, together with the island itself, be destroyed. If the Captain is to be changed next year, then send no other than the Captain Elserach, who understands the Japanese laws and Customs, and knows how to dispatch matters speedily; but if you should send an inexperienced person, then everything will be delayed. The Governor Phesodonne, and all the great ones of Nangasacqui [Nagasaki–Ed.], as also everyone from the neighboring districts, have a high opinion of Captain Elserach, and if he should come again in Nangasacqui [Nagasaki–Ed.], trade will certainly be brisk.

In the event that you find it good to ordain that Christianity should be kept secretly, and nothing thereof appear to view, you will obtain all you ask, suffer no let nor hindrance, and be held in higher esteem. Nangasacqui [Nagasaki–Ed.] is much better situated than Firando [another city in Japan–Ed.], and the Company will be able to trade there more advantageously than in Firando, though in the event of punishment being meted out, this may fall rather heavily; but provided you be pleased to order that no Christian things be brought nor any mention be made of the Christian belief, then shall you grow to be a great tree, flourishing eternally with many branches; and then you may send as many ships to Japan as you choose, since we shall order everything, with the help of the Captain, to the best advantage of the Company.

Together with this Letter I send you a pot of Cha, as also a copper beaker and lamp, being merely an acknowledgement. What else I have to say, I have told Captain Elserach verbally, from whom you can understand everything.

QUESTIONS TO CONSIDER

1. Why were Dutch traders tolerated in Japan when other Europeans were not? What concerns do the Japanese express about Europeans in general?
2. What benefits does each side—Dutch and Japanese—seem to seek from the trading arrangement at Nagasaki? In what ways does this relationship reflect global issues in the seventeenth century?

4.5 "PROHIBIT THE TRAFFIC IN THE ABOVE-MENTIONED MERCHANDISE FROM CHINA." *SPANISH EMPIRE CORRESPONDENCE*, 1586

Trade, even long-distance trade between continents, was not new in the sixteenth century. Maritime trade across both the Atlantic and Pacific oceans, however, did not become commonplace until the late 1500s. The realization that North and South America lay between the west coast of Europe and the east coast of Asia fundamentally transformed European understandings of the world, but trade with Asia remained an important goal of most European governments as the sixteenth century began.

One of the most important instances of this trade was the so-called Manila Galleon, a fleet of Spanish ships that traveled between the west coast of New Spain (modern Mexico) and the islands now known as the Philippines, which Spanish explorers named for their king (Philip II) in 1542. Chinese merchants had dominated trade across the South China Sea for centuries, and an active market existed in the islands long before the Spanish arrived. Establishing a presence in the Philippines, however, gave the Spanish access to the Chinese markets they sought. Combined with the tremendous natural resources—especially gold and silver—the Spaniards brought from the Americas, the Galleon trade became a powerful economic engine that linked five continents.

The document presented here is a letter to the Spanish king describing the trade Spaniards conducted out of Manila in 1586, focusing on trade with China.

Source: Emma Helen Blair and James Alexander Robertson, eds., *The Philippine Islands 1493–1898*, Vol. VI, 1583–1588 (Cleveland, Ohio: Arthur H. Clark Company, 1903), 279–281.

Sacred Royal Catholic Majesty:

In order to discuss your Majesty's commands regarding the commerce between the Philipinas Islands and Nueva España, Don Cristobal Mora and I met yesterday and examined a long report which Ledesma had drawn up from many papers which have been sent from both sides, together with a certain clause of a letter to your Majesty by the viceroy, Don Martin Enriquez, written on the twentieth of March of the past year, eighty [five]. In this letter he says that the merchants of that country are greatly disappointed that trade with the Philipinas Islands should be taken away from them; for, although the satins, damasks, and other silken goods, even the finest of them, contain very little silk, and others are woven with grass (all of which is quite worthless), the people mainly resort to this cheap market, and the prices of silks brought from Spain are lowered. Of these latter, taffetas had come to be worth no more than eight reals, while satins and damasks had become very cheap. He feared that, if this went further, it would not be needful to import silks from España. He says, moreover, that all goods carried from the said islands are mere trifles, from which the land derives no profit—such as porcelains, escritoires, caskets, fans, and parasols, all flimsy and very unprofitable. We can trade with the Chinese only with gold and silver, since they have more than enough of everything else. The letter written to your Majesty by the commander of the fleet which is in Nueva España was also examined. He states therein that the trade in thin fabrics imported from these kingdoms to that land is steadily decreasing, on account of the trade which is carried on there with the Philipinas Islands. This letter was the occasion for issuing a decree, to which your Majesty was pleased to set your royal hand, calling for a report from the viceroy of Nueva España. This is an affair which requires a much more expeditious remedy. We have investigated the state of affairs in those regions, of which a detailed report was made to us. Besides the little value of those wares, a large amount of silver and coin is carried thither in exchange for them. Although a portion of this money

remains in those islands, all the rest is carried away by the Chinese who go thither from the mainland to sell these wares.

In this way the commerce of these kingdoms is falling away, and the bringing of money hither is impeded; both these are matters of consequence and importance. This is not the way to maintain our trade, since the settlement of the land must be through its richness and fertility, and the prospect of other discoveries that are being made daily, and not through trade. Those who are engaged in this trade are merely transients, and those islands are merely a place of lading for this commerce; for all, or the greater part; of the merchandise comes from China. The Spaniards derive two, three, or four thousand ducats from anchorage alone; this is the fee for the privilege of anchoring the ship. The lure of the cheapness of the merchandise overcomes all other considerations. This hinders the prosperity of the people, and furnishes them no aid in the most important thing, namely, the settlement of the islands, and the discovery and operation of the gold mines there. We came to the conclusion that the trade and commerce of the said islands, as far as the said merchandise is concerned, should be abolished, and that these wares should not be carried to Nueva España or other parts of the Indias, in order that the trade of these kingdoms—a most important matter—may continue. A communication to this effect should be addressed to the viceroy of Nueva España, recounting to him the aforesaid disadvantages; and advising him that, unless he shall encounter other obstacles so great as to prevent him from taking such action, he should prohibit the traffic in the above-mentioned merchandise from China, and order the cessation of such commerce with that country.

If he find too great difficulties in the way, then he should give advice thereof, together with his opinion. In the meantime, he should make such provision as he shall find most expedient. To save time, the decree in accordance with this recommendation accompanies the present communication; and it shall be sent by this fleet, if your Majesty will have the goodness to sign it.

Madrid, June 17, 1586.

QUESTIONS TO CONSIDER

1. What articles of trade do the Spanish and the Chinese desire? Can you assess the relative wealth of Spain and China based on this exchange?
2. What advantages and disadvantages does the writer of this report see in the trade with China at the time the document was written? How would he like to see it changed?

4.6 "GOLD AND SILVER COME AT LENGTH TO BE SWALLOWED UP IN HINDOUSTAN." FRANÇOIS BERNIER, *TRAVELS IN THE MOGUL EMPIRE*, AD *1656–1668*, 1670

François Bernier (1620–1688) was a French physician who traveled widely during the second half of the seventeenth century. He lived in India for more than a decade, and even traveled in the entourage of the Emperor Aurangzeb (1618–1707) to the province of Kashmir. Bernier's letters to acquaintances in France formed the basis for the book *Histoire de la dernière révolution des états du Grand Mogol,* published in installments in France between 1670 and 1677. English translations of the book bore the more generic title, *Travels in the Mogul Empire.*

One of Bernier's correspondents was Jean Baptiste Colbert (1619–1683), who served as Finance Minister for French King Louis XIV from 1665 until 1683. Colbert believed that there was only a limited amount of wealth on the planet. Therefore, over the long term, a kingdom's power could only be maintained if it exported more goods than it imported and accumulated precious metals in the royal treasury. Colbert designed French policy based on this theory, called mercantilism, which many other policymakers at the time believed was the best and most accurate reflection of economic reality.

It was in Hindoustan, My Lord, whither your fame extends, and from which country I am lately returned after an absence of twelve years, that I first became acquainted with the happiness of France, and with the share which you have had in promoting it, by your unwearied attention and brilliant abilities. This is a theme on which I could fondly dwell; but why should I expatiate on facts already and universally admitted, when my present purpose is to treat of those which are new and unknown? It will be more agreeable to you if I proceed, according to my promise, to furnish such materials as may enable your lordship to form some idea of the actual state of the Indies. The maps of Asia point

Source: François Bernier, *Travels in the Mogul Empire,* AD *1656–1668. A Revised and Improved Edition Based upon Irving Block's Translation by Archibald Constable* (Westminster, UK: Constable, 1891), 201–204; Electronic reproduction (New York: Columbia University Libraries, 2006). JPEG use copy available via the World Wide Web.

out the mighty extent of the Great Mogol's empire, known commonly by the name of the Indies, or Hindoustan. I have not measured it with mathematical exactness; but judging from the ordinary rate of travel, and considering that it is a journey of three months from the frontier of the kingdom of Golkonda to Kazni, or rather beyond it, near to Kandahar, which is the first town in Persia, the distance between those two extreme points cannot be less than five hundred French leagues, or five times as far as from Paris to Lyons.

It is important to observe, that of this vast tract of country, a large portion is extremely fertile; the large kingdom of Bengale, for instance, surpassing Egypt itself, not only in the production of rice, corn, and other necessaries of life, but of innumerable articles of commerce which are not cultivated in Egypt; such as silks, cotton, and indigo. There are also many parts of the Indies, where the population is sufficiently abundant, and the land pretty well tilled; and where the artisan, although naturally indolent, is yet compelled by necessity or otherwise to employ himself in manufacturing carpets, brocades, embroideries, gold and silver cloths, and the various sorts of silk and cotton goods, which are used in the country or exported abroad.

It should not escape notice that gold and silver, after circulating in every other quarter of the globe, come at length to be swallowed up, lost in some measure, in Hindoustan. Of the quantity drawn from America, and dispersed among the different European states, a part finds its way, through various channels, to Turkey, for the payment of commodities imported from that country; and a part passes into Persia, by way of Smyrna, for the silks laden at that port. Turkey cannot dispense with the coffee, which she receives from Yemen, or Arabia Felix; and the productions of the Indies are equally necessary to Turkey, Yemen, and Persia. Thus it happens that these countries are under the necessity of sending a portion of their gold and silver to Moka, on the Red Sea, near Babel-mandel; to Bassora, at the top of the Persian Gulf; and to Bander Abassi or Gomeron, near Ormus; which gold and silver is exported to Hindoustan by the vessels that arrive every year, in the . . . season of the winds, at those three celebrated

ports, laden with goods from that country. Let it also be borne in mind that all the Indian vessels, whether they belong to the Indians themselves, or to the Dutch, or English, or Portuguese, which every year carry cargoes of merchandise from Hindoustan to Pegu, Tanasseri, Siam, Ceylon, Achem, Macassar, the Maldives, to Mozambic, and other places, bring back to Hindoustan from those countries a large quantity of the precious metals, which share the fate of those brought from Moka, Bassora, and Bunder-Abassi. And in regard to the gold and silver which the Dutch draw from Japan, where there are mines, a part is, sooner or later, introduced into Hindoustan; and whatever is brought directly by sea, either from Portugal or from France, seldom leaves the country, returns being made in merchandise.

I am aware, it may be said, that Hindoustan is in want of copper, cloves, nutmegs, cinnamon, elephants, and other things, with which she is supplied by the Dutch from Japan, the Moluccas, Ceylon, and Europe;—that she obtains lead from abroad, in part from England; broadcloths and other articles from France;—that she is in need of a considerable number of foreign horses, receiving annually more than five-and-twenty thousand from Usbec, a great many from Persia by way of Kandahar, and several from Ethiopia, Arabia, and Persia, by sea, through the ports of Moka, Bassora, and Bander-Abassi. It may also be observed that Hindoustan consumes an immense quantity of fresh fruit from Samarkand, Bali; Bocara, and Persia; such as melons, apples, pears and grapes, eaten at Delhi and purchased at a very high price nearly the whole winter; —and likewise dried fruit, such as almonds, pistachio and various other small nuts, plums, apricots, and raisins, which may be procured the whole year round ;—that she imports a small sea-shell from the Maldives, used in Bengale, and other places, as a species of small money ; ambergris from the Maldives and Mozambic; rhinoceros' horns, elephants' teeth, and slaves from Ethiopia; musk and porcelain from China, and pearls from Beharen, and Tutucoury, near Ceylon; and I know not what quantity of other similar wares, which she might well do without. The importation of all these articles into Hindoustan does not, however, occasion the export of gold and silver; because the merchants who bring them find it advantageous to take back, in exchange, the productions of the country. Supplying itself with articles of foreign growth or manufacture, does not, therefore, prevent Hindoustan from absorbing a large portion of the gold and silver of the world, admitted through a variety of channels, while there is scarcely an opening for its return.

QUESTIONS FOR CONSIDERATION

1. What is Bernier's assessment of the strengths and weaknesses of the economy of South Asia?
2. What would be the implications of this assessment for someone like Colbert, who believed in mercantilist economic policies?

CHAPTER 5

GLOBAL WAR AND IMPERIAL REFORM, 1655–1765

5.1 "THE REASON WHY MEN ENTER INTO SOCIETY IS THE PRESERVATION OF THEIR PROPERTY." JOHN LOCKE, *TWO TREATISES OF GOVERNMENT*, 1689

John Locke (1632–1704), was an English philosopher and physician who had an enormous influence on the development of the political philosophy of liberalism, with its emphasis on liberty, rights, the individual, and the contractual nature of politics. Locke lived through the political upheaval of the English civil wars in the seventeenth century. Between 1683 and 1688, out of favor with the Stuart Kings Charles II and James II, Locke lived in exile in the Netherlands. He returned to England when the Glorious Revolution brought more accommodating monarchs to power in King William and Queen Mary. William and Mary accepted a set of limits on the English monarchs' powers, known as the Bill of Rights, in 1689. Shortly thereafter, Locke published *Two Treatises of Government*, excerpted here.

OF THE STATE OF NATURE

Sec. 4. To understand political power right, and derive it from its original, we must consider, what state all men are naturally in, and that is, a state of perfect freedom to order their actions, and dispose of their possessions and persons, as they think fit, within the bounds of the law of nature, without asking leave, or depending upon the will of any other man. . . .

OF PATERNAL POWER

Sec. 53. Had but this one thing been well considered, without looking any deeper into the matter, it might perhaps have kept men from running into those gross mistakes, they have made, about this power of parents; which, however it might, without any great harshness, bear the name of absolute dominion, and regal authority, when under the title of paternal

Source: John Locke, *Two Treatises of Government: A Critical Edition with an Introduction and Apparatus Criticus by Peter Laslett*, 2nd ed. (London: Cambridge University Press, 1967), 287; 321–22; 339; 368–70; 399; 430–31; 437; 444–45.

power it seemed appropriated to the father, would yet have founded but oddly, and in the very name shewn the absurdity, if this supposed absolute power over children had been called parental; and thereby have discovered, that it belonged to the mother too: for it will but very ill serve the turn of those men, who contend so much for the absolute power and authority of the fatherhood, as they call it, that the mother should have any share in it; and it would have but ill supported the monarchy they contend for, when by the very name it appeared, that that fundamental authority, from whence they would derive their government of a single person only, was not placed in one, but two persons jointly. . . .

POLITICAL OR CIVIL SOCIETY

Sec. 82. But the husband and wife, though they have but one common concern, yet having different understandings, will unavoidably sometimes have different wills too; it therefore being necessary that the last determination, i.e. the rule, should be placed somewhere; it naturally falls to the man's share, as the abler and the stronger. But this reaching but to the things of their common interest and property, leaves the wife in the full and free possession of what by contract is her peculiar right, and gives the husband no more power over her life than she has over his; the power of the husband being so far from that of an absolute monarch, that the wife has in many cases a liberty to separate from him, where natural right, or their contract allows it; whether that contract be made by themselves in the state of nature, or by the customs or laws of the country they live in; and the children upon such separation fall to the father or mother's lot, as such contract does determine. . . .

PATERNAL, POLITICAL, AND DESPOTIC POWER CONSIDERED TOGETHER

Sec. 170. First, then, Paternal or parental power is nothing but that which parents have over their children, to govern them for the children's good, till they come to the use of reason, or a state of knowledge, wherein they may be supposed capable to understand that rule, whether it be the law of nature, or the municipal law of their country, they are to

govern themselves by: capable, I say, to know it, as well as several others, who live as freemen under that law. The affection and tenderness which God hath planted in the breast of parents towards their children, makes it evident, that this is not intended to be a severe arbitrary government, but only for the help, instruction, and preservation of their offspring. But happen it as it will, there is, as I have proved, no reason why it should be thought to extend to life and death, at any time, over their children, more than over anybody else; neither can there be any pretence why this parental power should keep the child, when grown to a man, in subjection to the will of his parents, any farther than having received life and education from his parents, obliges him to respect, honour, gratitude, assistance and support, all his life, to both father and mother. And thus, 'tis true, the paternal is a natural government, but not at all extending itself to the ends and jurisdictions of that which is political. The power of the father doth not reach at all to the property of the child, which is only in his own disposing.

OF THE ENDS OF POLITICAL SOCIETY AND GOVERNMENT

Sec. 123. If man in the state of nature be so free, as has been said; if he be absolute lord of his own person and possessions, equal to the greatest, and subject to no body, why will he part with his freedom? why will he give up this empire, and subject himself to the dominion and controul of any other power? To which it is obvious to answer, that though in the state of nature he hath such a right, yet the enjoyment of it is very uncertain, and constantly exposed to the invasion of others: for all being kings as much as he, every man his equal, and the greater part no strict observers of equity and justice, the enjoyment of the property he has in this state is very unsafe, very unsecure. This makes him willing to quit a condition, which, however free, is full of fears and continual dangers: and 'tis not without reason, that he seeks out, and is willing to join in society with others, who are already united, or have a mind to unite, for the mutual preservation of their lives, liberties and estates, which I call by the general name, property.

Sec. 124. The great and chief end, therefore, of men's uniting into commonwealths, and putting themselves under government, is the preservation of their property. To which in the state of nature there are many things wanting.

First, There wants an established, settled, known law, received and allowed by common consent to be the standard of right and wrong, and the common measure to decide all controversies between them: for though the law of nature be plain and intelligible to all rational creatures; yet men being biased by their interest, as well as ignorant for want of study of it, are not apt to allow of it as a law binding to them in the application of it to their particular cases.

Sec. 125. Secondly, In the state of nature there wants a known and indifferent judge, with authority to determine all differences according to the established law. For every one in that state being both judge and executioner of the law of nature, men being partial to themselves, passion and revenge is very apt to carry them too far, and with too much heat, in their own cases; as well as negligence, and unconcernedness, to make them too remiss in other men's.

Sec. 126. Thirdly, In the state of nature there often wants power to back and support the sentence when right, and to give it due execution, They who by any injustice offended, will seldom fail, where they are able, by force to make good their injustice; such resistance many times makes the punishment dangerous, and frequently destructive, to those who attempt it.

Sec. 127. Thus mankind, notwithstanding all the privileges of the state of nature, being but in an ill condition, while they remain in it, are quickly driven into society. Hence it comes to pass, that we seldom find any number of men live any time together in this state. The inconveniencies that they are therein exposed to, by the irregular and uncertain exercise of the power every man has of punishing the transgressions of others, make them take sanctuary under the established laws of government, and therein seek the preservation of their property. It is this makes them so willingly give up every one his single power of punishing, to be exercised by such alone, as shall be appointed to it amongst them; and by such rules as the community, or those authorized by them to

that purpose, shall agree on. And in this we have the original right and rise of both the legislative and executive power, as well as of the governments and societies themselves. . . .

OF THE DISSOLUTION OF GOVERNMENT

Sec. 222. The reason why men enter into society, is the preservation of their property; and the end why they chuse [*choose–Ed.*] and authorize a legislative, is, that there may be laws made, and rules set, as guards and fences to the properties of all the members of the society, to limit the power, and moderate the dominion, of every part and member of the society: for since it can never be supposed to be the will of the society, that the legislative should have a power to destroy that which every one designs to secure, by entering into society, and for which the people submitted themselves to legislators of their own making; whenever the legislators endeavour to take away, and destroy the property of the people, or to reduce them to slavery under arbitrary power, they put themselves into a state of war with the people, who are thereupon absolved from any farther obedience, and are left to the common refuge, which God hath provided for all men, against force and violence. Whensoever therefore the legislative shall transgress this fundamental rule of society; and either by ambition, fear, folly or corruption, endeavour to grasp themselves, or put into the hands of any other, an absolute power over the lives, liberties, and estates of the people; by this breach of trust they forfeit the power the people had put into their hands for quite contrary ends, and it devolves to the people, who have a right to resume their original liberty, and, by the establishment of a new legislative, (such as they shall think fit) provide for their own safety and security, which is the end for which they are in society. What I have said here, concerning the legislative in general, holds true also concerning the supreme executor, who having a double trust put in him, both to have a part in the legislative, and the supreme execution of the law, acts against both, when he goes about to set up his own arbitrary will as the law of the society. He acts also contrary to his trust, when he either employs the force, treasure, and offices of the society, to corrupt the representatives, and gain them to his purposes; or openly preengages the electors, and prescribes to their choice, such, whom he has, by solicitations, threats, promises, or otherwise, won to his designs; and employs them to bring in such, who have promised before-hand what to vote, and what to enact. . . .

Sec. 232. Whosoever uses force without Right . . . , who does it without law, puts himself into a state of war with those against whom he so uses it, and in that state all former ties are cancelled, all other rights cease, and everyone has a right to defend himself, and to resist the aggressor. . . .

Sec. 240. Here, it is like, the common question will be made, Who shall be judge, whether the prince or legislative act contrary to their trust? This, perhaps, ill-affected and factious men may spread amongst the people, when the prince only makes use of his due prerogative. To this I reply, the people shall be judge; for who shall judge whether his trustee or deputy acts well, and according to the trust reposed in him, but he who deputes him, and must, by having deputed him, have still a power to discard him, when he fails in his trust? If this be reasonable in particular cases of private men, why should it be otherwise in that of the greatest moment, where the welfare of millions is concerned, and also where the evil, if not prevented, is greater, and the redress very difficult, dear, and dangerous?

QUESTIONS TO CONSIDER

1. Locke is said to have proposed that governments emerge from a social contract. Based on the text presented here, how would you summarize the origins and purpose of forming a social contract to create a government? How do these principles relate to other forms of social hierarchy?

2. What are the potential challenges to political order that might emerge from the formation and maintenance of sovereign states based on Locke's ideas as articulated in these excerpts?

5.2 "DISCOVER AS MUCH AS POSSIBLE HOW TO PUT SHIPS TO SEA DURING A NAVAL BATTLE." PETER THE GREAT, *DECREES*, 1714 AND 1724

Tsar Peter the Great (1672–1725) of Russia embraced a number of the new ideas about the world summarized by the term *Enlightenment,* especially those related to administration and education. He attempted to bring the Russian Empire closer to western European states. Peter introduced a series of reforms that tell us much about Russia in the early eighteenth century but also illustrate how Peter, and others like him, thought a "modern" state should look.

The following documents are a small part of the so-called Petrine reforms, which also reformed the calendar, expanded the navy, and restructured the army. These excerpts focus on education reforms, which—along with military reforms—Peter saw as essential to Russia's move toward modernity.

Source: Basil Dmytryshyn, ed., *Imperial Russia: A Source Book, 1700–1917,* 3rd ed. (New York: Harcourt, Brace, Jovanovich, 1990), 15–16, 18, 21–23.

DECREE ON COMPULSORY EDUCATION OF THE RUSSIAN NOBILITY, 1714

Send to every gubernia *[the major administrative unit of the Russian Empire–Ed.]* some persons from mathematical schools to teach the children of the nobility—except those of freeholders and government clerks—mathematics and geometry; as a penalty [for evasion] establish a rule that no one will be allowed to marry unless he learns these [subjects]. Inform all prelates to issue no marriage certificates to those who are ordered to go to schools. . . .

AN INSTRUCTION TO RUSSIAN STUDENTS ABROAD STUDYING NAVIGATION, 1714

1. Learn [how to draw] plans and charts and how to use the compass and other naval indicators.
2. [Learn] how to navigate a vessel in battle as well as in a simple maneuver, and learn how to use all appropriate tools and instruments; namely, sails, ropes, and oars, and the like matters, on rowboats and other vessels.
3. Discover as much as possible how to put ships to sea during a naval battle. Those who cannot succeed in this effort must diligently ascertain what action should be taken by the vessels that do and those that do not put to sea during such a situation [naval battle]. Obtain from [foreign] naval officers written statements, bearing their signatures and seals, of how adequately you [Russian students] are prepared for [naval] duties.
4. If, upon his return, anyone wishes to receive [from the Tsar] greater favors for himself, he should learn, in addition to the above enumerated instructions, how to construct those vessels aboard which he would like to demonstrate his skills.
5. Upon his return to Moscow, every [foreign-trained Russian] should bring with him at his own expense, for which he will later be reimbursed, at least two experienced masters of naval science. They [the returnees] will be assigned soldiers, one soldier per returnee, to teach them [what they have learned abroad]. And if they do not wish to accept soldiers, they may teach their acquaintances or their own people. The treasury will pay for transportation and maintenance of soldiers. And if anyone other

than soldiers learns [the art of navigation], the treasury will pay 100 rubles for the maintenance of every such individual. . . .

A DECREE ON THE FOUNDING OF THE ACADEMY, 1724

His Imperial Majesty decreed the establishment of an academy, wherein languages as well as other sciences and important arts could be taught, and where books could be translated. On January 22 [1724], during His stay in the Winter Palace, His Majesty approved the project for the Academy, and with His own hand signed a decree that stipulates that the Academy's budget of 24,912 rubles annually should come from revenues, from custom dues and export-import license fees collected in the following cities: Narva, Dorpat, Pernov and Arensburg. . . .

Usually two kinds of institutions are used in organizing arts and sciences. One is known as a University; the other as an Academy or society of arts and sciences.

1. A University is an association of learned individuals who teach the young people the development of such distinguished sciences as theology and jurisprudence (the legal skill), and medicine and philosophy. An Academy, on the other hand, is an association of learned and skilled people who not only know their subjects to the same degree [as their counterparts in the University] but who, in addition, improve and develop them through research and inventions. They have no obligation to teach others.
2. While the Academy consists of the same scientific disciplines and has the same members as the University, these two institutions, in other states, have no connection between themselves in training many other well-qualified people who could organize different societies. This is done to prevent interference into the activity of the Academy, whose sole task is to improve arts and sciences through theoretical research that would benefit professors as well as students of universities. Freed from the pressure of research, universities can concentrate on educating the young people.

3. Now that an institution aimed at the cultivation of arts and sciences is to be chartered in Russia, there is no need to follow the practice that is accepted in other states. It is essential to take into account the existing circumstances of this state [Russia], consider [the quality of Russian] teachers and students, and organize such an institution that would not only immediately increase the glory of this [Russian] state through the development of sciences, but would also, through teaching and dissemination [of knowledge], benefit the people [of Russia] in the future.

4. These two aims will not be realized if the Academy of Sciences alone is chartered, because while the Academy may try to promote and disseminate arts and sciences, these will not spread among the people. The establishment of a university will do even less, simply because there are no elementary schools, gymnasia, or seminaries [in Russia] where young people could learn the fundamentals before studying more advanced subjects [at the University] to make themselves useful. It is therefore inconceivable that under these circumstances a university would be of some value [to Russia].

5. Consequently, what is needed most [in Russia] is the establishment of an institution that would consist of the most learned people, who, in turn, would be willing: (a) to promote and perfect the sciences while at the same time, wherever possible, be willing (b) to give public instruction to young people (if they feel the latter are qualified) and (c) instruct some people individually so that they in turn could train young people [of Russia] in the fundamental principles of all sciences.

6. As a result, and with only slight modifications, one institution will perform as great a service [in Russia] as the three institutions do in other states. . . .

7. Because the organization of this Academy is similar to that of Paris (except for this difference and advantage that the Russian Academy is also to do what a university and college are doing [in Paris]), I think that this institution can and should easily be called an Academy. Disciplines that can be organized in this Academy can easily be grouped in three basic divisions: The first division is to consist of mathematical and related sciences; the second of physics; and the third of humanities, history, and law.

QUESTIONS TO CONSIDER

1. What kind of state is Peter trying to build through these reforms? What problems is he trying to solve? What individuals or groups might resist these initiatives? Why? What costs, financial and otherwise, might reforms like these incur?

2. What inspirations do you see for these reforms? How do they compare to what is happening in other states at this time?

5.3 "ESTEEM MOST HIGHLY FILIAL PIETY AND BROTHERLY SUBMISSION." *THE SACRED EDICT OF THE YONGZHENG EMPEROR*, CA. 1723–1735

When the Manchus overthrew the Ming Dynasty in 1644, one of the greatest obstacles to their success was establishing the new Qing Dynasty's claim of legitimacy to rule China. One way they addressed this issue was through a series of "sacred edicts" that were read aloud in villages throughout China. These were designed to explain the foundations of political and social order in the empire and appealed to many traditional Chinese values, including Confucianism, a set of social and political ideas that originated in the first centuries BCE.

The practice of issuing edicts was not new to the Qing. They had been a common feature of the Ming Dynasty as well, which may have helped promote acceptance of the Qing as a legitimate dynasty in China. The edict presented here is an example from the reign of the Yongzheng Emperor (r. 1723–1735).

1. Esteem most highly filial piety and brotherly submission, in order to give due importance to human moral relations.
2. Behave with generosity toward your kindred, in order to illustrate harmony and benignity.
3. Cultivate peace and concord in your neighborhoods, in order to prevent quarrels and litigations.
4. Give importance to agriculture and sericulture, in order to ensure a sufficiency of clothing and food.
5. Show that you prize moderation and economy, in order to prevent the lavish waste of your means.
6. Foster colleges and schools, in order to give the training of scholars a proper start.
7. Do away with errant teachings, in order to exalt the correct doctrine.
8. Expound on the laws, in order to warn the ignorant and obstinate.
9. Explain ritual decorum and deference, in order to enrich manners and customs.
10. Attend to proper callings, in order to stabilize the people's sense of dedication [to their work].
11. Instruct sons and younger brothers, in order to prevent them from doing what is wrong.
12. Put a stop to false accusations, in order to protect the honest and good.
13. Warn against sheltering deserters, in order to avoid being involved in their punishment.
14. Promptly remit your taxes, in order to avoid being pressed for payment.
15. Combine in collective security groups (baojia), in order to put an end to theft and robbery.
16. Eschew enmity and anger, in order to show respect for the person and life.

QUESTIONS TO CONSIDER

1. What values do the Edict promote as most important? What goals might motivate the promotion of these values? What do these maxims reveal about the Qing government's concerns about ruling China?
2. In what ways, if any, do the goals these maxims promote seem unique to the Qing Dynasty or to China? Do you think they would be understood in other places or times?

Source: *Sources of the Chinese Tradition*, Vol. 2, compiled by William Theodore de Bary and Richard Lufrano, 2nd ed. (New York: Columbia University Press, 2000), 70–72.

5.4 "THEY WERE RESOLVED TO REGAIN THEIR LIBERTY IF POSSIBLE." WILLIAM SNELGRAVE, *A NEW ACCOUNT OF SOME PARTS OF GUINEA AND THE SLAVE TRADE*, 1734

William Snelgrave was a sea captain from Bristol, England, who participated in the African slave trade for three decades in the early eighteenth century. Snelgrave's *A New Account of Some Parts of Guinea and the Slave Trade,* published in 1734, provides details of his many years at sea, focusing primarily on the years between 1727 and 1730. In the book, Snelgrave interacts with pirates, political leaders (most notably the King of Dahomey), his crews, and African peoples caught up in the trans-Atlantic slave trade.

The Slave Voyages database *(slavevoyages.org)* records details on seven voyages made between 1717 and 1730 for which William Snelgrave served as captain, transporting enslaved humans from the Bight of Benin and the Gold Coast to Jamaica, Antigua, and elsewhere in the Americas. While almost 3,000 enslaved Africans departed on Snelgrave's ships, 370 died on the Middle Passage between Africa and the Americas, an appalling mortality rate exceeding 12 percent.

In the following excerpt, Snelgrave recounts rebellions against slave traders.

The first Mutiny I saw among the Negroes, happened during my first Voyage, in the Year 1704. It was on board the Eagle Galley of London, commanded by my Father, with whom I was as Purser. We had bought our Negroes in the River of Old Callabar in the Bay of Guinea. At the time of their mutinying we were in that River, having four hundred of them on board, and not above ten white Men who were able to do Service: For several of our Ship's Company were dead, and many more sick; besides, two of our Boats were just then gone with twelve People on Shore to fetch Wood, which lay in sight of the Ship. All these Circumstances put the Negroes on consulting how to mutiny, which they did at four o'clock in the Afternoon, just as they went to Supper. But as we had always carefully examined the Men's Irons, both Morning and Evening, none had got them off, which in a great measure contributed to our preservation. Three white men stood on the watch with cutlasses in the hands. One of them who was on the forecastle, a stout fellow, seeing some of the Men Negroes take hold of the chief Mate, in order to throw him overboard, he laid on them so heartily with the flat side of his Cutlace, that they soon quitted the Mate, who escaped from them, and run on the Quarter Deck to get Arms. I was then sick with an Ague [malaria], and lying on a Couch in the great Cabin, the Fit being just come on. However, I no sooner heard the Outcry, that the Slaves were mutinying, but I took two Pistols, and run on the Deck with them; where meeting with my Father and the chief Mate, I delivered a Pistol to each of them. Whereupon they went forward on the Booms, calling to the Negro Men that were on the Forecastle; but they did not regard their Threats, being busy with the Centry, (who had disengaged the chief Mate) and they would have certainly killed him with his own Cutlace, could they have got it from him; but they could not break the Line where—with the Handle was fastened to his Wrist. And so, tho' they had seized him, yet they could not make use of

Source: Robert O. Collins, ed., *Documents from the African Past* (Princeton, NJ: Markus Wiener, 2009), 128–135.

his Cutlace. Being thus disappointed, they endeavoured to throw him overboard, but he held so fast by one of them that they could not do it. My Father seeing this stout Man in so much Danger, ventured amongst the Negroes to save him; and fired his Pistol over their Heads, thinking to frighten them. But a lusty Slave struck him with a Billet [a round wooden bar] so hard, that he was almost stunned. The Slave was going to repeat his Blow, when a young lad about seventeen years old, whom we had been kind to, interposed his Arm, and received the Blow, by which his arm-bone was fractured. At the same instant the Mate fired his Pistol, and shot the Negroe that had struck my Father. At the sight of this the Mutiny ceased, and all the Men-Negroes on the Forecastle threw themselves flat on their Faces, crying out for Mercy.

Upon examining into the matter, we found, there were not above twenty Men Slaves concerned in this Mutiny; and the two Ringleaders were missing, having, it seems, jumped overboard as soon as they found their Project defeated, and were drowned. This was all the Loss we suffered on this occasion: For the Negroe that was shot by the Mate, the Surgeon, beyond all Expectation, cured. And I had the good Fortune to lose my Ague, by the fright and hurry I was put into. Moreover, the young Man, who had received the Blow on his Arm to save my Father, was cured by the Surgeon in our Passage to Virginia. At our Arrival in that place we gave him his Freedom; and a worthy Gentleman, one Colonel Carter, took him into his Service, till he became well enough acquainted in the Country to provide for himself.

I have been several Voyages, when there has been no Attempt made by our Negroes to mutiny; which I believe, was owing chiefly, to their being kindly used, and to my Officers Care in keeping a good Watch. But sometimes we meet with stout stubborn People amongst them, who are never to be made easy; and

these are generally some of the Cormantines, a nation of the Gold Coast. I went in the year 1721, in the *Henry* of London, a voyage to that part of the Coast and bought a good many of these People. We were obliged to secure them very well in irons, and watch them narrowly: yet they nevertheless mutinied, tho' they had little prospect of succeeding. I lay at that time near a place called Mumfort on the Gold Coast, having near five hundred Negroes on board, three hundred of which were Men. Our ship's company consisted of fifty white people, all in health: And I had very good Officers; so that I was very easy in all respects. . . .

After we had secured these People, I called the Linguists, and ordered them to bid the Men-Negroes between Decks be quiet; (for there was a great noise amongst them.) On their being silent, I asked, "What had induced them to mutiny?" They answered, "I was a great Rogue to buy them, in order to carry them away from their own Country, and that they were resolved to regain their Liberty if possible." I replied, "That they had forfeited their Freedom before I bought them, either by Crimes or by being taken in War, according to the Custom of their Country; and they being now my Property, I was resolved to let them feel my Resentment, if they abused my Kindness: Asking at the same time, Whether they had been ill used by the white Men, or had wanted for anything the Ship afforded?" To this they replied, "They had nothing to complain of." Then I observed to them, "That if they should gain their Point and escape to the Shore, it would be no Advantage to them, because their Countrymen would catch them, and sell them to other Ships." This served my purpose, and they seemed to be convinced of their Fault, begging, "I would forgive them, and promising for the future to be obedient, and never mutiny again, if I would not punish them this time. This I readily granted, and so they went to sleep.

QUESTIONS TO CONSIDER

1. How does William Snelgrave justify the actions he is taking, both broadly as a slave trader and narrowly in terms of his response to rebellion?
2. Researchers estimate that about one in ten slaving expeditions faced rebellions like the ones described by Snelgrave. What impact might the persistence of such rebellions have over time? How might you measure your hypothesis to see if it is credible?

5.5 "WE FEAR THE DAMAGE FROM A PUBLIC DISCLOSURE." JORGE JUAN AND ANTONIO DE ULLOA, *DISCOURSE AND POLITICAL REFLECTIONS ON THE KINGDOM OF PERU*, 1749

Jorge Juan y Santilla (1713–1773) and Antonio de Ulloa (1716–1795) trained at the Spanish naval academy at Cádiz. Together, they joined a scientific mission to the Americas in the mid-1730s. Upon returning to Spain, they published a massive account of the places they visited, called *Historical Report on a Voyage to America*. In addition to their scientific work, Juan and Ulloa completed a secret report for imperial officials that analyzed their perception of problems in Spain's Western Hemisphere empire. Excerpted here, this report found its way into the hands of enemies of the Spanish crown who published the document in England under the title *Secret Information on America*.

Among the many concerns which demand a sovereign's vigilance, two stand out above all: to insure the incomparable treasures of his subjects' eternal salvation and their earthly welfare. Religion and justice are his two principal responsibilities, and the paternal diligence and pious solicitude of any ruler should be directed toward upholding and preserving these two institutions. Both must be kept under constant consideration as part of Christian policy. To be successful, he must plan unexpected, quick action along whatever lines wisdom may dictate. To forestall future problems, he must apply preventive measures to avoid certain situations, or recognizing the damage already done, apply suitable remedies so as to restore affairs to a condition where justice based on reason ought to prevail without interruption.

The Indies are abundant, rich, and flourishing. As such, they are also exposed to indolence and luxury. Far removed from the king and his high ministers and governed by people who often neglect the public interest for their own, those areas are now in a bad state because of the longevity and deep-rooted character of these ills. Justice does not have sufficient

weight nor reason enough power to counteract disorder and vice. Consequently, it is not surprising that abuses have been introduced into all affairs of the republic: the harm done from disobedience of the law or introduction of unjust procedures; excesses on the part of ministers and people in power, seriously detrimental to the weak and the helpless; scandals in the licentious behavior of all; and an almost continuous general drift away from what is right, desirable, and necessary for well-ordered societies. With no good examples to follow and with the senseless spread of evil, it is not surprising that, with few exceptions, everyone is corrupted and powerless to re-establish conditions as they should be.

Although distance may help diminish knowledge of these facts, they cannot all be concealed. This is doubtless why the king included the following instructions among the other assignments he gave us when we went to the kingdoms of Peru: to collect with precision and the greatest attention to detail all the important facts which bear on government, administration of justice, customs and the state of affairs in those areas, and everything regarding civil, political, military, and economic conditions. . . .

Source: Jorge Juan and Antonio Ulloa, *Discourse and Political Reflections on the Kingdom of Peru*, ed. John J. TePaske (Tulsa: University of Oklahoma Press, 1978), 38–41, 70, 143, 155.

Our sole object has been to get at the truth, and now, to lay it open before the eyes of high ministers. Once these prevailing evils are revealed, suitable remedies can be applied as circumstances dictate, in time lessening the risk for such opportunities. The general public can have no interest in this report. Such information in its hands would lead to no good purpose and cause the natives of the area to be subject unjustifiably to general defamation. . . .

Divided into twelve chapters, the present work describes these confidential matters. We should warn that the information should be restricted to the sole purpose specified above because we fear the damage from a public disclosure. . . .

The tyranny suffered by the Indians stems from the insatiable desire for riches on the part of those who come from Spain to rule over them. The latter have no other means of satisfying this lust than by exploiting the Indians. Using every oppressive measure at their disposal, officials exact more through cruelty than they obtain from their own slaves. . . .

Corregidores *[local Spanish administrative officials–Ed.]* use many methods to enrich themselves at the expense of the Indians, and we shall start with the collection of tribute. In this matter they institute severe treatment, ignore justice, forget charity, and totally disregard the fear of God. Tribute *[a tax on indigenous people–Ed.]* is one revenue that corregidores count as profit or personal gain from their corregimiento *[the territory under a corregidor's jurisdiction–Ed.]*. Clearly if they made collections honestly, they would not profit personally from the tribute, would do no harm to the Indians, and would not defraud the king; but all three result from their corrupt conduct. Their insatiable greed seeks nothing but its own satisfaction; overwhelmed by avarice, corregidores satisfy it by any means possible. . . .

It may seem a great exaggeration to defend and exonerate the Indians and blame the Spaniards for the natives' indolence, but both past experience and recent events bear out our judgment. One has only to look back at pre-conquest days to be astounded by the Indians' admirable achievements, even though today we find it difficult to believe what marvelous things they could accomplish. Let us leave aside the magnificent accounts in the histories, which might perhaps lead us to suspect their validity, and point to the extant remains of their accomplishments. This is enough, not only to dispel prejudiced opinions but also to demonstrate the Indians' initiative and industry. Are not the scrupulously developed irrigation projects testimony to the Indians' ambition? To cultivate a bit of arid land, worthless without water, they devised irrigation ditches. With dams built to store the torrents of rain flowing off the mountains, they diverted water more than thirty leagues, depending upon the terrain, until they achieved their purpose. Irrigation enabled them to cultivate small parcels of land and to make them fertile. Truly lasting achievements, the irrigation ditches have remained in such good condition that the Spaniards now use them. Although we state it ruefully, the Spaniards themselves have been lamentably careless and have neglected and destroyed many of those projects which they now need. . . .

One thing which made us most compassionate toward those people was seeing them totally despoiled of their land. At the beginning of the conquest when towns were established, some lands were assigned to the caciques *[indigenous political leaders–Ed.]* and the Indians under their control. Now, greed has sharply reduced the amount of land under their control. The majority of Indians have nothing, some because ownership has been usurped. Others because owners of nearby haciendas have forced them to sell, and still others because they have been persuaded by deceitful means to give up their land.

QUESTIONS TO CONSIDER

1. What kinds of problems are Juan and Ulloa reporting to the imperial government? What are the root causes?
2. What relationships can you infer between a report like this and changes in Spanish imperial policy in the eighteenth century?

5.6 "OUR HEARTY THANKS FOR THE CARE YOU TAKE OF US IN SUPPLYING US WITH AMMUNITION." *MEETINGS BETWEEN A BRITISH GENERAL AND LEADERS OF THE MOHAWKS, ONEIDAS, AND TUSCARORAS, 1755–1756*

William Johnson (ca. 1715–1774) was born in Ireland and moved to New York in the 1730s to manage an estate for his uncle. The estate was located in territory dominated by the Mohawks, one of the six indigenous nations that constituted the Iroquois League. Johnson learned the language of the Mohawks, commanded a troop of Iroquois and English colonists during the Seven Years' War, and was appointed British Superintendent of Indian Affairs for the northern colonies in 1756. The following sources contain summaries of communications between Iroquois leaders and Johnson at Fort Johnson in Albany, New York, in the midst of the war, known in US history as the French and Indian War

SPEECHES FROM IROQUOIS LEADERS TO GENERAL JOHNSON, DECEMBER 1755

1. We return you our hearty thanks for the care you take of us in supplying us with ammunition, large guns and paint; as we do not know how soon the enemy will come upon us. We have been speaking to our elder brothers these four years, about having a place of defense made against the French, but could never bring them to a conclusion until now, having promised to join and assist our brothers the English against any attempts which the French shall make upon them.

2. We join with our brothers, the Tuscaroras, in returning you our hearty thanks for advising us to be upon our guard against the malicious designs of the French, and that you would supply us with ammunition, large guns, paint, etc.

3. We own we have been soft or drunk these several years past, in not listening to you and our youngest brothers in joining the two castles together; but we have now opened our ears which have been stopped, and are determined to live and die with you.

4. You acquainted us some time ago, of the designs of the French in encroaching upon our hunting-grounds, and advised us to be upon our guard against them, or otherwise they would come and dispossess and destroy us all; it seems to us now that they had blinded our eyes, and it is plain to us as the sun that rises in the morning, that they had it in view. No doubt but you have heard that the French had invited us to meet them at Swegatsy; but we have taken a firm resolution never to listen to any but yourself: we don't speak this from our lips only, but it comes from the bottom of our hearts.

5. You blame us for not taking care of our allies to the southward, but we assure you we have some time ago sent four large belts to them, desiring they would not join with any but whom the five nations joined; and since we are informed that

Source: *An Account of Conferences Held and Treaties Made between Major-General Sir William Johnson, Bart. and the Chief Sachems and Warriors of the . . . Indian Nations in North America* (London: A. Millar, 1756), 5–9.

the belts and messages we sent were directly made known to the French. Now, brother, we have sent another message, desiring that they would come and speak with us; and be assured we will do our utmost endeavors to put a stop to any more bloodshed that way; and we hope, that you will desire the governors to do their utmost in bringing them over to us, as we are sure there is nothing draws them from us but the large presents which the French make them.

6. We have sent to the River-Indians and Shawanese to come to our castle, to hear from their own mouths what they have to say for their killing so many of our brothers; and if they should not come upon our message, we the Oneidas, and Tuscaroras Sachems, are determined to go to them and know the reason of it. Governor Shirley promised to have a fort built for us, and men to garrison it; and not hearing anything about it since, we think he will defer it until spring; so hope that you will have a fort built immediately, and men to garrison it, as we are certain the French only wait a favourable opportunity to fall upon us.

JOHNSON'S COMMUNICATIONS WITH IROQUOIS LEADERS, FEBRUARY 1756

1. I received the friendly speech which you made at my house when I was at New-York, together with your acknowledgments for the arms, ammunition, &c. I gave your nation; I heartily wish they may answer the end they were designed for, which was to enable you to secure yourselves against any attempts of the French, or any other enemy. I highly approve of your wisdom and timely advice to your elder brothers the Oneidas, and am extremely glad that you and they have at last agreed to build a place of defense, and to join your brethren the English against any attempts of your and our common enemy the French.

2. It highly pleases me to find you so grateful for the advice I have given you, and the assistance I promised you should have, as well as your brethren the Tuscaroras; and I expect you and they, together with the Skaniadaradighronos, will live so compact, and have your castle fortified in such a manner, as may enable you to make a bold defense, should any attempts be made against you. If you do this, and have a good officer with a party of men there, nothing can hurt you.

3. Nothing can give me greater satisfaction, than to find you have at last come to your senses, and to the use of your hearing, of which you have acknowledged to have been bereft some time. As I have a great regard for you, I most sincerely wish you may continue in your senses, that you may follow the wholesome advice which your brother the Tuscarora, although younger, has given you, and that which I shall from time to time give you.

4. Had you been in your right senses, and your eyes open when I timely acquainted you with the designs of the French encroaching on your hunting-grounds, and destroying you, and had followed my advice, the French would not have been now in possession of the best part of your country, and bid you defiance as they now do. Shake away then that infatuation, which has so long had the better of you, and exert yourselves now in conjunction with your Father the King's troops, and you may still recover your lands and be a happy people, which is the sincere wish of your Father and all your brethren. Your not complying with the governor of Canada's invitation to meet him at Swegatfy, was quite right; and I am glad you have taken so firm a resolution of adhering to your engagements: had you acted otherwise, it would have been a breach of the many solemn promises you have made to me on that head.

QUESTIONS TO CONSIDER

1. What is Johnson hoping to achieve in these exchanges with indigenous leaders and peoples? What are the indigenous leaders hoping to achieve?
2. What do these exchanges tell us about the balance of powers among various peoples and their governments in North America in the middle of the eighteenth century?

5.7 "THE SOVEREIGN IS ABSOLUTE."
CATHERINE II OF RUSSIA, *INSTRUCTIONS FOR A NEW LAW CODE*, 1767

Born into a noble German family, Princess Sophie Auguste Frederike von Anhalt-Zerbst (1729–1796) married the heir to the Russian throne in 1745. Her husband, Peter III, came to power in 1762 but immediately alienated key elites in the empire. He withdrew Russian forces from the Seven Years' War and ceded territory to Prussia. He was drawn to Protestantism rather than Russian Orthodox Christianity. Soon after his coronation, he was deposed by a group of nobles allied with his wife, who took the throne for herself and the royal name of Empress Catherine II. She served as Russia's longest-reigning female ruler—in power from 1762 until her death in 1796.

During much of her life leading up to her coronation, Catherine had both studied and personally experienced the intrigues and challenges of rulership during this age of global war and imperial reform. She kept a diary of her observations and corresponded with numerous intellectuals, including French philosophers Voltaire and Denis Diderot. Early in her reign, she began to draft a set of guiding principles for rulership. By the time Catherine was finished, the document contained twenty-two chapters and 655 clauses. She delivered the revised document, excerpted here, as a set of guidelines for a legislative commission that she convened in 1767 to revise the Russian legal code.

6. Russia is an European State.

7. This is clearly demonstrated by the following Observations: The Alterations which Peter the Great undertook in Russia succeeded with the greater Ease, because the Manners, which prevailed at that Time, and had been introduced amongst us by a Mixture of different Nations, and the Conquest of foreign Territories, were quite unsuitable to the Climate. Peter the First, by introducing the Manners and Customs of Europe among the European People in his Dominions, found at that Time such Means as even he himself was not sanguine enough to expect. . . .

9. The Sovereign is absolute; for there is no other authority but that which centers in his single Person that can act with a Vigour proportionate to the Extent of such a vast Dominion. . . .

11. Every other Form of Government whatsoever would not only have been prejudicial to Russia, but would even have proved its entire Ruin. . . .

13. What is the true End of Monarchy? Not to deprive People of their natural Liberty; but to correct their Actions, in order to attain the supreme Good.

14. The Form of Government, therefore, which best attains this End, and at the same Time sets less Bounds than others to natural Liberty, is that which coincides with the Views and Purposes of rational Creatures, and answers the End, upon which we ought to fix a steadfast Eye in the Regulations of civil Polity.

15. The Intention and the End of Monarchy is the Glory of the Citizens, of the State, and of the Sovereign.

Source: W. F. Reddaway, ed., *Documents of Catherine the Great; the Correspondence with Voltaire and the Instruction of 1767 in the English text of 1768* (New York: Russell & Russell, 1971), 216–217, 225, 248–249, 273, 275, 293–294.

16. But, from this Glory, a Sense of Liberty arises in a People governed by a Monarch; which may produce in these States as much Energy in transacting the most important Affairs, and may contribute as much to the Happiness of the Subjects, as even Liberty itself. . . .

80. Of Punishments.

81. The Love of our Country, Shame, and the Dread of public Censure are Motives which restrain, and may deter Mankind from the Commission of a Number of Crimes.

82. The greatest Punishment for a bad Action, under a mild Administration, will be for the Party to be convinced of it. The civil Laws will there correct Vice with the more Ease, and will not be under a Necessity of employing more rigorous Means.

83. In these Governments, the Legislature will apply itself more to prevent Crimes than to punish them, and should take more Care to instil Good Manners into the Minds of the Citizens, by proper Regulations, than to dispirit them by the Terror of corporal and capital Punishments. . . .

209. Whether the punishment of death is really useful and necessary in a community for the preservation of peace and good order.

210. Proofs from fact demonstrate to us that the frequent use of capital punishment never mended the morals of a people. . . . The death of a citizen can only be useful and necessary in one case: which is, when, though he be deprived of liberty, yet he has such power by his connections as may enable him to raise disturbances dangerous to the public peace. This case can happen only when a People either loses or recovers their liberty, or in a time of anarchy, when the disorders themselves hold the place of laws. But in a reign of peace and tranquility, under a Government established with the united wishes of a whole People, in a state well fortified against external enemies and protected within by strong supports, that is, by its own internal strength and virtuous sentiments rooted in the minds of the citizens, and where the whole power is lodged in the hands of a Monarch: in such a state there can be no necessity for taking away the life of a citizen. . . .

361. As amongst mankind there were some more virtuous than others, and who at the same time distinguished themselves more eminently by their merit, the people in ancient times agreed to dignify the most virtuous and the most deserving, by this honourable appellation, or title, and determined to invest them with many privileges which are founded upon the principal rules of virtue and honour. . . .

363. Virtue with merit raises people to the rank of nobility. . . .

377. In whatever state the fundamental qualification for the rank of nobility is established, conformably with the rules prescribed . . . , it is no less useful to establish the qualification of citizens upon principles productive of good manners and industry, by which the people we here treat of, will enjoy that situation.

378. This sort of people, of whom we ought now to speak, and from whom the state expects much benefit, are admitted into the middling rank, if their qualifications are firmly established upon good manners and incitements to industry.

379. People of this rank will enjoy a state of liberty, without intermixing either with the nobility or the husbandmen [owners of agricultural property–Ed.].

380. To this rank of people we ought to annex all those who are neither gentlemen nor husbandmen but employ themselves in arts, science, navigation, commerce, or handicraft trades. . . .

383. As the whole qualification, which intitles people to this middling rank, is founded upon good manners and industry; the violation of these rules will serve, on the contrary, for their exclusion from it; as for instance perfidiousness and breach of promise, especially if caused by idleness and treachery.

Conclusions: Perhaps some persons may object, after perusing these instructions, that they will not be intelligible to everyone. To this it may be answered: it is true, they will not be readily understood by every person, after one slight perusal only; but every person may comprehend these instructions, if he reads them with care and attention, and selects occasionally such articles as may serve to direct him, as a rule, in whatever he undertakes. The instructions ought to be frequently perused, to render them more familiar. . . . To render this difficult affair more easy; these instructions are to be read over once at the beginning of every month, in the commission for composing the New Code of Laws.

QUESTIONS TO CONSIDER

1. What can these clauses tell us about Catherine's concerns regarding the state of the Russian Empire at the beginning of her reign? What does she appear intent on accomplishing with this guidance to the legislators?
2. How would you characterize Catherine's ideas about government and rulership compared to other documents you have read, especially those of her Russian predecessor Peter the Great (Source 5.2)? What parts of the document appear similar to that which came before, and what parts appear to be moving in a new direction? How might one account for this?

CHAPTER 6

A NEW ORDER FOR THE AGES, 1755–1839

6.1 "WE HOLD THESE TRUTHS TO BE SELF-EVIDENT." *THE US DECLARATION OF INDEPENDENCE*, 1776

After the 1756–1763 Seven Years' War (what we have called "World War 0" in *Forging the Modern World*), Great Britain imposed higher costs and closer controls on its North American colonies. These measures exacerbated resentment among many colonists in the thirteen southernmost colonies on the North American mainland and prompted protests against British rule. After several years of intensifying protests and increasing repression, armed conflict broke out in April 1775 in the outskirts of Boston. Although many colonists were dissatisfied with British rule, there was no consensus about how to proceed. It was not until the summer of 1776 that representatives of the thirteen colonies met in Philadelphia and drafted a document that would declare the colonies to be an independent United States of America. Thomas Jefferson was charged with writing the original draft, which was then edited and revised by the Continental Congress.

The document reproduced here has become one of the most important statements about political governance in history, not just for its role in establishing the United States, but for its influence on other revolutionary movements around the world for centuries to follow.

When in the course of human events it becomes necessary for one people to dissolve the political bands which have connected them with another and to assume among the powers of the earth, the separate and equal station to which the Laws of Nature and of Nature's God entitle them, a decent respect to the opinions of mankind requires that they should declare the causes which impel them to the separation.

We hold these truths to be self-evident, that all men are created equal, that they are endowed by their Creator with certain unalienable Rights, that among these are Life, Liberty and the pursuit of Happiness.—That

Source: United States National Archives and Records Administration, http://www.archives.gov/founding-docs/declaration-transcript.

to secure these rights, Governments are instituted among Men, deriving their just powers from the consent of the governed, — That whenever any Form of Government becomes destructive of these ends, it is the Right of the People to alter or to abolish it, and to institute new Government, laying its foundation on such principles and organizing its powers in such form, as to them shall seem most likely to effect their Safety and Happiness. Prudence, indeed, will dictate that Governments long established should not be changed for light and transient causes; and accordingly all experience hath shewn that mankind are more disposed to suffer, while evils are sufferable than to right themselves by abolishing the forms to which they are accustomed. But when a long train of abuses and usurpations, pursuing invariably the same Object evinces a design to reduce them under absolute Despotism, it is their right, it is their duty, to throw off such Government, and to provide new Guards for their future security. — Such has been the patient sufferance of these Colonies; and such is now the necessity which constrains them to alter their former Systems of Government. The history of the present King of Great Britain is a history of repeated injuries and usurpations, all having in direct object the establishment of an absolute Tyranny over these States. To prove this, let Facts be submitted to a candid world.

He has refused his Assent to Laws, the most wholesome and necessary for the public good.

He has forbidden his Governors to pass Laws of immediate and pressing importance, unless suspended in their operation till his Assent should be obtained; and when so suspended, he has utterly neglected to attend to them.

He has refused to pass other Laws for the accommodation of large districts of people, unless those people would relinquish the right of Representation in the Legislature, a right inestimable to them and formidable to tyrants only.

He has called together legislative bodies at places unusual, uncomfortable, and distant from the depository of their Public Records, for the sole purpose of fatiguing them into compliance with his measures.

He has dissolved Representative Houses repeatedly, for opposing with manly firmness his invasions on the rights of the people.

He has refused for a long time, after such dissolutions, to cause others to be elected, whereby the Legislative Powers, incapable of Annihilation, have returned to the People at large for their exercise; the State remaining in the meantime exposed to all the dangers of invasion from without, and convulsions within.

He has endeavoured to prevent the population of these States; for that purpose obstructing the Laws for Naturalization of Foreigners; refusing to pass others to encourage their migrations hither, and raising the conditions of new Appropriations of Lands.

He has obstructed the Administration of Justice by refusing his Assent to Laws for establishing Judiciary Powers.

He has made Judges dependent on his Will alone for the tenure of their offices, and the amount and payment of their salaries.

He has erected a multitude of New Offices, and sent hither swarms of Officers to harass our people and eat out their substance.

He has kept among us, in times of peace, Standing Armies without the Consent of our legislatures.

He has affected to render the Military independent of and superior to the Civil Power.

He has combined with others to subject us to a jurisdiction foreign to our constitution, and unacknowledged by our laws; giving his Assent to their Acts of pretended Legislation:

For quartering large bodies of armed troops among us:

For protecting them, by a mock Trial from punishment for any Murders which they should commit on the Inhabitants of these States:

For cutting off our Trade with all parts of the world:

For imposing Taxes on us without our Consent:

For depriving us in many cases, of the benefit of Trial by Jury:

For transporting us beyond Seas to be tried for pretended offences:

For abolishing the free System of English Laws in a neighbouring Province, establishing therein an Arbitrary government, and enlarging its Boundaries so as to render it at once an example and fit instrument for introducing the same absolute rule into these Colonies:

For taking away our Charters, abolishing our most valuable Laws and altering fundamentally the Forms of our Governments:

For suspending our own Legislatures, and declaring themselves invested with power to legislate for us in all cases whatsoever.

He has abdicated Government here, by declaring us out of his Protection and waging War against us.

He has plundered our seas, ravaged our coasts, burnt our towns, and destroyed the lives of our people.

He is at this time transporting large Armies of foreign Mercenaries to compleat the works of death, desolation, and tyranny, already begun with circumstances of Cruelty & Perfidy scarcely paralleled in the most barbarous ages, and totally unworthy the Head of a civilized nation.

He has constrained our fellow Citizens taken Captive on the high Seas to bear Arms against their Country, to become the executioners of their friends and Brethren, or to fall themselves by their Hands.

He has excited domestic insurrections amongst us, and has endeavoured to bring on the inhabitants of our frontiers, the merciless Indian Savages whose known rule of warfare, is an undistinguished destruction of all ages, sexes and conditions.

In every stage of these Oppressions We have Petitioned for Redress in the most humble terms: Our repeated Petitions have been answered only by repeated injury. A Prince, whose character is thus marked by every act which may define a Tyrant, is unfit to be the ruler of a free people. Nor have We been wanting in attentions to our British brethren. We have warned them from time to time of attempts by their legislature to extend an unwarrantable jurisdiction over us. We have reminded them of the circumstances of our emigration and settlement here. We have appealed to their native justice and magnanimity, and we have conjured them by the ties of our common kindred to disavow these usurpations, which would inevitably interrupt our connections and correspondence. They too have been deaf to the voice of justice and of consanguinity. We must, therefore, acquiesce in the necessity, which denounces our Separation, and hold them, as we hold the rest of mankind, Enemies in War, in Peace Friends.

We, therefore, the Representatives of the united States of America, in General Congress, Assembled, appealing to the Supreme Judge of the world for the rectitude of our intentions, do, in the Name, and by Authority of the good People of these Colonies, solemnly publish and declare, That these united Colonies are, and of Right ought to be Free and Independent States, that they are Absolved from all Allegiance to the British Crown, and that all political connection between them and the State of Great Britain, is and ought to be totally dissolved; and that as Free and Independent States, they have full Power to levy War, conclude Peace, contract Alliances, establish Commerce, and to do all other Acts and Things which Independent States may of right do. — And for the support of this Declaration, with a firm reliance on the protection of Divine Providence, we mutually pledge to each other our Lives, our Fortunes, and our sacred Honor.

QUESTIONS TO CONSIDER

1. This document is considered one of the first written acknowledgments of a "social contract." How does the Declaration imply the existence of the social contract? How do the two sides (governor and governed) appear obligated to one another, and how did Social Contract theory help the authors of the Declaration to justify their rebellion?

2. The Declaration is one of the most influential statements across time and space. What features of it have been taken up by other revolutionaries? Can you find examples in this book that have taken inspiration from the Declaration?

3. What influences helped shape the Declaration of Independence? How did those influences contribute to the grievances listed here?

6.2 "THE STATE OUGHT NOT TO BE CONSIDERED AS NOTHING BETTER THAN A PARTNERSHIP AGREEMENT." EDMUND BURKE, *REFLECTIONS ON THE REVOLUTION IN FRANCE*, 1790

Born in Ireland, Edmund Burke (1729–1797) had a long career in British politics, serving as a Member of Parliament (House of Commons) from 1766 to 1794. During the growing dispute between the crown and its North American colonies, Burke advocated for compromise and pragmatism on the part of the imperial government. The outbreak of the French Revolution in 1789, together with the enthusiastic embrace of the revolutionary ethos in some English quarters, led Burke to write his most famous work, *Reflections on the Revolution in France* (1790), excerpted here. It is this work that earned Burke his reputation as "father of modern conservative political thought."

But now all is to be changed. All the pleasing illusions, which made power gentle, and obedience liberal, which harmonized the different shades of life, and which, by a bland assimilation, incorporated into politics the sentiments which beautify and soften private society, are to be dissolved by this new conquering empire of light and reason. All the decent drapery of life is to be rudely torn off. All the superadded ideas, furnished from the wardrobe of a moral imagination, which the heart owns, and the understanding ratifies, as necessary to cover the defects of our naked shivering nature, and to raise it to dignity in our own estimation, are to be exploded as a ridiculous, absurd, and antiquated fashion.

On this scheme of things, a king is but a man; a queen is but a woman; a woman is but an animal; and an animal not of the highest order. All homage paid to the sex in general as such, and without distinct views, is to be regarded as romance and folly. Regicide, and parricide, and sacrilege, are but fictions of superstition, corrupting jurisprudence by destroying its simplicity. The murder of a king, or a queen, or a bishop, or a father, are only common homicide; and if the people are by any chance, or in any way gainers by it, a sort of homicide much the most pardonable,

and into which we ought not to make too severe a scrutiny.

On the scheme of this barbarous philosophy, which is the offspring of cold hearts and muddy understandings, and which is as void of solid wisdom, as it is destitute of all taste and elegance, laws are to be supported only by their own terrors, and by the concern, which each individual may find in them, from his own private speculations, or can spare to them from his own private interests. In the groves of their academy, at the end of every vista, you see nothing but the gallows. Nothing is left which engages the affections on the part of the commonwealth.

On the principles of this mechanic philosophy, our institutions can never be embodied, if I may use the expression, in persons; so as to create in us love, veneration, admiration, or attachment. But that sort of reason which banishes the affections is incapable of filling their place. These public affections, combined with manners, are required sometimes as supplements, sometimes as correctives, always as aids to law. The precept given by a wise man, as well as a great critic, for the construction of poems, is equally true as to states. *Non satis est pulchra esse poemata, dulcia sunto. [This is a quote from the Roman poet Horace (65 BC–8 BC): "It is not*

Source: Edmund Burke, *Reflections on the Revolution in France* (New York: E. P. Dutton, 1910 [1951]), 73–77, 93–94.

enough for poems to be beautiful; they must also be sweet, and divert the mind of the listener"–Ed.]. There ought to be a system of manners in every nation which a well-formed mind would be disposed to relish. To make us love our country, our country ought to be lovely.

But power, of some kind or other, will survive the shock in which manners and opinions perish; and it will find other and worse means for its support. The usurpation which, in order to subvert ancient institutions, has destroyed ancient principles, will hold power by arts similar to those by which it has acquired it. When the old feudal and chivalrous spirit of Fealty, which, by freeing kings from fear, freed both kings and subjects from the precautions of tyranny, shall be extinct in the minds of men, plots and assassinations will be anticipated by preventive murder and preventive confiscation, and that long roll of grim and blood maxims, which form the political code of all power, not standing on its own honor, and the honor of those who are to obey it. Kings will be tyrants from policy when subjects are rebels from principle.

When ancient opinions and rules of life are taken away, the loss cannot possibly be estimated. From that moment we have no compass to govern us; nor can we know distinctly to what port we steer. Europe undoubtedly, taken in a mass, was in a flourishing condition the day on which your Revolution was completed. How much of that prosperous state was owing to the spirit of our old manners and opinions is not easy to say; but as such causes cannot be indifferent in their operation, we must presume, that, on the whole, their operation was beneficial. . . .

Society is indeed a contract. Subordinate contracts for objects of mere occasional interest may be dissolved at pleasure—but the state ought not to be considered as nothing better than a partnership agreement in a trade of pepper and coffee, callico or tobacco, or some other such low concern, to be taken up for a little temporary interest, and to be dissolved by the fancy of the parties. It is to be looked on with other reverence; because it is not a partnership in things subservient only to the gross animal existence of a temporary and perishable nature. It is a partnership in all science; a partnership in all art; a partnership in every virtue, and in all perfection. As the ends of such a partnership cannot be obtained in many generations, it becomes a partnership not only between those who are living, but between those who are living, those who are dead, and those who are to be born. Each contract of each particular state is but a clause in the great primaeval contract of eternal society, linking the lower with the higher natures, connecting the visible and invisible world, according to a fixed compact sanctioned by the inviolable oath which holds all physical and all moral natures, each in their appointed place. This law is not subject to the will of those, who by an obligation above them, and infinitely superior, are bound to submit their will to that law. The municipal corporations of that universal kingdom are not morally at liberty at their pleasure, and on their speculations of a contingent improvement, wholly to separate and tear asunder the bands of their subordinate community, and to dissolve it into an unsocial, uncivil, unconnected chaos of elementary principles. It is the first and supreme necessity only, a necessity that is not chosen but chooses, a necessity paramount to deliberation, that admits no discussion, and demands no evidence, which alone can justify a resort to anarchy. This necessity is no exception to the rule; because this necessity itself is a part too of that moral and physical disposition of things to which man must be obedient by consent or force; but if that which is only submission to necessity should be made the object of choice, the law is broken, nature is disobeyed, and the rebellious are outlawed, cast forth, and exiled, from this world of reason, and order, and peace, and virtue, and fruitful penitence, into the antagonist world of madness, discord, vice, confusion, and unavailing sorrow.

QUESTIONS TO CONSIDER

1. What characteristics of Burke's analysis render this a work of "conservative" political philosophy?
2. Would it be right to think of Burke as an Enlightenment thinker? What aspects of Enlightenment thought does he seem to embrace? Reject?

6.3 "WOMAN IS BORN FREE AND LIVES EQUAL TO MAN IN HER RIGHTS." OLYMPE DE GOUGES, *DECLARATION OF THE RIGHTS OF WOMAN AND THE FEMALE CITIZEN*, 1791

Olympe de Gouges (1748–1793) was born Marie Gouze in southwestern France. A young widow with a child, she moved to Paris in 1770, where she became involved in the artistic and intellectual circles of the French Enlightenment. She wrote plays, a memoir, and literary criticism, and became one of the most outspoken and articulate women in the early days of the French Revolution. Frustrated by the exclusion of women from the French revolutionary agenda, in 1791, she wrote the *Declaration of the Rights of Woman and the Female Citizen*, excerpted here. The document directly challenged the inferiority presumed of women by the Declaration of the Rights of Man, issued by the French National Assembly in 1789, and subsequent actions of the revolutionary government. Her advocacy on behalf of women's rights was deemed treasonous. She was arrested and executed by guillotine in November 1793. She was among more than 16,000 people executed by guillotine during the height of revolutionary fervor, only a handful of whom were women.

Declaration of the Rights of Woman and the Female Citizen

For the National Assembly to decree in its last sessions, or in those of the next legislature:

PREAMBLE

Mothers, daughters, sisters [and] representatives of the nation demand to be constituted into a national assembly. Believing that ignorance, omission, or scorn for the rights of woman are the only causes of public misfortunes and of the corruption of governments, [the women] have resolved to set forth a solemn declaration [of] the natural, inalienable, and sacred rights of woman in order that this declaration, constantly exposed before all members of the society, will ceaselessly remind them of their rights and duties; in order that the authoritative acts of women and the authoritative acts of men may be at any moment compared with and respectful of the purpose of all political institutions; and in order that

citizens' demands, henceforth based on simple and incontestable principles, will always support the constitution, good morals, and the happiness of all.

Consequently, the sex that is as superior in beauty as it is in courage during the sufferings of maternity recognizes and declares in the presence and under the auspices of the Supreme Being, the following Rights of Woman and of Female Citizens.

ARTICLE I

Woman is born free and lives equal to man in her rights. Social distinctions can be based only on the common utility.

ARTICLE II

The purpose of any political association is the conservation of the natural and imprescriptible rights of woman and man; these rights are liberty, property, security, and especially resistance to oppression.

Source: Darline Gay Levy, Harriet Branson Applewhite, and Many Durham Johnson, eds., *Women in Revolutionary Paris, 1789–1795* (Urbana: University of Illinois Press, 1980), 87–96.

ARTICLE III

The principle of all sovereignty rests essentially with the nation, which is nothing but the union of woman and man; no body and no individual can exercise any authority which does not come expressly from it (the nation).

ARTICLE IV

Liberty and justice consist of restoring all that belongs to others; thus, the only limits on the exercise of the natural rights of woman are perpetual male tyranny; these limits are to be reformed by the laws of nature and reason.

ARTICLE V

Laws of nature and reason proscribe all acts harmful to society; everything which is not prohibited by these wise and divine laws cannot be prevented, and no one can be constrained to do what they do not command.

ARTICLE VI

The law must be the expression of the general will; all female and male citizens must contribute either personally or through their representatives to its formation; it must be the same for all: male and female citizens, being equal in the eyes of the law, must be equally admitted to all honors, positions, and public employment according to their capacity and without other distinctions besides those of their virtues and talents.

ARTICLE VII

No woman is an exception; she is accused, arrested, and detained in cases determined by law. Women, like men, obey this rigorous law.

ARTICLE VIII

The law must establish only those penalties that are strictly and obviously necessary. . . .

ARTICLE IX

Once any woman is declared guilty, complete rigor is exercised by law.

ARTICLE X

No one is to be disquieted for his very basic opinions; woman has the right to mount the scaffold; she must equally have the right to mount the rostrum, provided that her demonstrations do not disturb the legally established public order.

ARTICLE XI

The free communication of thoughts and opinions is one of the most precious rights of woman, since that liberty assures recognition of children by their fathers. Any female citizen thus may say freely, I am the mother of a child which belongs to you, without being forced by a barbarous prejudice to hide the truth; (an exception may be made) to respond to the abuse of this liberty in cases determined by law.

ARTICLE XII

The guarantee of the rights of woman and the female citizen implies a major benefit; this guarantee must be instituted for the advantage of all, and not for the particular benefit of those to whom it is entrusted.

ARTICLE XIII

For the support of the public force and the expenses of administration, the contributions of woman and man are equal; she shares all the duties and all the painful tasks; therefore, she must have the same share in the distribution of positions, employment, offices, honors, and jobs.

ARTICLE XIV

Female and male citizens have the right to verify, either by themselves or through their representatives, the necessity of the public contribution. This can only apply to women if they are granted an equal share, not only of wealth, but also of public administration, and in the determination of the proportion, the base, the collection, and the duration of the tax.

ARTICLE XV

The collectivity of women, joined for tax purposes to the aggregate of men, has the right to demand an accounting of his administration from any public agent.

ARTICLE XVI

No society has a constitution without the guarantee of rights and the separation of powers; the constitution is null if the majority of individuals comprising the nation have not cooperated in drafting it.

ARTICLE XVII

Property belongs to both sexes whether united or separate; for each it is an inviolable and sacred right; no one can be deprived of it, since it is the true patrimony of nature, unless the legally determined public need obviously dictates it, and then only with a just and prior indemnity.

POSTSCRIPT

Woman, wake up; the tocsin of reason is being heard throughout the whole universe; discover your rights. The powerful empire of nature is no longer surrounded by prejudice, fanaticism, superstition, and lies. The flame of truth has dispersed all the clouds of folly and usurpation. Enslaved man has multiplied his strength and needs recourse to yours to break his chains. Having become free, he has become unjust to his companion. Oh, women, women! When will you cease to be blind? What advantage have you received from the Revolution? A more pronounced scorn, a more marked disdain. In the centuries of corruption you ruled only over the weakness of men. The reclamation of your patrimony, based on the wise decrees of nature—what have you to dread from such a fine undertaking? The *bon mot* of the legislator of the marriage of Cana? Do you fear that our French legislators, correctors of that morality, long ensnared by political practices now out of date, will only say again to you: women, what is there in common between you and us? Everything, you will have to answer. If they persist in their weakness in putting this non sequitur in contradiction to their principles, courageously oppose the force of reason to the empty pretentions of superiority; unite yourselves beneath the standards of philosophy; deploy all the energy of your character, and you will soon see these haughty men, not groveling at your feet as servile adorers, but proud to share with you the treasures of the Supreme Being. Regardless of what barriers confront you, it is in your power to free yourselves; you have only to want to. . . .

Marriage is the tomb of trust and love. The married woman can with impunity give bastards to her husband, and also give them the wealth which does not belong to them. The woman who is unmarried has only one feeble right; ancient and inhuman laws refuse to her for her children the right to the name and the wealth of their father; no new laws have been made in this matter. If it is considered a paradox and an impossibility on my part to try to give my sex an honorable and just consistency, I leave it to men to attain glory for dealing with this matter; but while we wait, the way can be prepared through national education, the restoration of morals, and conjugal conventions.

FORM FOR A SOCIAL CONTRACT BETWEEN MAN AND WOMAN

We, _____ and _____, moved by our own will, unite ourselves for the duration of our lives, and for the duration of our mutual inclinations, under the following conditions: We intend and wish to make our wealth communal, meanwhile reserving to ourselves the right to divide it in favor of our children and of those toward whom we might have a particular inclination, mutually recognizing that our property belongs directly to our children, from whatever bed they come, and that all of them without distinction have the right to bear the name of the fathers and mothers who have acknowledged them, and we are charged to subscribe to the law which punishes the renunciation of one's own blood. We likewise obligate ourselves, in case of separation, to divide our wealth and to set aside in advance the portion the law indicates for our children, and in the event of a perfect union, the one who dies will divest himself of half his property in his children's favor, and if one dies childless, the survivor will inherit by right, unless the dying person has disposed of half the common property in favor of one whom he judged deserving.

That is approximately the formula for the marriage act I propose for execution. Upon reading this strange document, I see rising up against me the hypocrites, the prudes, the clergy, and the whole infernal sequence. But how it [my proposal] offers to the wise the moral means of achieving the perfection of a happy government! . . .

Moreover, I would like a law which would assist widows and young girls deceived by the false promises of a man to whom they were attached; I would like, I say, this law to force an inconstant man to hold to his obligations or at least [to pay] an indemnity equal to his wealth. Again, I would like this law to be rigorous against women, at least those who have the effrontery to have recourse to a law which they themselves had violated by their misconduct, if proof of that were given. At the same time, as I showed in *Le Bonheur primitif de l'homme, ["Man's Original Happiness"–Ed.]* in 1788, that prostitutes should be placed in designated quarters. It is not prostitutes who contribute the most to the depravity of morals, it is the women of society. In regenerating the latter, the former are changed. This link of fraternal union will first bring disorder, but in consequence it will produce at the end a perfect harmony.

I offer a foolproof way to elevate the soul of women; it is to join them to all the activities of man; if man persists in finding this way impractical, let him share his fortune with woman, not at his caprice, but by the wisdom of laws. Prejudice falls, morals are purified, and nature regains all her rights. Add to this the marriage of priests and the strengthening of the king on his throne, and the French government cannot fail.

QUESTIONS TO CONSIDER

1. What changes did Olympe de Gouges demand in French society in order for true equality among citizens to be achieved? How do her demands differ from those of other revolutionary tracts and political ideas discussed in the sources in this chapter?

2. Which ideas presented in this document do you think were seen as the most radical for their time period? Why? How many of the ideas presented here do you think have been incorporated into modern understandings of a good, correct, or desirable democratic political order?

6.4 "WE WILL DISTANCE FOREVER FROM THIS COLONY THE HORRIBLE EVENTS." TOUSSAINT LOUVERTURE, *PROCLAMATION*, 1801

François Toussaint-Louverture (ca. 1746–1803) was born into slavery in the French Caribbean colony of Saint-Domingue. He labored as a stable hand and coach driver. Primary source records reveal that, well before the French Revolution erupted in 1789, Toussaint had become a free man and property owner. Scholars disagree on Toussaint's role in the first stages of the mass uprising of slaves that began in 1791, leading eventually to Haiti's independence, but he emerged in the documentary record as a military leader the next year. First fighting against the French, Toussaint later declared allegiance to the French Republic in 1794, about the time the republican government abolished slavery.

Source: Victor Schoelcher, *Vie de Toussaint*, Mitch Abidor, trans. (Paris: Paul Ollendorf, 1889). Toussaint Louverture Archive: https://www.marxists.org/reference/archive/toussaint-louverture/1801/dictatorial.htm.

While continuing to proclaim loyalty to France, Toussaint acted with great autonomy, even signing treaties with other countries and creating a new constitution in July 1801 that made him ruler for life. Napoleon Bonaparte (1769–1821), who came to power in France in 1799, had different plans for Haiti. Bonaparte wrote to Toussaint rejecting the Haitian Constitution. Soon thereafter, a French expedition arrived to reclaim Haiti. The invasion force captured Toussaint, who died in prison in 1803, but the French did not prevail. Led by Jean-Jacques Dessalines (1758–1806), another former slave, Haiti secured its independence in 1804.

The following excerpt is from a proclamation issued by Toussaint in November 1801. At the time of the proclamation, Toussaint was responding both to Napoleon's threats and to a major internal uprising on the north of the island, which was brutally suppressed.

NOVEMBEFR 25, 1801

Since the revolution, I have done all that depended upon me to return happiness to my country and to ensure liberty for my fellow citizens. Forced to combat internal and external enemies of the French Republic, I made war with courage, honor and loyalty. I have never strayed from the rules of justice with my enemies; as much as was in my power I sought to soften the horrors of war, to spare the blood of men. . . . Often after victory I received as brothers those who, the day before, were under enemy flags. Through the overlooking of errors and faults I wanted to make even its most ardent enemies love the legitimate and sacred cause of liberty.

I constantly reminded my brothers in arms, general and officers, that the ranks to which they'd been raised were nothing but the reward for honor, bravery and irreproachable conduct. That the higher they were above their fellow citizens, the more irreproachable all their actions and words must be; that scandals caused by public men had consequences even more dire for society than those of simple citizens; that the ranks and functions they bore hadn't been given to them to serve only their ambition, but had as cause and goal the general good. . . .

Nevertheless, how negligently fathers and mothers raise their children, especially in cities. They leave them in a state of idleness and in ignorance of their principal obligations. They seem to inspire in children contempt for agriculture, the first, the most honorable, and the most useful of all states. . . .

The same reproaches equally apply to cultivators on the habitations. Since the revolution perverse men have told them that freedom is the right to remain idle and to follow only their whims. Such a doctrine could not help but be accepted by all the evil subjects, thieves and assassins. It is time to hit out at the hardened men who persist in such ideas. . . .

An object worthy of its attention is the surveillance of foreigners who arrive in the colony. Some among them, knowing only through the reports of enemies of the new order of things, of the changes that have taken place, make statements which are all the more dangerous in that they are avidly listened to by those who, basing their hopes on the troubles, ask only for pretexts. Such straying must be severely punished. . . .

The most holy of all institutions among men who live in society, that from which flows the greatest good, is marriage. . . . Thus a wise government must always occupy itself with surrounding happy couples with honor, respect and veneration. It should only rest after having extirpated immorality to the last root. . . .

Idleness is the source of all disorders, and if it is allowed with one individual I shall hold the military commanders responsible, persuaded that those who tolerate the lazy and vagabonds are secret enemies of the government. . . .

In keeping with his faculties, no one under any pretext is to be exempt from some task. It is through these means that useful and respectable citizens will be formed, and we will distance forever from this colony the horrible events whose memory should never be effaced from our minds.

Consequently, I decree the following:

Any commander who during the late conspiracy had knowledge of the troubles which were to break out and who tolerated pillage and murder or who, able to prevent or block the revolt allowed the law that declares that "life, property and the asylum of every citizen are sacred and inviolable" to be broken, will be brought before a special tribunal and punished in conformity with the law of August 10, 1801. Any military commander who, by lack of foresight or negligence, has not stopped the disorders that have been committed, will be discharged and punished with one year in prison. In consequence of this a rigorous inquest will be carried out, according to which the government will pronounce on his destiny. . . .

4. Any individual, man or woman, whatever his or her color, who shall be convicted of having pronounced serious statements tending to incite sedition shall be brought before a court martial and punished in conformity with the law.

5. Any Creole [native-born Haitian–Ed.] individual, man or woman, convicted of making statements tending to alter public tranquility but who shall not be worthy of death shall be sent to the fields to work with a chain on one foot for six months. . . .

7. In all the communes of the colony where municipal administrations exist, all male and female citizens who live in them, whatever their quality or condition, must obtain a security card. Such card shall contain the name, family name, address, civil state, profession and quality, age and sex of those who bear them.

8. It is expressly ordered that municipal administrators are only to deliver security cards to persons having a known profession or state, irreproachable conduct and well assured means of existence. All those who cannot fulfill the conditions rigorously necessary to obtain it will be sent to the fields if they are Creole, or sent away from the colony if they are foreigners.

9. Dating two weeks after the publication of the present act all managers and drivers on habitations are to send to the commanders of their quarter the exact list of all the cultivators on their habitations of every age and sex, under penalty of one week in prison. Every manager and driver is the first overseer of his habitation. He is declared personally responsible for any kind of disorder that shall be committed, and for the laziness and vagabondage of the cultivators. . . .

15. Any captain or commander of a section who through negligence allowed a foreign cultivator on a habitation in his section for more than three days shall be discharged. . . .

17. It is forbidden for any soldier to go to a habitation, unless it is to see his father or mother and with a limited permit from his chief. If he fails to return to his corps at the stated hour he shall be punished in accordance with military ordinances. . . .

19. Any person convicted of having disturbed or attempted to disturb a married couple shall be denounced to the civil and military authorities, who shall render an account to the governor, who shall pronounce on their fate in accordance with the needs of the case.

QUESTIONS TO CONSIDER

1. What is the logic Toussaint used to justify the orders contained in the proclamation? How does this compare in logic and content with the proclamations contained in Chapter 5 in this sourcebook (see Sources 5.2 and 5.3)?

2. What does this proclamation reveal about the challenges that would face independent Haiti, whether or not Toussaint Louverture remained in power?

6.5 "I HAVE SIMPLY BEEN A MERE PLAYTHING OF THE REVOLUTIONARY STORM." SIMÓN BOLÍVAR, *ADDRESS TO THE CONGRESS OF ANGOSTURA*, 1819

Simón Bolívar (July 24, 1783–December 17, 1830) was born in Caracas (today the capital of Venezuela) and was a member of an important and wealthy family that had settled in the New World in the sixteenth century. Like many children of elite Spanish American families, Bolívar received an education in Spain. Upon his return to Venezuela, he became a leader of the cause of South American independence. During that long struggle, he spent time in exile, revised his views about the path toward independence, and eventually became one of the key military and political leaders who secured independence for all of Spanish South America by the mid-1820s.

While the war was still being fought, a constitutional convention met at Angostura (today called Ciudad Bolívar, Venezuela) to revise the original political plan for the independent state. The congress met from February 1819 to July 1821. At the congress's inaugural session, Bolívar gave what would become one of his most famous public statements, which is excerpted here. While Bolívar was perhaps the most important leader on the continent at the time he gave this speech, not all of his proposals were accepted by the congress.

The epoch in the life of the Republic over which I have presided has not been a mere political storm; it has been neither a bloody war, nor yet one of popular anarchy. It has been indeed, the development of all disorganizing elements; it has been the flooding of an infernal torrent which has overwhelmed the land of Venezuela. A man, aye, such a man as I am, what check could he offer to the march of such devastation? In the midst of this sea of woes I have simply been a mere plaything of the revolutionary storm, which tossed me about like a frail straw. I could do neither good nor harm. Irresistible forces have directed the trend of our events. To attribute this to me would not be fair, it would be assuming an importance which I do not merit. Do you desire to know who are the authors of past events and the present order of things? Consult then the Annals of Spain, of America, of Venezuela; examine the Laws of the Indies, the rule of the old executives; the influence of religion and of foreign domination; observe the first acts of the Republican Government, the ferocity of our enemies and our national temperament. Do not ask me what are the effects of such mishaps, ever to be lamented. I can scarcely be accounted for but as a mere instrument of the great forces which have been at work in Venezuela. . . .

By casting a glance over the past, we shall see what is the basic element of the Republic of Venezuela. America, on becoming separated from the Spanish monarchy, found itself like the Roman Empire, when that enormous mass fell to pieces in the midst of the ancient world. Each dismembered portion formed then an independent nation in accordance with its situation or its interests, the difference being that those members established anew their former associations. We do not even preserve the vestiges of what once we were; we are not Europeans, we are not

Source: Simón Bolívar, *An Address of Bolivar at the Congress of Angostura (February 15, 1819)*, reprint ordered by the Government of the United States of Venezuela to Commemorate the Centennial of the Opening of the Congress (Caracas, 1919), 17–23.

Indians, but an intermediate species between the aborigines and the Spaniards—Americans by birth and Europeans in right, we are placed in the dilemma of disputing with the natives our titles of possession and maintaining ourselves in the country where we were born, against the opposition of the invaders. Thus, ours is a most extraordinary and complicated case. Moreover, our part has always been a purely passive one; our political existence has always been null, and we find ourselves in greater difficulties in attaining our liberty than we ever had when we lived on a plane lower than servitude, because we had been robbed not only of liberty but also of active and domestic tyranny. Allow me to explain this paradox.

In an absolute regime, authorized power does not admit any limits. The will of the despot is the supreme law, arbitrarily executed by the subordinates who participate in the organized oppression according to the measure of the authority they enjoy. The people of America having been held under the triple yoke of ignorance, tyranny and vice, have not been in a position to acquire either knowledge, power or virtue. Disciples of such pernicious masters, the lessons we have received and the examples we have studied, are most destructive. We have been governed more by deception than by force, and we have been degraded more by vice than by superstition. Slavery is the offspring of Darkness; an ignorant people is a blind tool, turned to its own destruction; ambition and intrigue exploit the credulity and inexperience of men foreign to all political, economical or civil knowledge; mere illusions are accepted as reality, license is taken for liberty, treachery for patriotism, revenge for justice. . . .

Notwithstanding such bitter reflections, I am filled with unbounded joy because of the great strides made by our republic since entering upon its noble career. Loving that which is most useful, animated by what is most just and aspiring to what is most perfect, Venezuela in separating from the Spanish Nation has recovered her independence, her freedom, her equality, her national sovereignty. In becoming a democratic republic, she proscribed monarchy, distinctions, nobility, franchises and privileges; she declared the rights of man, the liberty of action, of thought, of speech, of writing. These preeminently liberal acts will never be sufficiently admired for the sincerity by which they are inspired. The first Congress of Venezuela has impressed upon the annals of our legislation with indelible characters the majesty of the people, so fittingly expressed in the consummation of the social act best calculated to develop the happiness of a Nation. . . .

The more I admire the excellence of the Federal Constitution of Venezuela, the more I am persuaded of the impossibility of its application in our State. And, in my opinion, it is a wonder that its model in North America may endure so successfully, and is not upset in the presence of the first trouble or danger. Notwithstanding the fact that that people is a unique model of political virtues and moral education; notwithstanding that it has been cradled in liberty, that it has been reared in freedom and lives on pure liberty, I will say more, although in many respects that people is unique in the history of humanity, it is a prodigy, I repeat, that a system so weak and complicated as the federal system should have served to govern that people in circumstances as difficult and delicate as those which have existed. But, whatever the case may be, as regards the American Nation, I must say that nothing is further from my mind than to try to assimilate the conditions and character of two nations as different as the Anglo-American and the Spanish-American.

QUESTIONS TO CONSIDER

1. According to Bolívar, what key factors must be considered by the congress in order to design a more durable state and constitution? Comparing this document to the US Declaration of Independence (see Source 6.1), what differences and similarities do you see in the justifications for claiming independence from colonial rule?
2. How did Bolívar address questions of race and ethnicity? How does his approach compare with the ways other American revolutionary states (for example, Haiti and the United States) dealt with these issues? What consequences did their decisions have?

6.6 "GREAT REVOLUTIONS ARE THE WORK RATHER OF PRINCIPLES THAN OF BAYONETS." GIUSEPPE MAZZINI, *MANIFESTO OF YOUNG ITALY*, 1831

Giuseppe Mazzini (1805–1872) was born in Genoa (then part of the Ligurian Republic ruled by the French Empire) and began a career in politics and law at a very young age, entering university at age 14. In the 1830s, Mazzini was a founder of "Young Italy," an organization dedicated to establishing "one, free, independent, republican nation." Mazzini spent most of his life organizing revolutionary movements and fleeing authorities, living in exile or hiding in Switzerland, London, and Italy. He allied "Young Italy" with similar organizations throughout the continent, creating a "Young Europe" movement that aspired to national, republican revolutions in many countries, including Germany and Poland. Many of these activists, including Mazzini, saw European unification as a further natural progression beyond national unification movements.

When Italian unification did occur, in the 1860s, Mazzini did not support it because it established a monarchy. Unlike some of his earlier allies, like Giuseppe Garibaldi (1807–1882), who compromised on the question of republicanism and served the newly unified state, Mazzini refused a seat in the new Italian parliament and attempted a rebellion against the Kingdom of Italy in 1870, just two years before he died.

If we thought that a journal, issued by wandering exiled Italians, whom fate has cast among a foreign people, their hearts fed by rage and grief, and unconsoled save by a hope, was to prove but a barren expression of protest and lament, we should be silent. Too much time has hitherto been spent in words amongst us, too little in acts; and were we simply to regard the suggestions of our individual tendencies, silence would appear the fittest reply to undeserved calumny and overwhelming misfortune; the silence of the indignant soul burning for the moment of solemn justification.

But in consideration of the actual state of things, and the desire expressed by our Italian brothers, we feel it a duty to disregard our individual inclinations for the sake of the general good. We feel it urgent to speak out frankly and freely, and to address some words of severe truth to our fellow-countrymen, and to those peoples who have witnessed our misfortune.

Great revolutions are the work rather of principles than of bayonets, and are achieved first in the moral, and afterwards in the material sphere. Bayonets are truly powerful only when they assert or maintain a right; the rights and duties of society spring from a profound moral sense which has taken root in the majority. Blind brute force may create victors, victims, and martyrs; but tyranny results from its triumph, whether it crown the brow of prince or tribune, if achieved in antagonism to the will of the majority. . . .

There is a class of men of civic ability and influence who imagine that revolutions are to be conducted with diplomatic caution and reserve, instead of the energy of an irrevocable faith and will. They admit our principles, but reject their consequences;

Source: *Life and Writings of Joseph Mazzini, Vol. 1. Autobiographical and Political* (London: Smith, Elder, 1890), 117–128.

deplore extreme evils, yet shrink from extreme remedies, and would attempt to lead the peoples to liberty with the same cunning and artifice adopted by tyranny to enslave them. Born and educated at a time when the conscience of a free man was a thing almost unknown in Italy, they have no faith in the power of a people rising in the name of their rights, their past glories, their very existence. They have no faith in enthusiasm, nor indeed in aught beyond the calculations of that diplomacy by which we have a thousand times been bought and sold, and the foreign bayonets by which we have been a thousand times betrayed.

They know nothing of the elements of regeneration that have been fermenting for the last half century in Italy, nor of that yearning after better things which is the heart's desire of our masses at the present day. They do not understand that, after many centuries of slavery, a nation can only be regenerated through virtue, or through death. They do not understand that twenty-six millions of men, strong in a good cause and an inflexible will, are invincible. They do not believe in the possibility of uniting them in a single aim and purpose. But have they ever earnestly attempted this? Have they shown themselves ready to die for this? Have they ever proclaimed an Italian crusade? Have they ever taught the people that there is but one path to salvation; that a movement made in their cause must be upheld and sustained by themselves; that war is inevitable—desperate and determined war that knows no truce save in victory or the grave?

No; they have either stood aloof, dismayed by the greatness of the enterprise, or advanced doubtfully and timidly, as if the glorious path they trod were the path of illegality or crime. . . .

But now, in this nineteenth century, Italy does know that unity of enterprise is a condition without which there is no salvation; that all true revolution is a declaration of war unto death between two principles—that the fate of Italy must be decided upon the plains of Lombardy, and that peace may only be signed beyond the Alps. Italy does know that there is no true war without the masses; that the secret of raising the masses lies in the hands of those who show themselves ready to fight and conquer

at their head; that new circumstances call for new men—men untrammeled by old habits and systems, with souls virgin of interest or greed, and in whom the Idea is incarnate; that the secret of power is faith; that true virtue is sacrifice, and true policy to be and to prove one's self strong.

Young Italy knows these things. It feels the greatness of its mission, and will fulfil it. We swear it by the thousands of victims that have fallen during the last ten years to prove that persecutions do not crush, but fortify conviction; we swear it by the human soul that aspires to progress; by the youthful combatants of Rimini; by the blood of the martyrs of Modena.

There is a whole religion in that blood; no power can exterminate the seed of liberty when it has germinated in the blood of brave men. Our religion of to-day is still that of martyrdom; tomorrow it will be the religion of victory. And for us, the young—for us who are believers in the same creed—it is a duty to further the sacred cause by every means in our power. Since circumstances forbid us the use of arms, we will write. . . .

We will uncover our wounds, and show to foreign nations our blood flowing as the price of that peace for which we have been sacrificed by the fears of diplomatists; we will declare the duties of other nations towards us, and unveil the falsehoods by which we have been overcome.

We will drag forth from the prisons and the darkness of despotism, documentary evidence of our wrongs, our sorrows, and our virtues.

We will descend into the dust of our sepulchres, and display the bones of our martyrs and the names of our unknown great in the eyes of foreign nations; mute witnesses of our sufferings, our constancy, and their guilty indifference. A cry of fearful anguish goes up from those ruins upon which Europe gazes in cold indifference, forgetful that they have twice shed the light of liberty and civilization upon her. . . .

We have given ear unto that cry, and we will repeat it to Europe until she learn the greatness of the wrong done ; we will say unto the peoples, such are the souls you have bought and sold; such is the land you have condemned to isolation and eternal slavery!

QUESTIONS TO CONSIDER

1. What features does Mazzini consider essential for the formation of a nation? Why does he believe in national unification?
2. On precisely which principles does Mazzini base his call for revolution? What similarities and differences do you see when comparing Mazzini's ideas with those of other revolutionaries of this era?

6.7 "THE BENEFIT OF A GOOD ADMINISTRATION." *THE RESCRIPT OF GÜLHANE*, 1839

Like many other states around the world, the Ottoman Empire attempted a series of reforms in the nineteenth century to address changing internal and external conditions. These reforms, as elsewhere, had as one goal the "modernization" of the empire. The following document was pronounced in 1839 in the Gülhane (Rose Bower) of Topkapi Palace, the seat of Ottoman political authority. The implementation of ideas it contained began the Tanzimat ("Reform") era in Ottoman history. The greatest influence over the content of this document was attributed to Grand Vizier Mustafa Resid Pasha, who served as Ottoman Ambassador to England and France before becoming Minister of Foreign Affairs. The reforms of the Tanzimat era share similarities with the imperial reforms seen across the world during the nineteenth century, including rationalization of revenues and taxes, standardization of the bureaucracy and the military, and an emphasis on secularism.

All the world knows that in the first days of the Ottoman monarchy, the glorious precepts of the Quran and the laws of the empire were always honored. The empire in consequence increased in strength and greatness, and all its subjects, without exception, had risen in the highest degree to ease and prosperity. In the last one hundred and fifty years a succession of accidents and divers causes have arisen which have brought about a disregard for the sacred code of laws and the regulations flowing therefrom, and the former strength and prosperity have changed into weakness and poverty; an empire in fact loses all its stability so soon as it ceases to observe its laws.

These considerations are ever present to our mind, and ever since the day of our advent to the throne the thought of the public weal, of the improvement of the state of the provinces, and of relief to the (subject) peoples, has not ceased to engage it. If, therefore, the geographical position of the Ottoman provinces, the fertility of the soil, the aptitude and intelligence of the inhabitants are considered, the conviction will remain that by striving to find efficacious means, the result, which by the help of God we hope to attain,

Source: Kemal Gözler, *Turkish Constitutional Law Materials in English*, https://www.anayasa.gen.tr/gulhane.htm.

can be obtained within a few years. Full of confidence, therefore, in the help of the Most High, and certain of the support of our Prophet, we deem it right to seek by new institutions to give to the provinces composing the Ottoman Empire the benefit of a good administration.

These institutions must be principally carried out under three heads, which are:

1. The guarantees insuring to our subjects perfect security for life, honor, and fortune.
2. A regular system of assessing and levying taxes.
3. An equally regular system for the levying of troops and the duration of their service.

And, in fact, are not life and honor the most precious gifts to mankind? What man however much his character may be against violence, can prevent himself from having recourse to it, and thereby injure the government and the country, if his life and honor are endangered? If, on the contrary, he enjoys in that respect perfect security, he will not depart from the ways of loyalty, and all his actions will contribute to the good of the government and of his brothers.

If there is an absence of security as to one's fortune, everyone remains insensible to the voice of the Prince and the country; no one interests himself in the progress of public good, absorbed as he is in his own troubles. If, on the contrary, the citizen keeps possession in all confidence of all his goods, then, full of ardor in his affairs, which he seeks to enlarge in order to increase his comforts, he feels daily growing and bubbling in his heart not only his love for the Prince and country, but also his devotion to his native land. These feelings become in him the source of the most praiseworthy actions.

As to the regular and fixed assessment of the taxes, it is very important that it be regulated; for the state which is forced to incur many expenses for the defense of its territory cannot obtain the money necessary for its armies and other services except by means of contributions levied on its subjects. Although, thanks be to God, our empire has for some time past been delivered from the scourge of monopolies, falsely considered in times of war as a source of revenue, a fatal custom still exists, although it can only have disastrous consequences; it is that of venal

concessions, known under the name of "iltizam" *[a tax system that would be eliminated–Ed.]*.

Under that name the civil and financial administration of a locality is delivered over the passions of a single man; that is to say, sometimes to the iron grasp of the most violent and avaricious passions, for if that contractor is not a good man, he will only look to his own advantage. It is therefore necessary that henceforth each member of Ottoman society should be taxed for a quota of a fixed tax according to his fortune and means, and that it should be impossible that anything more could be exacted from him. It is also necessary that special laws should fix and limit the expenses of our land and sea forces.

Although, as we have said, the defense of the country is an important matter, and that it is the duty of all the inhabitants to furnish soldiers for that object, it has become necessary to establish laws to regulate the contingent to be furnished by each locality according to the necessity of the time, and to reduce the term of military service to four or five years. For it is at the same time doing an injustice and giving a mortal blow to agriculture and to industry to take, without consideration to the respective population of the localities, in the one more, in the other less, men that they can furnish; it is also reducing the soldiers to despair and contributing to the depopulation of the country by keeping them all their lives in the service.

In short, without the several laws, the necessity for which has just been described, there can be neither strength, nor riches, nor happiness, nor tranquility for the empire; it must, on the contrary, look for them in the existence of these new laws. From henceforth, therefore, the cause of every accused person shall be publicly judged, as the divine law requires, after inquiry and examination, and so long as a regular judgment shall not have been pronounced, no one can secretly or publicly put another to death by poison or in any other manner.

No one shall be allowed to attack the honor of any other person whatever.

Each one shall possess his property of every kind, and shall dispose of it in all freedom, without let or hindrance from any person whatever; thus, for example, the innocent heirs of a criminal shall not be deprived of their legal rights, and the property of the criminal shall not be confiscated. These imperial concessions shall extend to all our subjects, of whatever religion or sect they may be; they shall enjoy them without exception. We therefore grant perfect security to the inhabitants of our empire in their lives, their honor, and their fortunes, as they are secured to them by the sacred text of the law.

As for the other points as they must be settled with the assistance of enlightened opinions, our council of justice (increased by new members as shall be found necessary), to whom shall be joined, on certain days which we shall determine, our ministers and the notabilities of the empire, shall assemble in order to frame laws regulating the security of life and fortune and the assessment of the taxes. Each one in those assemblies shall freely express his ideas and give his advice.

The laws [regulating] the military service shall be discussed by a military council holding its sittings at the palace of Serasker. As soon as a law shall be passed, in order to be forever valid, it shall be presented to us; we shall give it our approval, which we will write with our imperial sign-manual.

As the object of those institutions is solely to revivify religion, government, the nation, and the empire, we engage not to do anything which is contrary thereto.

In testimony of our promise we will, after having deposited these presents in the hall containing the glorious mantle of the prophet, in the presence of all the ulemas *[Islamic scholars–Ed.]* and the grandees of the empire, take oath thereto in the name of God, and shall afterwards cause the oath to be taken by the ulemas and the grandees of the empire.

After that, those from among the ulemas or the grandees of the empire, or any other persons whatsoever who shall infringe these institutions, shall undergo, without respect of rank, position, and influence, the punishment corresponding to his crime, after having been well authenticated. A penal code shall be compiled to that effect.

As all the public servants of the empire receive a suitable salary, and as the salaries of those whose duties have not up to the present time been sufficiently remunerated are to be fixed, a rigorous law shall be passed against the traffic of favoritism and bribery (rüşvet), which the Divine law reprobates, and which is one of the principal causes of the decay of the empire.

The above dispositions being a thorough alteration and renewal of ancient customs the imperial rescript shall be published at Istanbul and in all places of our empire, and shall be officially communicated to all the ambassadors of the friendly powers resident in Istanbul, that they may be witnesses to the granting of these institutions, which, should it please God, shall last forever. Wherein may the Most High have us in His holy keeping. May those who shall commit an act contrary to the present regulations be the object of Divine malediction, and be deprived forever of every kind of (protection or) happiness.

QUESTIONS TO CONSIDER

1. What are the most important goals this rescript is trying to attain? What groups would most likely support these goals? Who might oppose them? Why?
2. In what ways do these reforms suggest that a different kind of state will emerge in the Ottoman Empire from that which preceded it? What common features and differences can be seen in the reforms introduced here compared with those of other states during this era?

CHAPTER 7

THE ENGINES OF INDUSTRIALIZATION, 1787–1868

7.1 "THE PRINCIPLE OF THE FACTORY SYSTEM THEN IS, TO SUBSTITUTE MECHANICAL SCIENCE FOR HAND SKILL." ANDREW URE, *THE PHILOSOPHY OF MANUFACTURES*, 1835

Andrew Ure (1778–1857), born in Glasgow, Scotland, defies easy characterization. At various times in his life he was a physician, chemist, physicist, industrial consultant, university professor, and astronomer. He was one of the first theorists of efficiency, proposing how industrialization would improve not only the quality and consistency of manufactures but also the lives of workers and the general public. The work excerpted here, *The Philosophy of Manufactures*, is his most important contribution to this field.

In the book, which runs nearly 500 pages in the original, Ure lays out technical details of the manufacturing process and advice for how to manage workers' hours and tasks for the greatest efficiency. He also asserts his belief that limited regulation and unlimited capital will lead to progress in almost every aspect of society.

In the recent discussions concerning our factories, no circumstance is so deserving of remark, as the gross ignorance evinced by our leading legislators and economists, gentlemen well informed in other respects relative to the nature of those stupendous manufactures which have so long provided the rulers of the kingdom with the resources of war, and a great body of the people with comfortable subsistence; which have, in fact, made this island the arbiter of many nations, and the benefactor of the globe itself. Till this ignorance be dispelled, no sound legislation need be expected on manufacturing subjects. To effect this purpose is a principal, but not the sole aim of the present volume, for it is intended also

Source: *The Philosophy of Manufactures: Or an Exposition of the Scientific, Moral, and Commercial Economy of the Factory System of Great Britain* (London: Charles Knight, 1835), 6–7, 20–21, 30.

to convey specific information to the classes directly concerned in the manufactures, as well as general knowledge to the community at large and particularly to young persons about to make the choice of a profession.

The blessings which physico-mechanical science has bestowed on society, and the means it has still in store for ameliorating the lot of mankind, have been too little dwelt upon; while, on the other hand, it has been accused of lending itself to the rich capitalists as an instrument for harassing the poor, and of exacting from the operative an accelerated rate of work. It has been said, for example, that the steam-engine now drives the power looms with such velocity as to urge on their attendant weavers at the same rapid pace; but that the handweaver, not being subjected to this restless agent, can throw his shuttle and move his treadles at his convenience. There is, however, this difference in the two cases, that in the factory, every member of the loom is so adjusted, that the driving force leaves the attendant nearly nothing at all to do, certainly no muscular fatigue to sustain, while it procures for him good, unfailing wages, besides a healthy workshop *gratis:* whereas the nonfactory weaver, having everything to execute by muscular exertion, finds the labour irksome, makes in consequence innumerable short pauses, separately of little account, but great when added together; earns therefore proportionally low wages, while he loses his health by poor diet and the dampness of his hovel. Dr. Carbutt of Manchester says, "With regard to Sir Robert Peel's assertion a few evenings ago that the hand-loom weavers are mostly small farmers, nothing can be a greater mistake; they live, or rather they just keep life together, in the most miserable manner, in the cellars and garrets of the town, working sixteen or eighteen hours for the merest pittance."

The constant aim and effect of scientific improvement in manufactures are philanthropic, they tend to relieve the workmen either from niceties of adjustment which exhaust his mind and fatigue his eyes, or from painful repetition of effort which distort or wear out his frame. At every step of each manufacturing process described in this volume, the humanity of science will be manifest.

New illustrations of this truth appear almost every day, of which a remarkable one has just come to my knowledge. In the woolen-cloth trade there is a process between carding and spinning the wool, called slubbing, which converts the spongy rolls, turned off from the cards, into a continuous length of fine porous cord. Now, though carding and spinning lie within the domain of automatic science, yet slubbing is a handicraft operation, depending on the skill of the slubber, and participating therefore in all his irregularities. If he be a steady, temperate man, he will conduct his business regularly, without needing to harass his juvenile assistants, who join together the series of card rolls, and thus feed his machine; but if he be addicted to liquor, and passionate, he has it in his power to exercise a fearful despotism over the young pieceners [*workers who repair broken threads–Ed.*], in violation of the proprietor's benevolent regulations. This class of operatives, who, though inmates of factories are not, properly speaking, factory workers, being independent of the moving power, have been the principal source of the obloquy so unsparingly cast on the cotton and other factories, in which no such capricious practices or cruelties exist. The wool slubber, when behind hand with his work, after a visit to the beer-shop, resumes his task with violence, and drives his machine at a speed beyond the power of the pieceners to accompany; and if he finds them deficient in the least point, he does not hesitate to lift up the long wooden rod from his slubbing-frame, called a billy-roller, and beat them unmercifully. I rejoice to find that science now promises to rescue this branch of the business from handicraft caprice, and to place it, like the rest, under the safeguard of automatic mechanism. . . .

The principle of the factory system then is, to substitute mechanical science for hand skill, and the partition of a process into its essential constituents, for the division or graduation of labour among artisans. On the handicraft plan, labour more or less skilled, was usually the most expensive element of production—*Materiam superabat opus* [*"the workmanship surpasses the material,"—Ure is quoting the Roman poet Ovid (43 BCE-17 CE)–Ed.*]; but on the automatic plan, skilled labour gets progressively superseded, and will, eventually, be replaced by mere overlook-ers of machines. By the infirmity of human nature it happens that the more skillful the workman, the more self-willed and intractable he is apt to become, and, of course, the less fit a component of a mechanical system, in which, by occasional irregularities, he may do great damage to the whole. The grand object therefore of the modem manufacturer is, through the union of capital and science, to reduce the task of his work-people to the exercise of vigilance and dexterity,—faculties, when concentrated to one process, speedily brought to perfection in the young. In the infancy of mechanical engineering, a machine-factory displayed the division of labour in manifold gradations—the file, the drill, the lathe, having each its different workmen in the order of skill: but the dexterous hands of the filer and driller are now superseded by the planning, the key-groove cutting, and the drilling-machines; and those of the iron and brass turners, by the self-acting slide-lathe. Mr. Anthony Strutt, who conducts the mechanical department of the great cotton factories of Belper and Milford, has so thoroughly departed from the old routine of the schools, that he will employ no man who has learned his craft by regular apprenticeship; but in contempt, as it were, of the division of labour principle, he sets a ploughboy to turn a shaft of perhaps several tons weight, and never has reason to repent his preference, because he infuses into the turning apparatus a precision of action, equal, if not superior, to the skill of the most experienced journeyman. An eminent mechanician in Manchester told me that he does not choose to make any steam-engines at present, because with his existing means, he would need to resort to the old principle of the division of labour, so fruitful of jealousies and strikes among workmen; but he intends to prosecute that branch of business whenever he has prepared suitable arrangements on the equalization of labour, or automatic plan. On the graduation system, a man must serve an apprenticeship of many years before his hand and eye become skilled enough for certain mechanical feats but on the system of decomposing a process into its constituents and embodying each part in an automatic

machine, a person of common care and capacity may be entrusted with any of the said elementary parts after a short probation, and may be transferred from one to another, on any emergency, at the discretion of the master. Such translations are utterly at variance with the old practice of the division of labour, which fixed one man to shaping the head of a pin, and another to sharpening its point, with most irksome and spirit-wasting uniformity, for a whole life.

It was indeed a subject of regret to observe how frequently the workman's eminence, in any craft, had to be purchased by the sacrifice of his health and comfort. To one unvaried operation, which required unremitting dexterity and diligence, his hand and eye were constantly on the strain, or if they were suffered to swerve from their task for a time, considerable loss ensued, either to the employer, or the operative, according as the work was done by the day or by the piece. But on the equalization plan of self-acting machines, the operative needs to call his faculties only into agreeable exercise; he is seldom harmed with anxiety or fatigue, and may find many leisure moments for either amusement or meditations, without detriment to his master's interests or his own. As his business consists in tending the work of a well regulated mechanism, he learns it in a short period; and when he transfers his services from one machine to another, he varies his task, and enlarges his views by thinking on those general combinations which result from his and his companions' labours. Thus, that cramping of the faculties, that narrowing of the mind, that stunting of the frame, which were ascribed, and not unjustly, by moral writers, to the division of labour, cannot, in common circumstances, occur under the equable distribution of industry. How superior in vigor and intelligence are the factory mechanics in Lancashire, where the latter system of labour prevails, to the handicraft artisans of London, who, to a great extent, continue slaves to the former! The one set is familiar with almost every physico-mechanical combination, while the other seldom knows anything beyond the pin-head sphere of his daily task.

It is, in fact, the constant aim and tendency of every improvement in machinery to supersede human labour altogether, or to diminish its cost, by substituting the industry of women and children for that of men; or that of ordinary labourers for trained artisans. In most of the water-twist, or throttle cotton mills, the spinning is entirely managed by females of sixteen years and upwards. The effect of substituting the self-acting mule for the common mule is to discharge the greater part of the men spinners, and to retain adolescents and children. The proprietor of a factory near Stockport states, in evidence to the commissioners, that by such substitution, he would save 50 [pounds] a week in wages, in consequence of dispensing with nearly forty male spinners, at about 25 [shillings] of wages each. This tendency to employ merely children with watchful eyes and nimble fingers, instead of journeymen of long experience, shows how the scholastic dogma of the division of labour into degrees of skill has been exploded by our enlightened manufacturers. . . .

Improvements in machinery have a three-fold bearing:

1. They make it possible to fabricate some articles which, but for them, could not be fabricated at all.
2. They enable an operative to turn out a greater quantity of work than he could before, time, labour, and quality of work remaining constant.

3. They effect a substitution of labour comparatively unskilled, for that which is more skilled.

The introduction of new machines into any manufacture, with the effect of superseding hand labour, is tempered by the system of patents, which maintains them for a certain time at a monopoly price, and thereby obstructs their rapid multiplication. Did we admit the principles on which the use of particular self-acting mechanisms is objected to by workmen, we should not be able, in any case, to define the limits of their application. Had parliament acted on such principles sixty years ago, none of our manufactures could have attained to their present state of profitable employment to either masters or men. The immediate causes of their vast augmentation may be ascribed, under the blessing of Providence, to the general spirit of industry and enterprise among a free and an enlightened people, left to the unrestrained exercise of their talents in the employment of a vast capital, pushing to the utmost the principle of the analysis of labour, summoning to their service all the resources of scientific research and mechanical ingenuity; and finally, availing themselves of all the benefits to be derived from visiting foreign countries, not only in order to form new and confirm old commercial connexions, but to obtain an intimate knowledge of the wants, the tastes, the habits, the discoveries and improvements, the productions, and fabrics of other civilized nations. . . .

QUESTIONS FOR CONSIDERATION

1. What are the advantages and disadvantages for different classes of society in the new manufacturing processes that Ure describes? Does Ure seem to favor any particular group of interests? What signs of political, as well as technological, change do we see in this document?
2. Compare this document with the selection from Gandhi's *Hind Swaraj* (Source 9.5). How do you explain the similarities and differences between these two men's descriptions of manufacturing and definitions of "civilization"?

7.2 "I HAVE WROUGHT IN THE BOWELS OF THE EARTH THIRTY-THREE YEARS." *THE CONDITION AND TREATMENT OF THE CHILDREN EMPLOYED IN THE MINES AND COLLIERIES, 1842*

Industrialization transformed almost every aspect of life in nineteenth-century Great Britain, which was one of the earliest societies to industrialize. Tremendous wealth and revolutionized transportation and communication occurred alongside environmental degradation, extreme poverty, and harsh labor conditions.

Coal, mined in small quantities for centuries, became a valuable commodity as steam power demanded great quantities of fuel. Often unhealthy and dangerous, coal mines were frequently worked by children—both boys and girls—because their size enabled them to work in smaller passageways and also because their pay could be lower than that of adults.

Reports of hazardous conditions in the mines led to parliamentary investigations. The document presented here includes excerpts collected from various sources for an 1842 report on conditions in Scotland and South Wales.

In the east of Scotland, as it has already been incidentally intimated, the method of carrying the coal is different, although, as in many other districts, males and females are indifferently employed in the severe labour it involves. Indeed, it is stated by Mr. Franks, to be a general rule, that "girls are invariably set at an earlier age than boys to their peculiar labour, from a notion very generally entertained amongst the parents, that girls are more acute and capable of making themselves useful at an earlier age than boys". . . . The persons employed in coal-bearing are almost always girls and women. Boys are sometimes engaged in the same labour, but that is comparatively rare. The coal-bearers have to carry coal on their backs in un-railed roads with burdens varying from 3/4 cwt. to 3 cwt. *[a cwt. is a "hundredweight," which in the United Kingdom was approximately 112 pounds. So, these burdens are between about 85 and 336 pounds–Ed.].* The Sub-Commissioner represents this labour as "a cruel slaving, revolting to humanity"; yet he found engaged in this labour a child, a beautiful girl, only six years old, whose age he ascertained, carrying in the pit ½ cwt. of coals, and regularly making with this load fourteen long and toilsome journeys a-day. . . .

Margaret Leveston, six years old, coal-bearer: "Been down at coal-carrying six weeks; makes 10 to 14 rakes a-day; carries full 56 lbs. of coal in a wooden backit. The work is na guid; it is so very sail. I work with sister Jesse and mother; dinna ken the time we gang; it is gai dark." [A most interesting child, and perfectly beautiful. I ascertained her age to be six years, 24th May, 1840; she was registered at Inverness]. . . .

William Burnside, ten years old, coal-bearer, same colliery: "I gang with brother and sister; have done so two months. I can fill one tub in the day; it takes me 17 journeys, as my back gets sore. A tub holds near 5 cwt. I follow sister with bits of coal

Source: Great Britain Commissioners for Inquiring into the Employment and Condition of Children in Mines and Manufactories, *The Condition and Treatment of Children Employed in the Mines and Colliers of the United Kingdom.* Carefully compiled from the appendix to the first report of the Commissioners with copious extracts from the evidence, and illustrative engravings (London, William Strange, 1842), 48–51. https://www.bl.uk/collection-items/report-on-child-labour-1842.

strapped over my head and back. The works fatigues me muckle". . . .

Ellison Jack, a girl eleven years old, coal-bearer: "I have been working below three years on my father's account; he takes me down at two in the morning, and I come up at one and two next afternoon. I go to bed at six at night to be ready for work next morning; the part of the pit I bear in the seams are much on the edge. I have to bear my burthen up four traps, or ladders, before I get to the main road which leads to the pit bottom. My task is four to five tubs; each tub holds 4 ¼ cwt. I fill five tubs in 20 journeys. I have had the strap when I did not do my bidding. Am very glad when my task is wrought, as it sore fatigues". . . .

A brief description of this child's place of work will better illustrate her evidence. She has first to descend a nine-ladder pit to the first rest, even to which a shaft is sunk, to draw up the baskets or tubs of coals filled by the bearers. She then takes her creel (a basket formed to the back, not unlike a cockle-shell flattened towards the neck, so as to allow lumps of coal to rest on the back of the neck and shoulders), and pursues her journey to the wall-face, or as it is called here, the room of work. She then lays down her basket, into which the coal is rolled, and it is frequently more than one man can do to lift the burden on her back. The tugs, or straps, are placed over the forehead, and the body bent in a semicircular form, in order to stiffen the arch. Large lumps of coal are then placed on the neck, and she then commences her journey with her burden to the pit bottom, first hanging her lamp to the cloth crossing her head. In this girl's case she has first to travel about 14 fathoms (84 feet) from the wall-face to the first ladder, which is 18 feet high; leaving the first ladder, she proceeds along the main road, probably 3 feet 6 inches to 4 feet 6 inches high, to the second ladder, 18 feet high, so on to the third and fourth ladders, till she reaches the pit bottom, where she casts her load, varying from 1 cwt. to 1 ½ cwt., into the tub. This one journey is designated a rake; the height ascended, and the distance along the roads added together exceed the height of St. Paul's Cathedral; and it not unfrequently happens that the tugs break, and the load falls upon those females who are following. "However incredible it may be," says Mr. Franks, "yet I have taken the evidence of

fathers who have ruptured themselves from straining to lift coal on their children's backs". . . .

Janet Cumming, eleven years old, bears coals, and says: "I gang with the women at five and come up at five at night; work all night on Fridays, and come away at twelve in the day. I carry the large bits of coal from the wall-face to the pit-bottom, and the small pieces, called chows, in a creel. The weight is usually a hundredweight; does not know how many pounds there are in a hundredweight, but it is some weight to carry; it takes three journeys to fill a tub of four hundredweight. The distance varies, as the work is not always on the same wall; sometimes 150 fathoms (1 fathom = 6 feet), whiles [other times it is] 250 fathoms. The roof is very low; I have to bend my back and legs, and the water comes frequently up to the calves of my legs. Has no liking for the work; father makes me like it. Never got hurt, but often obliged to scramble out of the pit when bad air was in". . . .

The following represents an older girl carrying coal.

Isabella Read, twelve years old: "I am wrought with sister and brother; it is very sore work. Cannot say how many rakes, or journeys, I make from pit-bottom to wall-face and back, thinks about thirty or twenty-five on the average; distance varies from 100 to 250 fathoms. I carry a hundredweight and a quarter on my back, and am frequently in water up to the calves of my legs. When first down, fell frequently asleep while waiting for coal, from heat and fatigue. I do not like the work, nor do the lassies, but they are made to like it. When the weather is warm, there is difficulty in breathing, and frequently the lights go out". . . .

Agnes Kerr, fifteen years old, coal-bearer, Dryden Colliery: "Was nine years old when commenced carrying coals; carry father's coal; make eighteen to twenty journeys a-day; a journey to and fro is about 200 to 250 fathoms; have to ascend and descend many ladders; can carry 1 ½ cwt.". . . .

Mary Duncan, sixteen years of age, coal-bearer: "Began to carry coals when twelve years old. Do not like the work, nor do the other women, many of whom have wrought from eight years of age, and know no other. My employment is carrying coals from wall-face to the daylight, up the stair-pit. I make forty to fifty journeys a-day, and can carry 2 cwt. as my burthen. Some females carry 2 to 3 cwt., but it is overstraining"....

Agnes Moffatt, seventeen years of age: "Began working at ten years of age. Works twelve and fourteen hours daily. Father took sister and I down; he gets our wages. I fill five baskets; the weight is more than 22 cwt.; it takes me five journeys. The work is o'er sair for females. Had my shoulder knocked out a short time ago, and laid idle some time. It is no uncommon thing for women to lose their burthen [load], and drop off the ladder down the dyke below. Margaret M'Neil did a few weeks since, and injured both legs. When the tugs which pass over the forehead break, which they frequently do, it is very dangerous to be under a load. The lassies hate the work altogether, but they canna run away from it"....

Jane Peacock Watson, aged forty, coal- bearer, Bearing Pits, Harlow Muir, Coaly Burn, Peebleshire: "I have wrought in the bowels of the earth thirty-three years. Have been married twenty-three years, and had nine children; six are alive, three died of typhus a few years since; have had two dead born; thinks they were so from the oppressive work. A vast of women have dead children, and false births, which are worse, as they are not able to work after"....

William Hunter, mining oversman Arniston Colliery: "I have been twenty years in the works of Robert Dundas, Esq., and had much experience m the manner of drawing coal, as well as the habits and practices of the collier people. Until the last eight months, women and lassies were brought below in these works, when Mr. Alexander Maxton, our manager, issued an order to exclude them from going below, having some months prior given intimation of the same. Women always did the lifting, or heavy part of the work, and neither they nor the children were treated like human beings; nor are they, where they are employed. Females submit to work in places where no man, or even lad, could be got to labour in; they work in bad roads, up to their knees in water, in a posture nearly double; they are below till last hour of pregnancy; they have swelled haunches and ankles, and are prematurely brought to the grave, or, what is worse, a lingering existence. Many of the daughters of the miners are now at respectable service. I have two who are in families at Leith, and who are much delighted with the change"....

Robert Bald, Esq., the eminent coal-viewer, states that "in surveying the workings of an extensive colliery underground, a married woman came forward, groaning under an excessive weight of coals, trembling in every nerve, and almost unable to keep her knees from sinking under her. On coming up she said, in a plaintive and melancholy voice, 'Oh, sir, this is sore, sore, sore work! I wish to God that the first woman who tried to bear coals had broke her back, and none would have tried it again!'...."

At the conclusion of his account of this employment, Mr. Franks says: "When the nature of this horrible labour is taken into consideration, its extreme severity, its regular duration of from twelve to fourteen hours daily, which, once a week at least, is extended through the whole of the night; the damp, heated, and unwholesome atmosphere in which the work is carried on; the tender age and sex of the workers; when it is considered that such labour is performed, not in isolated instances selected to excite compassion, but that it may be truly regarded as the type of the everyday existence of hundreds of our fellow-creatures— a picture is presented of deadly physical oppression and systematic slavery, of which I conscientiously believe no one unacquainted with such facts would credit the existence in the British dominions"....

QUESTIONS TO CONSIDER

1. What conditions seem to be of greatest concern for the reporters? Does it seem that the workers share these same concerns?
2. What seems to be the attitude of the workers toward their employment? What does their attitude toward industrialization seem to be?

7.3 "NO EXEMPTIONS FROM ATTACKS OF EPIDEMIC DISEASE." EDWIN CHADWICK, *REPORT ON THE SANITARY CONDITION OF THE LABOURING POPULATION*, 1842

The Industrial Revolution, in Britain as elsewhere, affected far more than just economic production. One of the most important effects was the growth of cities, encouraged by the need to concentrate labor, materials, and machinery in factory-based manufacturing. These rapidly growing cities became densely populated in a very short span of time, with consequences for those living there. Sanitary conditions declined rapidly, as greater population density compromised living conditions and strained facilities for sewage, water, and garbage collection. Water and air pollution, another effect of industrialization, also detracted from quality of life.

Sir Edwin Chadwick (1800–1890), a physician and social reformer, was undertaking a study of England's Poor Laws when he began to examine public health conditions in London's urban slums. In 1842, he published his *Report on the Sanitary Conditions of the Labouring Population*. The report, which documented mortality patterns and living conditions, was an important work of public health and established clear links between poor living standards and disease.

A conception may be formed of the aggregate effects of the several causes of mortality from the fact, that of the deaths caused during one year in England and Wales by epidemic, endemic, and contagious diseases, including fever, typhus, and scarlatina, amounting to 56,461, the great proportion of which are proved to be preventible, it may be said that the effect is as if the whole county of Westmoreland, now containing 56,469 souls, or the whole county of Huntingdonshire, or any other equivalent district, were entirely depopulated annually, and were only occupied again by the growth of a new and feeble population living under the fears of a similar visitation. The annual slaughter in England and Wales from preventible causes of typhus which attacks persons in the vigour of life, appears to be double the amount of what was suffered by the Allied Armies in the battle of Waterloo.

It will be shown that diseases such as those which now prevail on land, did within the experience of persons still living, formerly prevail to a greater extent at sea and have since been prevented by sanitary regulations; and that when they did so prevail in ships of war, the deaths from them were more than double in amount of the deaths in battle. But the number of persons who die is to be taken also as the indication of the much greater number of persons who fall sick, and who, although they escape, are subjected to the suffering and loss occasioned by attacks of disease. Thus it was found on the original inquiry in the metropolis, that the deaths from fever amounted to 1 in 10 of the number attacked. If this proportion held equally throughout the country, then a quarter of a million of persons will have been subjected to loss and suffering from an attack of fever during the year; and in so far as

Source: Edwin Chadwick, *Report on the Sanitary Condition of the Labouring Population and on the Means of Its Improvement* (London, 1842), 2, 10, 202–204.

the proportions of attacks to deaths is diminished, so it appears from the reports is the intensity and suffering from the disease generally increased. . . .

The report of Dr. Baron Howard, on the condition of the population of Manchester, and that of Dr. Duncan, on the condition of the population of Liverpool. . . .

The locality of the residences of the labouring classes are in respect to the surrounding atmosphere favourably situated, but their internal structure and economy the very reverse of favourable. The cottages are in general built more with a view to the percentage of the landlord than to the accommodation of the poor. The joiner's work is ill performed; admitting by the doors, windows, and even floors, air in abundance, which, however, in many cases, is not disadvantageous to the inmates. The houses generally consist of three apartments, viz., the day-room, into which the street-door opens, and two bedrooms, one above the other. There is likewise beneath the day-room a cellar, let off either by the landlord or tenant of the house, to a more improvident class of labourers; which cellar, in almost all cases, is small and damp, and often crowded with inhabitants to excess. These cellars are, in my opinion, the source of many diseases, particularly catarrh, rheumatic affections, and tedious cases of typhus mitior, which, owing to the over-crowded state of the apartment, occasionally pass into typhus gravior. I need scarcely add that the furniture and bedding are in keeping with the miserable inmates. The rooms above the day-room are often let separately by the tenant to lodgers, varying in number from one or two, to six or eight individuals in each; their slovenly habits, indolence, and consequent accumulation of filth go far to promote the prevalence of contagious and infectious diseases.

The houses already alluded to front the street, but there are houses in back courts still more unfavourably placed, which also have their cellars, and their tenants of a description worse, if possible. There is commonly only one receptacle for refuse in a court of eight, ten, or twelve densely crowded houses, In the year 1836–7, I attended a family of 13, twelve of whom had typhus fever, without a bed in the cellar,

without straw or timber shavings–frequent substitutes. They lay on the floor, and so crowded, that I could scarcely pass between them. In another house I attended 14 patients; there were only two beds in the house. All the patients, as lodgers, lay on the boards, and during their illness, never had their clothes off. I met with many cases in similar conditions, yet amidst the greatest destitution and want of domestic comfort, I have never heard during the course of twelve years' practice, a complaint of inconvenient accommodation."

RECAPITULATION OF CONCLUSIONS

That high prosperity in respect to employment and wages, and various and abundant food, have afforded to the labouring classes no exemptions from attacks of epidemic disease, which have been as frequent and as fatal in periods of commercial and manufacturing prosperity as in any others. . . .

That the annual loss of life from filth and bad ventilation are greater than the loss from death or wounds in any wars in which the country has been engaged in modern times. . . .

The primary and most important measures, and at the same time the most practicable, and within the recognized province of public administration, are drainage, the removal of all refuse of habitations, streets, and roads, and the improvement of the supplies of water. . . .

The removal of noxious physical circumstances, and the promotion of civic, household. and personal cleanliness, are necessary to the improvement of the moral condition of the population; for that sound morality and refinement in manners and health are not long found co-existant with filthy habits amongst any class of the community. . . .

The advantages of uniformity in legislation and in the executive machinery, and of doing the same things in the same way (choosing the best), and calling the same officers, proceedings, and things by the same names, will only be appreciated by those who have observed the extensive public loss occasioned by the legislation for towns which makes them independent of beneficent, as of what perhaps might have been deemed formerly aggressive legislation.

QUESTIONS TO CONSIDER

1. What does Chadwick establish as the consequences of living conditions like the ones he describes?
2. How do these conditions fit into understandings of progress that were common at the time? In what ways might Chadwick's report be said to both support and challenge the assumptions of the Enlightenment?
3. Compare this document to claims made by Gandhi (see Source 9.5). What would Gandhi say about the conditions Chadwick describes?

7.4 "THE STATUTES OF THE HEAVENLY DYNASTY CANNOT BUT BE OBEYED WITH FEAR AND TREMBLING!" *QIANLONG EMPEROR TO KING GEORGE III*, 1793 AND *LETTER FROM THE HIGH IMPERIAL COMMISSIONER LIN AND HIS COLLEAGUES TO QUEEN VICTORIA OF ENGLAND*, 1840

The Manchus, a people from what is now northeastern China, overthrew the Ming Dynasty and proclaimed Qing Dynasty rule over China in 1644. Over the long term, Qing China thrived. In the eighteenth century, it was perhaps the most prosperous society on earth. The stability afforded by several remarkably long imperial reigns, including that of the Kangxi Emperor (1661–1722) and that of his grandson, the Qianlong Emperor (1735–1796), contributed to Qing success.

In 1793, near the end of the Qianlong Emperor's reign, the British crown sent Lord George Macartney to China to seek more open diplomatic and trade relations between the two empires. The first document reproduced here contains excerpts from the Qianlong Emperor's response, rejecting the British request.

After the failure of the Macartney mission, Britain continued to trade with China under restrictions imposed by the Qing government. Seeking to reverse an imbalance between British exports to China and imports from China, Britain turned increasingly to opium, produced in British-controlled India and sold illegally in China. As sales and addiction increased amidst a global economic downturn, Qing officials again addressed the question of trade with Britain. This time, less than fifty years after the Qianlong Emperor rejected Britain's overtures, High

Source: First excerpt: E. Backhouse and J. O. P. Bland, *Annals and Memoirs of the Court of Peking* (Boston: Houghton Mifflin, 1914), 322–331. Second excerpt: *The Chinese Repository* 8, no. 10 (February 1840): 497–503.

Commissioner Lin Zexu, assigned by the Emperor to stop the opium trade, wrote to chastise Queen Victoria for conducting trade in poisonous drugs. In the second document excerpted here, Commissioner Lin beseeches the Queen to stop the opium trade, threatening that China will now imprison and even execute anyone who violates the prohibition on the opium trade.

EXCERPT FROM THE LETTER OF THE QIANLONG EMPEROR TO KING GEORGE III

I have perused your memorial: the earnest terms in which it is couched reveal a respectful humility on your part, which is highly praiseworthy. In consideration of the fact that your Ambassador and his deputy have come a long way with your memorial and tribute, I have shown them high favour and have allowed them to be introduced into my presence. To manifest my indulgence, I have entertained them at a banquet and made them numerous gifts. I have also caused presents to be forwarded to the Naval Commander and six hundred of his officers and men, although they did not come to Peking, so that they too may share in my all-embracing kindness.

As to your entreaty to send one of your nationals to be accredited to my Celestial Court and to be in control of your country's trade with China, this request is contrary to all usage of my dynasty and cannot possibly be entertained. It is true that Europeans, in the service of the dynasty, have been permitted to live at Peking, but they are compelled to adopt Chinese dress, they are strictly confined to their own precincts and are never permitted to return home. You are presumably familiar with our dynastic regulations. Your proposed Envoy to my Court could not be placed in a position similar to that of European officials in Peking who are forbidden to leave China, nor could he, on the other hand, be allowed liberty of movement and the privilege of corresponding with his own country; so that you would gain nothing by his residence in our midst.

Moreover, our Celestial dynasty possesses vast territories, and tribute missions from the dependencies are provided for by the Department for Tributary States, which ministers to their wants and exercises strict control over their movements. It would be quite impossible to leave them to their own devices. Supposing that your Envoy should come to our Court, his language and national dress differ from that of our people, and there would be no place in which to bestow him. It may be suggested that he might imitate the Europeans permanently resident in Peking and adopt the dress and customs of China, but it has never been our dynasty's wish to force people to do things unseemly and inconvenient. Besides, supposing I sent an Ambassador to reside in your country, how could you possibly make for him the requisite arrangements? Europe consists of many other nations besides your own: if each and all demanded to be represented at our Court, how could we possibly consent? The thing is utterly impracticable. How can our dynasty alter its whole procedure and system of etiquette, established for more than a century, in order to meet your individual views? If it be said that your object is to exercise control over your country's trade, your nationals have had full liberty to trade at Canton for many a year, and have received the greatest consideration at our hands. Missions have been sent by Portugal and Italy, preferring similar requests. The Throne appreciated their sincerity and loaded them with favours, besides authorising measures to facilitate their trade with China. You are no doubt aware that, when my Canton merchant, Wu Chao-ping, was in debt to the foreign ships, I made the Viceroy advance the monies due, out of the provincial treasury, and ordered him to punish the culprit severely. Why then should foreign nations advance this utterly unreasonable request to be represented at my Court? Peking is nearly two thousand miles from Canton, and at such a distance what possible control could any British representative exercise?

If you assert that your reverence for Our Celestial dynasty fills you with a desire to acquire our civilisation, our ceremonies and code of laws differ so completely from your own that, even if your Envoy were able to acquire the rudiments of our civilisation, you could not possibly transplant our manners and customs to your alien soil. Therefore, however adept the Envoy might become, nothing would be gained thereby.

Swaying the wide world, I have but one aim in view, namely, to maintain a perfect governance and to fulfil the duties of the State: strange and costly objects do not interest me. If I have commanded that the tribute offerings sent by you, O King, are to be accepted, this was solely in consideration for the spirit which prompted you to dispatch them from afar. Our dynasty's majestic virtue has penetrated unto every country under Heaven, and Kings of all nations have offered their costly tribute by land and sea. As your Ambassador can see for himself, we possess all things. I set no value on objects strange or ingenious, and have no use for your country's manufactures. This then is my answer to your request to appoint a representative at my Court, a request contrary to our dynastic usage, which would only result in inconvenience to yourself. I have expounded my wishes in detail and have commanded your tribute Envoys to leave in peace on their homeward journey. It behoves you, O King, to respect my sentiments and to display even greater devotion and loyalty in future, so that, by perpetual submission to our Throne, you may secure peace and prosperity for your country hereafter. Besides making gifts (of which I enclose an inventory) to each member of your Mission, I confer upon you, O King, valuable presents in excess of the number usually bestowed on such occasions, including silks and curios—a list of which is likewise enclosed. Do you reverently receive them and take note of my tender goodwill towards you!

[The following excerpt responds in further detail to requests from the British crown.–Ed.]

Yesterday your Ambassador petitioned my Ministers to memorialise me regarding your trade with China, but his proposal is not consistent with our dynastic usage and cannot be entertained. Hitherto, all European nations, including your own country's barbarian merchants, have carried on their trade with our Celestial Empire at Canton. Such has been the procedure for many years, although our Celestial Empire possesses all things in prolific abundance and lacks no product within its own borders. There was therefore no need to import the manufactures of outside barbarians in exchange for our own produce. But as the tea, silk and porcelain which the Celestial Empire produces, are absolute necessities to European nations and to yourselves, we have permitted, as a signal mark of favour, that foreign hongs *[merchant firms–Ed.]* should be established at Canton, so that your wants might be supplied and your country thus participate in our beneficence. But your Ambassador has now put forward new requests which completely fail to recognise the Throne's principle to "treat strangers from afar with indulgence," and to exercise a pacifying control over barbarian tribes, the world over. Moreover, our dynasty, swaying the myriad races of the globe, extends the same benevolence towards all. Your England is not the only nation trading at Canton. If other nations, following your bad example, wrongfully importune my ear with further impossible requests, how will it be possible for me to treat them with easy indulgence? Nevertheless, I do not forget the lonely remoteness of your island, cut off from the world by intervening wastes of sea, nor do I overlook your excusable ignorance of the usages of our Celestial Empire. I have consequently commanded my Ministers to enlighten your Ambassador on the subject, and have ordered the departure of the mission. But I have doubts that, after your Envoy's return he may fail to acquaint you with my view in detail or that he may be lacking in lucidity, so that I shall now proceed . . . to issue my mandate on each question separately. In this way you will, I trust, comprehend my meaning. . . .

(3) Your request for a small island near Chusan, where your merchants may reside and goods be warehoused, arises from your desire to develop trade. As there are neither foreign hongs nor interpreters in or near Chusan, where none of your ships have ever called, such an island would be utterly useless for your purposes. Every inch of the territory of our Empire is marked on the map and the strictest vigilance is exercised over it all: even tiny islets and far-lying sand-banks are clearly defined as part of the provinces to which they belong. Consider, moreover, that England is not the only barbarian land which wishes to establish . . . trade with our Empire:

supposing that other nations were all to imitate your evil example and beseech me to present them each and all with a site for trading purposes, how could I possibly comply? This also is a flagrant infringement of the usage of my Empire and cannot possibly be entertained.

(4) The next request, for a small site in the vicinity of Canton city, where your barbarian merchants may lodge or, alternatively, that there be no longer any restrictions over their movements at Aomen, has arisen from the following causes. Hitherto, the barbarian merchants of Europe have had a definite locality assigned to them at Aomen for residence and trade, and have been forbidden to encroach an inch beyond the limits assigned to that locality. . . . If these restrictions were withdrawn, friction would inevitably occur between the Chinese and your barbarian subjects, and the results would militate against the benevolent regard that I feel towards you. From every point of view, therefore, it is best that the regulations now in force should continue unchanged. . . .

(7) Regarding your nation's worship of the Lord of Heaven, it is the same religion as that of other European nations. Ever since the beginning of history, sage Emperors and wise rulers have bestowed on China a moral system and inculcated a code, which from time immemorial has been religiously observed by the myriads of my subjects. There has been no hankering after heterodox doctrines. Even the European (missionary) officials in my capital are forbidden to hold intercourse with Chinese subjects; they are restricted within the limits of their appointed residences, and may not go about propagating their religion. The distinction between Chinese and barbarian is most strict, and your Ambassador's request that barbarians shall be given full liberty to disseminate their religion is utterly unreasonable.

It may be, O King, that the above proposals have been wantonly made by your Ambassador on his own responsibility, or per adventure you yourself are ignorant of our dynastic regulations and had no intention of transgressing them when you expressed these wild ideas and hopes. . . . If, after the receipt of this explicit decree, you lightly give ear to the representations of your subordinates and allow your barbarian merchants to proceed to Chêkiang and Tientsin, with the object of landing and trading there, the ordinances of my Celestial Empire are strict in the extreme, and the local officials, both civil and military, are bound reverently to obey the law of the land. Should your vessels touch the shore, your merchants will assuredly never be permitted to land or to reside there, but will be subject to instant expulsion. In that event your barbarian merchants will have had a long journey for nothing. Do not say that you were not warned in due time! Tremblingly obey and show no negligence!

EXCERPT FROM COMMISSIONER LIN'S LETTER TO QUEEN VICTORIA

Delighted did we feel that the kings of your honorable nation so clearly understood the great principles of propriety, and were so deeply grateful for the heavenly goodness (of our emperor):—therefore, it was that we of the heavenly dynasty nourished and cherished your people from afar, and bestowed upon them redoubled proofs of our urbanity and kindness. It is merely from these circumstances, that your country—deriving immense advantage from its commercial intercourse with us, which has endured now two hundred years—has become the rich and flourishing kingdom that it is said to be!

But, during the commercial intercourse which has existed so long, among the numerous foreign merchants resorting hither, are wheat and tares, good and bad; and of the latter are some who, by means of introducing opium by stealth, have seduced our Chinese people, and caused every province of the land to overflow with that poison. These then know merely to advantage themselves; they care not about injuring others! This is a principle which heaven's Providence repugnates; and which mankind conjointly look upon with abhorrence! Moreover, the great emperor hearing of it, actually shivered with indignation, and especially dispatched me, the commissioner, to Canton, that in conjunction with the viceroy and lieut.governor of the province, means might be taken for its suppression!

Every native of the Inner Land who sells opium, as also all who smoke it, are alike adjudged to death. Were we then to go back and take up the crimes of the foreigners, who, by selling it for many years have induced dreadful calamity and robbed us of enormous wealth, and punish them with equal severity, our laws could not but award to them absolute annihilation! But, considering that these said foreigners did yet repent of their crime, and with a sincere heart beg for mercy; that they took 20,283 chests of opium piled up in their store-ships, and through Elliot, the superintendent of the trade of your said country, petitioned that they might be delivered up to us, when the same were all utterly destroyed, of which we, the imperial commissioner and colleagues, made a duly prepared memorial to his majesty; considering these circumstances, we have happily received a fresh proof of the extraordinary goodness of the great emperor, inasmuch as he who voluntarily comes forward, may yet be deemed a fit subject for mercy, and his crimes be graciously remitted him. But as for him who again knowingly violates the laws, difficult indeed will it be thus to go on repeatedly pardoning! He or they shall alike be doomed to the penalties of the new statute. . . .

We presume that you, the sovereign of your honorable nation, on pouring out your heart before the altar of eternal justice, cannot but command all foreigners with the deepest respect to reverence our laws! If we only lay clearly before your eyes, what is profitable and what is destructive, you will then know that the statutes of the heavenly dynasty cannot but be obeyed with fear and trembling!

We find that your country is distant from us about sixty or seventy thousand miles [*Mile is used here as a translation for a Chinese unit of distance. The sea voyage would have been in fact about 20,000 miles–Ed.*], that your foreign ships come hither striving the one with the other for our trade, and for the simple reason of their strong desire to reap a profit. . . .

By what principle of reason then, should these foreigners send in return a poisonous drug, which involves in destruction those very natives of China? Without meaning to say that the foreigners harbor such destructive intentions in their hearts, we yet positively assert that from their inordinate thirst after gain, they are perfectly careless about the injuries they inflict upon us! And such being the case, we should like to ask what has become of that conscience which heaven has implanted in the breasts of all men?

We have heard that in your own country opium is prohibited with the utmost strictness and severity: this is a strong proof that you know full well how hurtful it is to mankind. Since then you do not permit it to injure your own country, you ought not to have the injurious drug transferred to another country, and above all others, how much less to the Inner Land! Of the products which China exports to your foreign countries, there is not one which is not beneficial to mankind in some shape or other. There are those which serve for food, those which are useful, and those which are calculated for re-sale;—but all are beneficial. . . .

On the other hand, the things that come from your foreign countries are only calculated to make presents of, or serve for mere amusement. It is quite the same to us if we have them, or if we have them not. If then these are of no material consequence to us of the Inner Land, what difficulty would there be in prohibiting and shutting our market against them? It is only that our heavenly dynasty most freely permits you to take off her tea, silk, and other commodities, and convey them for consumption everywhere, without the slightest stint or grudge: for no other reason, but that where a profit exists, we wish that it be diffused abroad for the benefit of all the earth. . . .

Let your highness immediately, upon the receipt of this communication, inform us promptly of the state of matter, and of the measure you are pursuing utterly to put a stop to the opium evil. Please let your reply be speedy. Do not on any account make excuses or procrastinate. . . .

We annex an abstract of the new law, now about to be put in force. "Any foreigner or foreigners bringing opium to the Central Land, with design to sell the same, the principals shall most assuredly be decapitated, and the accessories strangled;—and all property (found on board the same ship) shall be confiscated." . . .

QUESTIONS TO CONSIDER

1. What differences between Chinese and British conceptions of trade and diplomacy can be inferred from these documents? What changes, if any, do these documents show in those conceptions, or in the relationship between China and Britain between the 1790s and 1830s?
2. In both of these cases, a monarch is refusing a foreign country's request. In the first, the Qianlong Emperor refuses a request from Britain. In the second, Queen Victoria is being called to task for refusing a request from China. What arguments could you make for or against these decisions? How might these rulers themselves explain their decisions in terms of their own power, sovereignty, and legitimacy?

7.5 "TO CARRY THE LAWS OF THE UNITED STATES INTO TURKEY AND CHINA." CALEB CUSHING, *OPINION OF THE ATTORNEY GENERAL*, 1855

Caleb Cushing (1800–1879) was an American diplomat, politician, and jurist who from 1843 to 1845 served as the first United States Ambassador to China. While there, he negotiated the first treaty between the United States and China, the Treaty of Wanghia, which was part of the treaty regime that ended the first Opium War (1839–1842).

One of the most important provisions of this treaty was the application of "extraterritoriality," which in effect extended the territory of treaty countries beyond their borders. Under the terms of extraterritoriality that Cushing was negotiating, US citizens were subject not to Chinese law but to US laws when in China. About a dozen other nations, including Great Britain, France, and Japan, enjoyed this privilege. This arrangement was not reciprocal (i.e., Chinese citizens did not enjoy extraterritorial protection when abroad) and remained in effect into the twentieth century. The United States and Great Britain renounced extraterritoriality in 1943, and the last country to claim extraterritorial privilege—Portugal—surrendered it in 1946. Extraterritoriality was practiced mainly by European states in East Asia.

The following document presents Cushing's justification for claiming extraterritoriality.

I entered China with the formed general conviction that the United States ought not to concede to any foreign state, under any circumstances, jurisdiction over the life and liberty of a citizen of the United States, unless that foreign state be of our own family of nations—in a word, a Christian state.

Source: *The Decisions of the United States Court for China from Its Beginning, Those Reviewing the Same by the Court of Appeals and the Leading Cases Decided by Other Courts on Questions of Extraterritoriality*, compiled and edited by Charles Sumner Lobingier (Manila: Bureau of Printing, 1920), 4–6.

The states of Christendom are bound together by treaties which confer mutual rights and prescribe reciprocal obligations. They acknowledge the authority of certain maxims and usages, received among them by common consent, and called the law of nations; but which, not being fully acknowledged and observed by the Mohammedan or Pagan states, which occupy the greater part of the globe, is, in fact, only the international law of Christendom. Above all, the states of Christendom have a common origin, a common religion, a common intellectuality; associated by which common ties, each permits to the subjects of the other, in time of peace, ample means of access to its dominions for the purpose of trade, full right to reside therein, to transmit letters by its mails, to travel in its interior at pleasure, using the highways, canals, stagecoaches, steamboats, and railroads of the country as freely as the native inhabitants.

And they hold a regular and systematic intercourse as governments, by means of diplomatic agents of each, residing in the courts of the others, respectively. All these facts impart to the states of Christendom many of the qualities of one confederated republic.

How different is the condition of things out of the limits of Christendom! From the greater part of Asia and Africa, individual Christians are utterly excluded, either by the sanguinary barbarism of the inhabitants, or by their phrenzied bigotry, or by the narrow-minded policy of their governments. To their courts, the ministers of Christian governments have no means of access except by force, and at the head of fleets and armies. As between them and us, there is no community of ideas, no common law of nations, no interchange of good offices; and it is only during the present generation that treaties, most of them imposed by force of arms or by terror, have begun to bring down the great Mohammedan and Pagan governments into a state of inchoate peaceful association with Christendom.

To none of the governments of this character, as it seemed to me, was it safe to commit the lives and liberties of citizens of the United States. In our treaties with the Barbary States, with Turkey, and with Muscat, I had the precedent of the assertion, on our part, of more or less of exclusion of the local jurisdiction, in conformity with the usage, as it is expressed in one of them, observed in regard to the subjects of other Christian states.

Mr. Urquhart thinks these concessions have not been wise on the part of the Mohammedan states. It may be so for them; but it will be time enough for them to obtain jurisdiction over Christian foreigners when these last can visit Mecca, Damascus, or Fez, as safely and freely as they do Rome and Paris, and when submission to the local jurisdiction becomes reciprocal.

Owing to the close association of the nations of Christendom, and the right their people mutually enjoy and exercise of free entry into each other's country, there is reciprocity in the recognition of the local jurisdiction. Not so in the case of the great Moslem or Pagan states of Asia and Africa, whose subjects do not generally frequent Europe and America, either for trade, instruction, or friendship.

In China, I found that Great Britain had stipulated for the absolute exemption of her subjects from the jurisdiction of the empire; while the Portuguese attained the same object through their own local jurisdiction at Macao. I deemed it, therefore, my duty, for all the reasons assigned, to assert a similar exemption on behalf of citizens of the United States. This exemption is agreed to in terms by the letter of the treaty of Wang Hiya. And it was fully admitted by the Chinese, in the correspondence which occurred contemporaneously with the negotiation of the treaty, on occasion of the death of Sha Aman. By that treaty, thus construed, the laws of the Union follow its citizens and its banner protects them, even within the domain of the Chinese Empire.

The treaties of the United States with the Barbary powers, and with Muscat, confer judicial functions on our consuls in those countries, and the treaty with Turkey places the same authority in the hands of the minister or consul, as the substitute for the local jurisdiction, which, in each case of controversy, would control it if it arose in Europe or America. These treaties are in this respect accordant with general usage, and with what I conceive to be the principles of the law of nations in relation to the non-Christian powers.

In extending these principles to our intercourse with China, seeing that I have obtained the concession of absolute and unqualified extraterritoriality,

I considered it well to use in the treaty terms of such generality, in describing the substitute jurisdiction, as, while they hold unimpaired the customary or law-of-nations jurisdiction, do also leave to Congress full and complete direction to define, if it please to do so, what officers, with what powers, and in what form of law, shall be the instruments for the protection and regulation of the citizens of the United States.

And it only remains, in case the treaty shall be ratified, to adopt such legislative provisions as the wisdom of the President and of Congress may desire or approve to give effect to the concessions which the Chinese government has made in this matter and which seem to me so important in principle and so material to the honor and interests of the United States.

QUESTIONS TO CONSIDER

1. What does extraterritoriality reveal about the nature of sovereignty, both in principle and in the context of nineteenth-century imperialism? According to Cushing, what would China have to do to recover its sovereign rights?
2. What are Cushing's justifications for claiming extraterritoriality in China? What do his reasons suggest about Enlightenment influences on the creation of the United States, at least as interpreted in the 1840s?

7.6 "ALL LIE STRETCHED IN THE MUD AND DUST, DRENCHED IN THEIR OWN BLOOD." HENRY DUNANT, *A MEMORY OF SOLFERINO*, 1859 AND FLORENCE NIGHTINGALE, *LETTER TO SIDNEY HERBERT*, 1855

Jean Henri Dunant (1828–1910) was born in Geneva, Switzerland. A businessman, Dunant was traveling in Lombardy (a region in Italy) when he witnessed the Battle of Solferino, pitting the Austrian army against troops from France and the Kingdom of Piedmont-Sardinia. The chaotic fighting resulted in almost 30,000 casualties between the two sides. In the battle's aftermath, Dunant helped to organize the civilian population to care for the wounded on both sides. Excerpted here, Dunant's *A Memory of Solferino* (1862), contained an appeal to the global community to do something to ameliorate the horrors of modern warfare. Within two years, the International Committee of the Red Cross was founded, and twelve European states signed the First Geneva Convention, which acknowledged that wounded combatants should be treated with impartiality and that civilians providing aid to the wounded should be protected. Updated and

Source: Excerpt 1: Henry Dunant, *A Memory of Solferino*, English Version, American Red Cross (1939, 1959), Reprinted by the International Committee of the Red Cross by Courtesy of the American Red Cross, 17–22, 24–26, 49. Excerpt 2: Lynn McDonald, ed., *Florence Nightingale: The Crimean War: Collected Works of Florence Nightingale*, Vol. 14 (Waterloo, Belgium: Wilfrid Laurier University Press, 2010), 108–112.

expanded repeatedly over the ensuing decades (e.g., 1906, 1929, 1949), the Geneva Conventions provided a framework by which signatory countries agreed to treat both military forces and civilians in wartime.

Florence Nightingale (1820–1930) was born in the city of Florence (in Italy today) into a wealthy British family. While women from her elite class were discouraged from working, Nightingale grew interested in medicine and health care. She trained as a nurse and became the superintendent of the Institute for the Care of Sick Gentlewomen in London. Reading of the horrors of the Crimean War battlefields, Nightingale organized and trained a contingent of nurses to travel to that region to care for the wounded. After the war, she continued her work in the field of nursing, training health care professionals and writing about health care. In 1860, she established a training facility for nurses at King's College London, which became known as the Florence Nightingale School of Nursing and Midwifery. The second document presented here is an excerpt from one of many letters Nightingale sent to Sidney Herbert, Great Britain's Secretary of War, who had asked Nightingale to serve during the Crimean War. In this letter, dated January 8, 1855, Nightingale describes the state of affairs at the Scutari Army Barracks hospital in Istanbul.

EXCERPT 1, FROM HENRY DUNANT, *A MEMORY OF SOLFERINO* (1859)

By six o'clock firing has begun in earnest. The Austrians advance, in perfect formation, along the beaten paths, with their yellow and black battle flags, blazoned with the German Imperial Eagle, floating above the compact masses of white-coats. Among all the troops which are to take part in the battle, the French Guard affords a truly imposing sight. The day is dazzlingly clear, and the brilliant Italian sunlight glistens on the shining armour of Dragoons and Guides, Lancers and Cuirassiers. . . .

The first encounter took place amid the difficulties of ground which was entirely strange to the Allies. The French Army was forced to beat a way through row upon row of mulberry trees with grapevines strung between them, amounting to a real obstacle. The ground was broken up in many places by great dried-up ditches, and by long walls some three or five feet high, wide at the base and tapering to the top. The horses had to clear these walls, and cross the ditches.

The Austrians, from their vantage points, on the hills, swept the French with artillery fire and rained on them a steady hail of shells, case- and grape-shot. Soil and dust, raised by this immense cloud of projectiles as they thundered into the ground, mingled with the thick fumes of smoking guns and shells. Facing the thunder of these batteries, roaring and spitting forth death upon them, the French rushed forward like an opposing storm sweeping from the plain, to attack the positions they were determined to secure.

During the torrid midday heat, the fighting that rages on all sides grows more and more furious. Compact columns of men throw themselves upon each other with the impetuosity of a destructive torrent that carries everything before it; French regiments, in skirmishing order, fling themselves upon the Austrian masses, which are constantly reinforced, and become more and more solid and menacing, resisting attack with the strength of steel walls. Whole divisions threw off their knapsacks in order to be able to charge the enemy more freely with fixed bayonets. As one battalion is repulsed, another immediately replaces it. Every mound, every height, every rocky crag, is the scene of a fight to the death; bodies lie in heaps on the hills and in the valleys. Here is a hand-to-hand struggle in all its horror and frightfulness; Austrians and Allies trampling each other under foot, killing one another on piles of bleeding corpses, felling their enemies with their rifle butts, crushing skulls, ripping bellies open with sabre and bayonet. No quarter is given; it is a sheer butchery; a struggle between savage beasts, maddened with blood and fury. Even the wounded fight to the last gasp. When they have no weapon left, they seize their enemies by the throat and tear them with their teeth.

A little further on, it is the same picture, only made the more ghastly by the approach of a squadron of cavalry, which gallops by, crushing dead and dying beneath its horses' hoofs. One poor wounded man has his jaw carried away; another his head shattered; a third, who could have been saved, has his chest beaten in. Oaths and shrieks of rage, groans of anguish and despair, mingle with the whinnying of horses.

Here come the artillery, following the cavalry, and going at full gallop. The guns crash over the dead and wounded, strewn pell-mell on the ground. Brains spurt under the wheels, limbs are broken and torn, bodies mutilated past recognition—the soil is literally puddled with blood, and the plain littered with human remains. The French troops climbed the mounds, and clambered up the steep hills and rocky slopes with the most fiery ardour, under the Austrian fire, with shells and grape-shot bursting over them. A few detachments of picked men, worn out with their efforts and bathed in sweat, would just manage to gain the top of a hill—then at once they would fall again like an avalanche on the Austrians, smashing into them, driving them from another position, scattering them and pursuing them to the very bottoms of ravines and ditches.

The positions of the Austrians were excellent ones, entrenched as they were in the houses and churches of Medola, Solferino and Cavriana. But nothing stopped the carnage, arrested or lessened it. There was slaughter in the mass, and slaughter man by man; every fold of ground was carried at the point of the bayonet; every position was defended foot by foot. Villages were won, house after house and farm after farm; each in turn became the stage of a siege. Every door, window, and courtyard was a ghastly scene of butchery.

Frightful disorder was caused in the Austrian lines by the French grape-shot, which was effective at prodigious ranges. It covered the hills with dead, and inflicted casualties even among the distant reserves of the German Army. But if the Austrians gave

ground, it was only step by step, and they soon resumed the offensive; they rallied again and again, only to be scattered once more.

On the plain, clouds of dust from the roads were thrown skyward by the wind, making dense clouds that darkened the air and blinded the fighting troops.

Now and again the fighting somewhere would seem to stop for a time, only to be renewed with greater force. The gaps made in the Austrian lines by the determined, murderous French attack, were immediately filled by fresh reserves. First from one side, then from another, drums would beat and bugles sound for the charge. . . .

The most powerful positions were taken, lost and retaken, only to be lost again and again recaptured. Everywhere men fell by thousands, with gaping wounds in limbs or bellies, riddled with bullets, mortally wounded by shot and shell of every kind. . . .

A son idolized by his parents, brought up and cherished for years by a loving mother who trembled with alarm over his slightest ailment; a brilliant officer, beloved by his family, with a wife and children at home; a young soldier who had left sweetheart or mother, sisters or old father, to go to war; all lie stretched in the mud and dust, drenched in their own blood!

EXCERPT 2, FROM A LETTER FROM FLORENCE NIGHTINGALE TO SIDNEY HERBERT, JANUARY 8, 1855

I feel that this is no time for compliments or false shame and that you will never hear the whole truth, troublesome as it is, except from one independent of promotion. . . .

As your official servant, you will say that I ought to have reported these things before. But I did not wish to be made a spy. I thought it better if the remedy could be brought quietly and I thought the commission was to bring it. But matters are worse than they were two months ago and will be worse two months hence than they are now. . . .

[T]he purveying is nil: that is the whole truth, beyond bedding, bread, meat, cold water, fuel. Beyond the boiling en masse in the great coppers of [the] general kitchen, the meat is not cooked; the water is not boiled except what is done in my subsidiary kitchens. My schedule will show what I have purveyed. I have refused to go on purveying for the third hospital, the Sultan's Serail—the demands upon me there having been begun with twelve hundred articles, including shirts, the first night of our occupying it. I refer you to a list of what was not in store and to a copy of one requisition upon me—sent last letter.

The extraordinary circumstance of a whole army having been ordered to abandon its kits, as was done when we landed our men before Alma, has been overlooked entirely in all our system. The fact is that I am now clothing the British Army. The sick were re-embarked at Balaclava for these hospitals without resuming their kits, also half-naked besides. And when discharged from here, they carry off, small blame to them! even my knives and forks—shirts, of course, and hospital clothing also. The men who were sent to Abydos as convalescents were sent in their hospital dresses, or they must have gone naked. The consequence is that not one single hospital dress is now left in store and I have substituted Turkish dressing gowns from Stamboul [Istanbul–Ed.]. . . .

To purvey this hospital is like pouring water into a sieve, and will be till regimental stores have been sent out from England enough to clothe the naked and refill the kit. I have requisitions for uniform trousers, for each and all of the articles of a kit sent in to me. We have not yet heard of boots being sent out—the men come into hospital half shod. In a time of such calamity, unparalleled in the history, I believe, of calamity, I have a little compassion left even for the wretched purveyor, swamped amid demands he never expected. But I have no compassion for the men who would rather see hundreds of lives lost than waive one scruple of the official conscience. . . .

The orderlies ought to be well paid, well fed, well housed. They are now overworked, ill-fed and underpaid. The sickness and mortality among them is extraordinary—ten took sick in one division tonight. They have only 4d a day as orderlies additional to their pay. If the Patriotic Fund would give them 1/ per day additional, query, would not such money be much better employed than among the widows, some of which ladies marry within six weeks of their husbands' deaths? . . .

[Nightingale recommends–Ed.] that the patient cease to be a soldier and become a patient from the moment he cross the hospital doors—that he leaves his clothes, blanket and kit behind in a storeroom for the purpose—whence it is taken away to the pack store, an inventory being given him of such articles and of any money, etc., which he may also leave if he choose—that, unless in exceptional or moribund cases, he have a warm bath after which he has a clean shirt and hospital suit given him, and goes up to his bed or is carried upon a stretcher with clean blankets. . . .

[Nightingale recommends–Ed.] that the cooking be done not by drunken soldiers but by cooks, and that the kitchens be multiplied or added to and the cooked food inspected daily. It is inspected now, but not really.

QUESTIONS TO CONSIDER

1. What are the most important decisions that military officers have to make in the kinds of situations described by Dunant and Nightingale? What role did individual soldiers and modern medicine play in nineteenth-century warfare?

2. Placing these documents within the broader context of change occurring in the nineteenth century, why do you think events such as the Crimean War and the Battle of Solferino contributed to the formation of the International Red Cross and the signing of the Geneva Convention?

7.7 "THE BEST ADAPTED TO ALL THE CROPS CULTIVATED IN THIS COUNTRY." SOLON ROBINSON, *GUANO: A TREATISE OF PRACTICAL INFORMATION*, 1853

Dramatic changes in agricultural production both facilitated and accompanied industrialization. Higher crop yields released more laborers for industry. Faster transportation and communications networks allowed for larger scale long-distance trade in agricultural inputs and outputs. In the decades after it gained independence from Spain in the 1820s, the new republic of Peru integrated into this global transformation by providing rich fertilizer–bird guano found in readily accessible and ample supply on islands just off the Peruvian coast.

By the mid-nineteenth century, guano was Peru's key export. The Peruvian government signed concession agreements for exploitation of the guano supply, sharing revenues with private investors. At the height of the guano boom in the 1860s, average annual sales approached $20 million. Some public works projects, like railroad lines, were begun, and Lima, the capital, became a cosmopolitan city with amenities rivaling those of other modern metropolitan areas. Borrowing against expected future returns from this booming industry created a fiscal crisis in Peru when the global economy experienced a downturn in the 1870s. The Peruvian government defaulted on its foreign loans. By the end of the nineteenth century, industrial fertilizers were replacing organic fertilizers in the agriculture supply chain. The guano boom was over.

The primary source excerpted below was written Solon Robinson (1803–1880). Robinson was born in Connecticut in the eastern United States. After moving to Indiana in the 1830s, Robinson became known as the "Squatter King" for the way he organized an armed group to attend a government land auction and set their own price for purchase of land upon which they had already settled. He later became country clerk and justice of the peace of Lake County, Indiana, and gained a reputation as a writer, an authority on farming, and an advocate for common folk. Robinson was paid by the government of Peru to write the pamphlet, a fact that Robinson did not hide: in fact, he mentioned it on the very first page of the document.

Of all manures procurable by the American Farmer, guano from the rainless islands of Peru, is perhaps not only the most concentrated—the most economical to the purchaser—but by its composition, as we will show by analysis, the best adapted to all the crops cultivated in this country requiring manure. For wheat, especially, it is the one thing needful. The mineral constituents of cultivated plants, as will also be shown by analysis, are chiefly lime, magnesia, potash, soda, chlorine, sulphuric and phosphoric acid; all of

Source: Solon Robinson, *Guano: A Treatise of Practical Information for Farmers: Containing Plain Directions How to Apply Peruvian Guano to the Various Crops and Soils of America, with a brief synopsis of its history, locality, quantity, method of procuring, prospect of continued supply, and price; analysis of its composition, and value as a fertilizer, over all other manures* (New York: Prepared and Published by Solon Robinson for F. Barreda and Brother, Agents of the Peruvian Government at Baltimore and Theodore W. Riley, Esq., Their Agent in New York, 1853), 5–6, 76, 78–79; http://chla.library.cornell.edu/cgi/t/text/text-idx?c=chla;idno=2903904.

which will be found in Peruvian guano. Nitrogen, the most valuable constituent of stable or compost manures, exists in great abundance in guano, in the exact condition required by plants to promote rapid vegetation. The concentration of all these valuable properties in the small bulk of guano renders it particularly valuable to farms situated in districts unprovided with facilities of cheap transportation. In some hilly regions, it would be utterly impossible to make any ordinary manure pay for transportation.

With guano the case is very different—one wagon will carry enough with a single pair of horses to dress 12 or 15 acres; while of stable manure it would require as many or more loads to each acre to produce the same effect. But this is not the greatest advantage in the use of this fertilizer; the first application puts the land in such condition that judicious after cultivation renders it continuously fertile by its own action of productiveness and reproductiveness of wheat, clover and wheat, by turning in the clover of one year for the wheat of the next, and by returning the straw back to the ground where it grew, spread upon the surface to shade the plants of clover and manure ills roots, which in turn manure the corn or wheat.

As a source of profit alone, we should recommend the continuous application of guano; knowing as we do, from our extensive means of observation, that no outlay of capital ever made by the farmer is so sure and certain to bring him back good returns for his money, as when he invests it in this invaluable fertilizer for his impoverished soil. . . .

The price of guano is owing mainly, if not entirely, to this *[Peruvian government–Ed.]* monopoly in the import trade; and it would be the same thing, and a monopoly still, whether in the hands of English or American merchants; with also, about the same amount of liberality to be looked for, from one as from the other.

Is there anything so unfair in this, that we should cry out "wicked monopoly." The Peruvian government, after the revolution, finds itself deeply in debt, and greatly in want of money, and in possession of one of the most valuable fertilizing substances in the world, which the people of other governments are in want of, or rather, may profit by the use of, which she offers to sell at what she deems a fair price; and

for the purpose of enabling her to borrow money for immediate necessities, as well as to pay the war debt, she has given some of her citizens rich merchants, who can advance money, certain privileges and advantages in the guano trade, upon condition that they will send a supply to all the countries where it can be sold, and in as great quantities as they will buy at fixed prices. This is the monopoly. A parallel case can be found nearer home. The government of the United States also incurred a revolutionary war debt, and also came in possession of an article which the people of all other countries want, and unlike that possessed by Peru, an article which they must have. Upon this necessity of life, our government has fixed a price, which any one may pay or let it alone—buy or not, just as he pleases. The government will neither sell to citizens or strangers at half price, nor let them have the use of it without pay; in fact, will not let us carry away anything of value from this property, although it might not materially injure the sale of the principal and most valuable portion, which is immovable. Such is the "guano monopoly" of one government, and such is the "land monopoly" of the other. Which is most wicked?

Of the right of each government, no honest man will dispute. That Peru has as much right to the guano upon her desert islands as the United States has to the live oak timber in the deserts of Florida; or as England has to the codfish in the waters of Newfoundland, seem to be as clear as any right ever exercised by any power on earth. Each protect their own by hired agents, so far as they are able, to prevent dishonest men from carrying away that which each considers valuable. . . .

All the guano islands are uninhabited, except by the laborers, mostly Indians or poor Chinamen, who are employed in the work of digging, carrying and loading the guano into the ships. When a vessel is ready to take in cargo, she is moored alongside of the rocks almost mast head high, from the top of which the guano is sent down through a canvass chute directly into the hold of the ship. Thus, several hundred tons can be put to board in a day. The trimming of the cargo is a very unpleasant part of the labor. The dust and odor is almost overpowering; so the men are obliged to come often on deck for fresh air. The rule is to remain below as long as a candle will burn; when that goes out, the air is considered unfit for respiration. If the labor had to be performed by a Yankee, he would think it unfit at first; and thereupon set his ready wit at work to construct a machine to spread the guano as it fell, from one end of the hold to the other.

The guano in position upon the island is so compact it has to be dug up with picks. It is then carried to a contrivance made of cane, at the edge of the rock, which conveys it into the canvass conductors. The mass is cut down in steps, receding and rising from the point of commencement, and has not yet attained a depth of 100 feet, and with all the labor of hundreds of men digging, and numerous ships carrying away to the several countries using it, there is but a bare beginning of removal made upon the mass upon one island only. . . .

Supposing like many others, the supply of Peruvian guano was . . . destined to run out—that is, all be dug up and carried away; we inquired of an intelligent captain of a ship just returned with a load, how long it would be before the supply would be exhausted. "Exhausted!" said he, with a look over the gangway, as much as to say how long would it take to exhaust the ocean with a pint cup; "why, not in one hundred years, if every ship afloat should go into the trade, and load and unload as fast as it would be possible to perform the labor; no, not from the Chincha islands alone. Exhausted! They never will be exhausted."

QUESTIONS TO CONSIDER

1. What is Robinson's assessment of the plusses and minuses of the guano industry—how it is organized, how guano is extracted, who is in the labor force, what the future looks like?
2. In what ways can these passages about the guano industry inform discussion about the nature of the global economy in general in the mid-nineteenth century? What kinds of questions can't be answered from a single document like this?

CHAPTER 8

MODERNITY ORGANIZED, 1840–1889

8.1 "WORKING MEN OF ALL COUNTRIES, UNITE." KARL MARX AND FRIEDRICH ENGELS, *MANIFESTO OF THE COMMUNITY PARTY*, 1848

Karl Marx (1818–1883) was born in Trier, in present-day Germany. He studied philosophy and began his career as a journalist in Cologne. His radical writing angered local leaders, leading Marx to move to Paris, where he met Friedrich Engels (1820–1892). Engels, like Marx, had studied philosophy and had begun collecting information and writing about conditions in the factory towns of Europe, including Manchester, England, where his family owned a mill. Marx and Engels began to collaborate in their writing, and both moved to London.

Amidst the political and social upheaval of the 1840s, Engels and Marx published *The Communist Manifesto* in 1848. This lengthy pamphlet was designed to serve as both a scientific explanation of how and why historical change occurs and a call to revolutionary action on the part of the working class and its allies. The *Manifesto* had little direct impact on political movements in the years immediately following its publication, but it became over time, along with other works by Marx and Engels, foundational theory for modern communist movements around the world.

A spectre is haunting Europe—the spectre of communism. All the powers of old Europe have entered into a holy alliance to exorcise this spectre. . .

It is high time that Communists should openly, in the face of the whole world, publish their views, their aims, their tendencies, and meet this nursery tale of the Spectre of Communism with a manifesto of the party itself. To this end, Communists of various nationalities have assembled in London and sketched the following manifesto, to be published in the English, French, German, Italian, Flemish and Danish languages. . . .

The history of all hitherto existing society is the history of class struggles. Freeman and slave, patrician and plebeian, lord and serf, guild-master and journeyman, in a word, oppressor and oppressed, stood in constant opposition to one another, carried on an uninterrupted, now hidden, now open fight, a

Source: *Marx/Engels Selected Works*, Vol. 1 (Moscow: Progress Publishers, 1969), 98–137. www.marxists.org/archive/marx/works/download/pdf/Manifesto.pdf

fight that each time ended, either in a revolutionary reconstitution of society at large, or in the common ruin of the contending classes. . . .

The modern bourgeois society that has sprouted from the ruins of feudal society has not done away with class antagonisms. It has but established new classes, new conditions of oppression, new forms of struggle in place of the old ones.

Our epoch, the epoch of the bourgeoisie, possesses, however, this distinct feature: it has simplified class antagonisms. Society as a whole is more and more splitting up into two great hostile camps, into two great classes directly facing each other—Bourgeoisie and Proletariat.

[In the 1888 English translation of the Manifesto, Engels provides the following definition of bourgeoisie and proletariat in a note to the reader: "By bourgeoisie is meant the class of modern capitalists, owners of the means of social production and employers of wage labour. By proletariat, the class of modern wage labourers who, having no means of production of their own, are reduced to selling their labour power in order to live."–Ed.]. . . .

Modern industry has established the world market, for which the discovery of America paved the way. This market has given an immense development to commerce, to navigation, to communication by land. This development has, in its turn, reacted on the extension of industry; and in proportion as industry, commerce, navigation, railways extended, in the same proportion the bourgeoisie developed, increased its capital, and pushed into the background every class handed down from the Middle Ages. . . .

Modern bourgeois society, with its relations of production, of exchange and of property, a society that has conjured up such gigantic means of production and of exchange, is like the sorcerer who is no longer able to control the powers of the nether world whom he has called up by his spells. For many a decade past the history of industry and commerce is but the history of the revolt of modern productive forces against modern conditions of production, against the property relations that are the conditions for the existence of the bourgeois and of its rule. . . .

In proportion as the bourgeoisie, i.e., capital, is developed, in the same proportion is the proletariat, the modern working class, developed—a class of labourers, who live only so long as they find work, and who find work only so long as their labour increases capital. These labourers, who must sell themselves piecemeal, are a commodity, like every other article of commerce, and are consequently exposed to all the vicissitudes of competition, to all the fluctuations of the market.

Owing to the extensive use of machinery, and to the division of labour, the work of the proletarians has lost all individual character, and, consequently, all charm for the workman. He becomes an appendage of the machine, and it is only the most simple, most monotonous, and most easily acquired knack, that is required of him. Hence, the cost of production of a workman is restricted, almost entirely, to the means of subsistence that he requires for maintenance, and for the propagation of his race. . . .

The less the skill and exertion of strength implied in manual labour, in other words, the more modern industry becomes developed, the more is the labour of men superseded by that of women. Differences of age and sex have no longer any distinctive social validity for the working class. All are instruments of labour, more or less expensive to use, according to their age and sex. No sooner is the exploitation of the labourer by the manufacturer, so far, at an end, that he receives his wages in cash, than he is set upon by the other portions of the bourgeoisie, the landlord, the shopkeeper, the pawnbroker, etc. . . .

But with the development of industry, the proletariat not only increases in number; it becomes concentrated in greater masses, its strength grows, and it feels that strength more. The various interests and conditions of life within the ranks of the proletariat are more and more equalised, in proportion as machinery obliterates all distinctions of labour, and nearly everywhere reduces wages to the same low level. The growing competition among the bourgeois, and the resulting commercial crises, make the wages of the workers ever more fluctuating. The increasing improvement of machinery, ever more rapidly developing, makes their livelihood more and more precarious; the collisions between individual workmen and individual bourgeois take more and more the character of collisions between two classes. . . .

Of all the classes that stand face to face with the bourgeoisie today, the proletariat alone is a really revolutionary class. The other classes decay and finally disappear in the face of Modern Industry; the proletariat is its special and essential product. . . .

The Communists fight for the attainment of the immediate aims, for the enforcement of the momentary interests of the working class; but in the movement of the present, they also represent and take care of the future of that movement. . . .

The Communists disdain to conceal their views and aims. They openly declare that their ends can be attained only by the forcible overthrow of all existing social conditions. Let the ruling classes tremble at a Communistic revolution. The proletarians have nothing to lose but their chains. They have a world to win. Working Men of All Countries, Unite!

QUESTIONS TO CONSIDER

1. According to Marx and Engels, what is going to happen in the industrialized countries in the nineteenth century? Why?
2. How would you compare Marx and Engels's analysis of industrial society with that of Andrew Ure (Source 7.1) or Mohandas Gandhi (Source 9.5)? What are the significant similarities and differences in the way they describe the impact of industrialization on work and workers?

8.2 "PARIS IN AMERICA." HERBERT H. SMITH, *BRAZIL, THE AMAZONS, AND THE COAST*, 1879

Herbert H. Smith (1851–1919) was an American author and naturalist who first traveled to Brazil in 1870 as a member of an expedition studying and collecting Amazonian wildlife. Returning to live and work in Brazil several times over the following years, he contributed a series of articles on Brazil for *Scribner's*, a popular magazine of the era. These articles formed the basis of a book, published in 1879. Much of the book focuses on Brazil's natural environment and economy, with shorter sections on social, cultural, and political observations, such as the excerpts presented in this section.

Smith's visits to Brazil coincided with the last years of institutional slavery. In 1871, the imperial government passed a law stating that in the future all children born of current slaves would be free, though masters retained the right to the children's labor until the age of 21. Outright abolition would not occur until 1888, almost a decade after Smith's book was published.

Here, as everywhere else, it takes all sorts of people to make up a community. Only, in Brazil, the proportion of really good families, refined, educated ones, is very much smaller than in the United States: too small as yet, to exercise much influence over the country. When you meet with these families you find

Source: E. Bradford Burns, ed., *A Documentary History of Brazil* (New York: Alfred A. Knopf, 1966), 274–277.

a social life differing very little from that to which we are accustomed at home; pure manners, intelligent conversation, and a hearty respect for every true lady. The ladies themselves are quick-witted, lively, brilliant; one of them would flash all over a northern drawing-room, to the utter extinction of dull conversation.

But the mass of Rio society is much lower; it is a bad imitation of the Parisian: I think, indeed, that there is a deal of unconscious truth in the boastful title which the people have given to their city—"Paris in America." French fashions, French literature, French philosophy, French morals, are spread broadcast through the educated circles. . . .

Ladies go about with their husbands and fathers, and are always treated with politeness; they are witty and lively, but often superficial. The time is past when women were shut up like nuns, behind latticed windows, invisible to the street; when they were only shown at balls and on state occasions. But true social freedom is hardly more accorded to them than it was a hundred years ago. . . .

So far, we have been considering only that portion of the population which would be distinguished as the "society" of Rio; people who, by birth, or education, or wealth, are able to retain a certain standing, which separates them from the mass of their countrymen. Classes are strongly marked in Brazil. Below this "society" stratum, we may distinguish three others, pretty sharply defined: the mechanics and small shop-keepers, the laborers and peasants, and the slaves.

In the United States we have nothing precisely parallel to the second Brazilian class. . . . In Brazil, the importance of the second class is very much underrated, simply because official statistics do not recognize it as a class at all. In it we may include peddlers, shop-keepers in the smallest way, low eating-house keepers, and finally, every mechanic who does any honest work; for mind you, in Brazil a mechanic is no more admitted into society than a boot-black would be at home. These men are mostly Portuguese immigrants; sometimes white or half-breed Brazilians. They work hard to keep themselves above the common laborers, whom they look down

on; they never aspire to the magnificence of the privileged class, the educated ones, who look down on them, or rather ignore them, except as they must make use of their services. With this lower stratum, education never extends beyond writing and accounts, but even that is enough to secure the respect of the *sans culottes [literally, "without breeches": a term derived from the French revolution referring to the lower classes–Ed.]*, who, very often, cannot even read. Then there is the added dignity of proprietorship; the owner of a street-corner pagoda, who sells coffee and lottery tickets at his windows, is a superior being to the porter or boatman, or even to the cartman, who may get his morning lunch there.

Rather a negative element is the stratum next below this—the free laborers. In this class I may include, not only the porters and cartmen and market-men of Rio and the other cities, but all the peasantry of Brazil, . . . stationary people, who work only when they must, and never accumulate property. . . .

In Rio, this class includes Portuguese and free Negroes; the latter, probably, the more intelligent and honest. There are boatmen and cartmen, porters waiting for a job at every street corner, hawkers of fish and fruit and poultry; thousands who have no regular employment, but pick up their living by doing "odd jobs." Our boot-blacks, and news-boys, and street Arabs, generally, might belong to this class; the "longshoremen" are a grade above it. . . .

So we come to the fourth and lowest class in Brazil—the slaves. The class that originated in barbarism and selfishness, the class which Brazil, for very shame, is trying to get rid of, but whose influence will curse the children with the sins of their fathers for dreary years. . . .

I came to Brazil with an honest desire to study this question of slavery in a spirit of fairness, without running to emotional extremes. Now, after four years, I am convinced that all other evils with which the country is cursed, taken together, will not compare with this one. . . .

In mere animal matters, of food and clothing, no doubt many of the Negroes are better off than they were in Africa; no doubt, also, they have learned some lessons of peace and civility; even a groping outline of Christianity. But it would be hard to prove that the plantation slave, dependent, like a child, on his master, and utterly unused to thinking for himself, is better, mentally, than the savage who has his faculties sharpened by continual battling with the savage nature around him. . . .

The treatment of slaves in Brazil depends, of course, on the master; largely, too, on the district. In the provinces north of the Sao Francisco, I am bound to say that they are treated with great kindness; on the Amazons, they would be, from necessity, if not from choice, for every ill-used slave would run off to the woods, as many have done. . . . But

around Rio and Bahia, where the vast majority of the slaves are now owned, they are masters who treat their servants with a severity that is nothing short of barbarism. . . .

Yet Brazil should have a certain credit above other slaveholding countries, present and past; for she alone has voluntarily set herself to getting rid of her shame. Other nations have done it by revolutions, or because they were forced to by a stronger power, or because the system died out of itself. But Brazil, among all, has had the nerve to cut away the sore flesh with her own hand; to cut it away while it was yet strong, while it seemed her best vitality. . . .

QUESTIONS TO CONSIDER

1. Smith thought of this book as an exercise in scientific objectivity. How would you assess the strengths and weaknesses of the way Smith constructs arguments and uses evidence?
2. What does this excerpt tell us about Brazil in the 1870s? What does it tell us about Herbert Smith's understanding of the modern world?

8.3 "THE HISTORY OF MANKIND IS A HISTORY OF REPEATED INJURIES AND USURPATIONS ON THE PART OF MAN TOWARD WOMAN." ELIZABETH CADY STANTON, *DECLARATION OF SENTIMENTS*, 1848

Elizabeth Cady Stanton (1815–1902) was born to a progressive family in upstate New York and became involved in the abolitionist movement. She attended the World Antislavery Convention in London in 1840, but was excluded from participation because she was a woman. This experience helped motivate her to focus her political activities on women's rights, which she did from then on. Together with Lucretia Mott (1793–1880) and others, she organized the first women's rights convention, at Seneca Falls, New York, in 1848.

Stanton's career was controversial. She opposed passage of the Fourteenth and Fifteenth amendments to the US Constitution because she objected to African American men being given legal

Source: Elizabeth Cady Stanton, *A History of Woman Suffrage*, Vol. 1 (Rochester, NY: Fowler and Wells, 1889), 70–71.

protections and the right to vote without women receiving those same rights. She also opposed organized religion, leading to divisions with other, often Christian, abolitionists and suffragists.

The document reproduced here, the Declaration of Sentiments (sometimes called the Seneca Falls Declaration), emerged from the 1848 Convention. It became a foundational document for the movement for women's rights in the United States and elsewhere

---

When, in the course of human events, it becomes necessary for one portion of the family of man to assume among the people of the earth a position different from that which they have hitherto occupied, but one to which the laws of nature and of nature's God entitle them, a decent respect to the opinions of mankind requires that they should declare the causes that impel them to such a course.

We hold these truths to be self-evident; that all men and women are created equal; that they are endowed by their Creator with certain inalienable rights; that among these are life, liberty, and the pursuit of happiness; that to secure these rights governments are instituted, deriving their just powers from the consent of the governed. Whenever any form of government becomes destructive of these ends, it is the right of those who suffer from it to refuse allegiance to it, and to insist upon the institution of a new government, laying its foundation on such principles, and organizing its powers in such form, as to them shall seem most likely to effect their safety and happiness. Prudence, indeed, will dictate that governments long established should not be changed for light and transient causes; and, accordingly, all experience hath shown that mankind are more disposed to suffer, while evils are sufferable, than to right themselves by abolishing the forms to which they were accustomed. But when a long train of abuses and usurpations, pursuing invariably the same object, evinces a design to reduce them under absolute despotism, it is their duty to throw off such government, and to provide new guards for their future security. Such has been the patient sufferance of the women under this government, and such is now the necessity which constrains them to demand the equal station to which they are entitled.

The history of mankind is a history of repeated injuries and usurpations on the part of man toward woman, having in direct object the establishment of an absolute tyranny over her. To prove this, let facts be submitted to a candid world.

He has never permitted her to exercise her inalienable right to the elective franchise.

He has compelled her to submit to laws, in the formation of which she had no voice.

He has withheld from her rights which are given to the most ignorant and degraded men—both natives and foreigners.

Having deprived her of this first right as a citizen, the elective franchise, thereby leaving her without representation in the halls of legislation, he has oppressed her on all sides.

He has made her, if married, in the eye of the law, civilly dead.

He has taken from her all right in property, even to the wages she earns.

He has made her morally, an irresponsible being, as she can commit many crimes with impunity, provided they be done in the presence of her husband. In the covenant of marriage, she is compelled to promise obedience to her husband, he becoming, to all intents and purposes, her master—the law giving him power to deprive her of her liberty, and to administer chastisement.

He has so framed the laws of divorce, as to what shall be the proper causes of divorce, in case of separation, to whom the guardianship of the children shall be given; as to be wholly regardless of the happiness of the women—the law, in all cases, going upon a false supposition of the supremacy of man, and giving all power into his hands.

After depriving her of all rights as a married woman, if single and the owner of property, he has taxed her to support a government which recognizes her only when her property can be made profitable to it.

He has monopolized nearly all the profitable employments, and from those she is permitted to follow, she receives but a scanty remuneration.

He closes against her all the avenues to wealth and distinction, which he considers most honorable to himself. As a teacher of theology, medicine, or law, she is not known.

He has denied her the facilities for obtaining a thorough education—all colleges being closed against her.

He allows her in church, as well as State, but a subordinate position, claiming Apostolic authority for her exclusion from the ministry, and, with some exceptions, from any public participation in the affairs of the Church.

He has created a false public sentiment by giving to the world a different code of morals for men and women, by which moral delinquencies which exclude women from society, are not only tolerated but deemed of little account in man.

He has usurped the prerogative of Jehovah himself, claiming it as his right to assign for her a sphere of action, when that belongs to her conscience and her God.

He has endeavored, in every way that he could to destroy her confidence in her own powers, to lessen her self-respect, and to make her willing to lead a dependent and abject life.

Now, in view of this entire disfranchisement of one-half the people of this country, their social and religious degradation, —in view of the unjust laws above mentioned, and because women do feel themselves aggrieved, oppressed, and fraudulently deprived of their most sacred rights, we insist that they have immediate admission to all the rights and privileges which belong to them as citizens of these United States.

In entering upon the great work before us, we anticipate no small amount of misconception, misrepresentation, and ridicule; but we shall use every instrumentality within our power to effect our object. We shall employ agents, circulate tracts, petition the State and national Legislatures, and endeavor to enlist the pulpit and the press in our behalf. We hope this Convention will be followed by a series of Conventions, embracing every part of the country.

Firmly relying upon the final triumph of the Right and the True, we do this day affix our signatures to this declaration.

QUESTIONS TO CONSIDER

1. Why do you think Stanton and her co-authors modeled this document on the US Declaration of Independence? How does the way they use, and respond to, the Declaration compare to the way other authors built documents modeled on famous predecessors (e.g., Olympe de Gouges in Source 6.3 or Ho Chi Minh in Source 12.3)?

2. One of the most controversial aspects of this document at the Convention was its insistence that women be given the right to vote. Why would this be considered such an important—and to many the most objectionable—part of the document?

8.4 "DEMAND RIGHTS FOR WOMEN." FLORA TRISTÁN, *WORKERS' UNION*, 1843 AND SOJOURNER TRUTH, *ADDRESS TO THE FIRST ANNUAL MEETING OF THE AMERICAN EQUAL RIGHTS ASSOCIATION*, 1867

Flora Tristán (1803–1844) was born in Paris to a French mother and a Spanish father. Impoverished after her father's death, she joined the labor force, found herself in an unhappy marriage with two children, and left her household while pregnant with a third. For more than a decade, while simultaneously writing, traveling, and studying, Tristán engaged in legal battles with her estranged husband (he would later shoot her—she survived—and be sentenced to twenty years in prison).

Beginning in the mid-1820s, Tristán worked, wrote, and agitated for women's and workers' rights. She traveled extensively—to England for work, to Peru in search of her father's relatives, and across France. By the early 1840s, Tristán's vision of a better future solidified, resulting in publication of the book *Worker's Union* (1843), which is excerpted here. Tristán died in 1844 while traveling across France, espousing the beliefs encapsulated in the book.

Sojourner Truth (1797–1883) was born into slavery in rural New York State but escaped with her daughter in 1826, the year before the New York Emancipation Act passed. Truth performed household work and later became a preacher. In the 1840s, she came into contact with leading abolitionists such as Frederick Douglass and William Lloyd Garrison, as well as women's rights activists Elizabeth Cady Stanton, Lucretia Mott, and others. She began making public appearances as an outspoken abolitionist and supporter of women's rights. Her memoir, *The Narrative of Sojourner Truth*, was published in 1850.

During the US Civil War, Truth met President Abraham Lincoln and contributed to assistance efforts for black refugees from the South. After the war, she advocated for equal rights and opportunities for all people. The excerpt presented here is from a speech delivered to the 1867 meeting of the American Equal Rights Association, which had formed one year before. Other speakers at the conference included Elizabeth Cady Stanton, Lucretia Mott, and Henry Ward Beecher.

EXCERPT 1: FROM FLORA TRISTÁN, *WORKERS' UNION* (1843)

I know of nothing so powerful as the forced, inevitable logic that issues from a principle laid down or from the hypothesis that represents it. Once woman's inferiority is proclaimed and posed as a principle, see what disastrous consequences result for the universal well-being of all men and all women.

Believing that woman, because of her structure, lacked strength, intelligence, and ability and was

Source: Doris and Paul Beik, *Flora Tristán: Utopian Feminist* (Bloomington: Indiana University Press, 1993), 104–123; Sojourner Truth, *Proceedings of the First Anniversary of the American Equal Rights Association, Held at the Church of the Puritans, New York, May 9 and 10, 1867* (New York: Robert J. Johnson, 1867), https://www.loc.gov/resource/rbnawsa.n3542/?sp=3.

unsuited for serious and useful work, it has been concluded very logically that it would be a waste of time to give her a rational, solid, strict education capable of making her a useful member of society. Therefore, she has been raised to be an amiable doll and a slave destined to entertain her master and serve him. To be sure, from time to time a few intelligent and compassionate men, suffering for their mothers, wives, and daughters, have cried out against such barbarousness and absurdity and have protested energetically against so unjust a condemnation. . . .

Pay attention and you will see what frightful perturbations result solely from the acceptance of a false principle. . . .

Woman is everything in the life of the workers. She is their sole providence. If she fails them, everything fails them. Consequently, it is said: "It is the woman who makes or unmakes the household," and this is the exact truth; that is why a proverb has been made of it. But what education, what teaching, what direction, what moral or physical development does the woman of the common people receive? None. . . .

Women of the working class, observe well, I beseech you, that in pointing out here what now exists concerning your ignorance and your inability to raise your children, I have no intention of bearing the least accusation against you and your character. No, it is society that I accuse of leaving you thus untutored, you, women, you, mothers, who will so much need, on the contrary, to be educated and developed, in order to be able in your turn to educate and develop the men and the children entrusted to your care.

The women of the lower classes are generally brutal, mean, sometimes harsh. That is true; but where does this state of things come from that so little conforms to woman's sweet, good, sensitive, generous nature? Poor working women! They have so many irritations! First the husband. (It must be acknowledged that there are few workers' households that are happy.) The husband, with a bit more education, being the head by virtue of the law, and also by virtue of the money he brings into the household, believes himself (which he is in fact) very much superior to the woman, who brings only her small daily wage and is only a humble servant in the house.

Notice that in all the trades engaged in by men and women, the woman worker gets only half what a man does for a day's work, or, if she does piecework, her rate is less than half. Not being able to imagine such a flagrant injustice, the first thought to strike us is this: because of his muscular strength, man doubtless does double the work of woman. Well, readers, just the contrary happens. In all the trades where skill and finger dexterity are necessary, women do almost twice as much work as men. . . .

Workers, you have not foreseen the disastrous consequences that would result for you from a similar injustice done to the detriment of your mothers, sisters, wives, and daughters. What is happening? The manufacturers, seeing the women laborers work more quickly and at half price, day by day dismiss men from their workshops and replace them with women. Consequently, the man crosses his arms and dies of hunger on the pavement! That is what the heads of factories in England have done. Once started in this direction, women will be dismissed in order to replace them with twelve-year-old children. A saving of half the wages! Finally, one gets to the point of using only seven- and eight-year-old children. Overlook one injustice and you are sure to get thousands more. . . .

Do you begin to understand, you man who exclaim in horror before being willing to examine the question, why I claim Rights for women? Why I would like them to be placed in society on an absolutely equal footing with men, and enjoy it by virtue of the legal right that every person has at birth?

I demand rights for women because I am convinced that all the ills of the world come from this forgetfulness and scorn that until now have been inflicted on the natural and imprescriptible rights of the female. I demand rights for women because that is the only way that their education will be attended to and because on the education of women depends that of men in general, and particularly of the men of the people. I demand rights for women because it is the only means of obtaining their rehabilitation in the eyes of the church, the law, and society, and because that preliminary rehabilitation is necessary if the workers themselves are to be rehabilitated. All the ills of the working class are summed up by these two words: poverty and ignorance, ignorance and poverty. But to get out of this labyrinth, I see only one way: to start by educating women, because women are entrusted with raising the children, male and female.

Workers, under present conditions, you know what happens in your households. You, the man, the master having rights over your wife, do you live with her contentedly? Speak: are you happy?

No, no. It is easy to see that in spite of your rights, you are neither contented nor happy.

Between master and slave, there can only be fatigue from the weight of the chain that binds one to the other. Where the absence of liberty makes itself felt, happiness cannot exist. . . .

Workers, this little picture, barely sketched, of the position that the proletarian class would enjoy if women were recognized as the equals of men, must make you reflect on the evil that exists and on the good that could be attained. That should inspire you to great determination.

EXCERPT 2: FROM SOJOURNER TRUTH, *AMERICAN EQUAL RIGHTS ASSOCIATION ADDRESS* (1867)

My friends, I am rejoiced that you are glad, but I don't know how you will feel when I get through. I come from another field—the country of the slave. They have got their liberty—so much good luck to have slavery partly destroyed; not entirely. I want it root and branch destroyed. Then we will all be free indeed. I feel that if I have to answer for the deeds done in my body just as much as a man, I have a right to have just as much as a man. There is a great stir about colored men getting their rights, but not a word about the colored women; and if colored men get their rights, and not colored women theirs, you see the colored men will be masters over the women, and it will be just as bad as it was before. So I am for keeping the thing going while things are stirring; because

if we wait till it is still, it will take a great while to get it going again. . . .

I want you to consider on that chil'n [*The original document uses this abbreviation for "children."–Ed.*]. I call you chil'n; you are somebody's chil'n, and I am old enough to be mother of all that is here. I want women to have their rights. In the courts women have no right, no voice; nobody speaks for them. I wish woman to have her voice there among the pettifoggers. If it is not a fit place for women, it is unfit for men to be there. I am above eighty years old; it is about time for me to be going. I have been forty years a slave and forty years free, and would be here forty years more to have equal rights for all. I suppose I am kept here because something remains for me to do; I suppose I am yet to help to break the chain. I have done a great deal of work; as much as a man, but did not get so much pay. I used to work in the field and bind grain, keeping up with the cradler; but men doing no more, got twice as much pay;. . . .

I suppose I am about the only colored woman that goes about to speak for the rights of the colored women. I want to keep the thing stirring, now that the ice is cracked. What we want is a little money. You men know that you get as much again as women when you write, or for what you do. When we get our rights we shall not have to come to you for money, for then we shall have money enough in our own pockets; and may be you will ask us for money. But help us now until we get it. It is a good consolation to know that when we have got this battle fought we shall not be coming to you anymore. You have been having our rights so long, that you think, like a slaveholder, that you own us. I know that it is hard for one who has held the reins for so long to give up; it cuts like a knife. It will feel all the better when it closes up again. I have been in Washington about three years, seeing about these colored people. Now colored men have the right to vote. There ought to be equal rights now more than ever, since colored people have got their freedom. . . .

QUESTIONS TO CONSIDER

1. According to Tristán and Truth, what are the moral, political, and practical arguments in support of equal rights? What rights in particular do they specify in these excerpts? What are the similarities and differences between their observations and suggestions and those of

Elizabeth Cady Stanton (Source 8.3)? Why do you think these differences exist? What importance might these differences have in shaping the struggle for equal rights?

2. Like Marx and Engels (Source 8.1), Tristán and Truth suggest the need for radical change in the modern political and economic order. What are the similarities and differences among their recommendations for improving conditions for the poor and workers? What kinds of rhetorical devices and evidence do the authors use to try to persuade their audiences?

8.5 "EVIL CUSTOMS OF THE PAST SHALL BE BROKEN OFF." *THE CHARTER OATH* (JAPAN), 1868 AND *THE EMANCIPATION MANIFESTO* (RUSSIA), 1861

These two documents are from states grappling with reform and, in their own words attempting to become "modern" by looking outside their borders and appealing to international norms and innovations.

After opening to foreign trade in response to American demands in 1853, Japan radically revised its relationship to other countries. After an official policy of *sakoku* that had been in place since the 1600s, an intense debate took place about industrialization and international commerce. From this process emerged the Meiji Restoration, so called because it was the formal restoration of the Emperor to power in place of the Tokugawa shogun. The Charter Oath outlined the principles of the new government. The document presented here is composed of three drafts of the Charter Oath and the final version that was promulgated in 1868.

Although not isolated to the extent Japan was, Russia, too, maintained a largely feudal social structure that many perceived to be holding the empire back. More than a third of Russians were serfs, without political or economic rights. With such a large percentage of its population marginalized in this way, Russian leaders found it difficult to encourage industrialization, political reform, and other features of a "modern" state. Discussions about how to do away with serfdom took place among leaders throughout the nineteenth century, but it was not until after Tsar Alexander II was coronated in 1855 that the problem was acted upon. In 1861—in the same decade as Japan's Charter Oath—Russia's Emancipation Manifesto (excerpted here) liberated some 23 million serfs.

Sources: David Lu, ed., *Japan: A Documentary History* (Armonk, NY: M. E. Sharpe, 1997), 307–309.; Basil Dmytryshyn, ed., *Imperial Russia: A Source Book, 1700–1917*, 3rd ed. (New York: Harcourt, Brace, Jovanovich, 1990), 307–311.

EXCERPT 1: DRAFTS OF *THE CHARTER OATH* AND EXCERPTS FROM *THE DOCUMENT ON THE FORM OF GOVERNMENT* (JAPAN, 1868)

(a) Draft by Yuri Kimimasa

GENERAL OUTLINE ON LEGISLATIVE MATTERS

1. It is requested that a system be established under which common people may be permitted to pursue their respective callings so that there may be no discontent.
2. It is necessary for the samurai and common people to unite in carrying out vigorously the administration of economic and financial affairs.
3. Knowledge shall be sought throughout the world so as to widen and strengthen the foundations of imperial rule.
4. The term of office held by qualified men [selected by the *han*] must be limited. Thereafter they must yield their positions to talented men. *[Han are similar to feudal domains, or the lords of those domains, in medieval and early modern Europe–Ed.].*
5. All matters of state must be decided by open discussion [with the participation of all factions on *han* concerned] and must not be discussed privately. . . .

(b) Amended Draft by Fukuoka Takachika

A COMPACT

1. An assembly consisting of daimyo *[feudal lords–Ed.]* shall be established, and all matters of state shall be decided by open discussion.
2. It is requested that a system be established under which not only the civil and military officials, but also the common people may be permitted to pursue their respective callings so that there may be no discontent.
3. The high and low shall all unite in carrying out vigorously the administration of economic and financial affairs.
4. Knowledge shall be sought throughout the world so as to broaden and strengthen the foundations of imperial rule.

5. The term of office of those appointed [by the imperial government] must be limited. Thereafter they must yield their positions to talented men. . . .

(c) Draft by Kido Koin

OATH

1. An assembly consisting of daimyo shall be established, and all matters of state shall be decided by open discussion.
2. The high and low shall all unite in carrying out the administration of economic and financial affairs.
3. It is requested that a system be established under which not only the civil and military officials, but also the common people may be permitted to pursue their respective callings so that there may be no discontent.
4. Evil practices of the past shall be discarded and [all our actions] shall follow the accepted practices of the world.
5. Knowledge shall be sought throughout the world so as to broaden and strengthen the foundations of imperial rule.

EXCERPTS FROM *THE DOCUMENT ON THE FORM OF GOVERNMENT* (SEITAISHO), 1868

1. In determining the national policy and establishing a new system of government and regulations, the text of the Charter Oath shall become the guide.

   (1) A deliberative assembly shall be convoked on a broad basis, and all matters of state shall be decided by open discussion.
   (2) The high and low shall all unite in carrying out vigorously the administration of economic and financial affairs.
   (3) It is necessary to have a system under which not only the civil and military officials, but also the common people may be permitted to pursue their respective callings so that there may be no discontent.
   (4) Evil practices of the past shall be discarded and [all our actions] shall follow the just way of the world [i.e., international law].

(5) Knowledge shall be sought throughout the world so as to broaden and strengthen the foundations of imperial rule.

EXCERPT 2: *THE EMANCIPATION MANIFESTO* (RUSSIA, 1861)

Examining the condition of classes and professions comprising the state, we became convinced that the present state legislation favours the upper and middle classes, defines their obligations, rights, and privileges, but does not equally favour the serfs, so designated because in part from old laws and in part from custom they have been hereditarily subjected to the authority of landowners, who in turn were obligated to provide for their well-being. Rights of nobles have been hitherto very broad and legally ill-defined, because they stem from tradition, custom, and the good will of the noblemen. In most cases this has led to the establishment of good patriarchal relations based on the sincere, just concern and benevolence on the part of the nobles, and on affectionate submission on the part of the peasants. Because of the decline of the simplicity of morals, because of an increase in the diversity of relations, because of the weakening of the direct paternal attitude of nobles toward the peasants, and because noble rights fell sometimes into the hands of people exclusively concerned with their personal interests, good relations weakened. The way was opened for an arbitrariness burdensome for the peasants and detrimental to their welfare, causing them to be indifferent to the improvement of their own existence. . . .

We thus became convinced that the problem of improving the condition of serfs was a sacred inheritance bequeathed to Us by Our predecessors, a mission which, in the course of events, Divine Providence has called upon Us to fulfil.

We have begun this task by expressing Our confidence in the Russian nobility, which has proved on so many occasions its devotion to the Throne, and its readiness to make sacrifices for the welfare of the country.

We have left to the nobles themselves, in accordance with their own wishes, the task of preparing proposals for the new organisation of peasant life, proposals that would limit their rights over the peasants, and the realisation of which would inflict on them some material losses. Our confidence was justified. . . .

These proposals were diverse, because of the nature of the problem. They have been compared, collated, systematised, rectified, and finalised in the Main Committee instituted for that purpose; and these new arrangements dealing with the peasants and domestics of the nobility have been examined in the State Council.

Having invoked Divine assistance, We have resolved to execute this task.

On the basis of the above-mentioned new arrangements, the serfs will receive in time the full rights of free rural inhabitants.

The nobles, while retaining their property rights on all the lands belonging to them, grant the peasants perpetual use of their domicile in return for a specified obligation; and, to assure their livelihood as well as to guarantee fulfilment of their obligations toward the government, grant them a portion of arable land fixed by the said arrangements, as well as other property.

While enjoying these land allotments, the peasants are obliged, in return, to fulfil obligations to the noblemen fixed by the same arrangements. In this condition, which is temporary, the peasants are temporarily obligated.

At the same time, they are granted the right to purchase their domicile, and, with the consent of the nobles, they may acquire in full ownership the arable lands and other properties which are allotted them for permanent use. Following such acquisition of full ownership of land, the peasants will be freed from their obligations to the nobles for the land thus purchased and will become free peasant landowners.

A special decree dealing with domestics will establish a temporary status for them, adapted to their occupations and their needs. At the end of two years from the day of the promulgation of this decree, they shall receive full freedom and some temporary immunities.

In accordance with the fundamental principles of these arrangements, the future organisation of peasants and domestics will be determined, the order of general peasant administration will be established, and the rights given to the peasants and to the domestics will be spelled out in detail, as will the obligations imposed on them toward the government and the nobles. . . .

This new arrangement, because of its complexity, cannot be put into effect immediately; a time of not less than two years is necessary. During this period, to avoid all misunderstanding and to protect public and private interests, the order actually existing on the estates of nobles should be maintained until the new order shall become effective.

QUESTIONS FOR CONSIDERATION

1. What distinctions do the drafters of these documents make between "Western" and "modern"? Do they see these things as the same? Are they seen as positive or negative?
2. Both documents address the ability of people to choose their profession or occupation. Why is this seen as an important aspect of a "modern" society? Are there other fundamental features of modernity expressed or implied in these documents?

8.6 "THERE ARE ENDLESS CHANGES IN THE WORLD." ZENG GUOFAN AND LI HONGZHANG, *LETTER TO THE ZONGLI YAMEN*, 1871 AND XUE FUCHENG, *SUGGESTIONS ON FOREIGN AFFAIRS*, 1879

China's defeat by Great Britain in the Opium War (1839–1842) shocked many Qing Dynasty officials and initiated a series of crises that revealed just how weak the empire was. The Taiping War, a rebellion led by a Chinese scholar who claimed to be the younger brother of Jesus Christ, was the most serious of these crises, killing more than 20 million people and bringing the Qing to the brink of collapse. In the eighteenth century, Qing China had been perhaps the most powerful and prosperous state in the world. By the 1870s, it was barely surviving.

In response to these crises, Chinese thinkers sought ways to revive their country. The three authors represented here are among the most influential figures of the "self-strengthening" movement that sought knowledge from abroad to find a way to reform China from within so that it could avoid collapse or overthrow. Li Hongzhang (1823–1901) and his mentor Zeng Guofan (1811–1872) both came to prominence for their roles in fighting the Taiping. Xue Fucheng (1838–1894) was one of the Qing Dynasty's first diplomats and also an advocate for a strong navy.

Source: *Sources of the Chinese Tradition*, Vol. 2, compiled by William Theodore de Bary and Richard Lufrano, 2nd ed. (New York: Columbia University Press, 2000), 235–249.

EXCERPT 1: ZENG GUOFAN AND LI HONGZHANG, *LETTER TO THE ZONGLI YAMEN* (FOREIGN AFFAIRS OFFICE), 1871

Last autumn when I [Zeng] was at Tianjin, Governor Ding Richang frequently came to discuss with me proposals for the selection of intelligent youths to be sent to the schools of various Western countries to study military administration, shipping administration, infantry tactics, mathematics, manufacturing, and other subjects. We estimated that after more than ten years their training would have been completed and they could return to China so that other Chinese might learn thoroughly the superior techniques of the Westerners. Thus we could gradually plan for self-strengthening. . . . After Mr. Bin Chun and two other gentlemen, Zhigang and Sun Jiagu, had traveled in various countries at imperial command, they saw the essential aspects of conditions overseas, and they found that cartography, mathematics, astronomy, navigation, shipbuilding, and manufacturing are all closely related to military defense. It is the practice of foreign nations that those who have studied abroad and have learned some superior techniques are immediately invited upon their return by academic institutions to teach the various subjects and to develop their fields. Military administration and shipping are considered as important as the learning that deals with the mind and body, and nature and destiny of man. Now that the eyes of the people have been opened, if China wishes to adopt Western ideas and excel in Western methods, we should immediately select intelligent young men and send them to study in foreign countries. . . .

Some may say, "Arsenals have been established in Tianjin, Shanghai, and Fuzhou for shipbuilding and the manufacture of guns and ammunition. The Tongwen College [for foreign languages] has been established in Beijing for Manchu and Chinese youths to study under Western instructors. A language school has also been opened in Shanghai for the training of young students. It seems, therefore, that a beginning has been made in China and that there is no need for studying overseas." These critics, however, do not know that to establish arsenals for manufacturing and to open schools for instruction is just the beginning of our effort to rise again. To go to distant lands for study, to gather ideas for more advantageous use, can produce far-reaching and great results. Westerners seek knowledge for practical use. . . . If we Chinese wish to adopt their superior techniques and suddenly try to buy all their machines, not only will our resources be insufficient to do so but we will be unable to master the fundamental principles or to understand the complicated details of the techniques, unless we have actually seen and practiced them for a long time. . . .

We have heard that youths of Fujian, Guangdong, and Ningbo also occasionally have gone abroad to study, but merely attempted to gain a superficial knowledge of foreign written and spoken languages in order to do business with the foreigners for the purpose of making a living. In our plan, we must be doubly careful at the beginning of selection. The students who are to be taken to foreign countries will all be under the control of the commissioners. Specializing in different fields, they will earnestly seek for mastery of their subjects. There will be interpreters, and instructors to teach them Chinese learning from time to time, so that they will learn the great principles for the establishment of character, in the hope of becoming men with abilities of use to us.

EXCERPT 2: XUE FUCHENG, *SUGGESTIONS ON FOREIGN AFFAIRS*, 1879

Western nations rely on intelligence and energy to compete with one another. To come abreast of them, China should plan to promote commerce and open mines; unless we change, the Westerners will be rich and we poor. We should excel in technology and the manufacture of machinery; unless we change, they will be skillful and we clumsy. Steamships, trains, and the telegraph should be adopted; unless we change the Westerners will be quick and we slow. . . . Unless we change, the Westerners will cooperate with each other and we shall stand isolated; they will be strong and we shall be weak.

Some may ask: "If such a great nation as China imitates the Westerners, would it not be using barbarian ways to change China?" Not so. For while in clothing, language, and customs China is different from foreign countries, the utilization of the forces of nature for the benefit of the people is the same in China as in foreign countries. The Western people happen to be the first in adopting this new way of life, but how can we say that they alone should monopolize the secrets of nature? And how do we know that a few decades or a hundred years later China may not surpass them? . . . Now if we really take over the Westerners' knowledge of machinery and mathematics in order to protect the Way of our sage kings Yao and Shun, Yu and Tang, Wen and Wu, and the Duke of Zhou and Confucius, and so make the Westerners not dare to despise China, I know that if they were alive today, the sages would engage themselves in the same tasks, and their Way would also be gradually spread to the eight bounds of the earth. That is what we call using the ways of China to change the barbarians. . . .

Alas! There are endless changes in the world, and so there are endless variations in the sages' way of meeting these changes. To be born in the present age but to hold fast to ancient methods is to be like one who in the age of Shen nong [when people had learned to cook] still ate raw meat and drank blood. . . . Such a one would say, "I am following the methods of the ancient sages." But it is hardly possible that he should not become exhausted and fall. Moreover, the laws [or methods] that ought to be changed today can still [in their new form] embody the essence of the laws of the ancient sages.

QUESTIONS TO CONSIDER

1. What challenges do these men perceive to be the most important ones facing China in the 1870s? How do they propose to respond to these challenges, and what resistance does it appear they anticipate?
2. Should these documents be considered conservative? Radical? What is the nature of the changes they call for?

8.7 "CHINA IS JUST THE OPPOSITE." LI GUI, *GLIMPSES OF A MODERN SOCIETY*, 1876

This document brings together two important threads in world history during the nineteenth century. One is the opening of China to trade on European and American terms after the first Opium War (1839–1842). The second is the spread of world's fairs and international expositions.

As merchants and missionaries flooded into China, Chinese also went abroad gathering information and ideas from other countries. On one of these missions, Li Gui, a minor government official, traveled to the United States and visited the 1876 Centennial Exhibition in Philadelphia. Li reported on the exposition itself, focusing especially on technical and industrial innovations on display, but also on American society outside the fair. In the selection presented here, he comments on the Women's Pavilion at the fair, remarking on differences between Chinese and American women's roles, and describes his visit to a police station.

Source: R. David Arkush and Leo O. Lee, trans and ed., *Land without Ghosts: Chinese Impressions of America from the Mid-Nineteenth Century to the Present* (Berkeley: University of California Press, 1989), 41–48.

THE WOMEN'S PAVILION

Originally the exposition planned to have an exhibit of women's handicrafts as part of the general pavilion and not to erect a separate building. This made women of the whole country dissatisfied because they considered that slighting women's work was slighting women, so they devised a plan to raise funds themselves for a separate building for women's handicrafts. This building is to the east of the hall of agriculture, 192 square feet, with more than five acres of grounds. It has eight sides, like a tent, with eight gates. The central tower rises eighty feet high. The design of the building, supervision of construction, and decoration and setup were all done by women. It is novel and ingenious, and cost $100,000. Books, paintings, maps, and embroideries done by women, together with [demonstrations of] the techniques of each are gathered here. Another room was used to display women's school equipment and curricular materials; even the people in charge of this exhibition hall were women. I toured the entire exhibition hall and saw books on astronomy, geography, science, mathematics, and sewing and cooking separately on display. There were also many ingenious tools and mechanisms.

Whenever I asked a question, everyone was happy to explain things tirelessly, in an open manner. These women do not have the manner of girls who are kept at home, but the spirit of men; I greatly respect and like them. Western friends accompanying me said that the Western custom was to treat men and women equally and give women the same education as men; therefore women are quite capable of voicing opinions on large matters and performing great deeds. In May of this year a newspaper appeared in which a woman argued what a great injustice it is that all official positions are filled by men and that the president soon to be elected will certainly be a man, too—why cannot we women be elected as well? This is most unjust, she said. I have heard that in England, too, there are women who want to enter Parliament and participate in national affairs. Their arguments are very novel, but after hearing them they seem reasonable.

In recent years, schools for girls have been established in all countries. In English universities men and women take entrance examinations on the same basis. In Germany girls of eight must go to school or else their parents will be held responsible. In America there are as many as three or four million female teachers and students. Such things are increasing daily in order that women's abilities may be fully made use of. There are roughly as many women as men in the world; if only men and not women are educated, then out of ten people only five will be useful. In intelligence women are not second to men, and in some ways they are superior; they can apply themselves because they are tranquil in mind. If we do not teach and encourage them, their talents will be buried; does this not go against Heaven's intention in creating people? For this reason in other countries people are happy both when they have boys and when they have girls, without distinction.

China is just the opposite. Regarding women as inferior and drowning [infant] girls cannot be stopped by means of persuasion or prohibitions. I say they are caused by nothing other than the decay of women's education. I find that officials of the Zhou dynasty [ca. 1050–221 BCE] included priestesses and female clerks. The Han [202 BCE–220 CE] system had an office staffed by female officials which kept daily records of the Imperial concubines. Women's learning was made use of in the past. . . . In the early three dynasties female education flourished, but in later ages such things gradually declined. Today there is even the saying that, "Only a woman without accomplishments is virtuous." Alas! In my opinion, this one sentence injures all women. How can their accomplishments be limited to writing poetry about pretty things? If these are called accomplishments, then it would be better not to be virtuous. If we could revive women's education so that they could all study and learn, women's morality would be strengthened, their abilities would be made use of, the tendency to look down on them would be corrected, and the custom of drowning girls would naturally stop.

As for the opinions of English and American women, they are too extreme, as my Western friends emphatically agree. . . .

A POLICE STATION AND A COURT

In the evening I visited a police station. According to the captain there are altogether thirty-five precincts in New York with twenty-three hundred policemen.

This one was the seventeenth precinct, which has ninety-two policemen divided into two shifts of forty-four each and four deputy captains. It was midnight and they were just changing shifts. After the captain called the roll, the policemen marched out in formation, like a military drill. Each man must report the next morning what he has seen and heard at night, and this is written down in a book. I saw several policemen coming in with people under arrest, drunkards who had been making a disturbance or burglars and the like. The captain asked them their names and addresses, and recorded these in another book, and put them in cells. The cells are separate for men and women, each holding several to over a dozen people, and have stone walls and iron bars.

Today they had arrested sixty-eight people, including seven or eight good-looking young girls in gorgeous dress, who were put together in a cell as prisoners and appeared to be wailing together. I was very surprised, and on asking was told they were subject to arrest because they were nude entertainers who dirty people's minds, and that the next morning they would be sent to court. The following day I heard they had all been fined and released.

The court building contains jails, roughly five or six cells each for men, women, and juveniles, for those who have been arrested the day before and are to be sent to court in the morning. The courtroom is about fifty or sixty feet square. There is an elevated platform three feet high, like a [Chinese] heated compartment, with a desk at which three judges sit, each with paper and pen, asking questions and recording the answers. Three or four newspaper reporters sit at a table to the side. The clerk who calls the criminals to enter stands in front of the judges' desk. On the left is a chair for the plaintiff or witnesses. The criminals all stand outside a low railing to the left of the judges' desk. A religious book is placed on the left corner of the desk. The criminal is brought into the court by the policemen and first picks up the book, brushes it against his lips, and then puts it back. This is to swear by the book that he will not tell lies. Below the platform, twenty or thirty people, all lawyers or witnesses sit at five or six long tables with chairs. In the back of the court there may be hundreds of people who are allowed to watch. The judges are elected from among the people. There are dozens of cases every day. After being interrogated people are released, or fined, or released on bail; or if found guilty, they are sent to a government office for deliberation; or if the case is not finished, then they are put back in jail temporarily and interrogated again the next day. This system is the same as the Shanghai Mixed Court. I hear that New York has six such places, each for a certain district, clearly specified.

In Western countries no matter whether the case is big or small, people are allowed to gather and watch the litigation, and newspaper reporters can come and write about it so that everyone may be informed. In this way, how can there be irregularities? If people wanted to use improper means they would not be able to. But is it not making trouble for themselves to handle dozens of cases every day in one place? It must be that they want peace and order. Western nations should think hard about this. And as for swearing by a book, that is nonsense.

QUESTIONS TO CONSIDER

1. In this passage, Li Gui remarks that "China is just the opposite" of America in terms of women. What does he mean by this observation? How did the place of women differ in American and Chinese society during the nineteenth century? Does evidence from other documents in this chapter suggest a different view of women's status in the United States during this era?
2. What aspects of American society does Li Gui find most appealing in comparison to those in China? What does he see as less appealing? What goals does he seem to be advancing toward through this reporting?

CHAPTER 9

GLOBALIZATION AND ITS DISCONTENTS, 1878–1910

9.1 "TAKE UP THE WHITE MAN'S BURDEN." RUDYARD KIPLING, "THE WHITE MAN'S BURDEN," 1899 AND H. T. JOHNSON, "THE BLACK MAN'S BURDEN," 1899

One of the most famous writers in English of the nineteenth and early twentieth centuries, Rudyard Kipling (1865–1936) was born in India and spent much of his life there and in South Africa. In 1907, he became the first English-language writer to win the Nobel Prize for Literature.

Extremely popular in his time, since his death Kipling has become a controversial figure. Some regard him as an insightful narrator of empire and human relations. Others, however, see his depictions of colonial society as paternalistic and even racist. The poem presented here, *"The White Man's Burden,"* celebrates the motives and achievements of empire but warns colonizers not to expect thanks or appreciation.

Kipling's poem received many responses. The one reproduced here was written by H. T. Johnson (dates unknown), an African American pastor and editor of the *Christian Recorder.* *"The Black Man's Burden"* satirizes Kipling's approach to race relations, mocking Kipling's assertions that "The White Man" had helped other races by describing African Americans' experience of racism in the United States. Johnson also challenges Kipling's views of empire, suggesting that American expansionism in Hawai'i and Cuba, for example, represented violent exploitation rather than philanthropy.

EXCERPT 1: "THE WHITE MAN'S BURDEN," RUDYARD KIPLING

Take up the White Man's burden—
Send forth the best ye breed—

Go bind your sons to exile
To serve your captives' need;
To wait in heavy harness
On fluttered folk and wild—

Source: www.kiplingsociety.co.uk/poems_burden.htm; American Memory, Library of Congress, http://nationalhumanitiescenter.org/pds/gilded/empire/text7/johnson.pdf.

133

Your new-caught sullen peoples,
Half devil and half child.

Take up the White Man's burden—
In patience to abide
To veil the threat of terror
And check the show of pride;
By open speech and simple,
An hundred times made plain,
To seek another's profit,
And work another's gain.

Take up the White Man's burden—
The savage wars of peace—
Fill full the mouth of famine
And bid the sickness cease;
And when your goal is nearest
The end for others sought,
Watch Sloth and heathen Folly
Bring all your hopes to nought.

Take up the White Man's burden—
No tawdry rule of kings,
But toil of serf and sweeper—
The tale of common things.
The ports ye shall not enter,
The roads ye shall not tread,
Go make them with your living,
And mark them with your dead!
Take up the White Man's burden—
And reap his old reward,
The blame of those ye better,
The hate of those ye guard -
The cry of hosts ye humour
(Ah slowly!) towards the light:
"Why brought ye us from bondage,
"Our loved Egyptian night?"

Take up the White Man's burden—
Ye dare not stoop to less—
Nor call too loud on Freedom
To cloak your weariness;
By all ye cry or whisper,
By all ye leave or do,
The silent sullen peoples
Shall weigh your Gods and you.

Take up the White Man's burden—
Have done with childish days—
The lightly proffered laurel,
The easy, ungrudged praise.
Comes now, to search your manhood
Through all the thankless years,
Cold-edged with dear-bought wisdom,
The judgement of your peers.

EXCERPT 2: "THE BLACK MAN'S BURDEN," H. T. JOHNSON

Pile on the Black Man's burden,
  'Tis nearest at your door;
Why heed long-bleeding Cuba
  Or dark Hawaii's shore?
Halt Ye your fearless armies
  Which menace feeble folks,
Who fight with clubs and arrows
  And brook your rifle's smoke.

Pile on the Black Man's burden,
  His wail with laughter drown.
You've sealed the Red Man's problem
  And now take up the Brown
In vain ye seek to end it
  With bullets, blood, or death—
Better by far to defend it
  With honor's holy breath

Pile on the Black Man's burden,
  His back is broad though sore;
What though the weight oppress him
  He's borne the like before
Your Jim-Crow laws and customs,
  And fiendish midnight deed.
Though winked at by the nation
  Will some day trouble breed.

Pile on the Black Man's burden,
  At length 'twill Heaven pierce;
Then on you or your children
  Will reign God's judgments fierce.
Your battleships and armies
  May weaker ones appall.
But God Almighty's justice
  They'll not disturb at all.

QUESTIONS TO CONSIDER

1. Why does Kipling consider colonialism to be "a burden" to be carried by "the White Man"?
2. How does the "Black Man's Burden" satirize Kipling's poem?

3. How do you think Kipling might respond to Johnson's criticisms? Do you think he would accept his critiques, or would he defend himself with other evidence? How?
4. Kipling dedicated his poem, written in 1899, to the United States. Why? Does knowing this affect your reading of Johnson's poem?

9.2 "A MATTER OF VITAL IMPORTANCE FOR GERMANY'S DEVELOPMENT." FRIEDRICH FABRI, *DOES GERMANY NEED COLONIES?*, 1879

Friedrich Fabri (1824–1891) was a German Lutheran pastor. From 1857 to 1884, he served as director of the Barmen Rhine Missionary Society. Though Fabri himself never traveled abroad, the Society sent Christian missionaries to Africa and the East Indies. *Does Germany Need Colonies?*, excerpted here, was a long pamphlet, published in 1879, a time of economic crisis shortly after the unification of Germany. The pamphlet was widely read; Fabri (and others) claimed that it had an important influence on popular perceptions and elite actions related to Germany's role in the world. After its publication, Fabri helped to form and direct several organizations to promote the ideas articulated in the pamphlet. He also attempted to leverage his renown to serve political aspirations, running an unsuccessful campaign for the German Parliament.

In the new Reich we have of late got into an economic situation which is oppressive, which is truly alarming. It is poor comfort that the trade crisis, which has continued for so long, is putting a heavy strain on more or less all the civilised States. Relatively—leaving Russia and Austria out of account here—Germany can be said to be in the most unfavourable position. Great though the growth of our prosperity may have been in the last few decades compared with earlier times, yet we are still on the whole poor, and the strength and resilience of our national prosperity are not at all proportionate to the plenitude of political power which we have acquired. This could easily create serious difficulties for the continued healthy development of our great national community. Moreover, the situation is all the more fragile because, just when, in the aftermath of the financial boom, we thought ourselves to be very rich, we were suddenly and sharply reminded of our poverty. . . .

But it is also a patriotic duty to give careful consideration to all possibilities of a wider and more secure development of our national work and thus of our national prosperity. And among these tasks we assign very great importance to the question, "Does the German Reich need colonial possessions?" . . .

For it was in large part the all-prevailing influence of the free trade doctrine which up till now prevented us in Germany from giving any serious consideration to the colonial question. Here too we took at their word those English voices which assured us that, in the rosy dawn-light of general freedom of trade, we would, happily, no longer have to

Source: *Bedarf Deutschland der Colonien? Does Germany Need Colonies?*, trans., eds., and introductions by E. C. M. Bruening and M. E. Chamberlain (Lewiston, NY: Edwin Mellen Press, 1998), 47–53, 79–83, 87–99, 179–181.

cumber ourselves with the ballast of colonial possessions. As if Germany's position were not, in this respect too, widely different from that of Britain. With an industry which has, slowly but steadily, developed and grown powerful, with a quite incomparably higher level of national prosperity, with vast colonial possessions extending across all the zones and commercially entirely controlled by the mother country, with the opportunities afforded Britain by these circumstances of always appropriately evening out the economic consequences of her population increase, there could indeed, for Britain, be nothing more favourable or more right than to see all the remaining opportunities in the world opened up to the predominance of her commerce by means of the victorious assertion of the free trade doctrine. True, it might for some little while have begun to seem suspicious to unprejudiced minds that Britain herself not only did not discard her colonial possessions, but rather, advancing ceaselessly year by year, further enlarged them. . . .

There exist today two fundamental forms of colonial possession, which are categorised as *agrarian colonies* and *trading colonies*. . . .

Agrarian colonies are only possible in temperate zones, and these—apart from special conditions such as high altitudes or favourably structured coastlands—are on the whole confined to the nontropical regions. To put it another way, one could say that where climatic fevers prevail a natural limit is set upon the activities of the European farmer and cattle-breeder. . . .

Various conclusions which are significant from the point of view of cultural history may be drawn from this brief analysis of the essential nature and the development of agrarian colonies. First, that we have here a form of colonisation which is entirely peculiar to modern times. Second, that only a mother country which is able to produce a continuous supply of superfluous labour is qualified to found agrarian colonies; and that therefore it is today only for the Germanic race to engage in this more modern form of colonial creation. . . .

The basic character of the trading colonies is, as has been shown, governed by their being situated in

the tropics; and the method of their administration and exploitation is the more efficacious the more it is adapted to these natural givens. As in the climatic characteristics, so too in the ethnographic respect, we encounter a sharply defined distinction between trading and agrarian colonies. Whilst the former have but a thinly distributed native population, we find in the latter, the tropical colonies, a massive population of in part black, and in part brown skin colouring. Able to derive the few necessities of life without effort from nature's generous store, the basic character of this population—speaking here, of course, in quite general terms—is more or less lax, carefree and languid. Only in contact with and under the guidance of the European does the aptitude for work of the inhabitant of the tropics likewise gain in staying-power, his attitude became more resolute, his spiritual life grows capable of a higher degree of moral and cultural development. Hence in the tropical lands the rule of the European is indispensable if these lands are to be drawn into the orbit of the modem cultural movement or to be kept within it. Agrarian colonies, settled by white men, can, at a certain stage in their development, very well be left to themselves, when they may turn into mighty states; trading colonies can never be left to themselves, that is to say, to the native population, without at once degenerating. . . .

Just as the European market has long, and to a constantly increasing degree, had need of the tropics and their products, so also the founding of every new trading colony is a contribution to the general progress of civilisation. These colonies, however, require constant European supervision, though this should be animated, not by a violent lust for power, but by intelligent foresight and true humanity. . . .

It is, however, by no means purely commercial gain alone which makes the tropical colonies valuable to the mother country. The strengthening and enlargement of the shipping of the mother country which is bound to occur as a result of rich overseas possessions is also an important factor. . . .

But the possession of rich colonies furnishes yet another, much more far-reaching advantage. The whole of national life in all sections of the population is enhanced, enlivened and enriched by continuous contact with colonial possessions. It is true that trading colonies are never the goal of emigration as such, but nevertheless there does take place a steady, beneficial ebb and flow of certain sections of the population between the mother country and the colonies; primarily from the middle and upper levels of the population. Merchants, officials, military men, technicians, tradespeople, divines and missionaries, teachers and scholars in their thousands move back and forth in a steady stream. The great majority of these people are out to make money, and many of them attain their goal and return home after ten or twenty years of work with their more or less rich gains. Whilst in agrarian colonies this return to the mother country of those who have become rich and prosperous only occurs in exceptional cases, in trading colonies it is the rule. Britain today has hundreds of thousands, Holland tens of thousands of her native sons in her colonies, a floating population which, at intervals averaging some ten to fifteen years, constantly renews itself through in- and outflow. It is clear that this constant circulation, continuing over a long period, indeed over centuries, is bound to prove a most fruitful source of national prosperity. There is no doubt that in proportion to its size and number of inhabitants—Holland today possesses the largest capital reserves in the world. This low-lying land, which in terms of soil is among the poorest spots on earth, which is half sand and heath, and the other half of which, with its fertile marshes, had to be effortfully wrested from the sea and can be defended against that sea year in and year out only by labour and financial sacrifice. The solution to this paradox lies simply and solely in Holland's once so mighty activity at sea, in her trade which today is still important, and in the exploitation of her rich colonies. Similarly, for Britain too, her colonies which furnish the products of all the [climatic] zones are the real source of her capital wealth and of her power. In the days of Queen Elizabeth Germany's prosperity (as also, probably, the density of her population) far outstripped that of Great Britain. In the ensuing two centuries, during which, chiefly in consequence of the Thirty Years' War, Germany lay almost completely crushed, in economic as in political terms, this ratio

was completely reversed. The retrogression here, one could say, was as great as the political and economic progress there. Britain 's seafaring, her acquisition of rich colonies, the resultant growing trade, and finally her industrial development, based, entirely correctly and soundly, on these pre-conditions, are, as is plain to see, the sources of Britain's greatness and power.

No less important than the immediate economic gain, however, is, as has already been indicated, the significance of this interchange between mother country and colony for the general development of a nation. Where in Britain is there a family of any size which does not have many of its closest kin occupying the most various positions in life, somewhere in the British colonies that circle the globe! What a wealth of influences on the spirit of the nation lies in this one fact which has now been operative for centuries! Just as, whilst widening interests, it widens vision, so also a knowledge of the sea and the need to make one's way in all manner of walks of life strengthens the character and gives our Anglo-Saxon cousins that practical insight and that confidence of bearing which differentiate them so markedly from the inhabitants of our continental States. This national characteristic, it is true, rarely manifests itself in an exterior of captivating amiability; but whoever succeeds in penetrating more deeply into its nature and being will usually find, even under an often brusque and forbidding appearance, a great store of competence, reliability and strength. It is clear that the typical characteristics of the seafarer have contributed much to the British national character. It is, however, worthy of note that in Germany it is only in our Hanse towns, in Bremen and Hamburg, with their commercial brains, their spirit of enterprise, their success at sea and their extensive overseas connections, that we also glimpse a pleasing resemblance to the British national character. . . .

When, centuries ago, the German Reich stood at the head of the States of Europe, it was the foremost trading and seagoing power. If the new German Reich wishes to entrench and preserve its regained power for long years to come, then it must regard that power as a cultural mission and must no longer hesitate to resume its colonising vocation also.

QUESTIONS TO CONSIDER

1. How do Fabri's motivations for German expansion fit with your understanding of the "New Imperialism" of the nineteenth century?
2. What insights does Fabri's essay give us into nineteenth-century nationalism? How does Fabri's justification for colonialism fit into his vision of Germany?

9.3 "WHAT A PITY SHE WASN'T BORN A LAD." EMMELINE PANKHURST, *MY OWN STORY*, 1914

Emmeline Pankhurst (1858–1928) was born Emmeline Goulden in Manchester, England. Her parents were politically active, and she worked throughout her youth for progressive political causes. In the 1870s, she helped found the Women's Social and Political Union, a group dedicated to gaining women the vote, through violent tactics if necessary. Pankhurst was controversial—even within her own family: her continued advocacy of violence to win women the vote led many opponents to label her a terrorist. At the start of World War I, she called for a suspension of militant activism and support of the British government against Germany. Women over age 30 gained the right to vote in Britain in 1918.

Later in life, Pankhurst joined the Conservative Party to oppose communism, running for Parliament in the 1920s. The excerpt here is from Pankhurst's memoir, *My Own Story*, published in 1914.

A certain Saturday afternoon stands out in my memory, as on my way home from school I passed the prison where I knew the men had been confined. I saw that a part of the prison wall had been torn away, and in the great gap that remained were evidences of a gallows recently removed. I was transfixed with horror, and over me there swept the sudden conviction that hanging was a mistake—worse, a crime. It was my awakening to one of the most terrible facts of life—that justice and judgment lie often a world apart.

I relate this incident of my formative years to illustrate the fact that the impressions of childhood often have more to do with character and future conduct than heredity or education. I tell it also to show that my development into an advocate of militancy was largely a sympathetic process. I have not personally suffered from the deprivations, the bitterness and sorrow which bring so many men and women to a realization of social injustice. My childhood was protected by love and a comfortable home. Yet, while still a very young child, I began instinctively to feel that there was something lacking, even in my own home, some false conception of family relations, some incomplete ideal.

This vague feeling of mine began to shape itself into conviction about the time my brothers and I were sent to school. The education of the English boy, then as now, was considered a much more serious matter than the education of the English boy's sister. My parents, especially my father, discussed the question of my brothers' education as a matter of real importance. My

Source: Emmeline Pankhurst, *My Own Story* (New York: Hearst International Library, 1914, Kraus Reprints, 1971), 6-14.

education and that of my sister were scarcely discussed at all. Of course we went to a carefully selected girls' school, but beyond the facts that the head mistress was a gentlewoman and that all the pupils were girls of my own class *[The author is referring to socioeconomic class–Ed.]*, nobody seemed concerned. A girl's education at that time seemed to have for its prime object the art of "making home attractive"—presumably to migratory male relatives. It used to puzzle me to understand why I was under such a particular obligation to make home attractive to my brothers. We were on excellent terms of friendship, but it was never suggested to them as a duty that they make home attractive to me. Why not? Nobody seemed to know. The answer to these puzzling questions came to me unexpectedly one night when I lay in my little bed waiting for sleep to overtake me. It was a custom of my father and mother to make the round of our bedrooms every night before going themselves to bed. When they entered my room that night I was still awake, but for some reason I chose to feign slumber. My father bent over me, shielding the candle flame with his big hand. I cannot know exactly what thought was in his mind as he gazed down at me, but I heard him say, somewhat sadly, "What a pity she wasn't born a lad."

My first hot impulse was to sit up in bed and protest that I didn't want to be a boy, but I lay still and heard my parents' footsteps pass on toward the next child's bed. I thought about my father's remark for many days afterward, but I think I never decided that I regretted my sex. However, it was made quite clear that men considered themselves superior to women, and that women apparently acquiesced in that belief.

I found this view of things difficult to reconcile with the fact that both my father and my mother were advocates of equal suffrage. I was very young when the Reform Act of 1866 was passed, but I very well remember the agitation caused by certain circumstances attending it. This Reform Act, known as the Household Franchise Bill, marked the first popular extension of the ballot in England since 1832. Under its terms, householders paying a minimum of ten pounds a year rental were given the Parliamentary vote. While it was still under discussion in the House of Commons, John Stuart Mill moved an amendment to the bill to include women householders as well as men. The amendment

was defeated, but in the act as passed the word "man," instead of the usual "male person," was used. Now, under another act of Parliament it had been decided that the word "man" always included "woman" unless otherwise specifically stated. For example, in certain acts containing rate-paying clauses, the masculine noun and pronoun are used throughout, but the provisions apply to women rate-payers as well as to men. So when the Reform Bill with the word "man" in it became law, many women believed that the right of suffrage had actually been bestowed upon them. A tremendous amount of discussion ensued, and the matter was finally tested by a large number of women seeking to have their names placed upon the register as voters. In my city of Manchester 3,924 women, out of a total of 4,215 possible women voters, claimed their votes, and their claim was defended in the law courts by eminent lawyers, including my future husband, Dr. Pankhurst. Of course the women's claim was settled adversely in the courts, but the agitation resulted in a strengthening of the woman-suffrage agitation all over the country. . . .

I was fourteen years old when I went to my first suffrage meeting. Returning from school one day, I met my mother just setting out for the meeting, and I begged her to let me go along. She consented, and without stopping to lay my books down I scampered away in my mother's wake. The speeches interested and excited me, especially the address of the great Miss Lydia Becker, who was the Susan B. Anthony of the English movement, a splendid character and a truly eloquent speaker. She was the secretary of the Manchester committee, and I had learned to admire her as the editor of the *Women's Suffrage Journal*, which came to my mother every week. I left the meeting a conscious and confirmed suffragist.

I suppose I had always been an unconscious suffragist. With my temperament and my surroundings I could scarcely have been otherwise. The movement was very much alive in the early seventies, nowhere more so than in Manchester, where it was organised by a group of extraordinary men and women. Among them were Mr. and Mrs. Jacob Bright, who were always ready to champion the struggling cause. Mr. Jacob Bright, a brother of John Bright, was for many years member of Parliament for Manchester, and to the day of his death was an active supporter of woman suffrage. Two especially gifted women, besides Miss Becker, were members of the committee. These were Mrs. Alice Cliff Scatcherd and Miss Wolstentholm, now the venerable Mrs. Wolstentholm-Elmy. One of the principal founders of the committee was the man whose wife, in later years, I was destined to become, Dr. Richard Marsden Pankhurst.

When I was fifteen years old I went to Paris, where I was entered as a pupil in one of the pioneer institutions in Europe for the higher education of girls. This school, one of the founders of which was Madame Edmond Adam, who was and is still a distinguished literary figure, was situated in a fine old house in the Avenue de Neuilly. It was under the direction of Mlle. Marchef-Girard, a woman distinguished in education, and who afterward was appointed government inspector of schools in France. Mlle. Marchef-Girard believed that girls' education should be quite as thorough and even more practical than the education boys were receiving at that time. She included chemistry and other sciences in her courses, and in addition to embroidery she had her girls taught bookkeeping. Many other advanced ideas prevailed in this school, and the moral discipline which the pupils received was, to my mind, as valuable as the intellectual training. Mlle. Marchef-Girard held that women should be given the highest ideals of honour. Her pupils were kept to the strictest principles of truth-telling and candour. Myself she understood and greatly benefited by an implicit trust which I am sure I could not have betrayed, even had I felt for her less real affection. . . .

I was between eighteen and nineteen when I finally returned from school in Paris and took my place in my father's home as a finished young lady. I sympathised with and worked for the woman-suffrage movement, and came to know Dr. Pankhurst, whose work for woman suffrage had never ceased.

It was Dr. Pankhurst who drafted the first enfranchisement bill, known as the Women's Disabilities Removal Bill, and introduced into the House of Commons in 1870 by Mr. Jacob Bright. The bill advanced to its second reading by a majority vote of thirty-three, but it was killed in committee by Mr. Gladstone's peremptory orders. Dr. Pankhurst, as I have already said, with another distinguished

barrister, Lord Coleridge, acted as counsel for the Manchester women, who tried in 1868 to be placed on the register as voters. He also drafted the bill giving married women absolute control over their property and earnings, a bill which became law in 1882.

My marriage with Dr. Pankhurst took place in 1879.

I think we cannot be too grateful to the group of men and women who, like Dr. Pankhurst, in those early days lent the weight of their honoured names to the suffrage movement in the trials of its struggling youth. These men did not wait until the movement became popular, nor did they hesitate until it was plain that women were roused to the point of revolt. They worked all their lives with those who were organising, educating, and preparing for the revolt which was one day to come. Unquestionably those pioneer men suffered in popularity for their feminist views. Some of them suffered financially, some politically. Yet they never wavered.

My married life lasted through nineteen happy years. Often I have heard the taunt that suffragists are women who have failed to find any normal outlet for their emotions, and are therefore soured and disappointed beings. This is probably not true of any suffragist, and it is most certainly not true of me. My home life and relations have been as nearly ideal as possible in this imperfect world. About a year after my marriage my daughter Christabel was born, and in another eighteen months my second daughter Sylvia came. Two other children followed, and for some years I was rather deeply immersed in my domestic affairs.

I was never so absorbed with home and children, however, that I lost interest in community affairs. Dr. Pankhurst did not desire that I should turn myself into a household machine. It was his firm belief that society as well as the family stands in need of women's services. So while my children were still in their cradles I was serving on the executive committee of the Women's Suffrage Society, and also on the executive board of the committee which was working to secure the Married Women's Property Act. This act having passed in 1882, I threw myself into the suffrage work with renewed energy. A new Reform Act, known as the County Franchise Bill, extending the suffrage to farm labourers, was under discussion, and we believed that our years of educational propaganda work had prepared the country to support us in a demand for a women's suffrage amendment to the bill. For several years we had been holding the most splendid meetings in cities all over the kingdom. The crowds, the enthusiasm, the generous response to appeals for support, all these seemed to justify us in our belief that women's suffrage was near. In fact, in 1884, when the County Franchise Bill came before the country, we had an actual majority in favour of suffrage in the House of Commons.

But a favourable majority in the House of Commons by no means insures the success of any measure. I shall explain this at length when I come to our work of opposing candidates who have avowed themselves suffragists, a course which has greatly puzzled our American friends. The Liberal party was in power in 1884, and a great memorial was sent to the Prime Minister, the Right Honourable William E. Gladstone, asking that a women's suffrage amendment to the County Franchise Bill be submitted to the free and unbiased consideration of the House. Mr. Gladstone curtly refused, declaring that if a women's suffrage amendment should be carried, the Government would disclaim responsibility for the bill. The amendment was submitted nevertheless, but Mr. Gladstone would not allow it to be freely discussed, and he ordered Liberal members to vote against it. What we call a whip was sent out against it, a note virtually commanding party members to be on hand at a certain hour to vote against the women's amendment. Undismayed, the women tried to have an independent suffrage bill introduced, but Mr. Gladstone so arranged Parliamentary business that the bill never even came up for discussion.

QUESTIONS TO CONSIDER

1. How did questions of class and gender shape Pankhurst's early experiences with politics? What advantages and disadvantages did class and gender cause her in the excerpt reproduced here?
2. Do you see any indications in this excerpt that might lead one to expect Pankhurst's move toward radical, violent activism, and then her later move to join the Conservative Party? How do you reconcile this apparent contradiction?

9.4 "ONE KNOWS THE FUTILITY OF TRYING TO PREVENT THE ONSLAUGHT OF WESTERN CIVILIZATION." FUKUZAWA YUKICHI, *GOODBYE ASIA*, 1885

Fukuzawa Yukichi (1835–1901) was born into a low-ranking samurai family in Japan. After a traditional Confucian education, he went to study European languages at in Nagasaki (site of the Dutch trade mission to Japan) and became fluent in Dutch and later English. His European studies coincided with the expansion of foreign trade with Japan in the 1850s, and he became a prominent intellectual commenting on the state of Japanese foreign relations. He participated in the first Japanese

Source: David Lu, ed., *Japan: A Documentary History* (Armonk, NY: M. E. Sharpe, 1997), 351–353.

diplomatic mission to both the United States, in 1859, and to Europe, in 1862. He was one of the founders of Keio University, now one of Japan's most important universities, as a school of Western Studies.

The following essay, presented in its entirety, appeared as an Editorial in the newspaper *Jiji Shimpo*. It was published anonymously in 1885 and was only attributed to Fukuzawa after his death.

Transportation has become so convenient these days that once the wind of Western civilization blows to the East, every blade of grass and every tree in the East follow what the Western wind brings. Ancient Westerners and present-day Westerners are from the same stock and are not much different from one another. The ancient ones moved slowly, but their contemporary counterparts move vivaciously at a fast pace. This is possible because present-day Westerners take advantage of the means of transportation available to them. For those of us who live in the Orient, unless we want to prevent the coming of Western civilization with a firm resolve, it is best that we cast our lot with them. If one observes carefully what is going on in today's world, one knows the futility of trying to prevent the onslaught of Western civilization. Why not float with them in the same ocean of civilization, sail the same waves, and enjoy the fruits and endeavors of civilization?

The movement of a civilization is like the spread of measles. Measles in Tokyo start in Nagasaki and come eastward with the spring thaw. We may hate the spread of this communicable disease, but is there any effective way of preventing it? I can prove that it is not possible. In a communicable disease, people receive only damages. In a civilization, damages may accompany benefits, but benefits always far outweigh them, and their force cannot be stopped. This being the case, there is no point in trying to prevent their spread. A wise man encourages the spread and allows our people to get used to its ways.

The Opening to the modern Civilization of the West began in the reign of Kaei (1848–58). Our people began to discover its utility and gradually and yet actively moved toward its acceptance. However there was an old-fashioned and bloated government that stood in the way of progress. It was a problem impossible to solve. If the government were allowed to continue, the new civilization could not enter. The modern civilization and Japan's old conventions were mutually exclusive. If we were to discard our old conventions, that government also had to be abolished. We could have prevented the entry of this civilization, but it would have meant loss of our national independence. The struggles taking place in the world civilization were such that they would not allow an Eastern island nation to slumber in isolation. At that point, dedicated men *(shijin)* recognized the principle of "the country is more important than the government," relied on the dignity of the Imperial Household, and toppled the old government to establish a new one. With this, public and the private sectors alike, everyone in our country accepted the modern Western civilization. Not only were we able to cast aside Japan's old conventions, but we also succeeded in creating a new axle toward progress in Asia. Our basic assumptions could be summarized in two words: "Good-bye Asia *(Datsu-a)*."

Japan is located in the eastern extremities of Asia, but the spirit of her people has already moved away from the old conventions of Asia to the Western civilization. Unfortunately for Japan, there are two neighboring countries. One is called China and another Korea. These two peoples, like the Japanese people, have been nurtured by Asiatic political thoughts and mores. It may be that we are different races of people, or it may be due to the differences in our heredity or education; significant differences mark the three peoples. The Chinese and Koreans are more like each other and together they do not show as much similarity to the Japanese. These two peoples do not know how to progress either personally or as a nation. In this day and age with transportation becoming so convenient, they cannot be blind to the manifestations of Western civilization. But they say that what is seen or heard cannot influence the disposition of their minds. Their love affairs with ancient ways and old customs remain as strong as they were centuries ago. In this new and vibrant theater of civilization when we speak of education, they only refer back to Confucianism. As for school education, they can only cite [Chinese philosopher Mencius's] precepts of humanity, righteousness, decorum, and knowledge. While professing their abhorrence to ostentation, in reality they show their ignorance of truth and principles. As for their morality, one only has to observe their unspeakable acts of cruelty and shamelessness. Yet they remain arrogant and show no sign of self-examination.

In my view, these two countries cannot survive as independent nations with the onslaught of Western civilization to the East. Their concerned citizens might yet find a way to engage in a massive reform, on the scale of our Meiji Restoration, and they could change their governments and bring about a renewal of spirit among their peoples. If that could happen they would indeed be fortunate. However, it is more likely that would never happen, and within a few short years they will be wiped out from the world with their lands divided among the civilized nations. Why is this so? Simply at a time when the spread of civilization and enlightenment *(bummei kaika)* has a force akin to that of measles, China and Korea violate the natural law of its spread. They forcibly try to avoid it by shutting off air from their rooms. Without air, they suffocate to death. It is said that neighbors must extend helping hands to one another because their relations are inseparable. Today's China and Korea have not done a thing for Japan. From the perspectives of civilized Westerners, they may see what is happening in China and Korea and judge Japan accordingly, because of the three countries' geographical proximity. The governments of China and Korea still retain their autocratic manners and do not abide by the rule of law. Westerners may consider Japan likewise a lawless society. Natives of China and Korea are deep in their hocus pocus of nonscientific behavior. Western scholars may think that Japan still remains a country dedicated to the *yin* and *yang* and five elements. Chinese are mean-spirited and shameless, and the chivalry of the Japanese people is lost to the Westerners. Koreans punish their convicts in an atrocious manner, and that is imputed to the Japanese as heartless people. There are many more examples I can cite. It is not different from the case of a righteous man living in a neighborhood of a town known for foolishness, lawlessness, atrocity, and heartlessness. His action is so rare that it is always buried under the ugliness of his neighbors' activities. When these incidents are multiplied, that can affect our normal conduct of diplomatic affairs. How unfortunate it is for Japan.

What must we do today? We do not have time to wait for the enlightenment of our neighbors so that we can work together toward the development of Asia. It is better for us to leave the ranks of Asian nations and cast our lot with civilized nations of the West. As for the way of dealing with China and Korea, no special treatment is necessary just because they happen to be our neighbors. We simply follow the manner of the Westerners in knowing how to treat them. Any person who cherishes a bad friend cannot escape his bad notoriety. We simply erase from our minds our bad friends in Asia.

QUESTIONS TO CONSIDER

1. Fukuzawa Yukichi compares Western civilization to "measles." Having read the entire essay, do you think this is an appropriate metaphor? Why do you think Fukuzawa chose this comparison? What considerations are motivating his attitude toward both the West and Japan's neighbors in Asia?

2. Two important issues confronting many countries, including Japan, at this time were modernization and Westernization. What does this essay suggest about Fukuzawa Yukichi's attitude toward these questions? Do modernization and Westernization appear to be distinct in his mind? If so, what differences exist between them?

9.5 "CIVILISATION IS NOT AN INCURABLE DISEASE, BUT IT SHOULD NEVER BE FORGOTTEN THAT THE ENGLISH PEOPLE ARE AT PRESENT AFFLICTED BY IT." MOHANDAS K. GANDHI, "CIVILISATION" FROM *HIND SWARAJ*, 1909

Mohandas Gandhi (1869–1948) was born in India, educated in Britain, and worked as a lawyer in South Africa before returning to India. He rose to prominence for his campaign against British rule in India, particularly for his insistence on nonviolence. Soon after achieving independence for India, he was assassinated by a Hindu extremist, in 1948.

This excerpt from his 1909 book *Hind Swaraj ("Indian Home-rule")* addresses the concept of "civilization," which some advocates of empire promoted as justifying Britain's colonial rule. Gandhi takes an unusual approach: rather than rejecting claims that India was "uncivilized," he attacks the very concept of "civilization" as antihuman and harmful. The book is conducted in a question–answer format, with Gandhi ("editor") providing answers to questions posed by a "reader."

CHAPTER VI: CIVILISATION

READER: Now you will have to explain what you mean by civilisation.

EDITOR: It is not a question of what I mean. Several English writers refuse to call that civilisation which passes under that name. Many books have been written upon that subject. Societies have been formed to cure the nation of the evils of civilisation. A great English writer has written a work called "Civilization: Its Cause and Cure." Therein he has called it a disease *[The author is Edward Carpenter and the work was published in 1889–Ed.]*.

READER: Why do we not know this generally?

EDITOR: The answer is very simple. We rarely find people arguing against themselves. Those who are intoxicated by modern civilisation are not likely to write against it. Their care will be to find out facts and arguments in support of it, and this they do unconsciously, believing it to be true. A man, whilst he is dreaming, believes in his dream; he is undeceived only when he is awakened from his sleep. A man labouring under the bane of civilisation is like a dreaming man. What we usually read are the works of defenders of modern civilisation, which undoubtedly claims among its votaries very brilliant and even some very good men. Their writings hypnotise us. And so, one by one, we are drawn into the vortex.

READER: This seems to be very plausible. Now will you tell me something of what you have read and thought of this civilisation?

EDITOR: Let us first consider what state of things is described by the word "civilisation." *[Gandhi uses the term "civilisation" in this text to refer to the way of life that has emerged in the West since the industrial revolution–Ed].* Its true test lies in the

Source: Mohandas K. Gandhi, *Hind Swaraj and Other Writings* (Cambridge, UK: Cambridge University Press, 2007), 34–38.

fact that people living in it make bodily welfare the object of life. We will take some examples. The people of Europe today live in better built houses than they did a hundred years ago. This is considered an emblem of civilisation, and this is also a matter to promote bodily happiness. Formerly, they wore skins and used as their weapons spears. Now, they wear long trousers, and, for embellishing their bodies they wear a variety of clothing, and, instead of spears, they carry with them revolvers containing five or more chambers. If people of a certain country, who have hitherto not been in the habit of wearing much clothing, boots, etc., adopt European clothing, they are supposed to have become civilised out of savagery. Formerly, in Europe, people ploughed their lands mainly by manual labour. Now, one man can plough a vast tract by means of steam-engines, and can thus amass great wealth. This is called a sign of civilisation. Formerly, the fewest men wrote books that were most valuable. Now, anybody writes and prints anything he likes and poisons people's mind. Formerly, men travelled in wagons; now they fly through the air in trains at the rate of four hundred and more miles per day. This is considered the height of civilisation. It has been stated that, as men progress, they shall be able to travel in airships and reach any part of the world in a few hours. Men will not need the use of their hands and feet. They will press a button and they will have their clothing by their side. They will press another button and they will have their newspaper. A third, and a motorcar will be in waiting for them. They will have a variety of delicately dished-up food. Everything will be done by machinery. Formerly, when people wanted to fight with one another, they measured between them their bodily strength; now it is possible to take away thousands of lives by one man working behind a gun from a hill. This is civilisation. Formerly, men worked in the open air only so much as they liked. Now, thousands of workmen meet together and for the sake of maintenance work in factories or mines. Their condition is worse than that of beasts. They are obliged to work, at the risk of their lives, at most dangerous occupations, for the sake of millionaires. Formerly, men were made slaves under physical compulsion; now they are enslaved by temptation of money and of the luxuries that money can buy. There are now diseases of which people never dreamt before, and an army of doctors is engaged in finding out their cures, and so hospitals have increased. This is a test of civilisation. Formerly, special messengers were required and much expense was incurred in order to send letters; today, anyone can abuse his fellow by means of a letter for one penny. True, at the same cost, one can send one's thanks also. Formerly, people had two or three meals consisting of homemade bread and vegetables; now, they require something to eat every two hours, so that they have hardly leisure for anything else. What more need I say? All this you can ascertain from several authoritative books. These are all true tests of civilisation. And, if anyone speaks to the contrary, know that he is ignorant. This civilisation takes note neither of morality nor of religion. Its votaries calmly state that their business is not to teach religion. Some even consider it to be a superstitious growth. Others put on the cloak of religion, and prate about morality. But, after twenty years' experience, I have come to the conclusion that immorality is often taught in the name of morality. Even a child can understand that in all I have described above there can be no inducement to morality. Civilisation seeks to increase bodily comforts, and it fails miserably even in doing so.

This civilisation is irreligion, and it has taken such a hold on the people in Europe that those who are in it appear to be half mad. They lack real physical strength or courage. They keep up their energy by intoxication. They can hardly be happy in solitude. Women, who should be the queens of households, wander in the streets, or they slave away in factories. For the sake of a pittance, half a million women in England alone are labouring under trying circumstances in factories or similar institutions. This awful fact is one of the causes of the daily growing suffragette movement *[The struggle for women's right to vote–Ed.].*

This civilisation is such that one has only to be patient and it will be self-destroyed. According to the teaching of Mahomed this would be considered a Satanic civilisation. Hinduism calls it the Black Age *[the worst segment in the Hindu cycle of time–Ed.]*. I cannot give you an adequate conception of it. It is eating into the vitals of the English nation. It must be shunned. Parliaments are really emblems of slavery. If you will sufficiently think over this, you will entertain the same opinion, and cease to blame the English. They rather deserve our sympathy. They are a shrewd nation and I, therefore, believe that they will cast off the evil. They are enterprising and industrious, and their mode of thought is not inherently immoral. Neither are they bad at heart. I, therefore, respect them. Civilisation is not an incurable disease, but it should never be forgotten that the English people are at present afflicted by it.

QUESTIONS TO CONSIDER

1. Why does Gandhi reject the concept of "civilization" as a path forward? What harm does he believe comes from being "civilized"?
2. How might Gandhi and Kipling ("The White Man's Burden," Source 9.1) discuss the role of Britain in India?
3. Colonialism in the nineteenth century included widespread promotion of the values of the Enlightenment? Does Gandhi embrace these values? Why or why not? What reasons might he have for rejecting them?

9.6 "THEY THOUGHT IT BETTER FOR A MAN TO DIE RATHER THAN LIVE IN SUCH TORMENT." ORAL HISTORIES ON THE OUTBREAK OF THE MAJI MAJI UPRISING OF 1905-1907, 1967

Germany was a latecomer to colonialism, but it spread its empire rapidly across Africa toward the end of the nineteenth century. In Tanganyika—the German colony in East Africa—German colonizers forced or encouraged the production of cash crops, reducing food production and leaving the colonies increasingly vulnerable to the vagaries of a global commodities market.

One response to German colonization was the Maji-Maji Rebellion, which lasted from 1905 to 1907. Neither the origins, aims, nor casualties of the war are well understood. It seems to have originated with a spirit medium named Kinjikitile Ngwale and claimed about 300,000 casualties, most of whom perished in a famine that followed the war itself and the German "scorched earth" response.

The documents reproduced here are from oral history interviews conducted by Tanzanian historians in the late 1960s. The interviews quoted here focus on the causes and beginning of the uprising, in 1905. The terms *jumbe* and *akida* used in the interviews are both titles for different local African officials.

Source: Historical Association of Tanzania Paper No. 4; G. C. K. Gwassa and John Iliffe, eds., *Records of the Maji Maji Rising, Part One* (Dar es Salaam, Tanzania: East African Publishing House, 1967), 3–5, 12–13, 19–20.

MZEE AMBROSE NGOMBALE MWIRU OF KIPATIMU, INTERVIEWED 26 SEPTEMBER 1967.

Then when that European arrived he asked, "Why did you not answer the call by drum to pay tax?" And they said, "We do not owe you anything. We have no debt to you. If you as a stranger want to stay in this country, then you will have to ask us. Then we will ask of you an offering to propitiate the gods. You will offer something and we will propitiate the gods on your behalf; we will give you land and you will get a place to stay in. But it is not for us as hosts to give you the offering. That is quite impossible."

MZEE NDUNDULE MANGAYA OF KIPATIMU, INTERVIEWED 2–10 SEPTEMBER 1967

The cultivation of cotton was done by turns. Every village was allotted days on which to cultivate at Samanga Ndumbo and at the jumbe's plantation. One person came from each homestead, unless there were very many people. Thus you might be told to work for five or ten days at Samanga. So a person would go. Then after half the number of days another man came from home to relieve him. If the new man did not feel pity for him, the same person would stay on until he finished. It was also like this at the jumbe's. If you returned from Samanga then your turn at the jumbe's remained, or if you began at the jumbe's you waited for the turn at Samanga after you had finished. No woman went unless her husband ran away; then they would say she had hidden him. Then the woman would go. When in a village a former clan head [Mpindo] was seized to go to cultivate, he would offer his slave in his stead. Then after arriving there you all suffered very greatly. Your back and your buttocks were whipped, and there was no rising up once you stooped to dig. The good thing about the Germans was that all people were the same before the whip; if a jumbe or akida made a mistake he received the whip as well. Thus there were people whose job was to clear the land of trees and undergrowth; others tilled the land; others would smooth the field and plant; another group would do the weeding and yet another the picking; and lastly others carried the bales of cotton to the coast beyond

Kikanda for shipping. Thus we did not know where it was taken. Then if that European gave out some *bakshishi [payment–Ed.]* to the akida or jumbe they kept it. We did not get anything. In addition, people suffered much from the cotton, which took three months [to ripen] and was picked in the fourth. Now digging and planting were in the months of Ntandatu and Nchimbi, and this was the time of very many wild pigs in this country. If you left the chasing of the pigs to the woman she could not manage well at night. In addition, they [the pigs] are very stubborn at that period and will not move even if you go within very close range. Only very few women can assist their husbands at night and these are the ones with very strong hearts. There were just as many birds, and if you did not have children it was necessary to help your wife drive away the birds, while at the same time you cleared a piece of land for the second maize crop, because your wife would not have time. And during this very period they still wanted you to leave your home and go to Samanga or to work on the jumbe's plantation. This was why people became furious and angry. The work was astonishingly hard and full of grave suffering, but its wages were the whip on one's back and buttocks. And yet he *[the German–Ed.]* still wanted us to pay him tax. Were we not human beings? And *[Matumbi, an ethnic and linguistic group of this region–Ed.]*, especially the Wawolo *[highlanders–Ed.]*, since the days of old, did not want to be troubled or ruled by any person. They were really fierce, ah! Given such grave suffering they thought it better for a man to die rather than live in such torment.

Thus they hated the rule which was too cruel. It was not because of agriculture, not at all. If it had been good agriculture which had meaning and profit, who would have given himself up to die? Earlier they had made troubles as well, but when he began to cause us to cultivate cotton for him and to dig roads and so on, then people said, "This has now become an absolute ruler. Destroy him." . . . .

MZEE NGAPATA MKUPALI OF MIPOTO CHUMO, INTERVIEWED 21 SEPTEMBER 1967

[Kinjikitele, the leader of the Maji Maji movement–Ed.] told them, "The Germans will leave. War will start from

up-country towards the coast and from the coast into the hinterland. There will definitely be war. But for the time being go and work for him. If he orders you to cultivate cotton or to dig his road or to carry his load, do as he requires. Go and remain quiet. When I am ready I will declare the war." Those elders returned home and kept quiet. They waited for a long time. Then the elders wondered. "This mganga [traditional healer with prophetic powers–Ed.] said he would declare war against the Germans. Why then is he delaying? When will the Europeans go? After all, we have already received the medicine and we are brave men. Why should we wait?" Then the Africans asked themselves, "How do we start the war? How do we make the Germans angry? Let us go and uproot their cotton so that war may rise."

MZEE KIBILANGE UPUNDA OF NANDETE, INTERVIEWED 6–22 SEPTEMBER 1967

Only a few shoots of cotton were affected, not the whole field.... Ngulumbalyo Mandai and Lindimyo Machela uprooted the first two shoots. Then Jumbe Mtemangani [of Nandete] sent a letter to Kibata through his wife Namchan jama Niponde. She was to report to the akida. People of Nandete had refused to be sent by Mtemangani to Kibata. The people had returned home to prepare for war. We waited for the akida or his spies to come to Nandete. Then we were ready. War broke out.

BW. ALI ABDALLAH KAPUNGU OF KIBATA, INTERVIEWED 23 AUGUST 1967

They heard that cotton had been uprooted in Wolo [Nandete]. The Arab [Germans appointed Arabs to oversee many of their plantations in East Africa–Ed.] at Kibata told Jumbe Kapungu to send his wife to investigate the reports of cotton uprooting. Jumbe Kapungu refused, saying, "If you have heard they have uprooted cotton you must realise that this is the beginning of war. So how can I send a woman to make enquiries?"... So my grandfather [Kapungu] and my father left for Wolo accompanied by others. They went up to Mundi at Kulita's. On seeing Kapungu, Kulita told him to hide himself, for if the Matumbi heard he was there they would slaughter him. At six in the evening the Matumbi called on Kulita and

said, "We have heard that the red earth is here. Is this true?" Kulita denied it, saying, "I cannot support the red earth." At the first cock Kulita escorted Kapungu and his men back to Kibata. But the Matumbi had caught wind that agents of the akida had come. So from Kipepele Hill onwards Kapungu was hotly pursued by the Matumbi. Near Mwando Hill Kapungu declared, "I cannot go on running like a woman. Here we will face them." They fought for two hour s until two in the afternoon. Kapungu's slave Manyanya fell dead. Kapungu and his friends ran back into Kibata.

MZEE NDUNDULE MANGAYA OF KIPATIMU, INTERVIEWED 7 AUGUST 1967

There at Kibata they began to fight. They fought for a whole week. Then the Arab ran out of ammunition. His village was surrounded by warriors. Then those jumbes who had gone to rescue him arranged for his escape to Miteja and thence to Kilwa. Then they plundered the shops and all property. But Kinjikitile had told them not to plunder. That was their mistake.

BW. ALI ABDALLAH KAPUNGU OF KIBATA, INTERVIEWED 23 AUGUST 1967

Bwana Undole heard of the approaching war of Maji Maji while he was staying at Kumwembe village.... The war had already reached Mngeta, which was near Merera [Undole's capital–Ed.]. When the news was announced, Undole sent one of the elders to Mngeta to investigate. On arrival, the envoy luckily met the people who had brought the maji medicine. The natives of Mngeta had already taken the maji and wore small pieces of reed on their heads. They advised the visitor to take the maji as well. But the visitor wanted first to know what was the meaning of drinking the maji. They told him, "We drink this maji medicine so that European and local wars will not harm us. If by bad luck war comes, bullets and spears will not harm us. Bullets and spears will not penetrate our skins." And they told him many more things in order to attract him. The man liked their news and wished to get the medicine. They told him, "If you want the medicine you must pay two cents." He paid the cents to those with the medicine, for that was what it cost. After he had drunk the medicine, they tied small pieces of reed around his head and made him wear one cent and told him he could return home. "That is the sign of comradeship. When you reach home tell all the people that they must dress like you. Those who will not dress like this will be taken for Swahili and will be killed." He bade his hosts farewell and returned to Merera.

When he arrived home he explained to his master all that he had seen. . . . Further, he told him how the maji comrades had promised to visit his country. After Undole had been told the news, the following morning he called a meeting of all elders and courtiers and explained to them the conditions regarding the maji. When the heads of the country arrived he harangued them, saying, "I do not want to hear that in my country there are

people who drink the maji. Further, I do not like to invite the maji carriers into my country." Maji Maji is a sham medicine brought by the Ngindo from Mponda's and if you agree to drink the maji do not complain to me later, for neither I nor my children will agree to take this maji. Europeans do not want this nonsense.". . .

After they had finished their business in Mngeta, the waganga of the maji proceeded to Mzee Masalika at Mkaja. There they cheated people, including Masalika who was made to drink the maji of immortality [maji ya uzima]. His people also took the maji, although Undole had tried very hard to prevent that. The waganga then left for Makuwa's at Lugoda. . . . He drank the maji as well.

QUESTIONS TO CONSIDER

1. Slavery had been abolished around the world during the nineteenth century. How do the conditions described in these interviews differ from those encountered by enslaved laborers? What do these differences, or their absence, suggest about colonialism and industrial capitalism in the early twentieth century?

2. Oral history is an important and rapidly growing field that presents challenges and opportunities for historians. What aspects of these interviews make them challenging as primary sources? Do you find them more or less reliable than other kinds of sources collected in this reader? Why?

9.7 "DO NOT TELL THE WHITE PEOPLE ABOUT THIS." *WOVOKA AND THE GHOST DANCE,* 1890

In 1890, a Paiute religious leader from Nevada named Wovoka (ca. 1856–1932), also known as Jack Wilson, reported a prophetic vision in which indigenous peoples in North America would again prosper, free of white domination, disease, and misery. To fulfill the prophecy, Wovoka asserted that indigenous peoples would have to follow certain rules and perform a sacred ritual known as the Ghost Dance. The message and movement quickly gained adherents. Fear of Ghost Dance gatherings, and efforts to dispel adherents, resulted in the massacre by US troops of 146 Sioux men, women, and children, including the Sioux leader Sitting Bull, at Wounded Knee, South Dakota, on December 29, 1890.

Source: James Mooney, "The Ghost-Dance Religion and the Sioux Outbreak of 1890," *14th Annual Report of the Bureau of American Ethnology, Part 2* (1896), 780–781, 916–917.

Born in New York, Z. A. Parker was a teacher at the Pine Ridge Reservation day school when she collected the description of the Ghost Dance excerpted here. James Mooney (1861–1921) worked for many decades at the Smithsonian Institution's Bureau of American Ethnology. He became the most well-informed nonindigenous expert on the Ghost Dance in the United States. Completing his field work, he met Wokova and gathered additional materials that allowed him to place the Ghost Dance movement in a comparative religions framework. Mooney was outraged by the Wounded Knee massacre.

We drove to this spot about 10.30 o'clock on a delightful October day. We came upon tents scattered here and there in low, sheltered places long before reaching the dance ground. Presently we saw over three hundred tents placed in a circle, with a large pine tree in the center, which was covered with strips of cloth of various colors, eagle feathers, stuffed birds, claws, and horns—all offerings to the Great Spirit. The ceremonies had just begun. In the center, around the tree, were gathered their medicine-men; also those who had been so fortunate as to have had visions and in them had seen and talked with friends who had died. A company of fifteen had started a chant and were marching abreast, others coming in behind as they marched. After marching around the circle of tents they turned to the center, where many had gathered and were seated on the ground.

I think they wore the ghost shirt or ghost dress for the first time that day. I noticed that these were all new and were worn by about seventy men and forty women. . . . They were of white cotton cloth. The women's dress was cut like their ordinary dress, a loose robe with wide, flowing sleeves, painted blue in the neck, in the shape of a three-cornered handkerchief, with moon, stars, birds, etc., interspersed with real feathers, painted on the waists, letting them fall to within 3 inches of the ground, the fringe at the bottom. In the hair, near the crown, a feather was tied. I noticed an absence of any manner of head ornaments, and, as I knew their vanity and fondness for them, wondered why it was. Upon making inquiries I found they discarded everything they could which was made by white men.

The ghost shirt for the men was made of the same material—shirts and leggings painted in red. Some of the leggings were painted in stripes running up and down, others running around. The shirt was painted blue around the neck, and the whole garment was fantastically sprinkled with figures of birds, bows and arrows, sun, moon, and stars, and everything they saw in nature. Down the outside of the sleeve were rows of feathers tied by the quill ends and left to fly in the breeze, and also a row around the neck and up and down the outside of the leggings. I noticed that a number had stuffed birds, squirrel heads, etc., tied in their long hair. The faces of all were painted red with a black half-moon on the forehead or on one cheek.

As the crowd gathered about the tree the high priest, or master of ceremonies, began his address, giving them directions as to the chant and other matters. After he had spoken for about fifteen minutes they arose and formed in a circle. As nearly as I could count, there were between three and four hundred persons. One stood directly behind another, each with his hands on his neighbor's shoulders. After walking about a few times, chanting, "Father, I come," they stopped marching, but remained in the circle, and set up the most fearful, heart-piercing wails I ever heard—crying, moaning, groaning, and shrieking out their grief, and naming over their departed friends and relatives, at the same time taking up handfuls of dust at their feet, washing their hands in it, and throwing it over their heads. Finally, they raised their eyes to heaven, their hands clasped high above their heads, and stood straight and perfectly still, invoking the power of the Great Spirit to allow them to see and talk with their people who had died. This ceremony lasted about fifteen minutes, when they all sat down where they were and listened to another address, which I did not understand, but which I afterwards learned were words of encouragement and assurance of the coming messiah.

They kept up dancing until fully 100 persons were lying unconscious. Then they stopped and seated themselves in a circle, and as each recovered from his trance he was brought to the center of the ring to relate his experience. . . .

WOVOKA'S MESSAGE

When you get home you must make a dance to continue five days. Dance four successive nights, and the last night keep up the dance until the morning of the fifth day, when all must bathe in the river and then disperse to their homes. You must all do in the same way.

I, Jack Wilson, love you all, and my heart is full of gladness for the gifts you have brought me. When you get home I shall give you a good cloud [rain?] which will make you feel good. I give you a good spirit and give you all good paint. I want you to come again in three months, some from each tribe there [the Indian Territory].

There will be a good deal of snow this year and some rain. In the fall there will be such a rain as I have never given you before.

Grandfather [a universal title of reverence among Indians and here meaning the messiah] says, when your friends die you must not cry. You must not hurt anybody or do harm to anyone. You must not fight. Do right always. It will give you satisfaction in life. This young man has a good father and mother. [Possibly this refers to Casper Edson, the young Arapaho who wrote down this message of Wovoka for the delegation.]

Do not tell the white people about this. Jesus is now upon the earth. He appears like a cloud. The dead are still alive again. I do not know when they will be here; maybe this fall or in the spring. When the time comes there will be no more sickness and everyone will be young again.

Do not refuse to work for the whites and do not make any trouble with them until you leave them. When the earth shakes [at the coming of the new world] do not be afraid. It will not hurt you.

I want you to dance every six weeks. Make a feast at the dance and have food that everybody may eat. Then bathe in the water. That is all. You will receive good words again from me some time. Do not tell lies.

QUESTIONS TO CONSIDER

1. Based on the descriptions of the ritual and the letter of Wovoka, what is the Ghost Dance religion asking indigenous peoples to do? Why do you think the movement gained popularity in the late nineteenth century?
2. Why do you think some people at the same time saw this movement as dangerous or disruptive?

CHAPTER 10

TOTAL WAR AND MASS SOCIETY, 1905–1928

10.1 "THINGS WILL NEVER BE AS THEY WERE." *CORRESPONDENCE OF VERA BRITTAIN, 1915 AND 1918*

Vera Brittain (1893–1970) was born in England in 1893. She began her studies at Oxford University in 1914 but left school to serve as a nurse with the Voluntary Aid Detachment (VAD) during World War I. She served with the VAD in France, Malta, and London. Brittain became one of the most important and well-known memoirists of twentieth-century England. *Testament of Youth* (1933) recounts her life as a child and young woman through 1925, including the World War I years. *Testament of Friendship* (1940) and *Testament of Experience* (1957) reflect on her later experiences.

Rather than extracting sections of the published memoirs, in the following we provide excerpts from Brittain's correspondence with two people during the war itself. You will find several passages from letters between Brittain and her fiancé, Roland Leighton (1895–1915), whom Brittain had met through her brother Edward (1895–1918). Leighton was shot by a sniper near Ypres, Belgium, in December 1915 and died from his wounds. Edward Brittain also died from a gunshot on the battlefield, in June 1918. We have also provided here excerpts from letters that Brittain wrote to her mother, Edith Bervon Brittain (1868–1948).

VERA TO ROLAND, BUXTON, APRIL 17, 1915

Nothing in the papers, not the most vivid & heart-rending descriptions, have made me realise war like your letters. Yet sometimes I feel that what I am reading is all a thrilling & terrible dream & that I shall wake & find things as they were. That cannot be; things will never be as they were, but if Heaven is kind perhaps one day I shall wake & find you with me again. Sometimes even your existence seems a dream too, and I have to look at your letters & the things you have given me to make myself feel it is real. . . .

Source: Alan Bishop and Mark Bostridge, eds., *Letters from a Lost Generation: First World War Letters of Vera Brittain and Four Friends* (Boston: Northeastern University Press, 1998), 83–84, 93–95, 97, 368–369, 377–378.

The presence of danger seems to make your gift shine out but the more brilliantly. You did not need to tell me you had not been afraid—your letter told me that very plainly, I think you will always be more afraid of fear than of the actual present dangers which terrify many people who were quite unmoved before they came to them. I can realise too how thin grows the barrier between life & death in those trenches out there. When I read about the ever-present dangers from snipers & bullets & German trenches 80 yards away, as well as the possibility of actual engagements, it seems hard to believe that anyone can escape. If ever you are tempted to hold your life too cheaply don't forget that you have left behind one or two people who do not, but who may hold theirs so if you fling yours away. How can you say: "Don't worry on my account?" You don't really want me not to & I don't believe I want not to either; after all, any number of weary apprehensive nights & days is not too high a price to pay for the happenings that have led to my being able to feel the anxiety I do. . . .

Kingsley's idea that "Men must work & women must weep," however untrue it ought to be, seems in one sense fairly correct just at present *[This is a line from the 1851 poem "Three Fishers," by Charles Kingsley (1819–1875)–Ed.].* I certainly try to do as much as possible of the former, & very rarely have an inclination towards the latter—but I do feel like it a little when you tell me you have been kissing my photograph. I envy the photograph; it is more fortunate than its original. She never seems quite to have got past your reserve or been able to know you properly. I suppose it is the nearness of death which breaks down the reserves & conventions which in the midst of elemental things are seen to matter so little after all. I never thought I should ever say to anyone the sort of things I write to you. At ordinary times one little knows how deeply one can be moved.

ROLAND TO VERA, FLANDERS, APRIL 29, 1915

Have just come back from my rounds. A French biplane went up a few minutes ago and is circling round and round over the German lines. They have got two anti-aircraft guns and a Maxim trying to hit him. It is a marvelous sight. Every minute there is a muffled report like the pop of a drawn cork magnified, and a fluffy ball of cotton wool appears suddenly in the air beside him. He is turning again now, the white balls floating all around him. You think how pretty it all is—white bird, white puffs of smoke, and the brilliant blue of the sky. It is hard to realise that there is danger up there, and daring, and the calculating courage that is true heroism.

He is out of range now. . . .

I am taking care of myself as much as I can, and don't put my head over the parapet. Only yesterday a man in the regiment we relieved was shot through the head through doing that. He died while being carried out. An officer who saw it happen gave me some gruesome details which I will not repeat. All I myself saw were the splashes of blood all the way along the plank flooring of the trench down which they carried him. It was his own fault, though, poor devil.

ROLAND TO VERA, FLANDERS MAY 13, 1915

Yesterday we got rushed off suddenly to occupy a line of support trenches, and had to stay in them till 3:30 a.m. this morning. We are to hold them again this evening, I believe; which, with nothing more inspiring to do than sit still in the rain for the most part of the night, does not sound inviting. Still, at the worst it is good practice, and you can listen to the undulating roar of a distant artillery bombardment from the direction of Ypres not with equanimity but with a certain tremulous gratitude that it is no nearer. Someone is getting hell, but it isn't you–yet.

This morning I took a digging party of 50 men about 2 miles the other side of our wood (we are not actually in it any longer, but we keep in the neighbourhood). They had to deepen a support trench on the slope of a hill behind our line. We were out of range of rifle fire but all the buildings near had suffered badly from the shells. It was a glorious morning and from where we were on the hill we could see the country for miles around. It looked rather like the clear cut landscape in a child's painting book. The basis was deep green with an occasional flame-coloured patch in the valley where a red-roofed farm house had escaped the guns. Just below the horizon and again immediately at our feet was a brilliant yellow mustard field. I left the men digging and went to look at some of the houses near. All the windows were without glass and the rooms a mass of debris—bricks, tiles, plaster, rafters, a picture or two, and even clothing buried among the rest. There were shell holes through most of the walls and often no walls at all. One large chateau had been left with only the outside walls standing at all. I enclose a rather pathetic souvenir that I found among the rubbish in the ruins of one of the rooms—some pages from a child's exercise book. Soon after I came back to the trench a German howitzer battery that had caught sight of us sent over 38 3.511 shells, which fortuitously hit nearby, though they were all within thirty or forty yards of us. Luckily you can always hear this sort coming and we had time to crouch down in the bottom of the trench, which is the safest place in these circumstances. When the shell hits the ground, it makes a circular depression like a pudding basin about a yard and a half across by 18 inches deep, burying itself deep down at the bottom. The explosion blows a cloud of earth and splinters of shell into the air, so that when they fire a salvo (all four guns together) the effect is rather terrifying, and you wonder if the next one will come a yard or two nearer and burst right in the trench on top of you. I do not mind rifle fire so much, but to be under heavy shell fire is a most nerve-racking job.

IN THE TRENCHES, FLANDERS, MAY 9, 1915

One of my men has just been killed—the first. I have been taking the things out of his pockets and tying them round in his handkerchief to be sent back somewhere to someone who will see more than a torn letter, and a pencil, and a knife and a piece of shell. He was shot through the left temple while firing over the parapet. I did not actually see it—thank Heaven. I only found him lying very still at the bottom of the trench with a tiny stream of red trickling down his cheek onto his coat. He has just been carried away. I cannot help thinking how ridiculous it was that so small a thing should make such a change. He could have walked down the trench himself an hour ago. I was talking to him only a few minutes before.

I do not quite know how I felt at the moment. It was not anger (—even now I have no feeling of

animosity against the man who shot him) only a great pity, and a sudden feeling of impotence. . . .

It is cruel of me to tell you this. Why should you have the horrors of war brought any nearer to you? And you have more time to think of them than I. At least, try not to remember: as I do.

VERA TO EDITH BRITTAIN, 24TH GENERAL HOSPITAL, ÉTAPLES, FRANCE, AUGUST 5, 1917

I arrived here yesterday afternoon; the hospital is about a mile out of the town, on the side of a hill, in a large clearing surrounded on three sides by woods. It is all huts & tents; I am working in a hut & sleeping under canvas, only not in a tent but in a kind of canvas shanty, with boarded floor & corrugated iron roof. . . . The hospital is frantically busy & we were very much welcomed. . . . You will be surprised to hear that at present I am nursing German prisoners. My ward is entirely reserved for the most acute German surgical cases; we have no cases but the very worst (26 beds) & a theatre is attached to the ward. . . .The majority are more or less dying; never, even at the 1st London during the Somme push, have I seen such dreadful wounds. Consequently, they are all too ill to be aggressive, & one forgets that they are the enemy and can only remember that they are suffering human beings. My half-forgotten German comes in very useful, & the Sisters were so glad to know I understood it & could speak a little as half the time they don't know what the poor things want. It gives one a chance to live up to our Motto "Inter Arma Caritas" ["In War, Charity"–Ed.], but anyhow one can hardly feel bitter towards dying men. It is incongruous, though, to think of Edward in one part of France trying to kill the same people whom in another part of France I am trying to save. . . .

Well, Malta was an interesting experience of the world, but this is War. There is a great coming & going all day long—men marching from one place "somewhere" in France to another, ambulances, transports, etc. passing all the time. One or two "courses" for officers are quite near here, & there are lots of troops training. Everything of war that one can imagine is here, except actual fighting, & one can even hear the distant rumble of that at times; usually by day the noise of things passing along the wide straight country road which runs right through the hospital drowns the more distant sounds. It is an enormous hospital—twice as many beds as at the 1st London.

OCTOBER 12, 1917

Someday perhaps I will try to tell you what this first half of October has been like, for I cannot even attempt to describe it in a letter & of course we are still in the middle of things; the rush is by no means over yet—Three times this week we have taken in convoys & evacuated to England, & the fourth came into our ward all at the same time. Every day since this day last week has been one long doing of the impossible—or what

seemed the impossible before you started. We have four of our twenty-five patients on the D.I.L. (dangerously ill list, which means their people can come over from England to see them) and any one of them would keep a nurse occupied all day but when there are only two of you for the whole lot you simply have to do the best you can. One does dressings from morning till night. I never knew anything approaching it in London, & certainly not in Malta. No one realises the meaning of emergencies who has not been in France. Nor does one know the meaning of "bad cases" for they don't get to England in the state we see them here; they either die in France or else wait to get better before they are evacuated.

QUESTIONS TO CONSIDER

1. What do these letters reveal about the authors' attitudes toward the Great War or war in general? Are there any indications that these attitudes changed over time?
2. How would you compare the battlefield and medical observations and experiences described in this source with those of Henri Dunant and Florence Nightingale (Source 7.6)? What has changed in the half-century between 1859 and 1914–1918? What is similar?

10.2 "A FREE, OPEN-MINDED, AND ABSOLUTELY IMPARTIAL ADJUSTMENT OF ALL COLONIAL CLAIMS." WOODROW WILSON, *ADDRESS TO US CONGRESS*, 1918 AND NGUYEN AI QUOC (HO CHI MINH), *LETTER TO US SECRETARY OF STATE*, 1919

These two documents illustrate some of the goals and principles that came into play at the peace conference following World War I and how they were received.

The first document is by US President Woodrow Wilson (1856–1921). Wilson was reelected in 1916 on a platform opposing US entry into the war that had begun two years earlier, but he came to

Sources: Excerpt one: Avalon Project, Yale Law School, *avalon.law.yale.edu/20th_century/wilson14.asp*; Excerpt two: Letter from Nguyen ai Quac (Ho Chi Minh) to Secretary of State Robert Lansing (with enclosure), 6/18/1919 [Electronic Record]. Trans. James Carter. Records of the American Commission to Negotiate Peace, 1914–1931. General Records, 1918–1931. Record Group 256; National Archives at College Park, College Park, MD [retrieved from the Access to Archival Databases at *www.archives.gov*, April 26, 2018].

advocate US involvement, which would play a crucial role in the Allied victory. The United States had not suffered the destruction that Europe did in the war, and Wilson attempted to negotiate "peace without victors" based on principles of democracy and national self-determination. The document presented here lists Wilson's "Fourteen Points" that he promoted as the foundation of a lasting peace.

These principles caught the attention of Vietnamese nationalist Ho Chi Minh (1890–1969) who was in Paris at the time. Believing that Wilson's ideals fit with his ambitions for Vietnamese independence from French colonialism, Ho (then going by the name Nguyen Ai Quoc) wrote the letter presented here to gain entry to the peace conference at Versailles. The letter included a petition, "Demands of the Annamite People," which is also reproduced here. He received no response to the letters, the originals of which are retained in the US National Archives. The rejection contributed to his move toward communism to support his anticolonial politics.

EXCERPT 1: WOODROW WILSON

It will be our wish and purpose that the processes of peace, when they are begun, shall be absolutely open and that they shall involve and permit henceforth no secret understandings of any kind. The day of conquest and aggrandizement is gone by; so is also the day of secret covenants entered into in the interest of particular governments and likely at some unlooked-for moment to upset the peace of the world. It is this happy fact, now clear to the view of every public man whose thoughts do not still linger in an age that is dead and gone, which makes it possible for every nation whose purposes are consistent with justice and the peace of the world to avow nor or at any other time the objects it has in view.

We entered this war because violations of right had occurred which touched us to the quick and made the life of our own people impossible unless they were corrected, and the world secure once for all against their recurrence. What we demand in this war, therefore, is nothing peculiar to ourselves. It is that the world be made fit and safe to live in; and particularly that it be made safe for every peace-loving nation which, like our own, wishes to live its own life, determine its own institutions, be assured of justice and fair dealing by the other peoples of the world as against force and selfish aggression. All the peoples of the world are in effect partners in this interest, and for our own part we see very clearly that unless justice be done to others it will not be done to us. The programme of the world's peace, therefore, is our programme; and that programme, the only possible programme, as we see it, is this:

I. Open covenants of peace, openly arrived at, after which there shall be no private international understandings of any kind, but diplomacy shall proceed always frankly and in the public view.

II. Absolute freedom of navigation upon the seas, outside territorial waters, alike in peace and in war, except as the seas may be closed in whole or in part by international action for the enforcement of international covenants.

III. The removal, so far as possible, of all economic barriers and the establishment of an equality of trade conditions among all the nations consenting to the peace and associating themselves for its maintenance.

IV. Adequate guarantees given and taken that national armaments will be reduced to the lowest point consistent with domestic safety.

V. A free, open-minded, and absolutely impartial adjustment of all colonial claims, based upon a strict observance of the principle that in determining all such questions of sovereignty the interests of the populations concerned must have equal weight with the equitable claims of the government whose title is to be determined. . . .

XIV. A general association of nations must be formed under specific covenants for the purpose of affording mutual guarantees of political independence and territorial integrity to great and small states alike.

In regard to these essential rectifications of wrong and assertions of right we feel ourselves to be intimate partners of all the governments and peoples associated together against the Imperialists. We cannot be separated in interest or divided in purpose. We stand together until the end.

For such arrangements and covenants we are willing to fight and to continue to fight until they are achieved; but only because we wish the right to prevail and desire a just and stable peace such as can be secured only by removing the chief provocations to war, which this programme does remove.

EXCERPT 2: PETITION FROM VIETNAMESE DELEGATION

We take the liberty of submitting to you the accompanying memorandum setting forth the claims of the Annamite people on the occasion of the Allied victory.

We count on your great kindness to honor our appeal by your support whenever the opportunity arises.

We beg your Excellency graciously to accept the expression of our profound respect. FOR THE GROUP OF ANNAMITE PATRIOTS [signed] Nguyen Ai Quoc (Ho Chi Minh) 56, rue Monsieur le Prince Paris

Revendications du Peuple Annamite [Claims of the Annamite People]

Since the victory of the Allies, all the subjugated people have trembled with hope at the prospect of an era of right that must open for them by virtue of the formal and solemn commitments made before the whole world by the powers of the Entente in the struggle of Civilization against barbarism.

While waiting for the principle of nationalism to pass from ideal to reality by the recognition of the sacred right of peoples to self-determination, the people of the former Empire of Annam, at present French Indo-China, present to the noble governments of the Allies in general, and to the honorable French Government in particular, the following humble claims:

(1) A general amnesty for all indigenous political convicts.
(2) Reform of the Indochinese justice by granting to the indigenous people the same judicial guarantees as Europeans, as well as the complete elimination of Special Tribunals which are instruments of terrorism and oppression against the most honest part of the Annamite people .
(3) Freedom of press and of expression.
(4) Freedom of association and assembly.
(5) Freedom to emigrate and travel abroad.
(6) Freedom of education and the creation in all provinces of technical and professional schools for the indigenous people.
(7) Replacement of the rule of arbitrary decree with the rule of law.
(8) A permanent delegation of indigenous people to the French parliament in order to inform parliament of their needs.

The Annamite people, in presenting the above claims, count on the global justice of all the Powers, and rely in particular on the benevolence of the noble French people who hold their fate in their hands and who, as a republic, have taken us under their protection. In claiming the protection of the French people, the Annamite people, far from humbling themselves, are honored, for they know that the French people represent freedom and justice, and will never give up their sublime ideal of universal brotherhood. As a result, listening to the voice of the oppressed, the French people will do their duty to France and to humanity.

QUESTIONS TO CONSIDER

1. What inspirations for Wilson's principles do you see? For Ho Chi Minh's Declaration of Annamite (Vietnamese) Patriots? What previous documents (in this collection or elsewhere) would you consider to be influences on either of these documents?
2. What elements of Wilson's declaration would have appealed most to Ho Chi Minh? Based on these, what outcomes might Ho Chi Minh and other nationalists and anticolonialists have expected in the years immediately following World War I? Which, if any, of these expectations were met in those years?

10.3 "THE NATION SHALL AT ALL TIMES HAVE THE RIGHT TO IMPOSE ON PRIVATE PROPERTY." *THE CONSTITUTION OF MEXICO, 1917*

The Mexican Revolution began in 1910 as a revolt against the authoritarian regime of Porfirio Díaz, who had ruled Mexico for four decades. After the overthrow of Díaz, the country descended into civil war among factions split by personal grievances, incompatible regional and socioeconomic priorities, and competing visions for the nation's future. In 1916, the major factions sent delegates to a constitutional convention with the intent of reconciling their differences and codifying a new set of laws to move the nation beyond the bloody civil war.

The resulting constitution took effect on May 1, 1917, though armed conflict among revolutionary factions continued into the 1920s. The 1917 Constitution remains the fundamental framework of the Mexican political system today, though it has been amended more than 300 times over the last century.

Article 27. Ownership of the lands and waters within the boundaries of the national territory is vested originally in the Nation, which has had, and has, the right to transmit title thereof to private persons, thereby constituting private property.

Private property shall not be expropriated except for reasons of public use and subject to payment of indemnity.

The Nation shall at all times have the right to impose on private property such limitations as the public interest may demand, as well as the right to regulate the utilization of natural resources which are susceptible of appropriation, in order to conserve them and to ensure a more equitable distribution of public wealth. With this end in view, necessary measures shall be taken to divide up large landed estates; to develop small landed holdings in operation; to create new agricultural centers, with necessary lands and waters; to encourage agriculture in general and to prevent the destruction of natural resources, and to protect property from damage to the detriment of society. Centers of population which at present either have no lands or water or which do not possess them in sufficient quantities for the needs of their inhabitants, shall be entitled to grants thereof, which shall be taken from adjacent properties, the rights of small landed holdings in operation being respected at all times.

In the Nation is vested the direct ownership of all natural resources of the continental shelf and the submarine shelf of the islands; of all minerals or substances, which in veins, ledges, masses or ore pockets, form deposits of a nature distinct from the components of the earth itself, such as the minerals from which industrial metals and metalloids are extracted; deposits of precious stones, rock-salt and the deposits of salt formed by sea water; products derived from the decomposition of rocks, when subterranean works are required for their extraction; mineral or organic deposits of materials susceptible of utilization as fertilizers; solid mineral fuels; petroleum and all solid, liquid, and gaseous hydrocarbons; and the space above the national territory to the extent and within the terms fixed by international law. . . .

It is exclusively a function of the general Nation to conduct, transform, distribute, and supply electric power which is to be used for public service. No concessions for this purpose will be granted to private persons and the Nation will make use of the property and natural resources which are required for these ends.

Source: Organization of American States, www.oas.org/juridico/mla/en/mex/en_mex-in-text-const.pdf.

Article 123. The Congress of the Union, without contravening the following basic principles, shall formulate labor laws which shall apply to: workers, day laborers, domestic servants, artisans and in a general way to all labor contracts:

I. The maximum duration of work for one day shall be eight hours.

II. The maximum duration of nightwork shall be seven hours. The following are prohibited: unhealthful or dangerous work by women and by minors under sixteen years of age; industrial nightwork by either of these classes; work by women in commercial establishments after ten o'clock at night and work (of any kind) by persons under sixteen after ten o'clock at night.

III. The use of labor of minors under fourteen years of age is prohibited. Persons above that age and less than sixteen shall have a maximum work day of six hours.

IV. For every six days of work a worker must have at least one day of rest.

V. During the three months prior to childbirth, women shall not perform physical labor that requires excessive material effort. In the month following childbirth they shall necessarily enjoy the benefit of rest and shall receive their full wages and retain their employment and the rights acquired under their labor contract. During the nursing period they shall have two special rest periods each day, of a half hour each, for nursing their infants.

VI. The minimum wage to be received by a worker shall be general or according to occupation. The former shall govern in one or more economic zones; the latter shall be applicable to specified branches of industry or commerce or to special occupations, trades, or labor. The general minimum wage must be sufficient to satisfy the normal material, social, and cultural needs of the head of a family and to provide for the compulsory education of his children. The occupational minimum wage shall be fixed by also taking into consideration the conditions of different industrial and commercial activities. Farm workers shall be entitled to a minimum wage adequate to their needs.

VII. Equal wages shall be paid for equal work, regardless of sex or nationality. . . .

XVI. Both employers and workers shall have the right to organize for the defense of their respective interests, by forming unions, professional associations, etc.

XVII. The laws shall recognize strikes and lockouts as rights of workmen and employers.

XVIII. Strikes shall be legal when they have as their purpose the attaining of an equilibrium among the various factors of production, by harmonizing the rights of labor with those of capital. . . .

XIX. Lockout shall be legal only when an excess of production makes it necessary to suspend work to maintain prices at a level with costs, and with prior approval of the Board of Conciliation and Arbitration.

XX. Differences or disputes between capital and labor shall be subject to the decisions of a Board of Conciliation and Arbitration, consisting of an equal number of workmen and employers, with one from the Government.

XXI. If an employer refuses to submit his differences to arbitration or to accept the decision rendered by the Board, the labor contract shall be considered terminated and he shall be obliged to indemnify the worker to the amount of three months' wages and shall incur any liability resulting from the dispute. This provision shall not be applicable in the case of actions covered in the following section. If the refusal is made by workers, the labor contract shall be considered terminated.

XXII. An employer who dismisses a worker without justifiable cause or because he has entered an association or union, or for having taken part in a lawful strike, shall be required, at the election of the worker, either to fulfill the contract or to indemnify him to the amount of three months' wages. . . .

XXIX. Enactment of a social security law shall be considered of public interest and it shall include insurance against disability, on life, against involuntary work stoppage, against sickness and accidents, and other forms for similar purposes. . . .

QUESTIONS TO CONSIDER

1. What details or concerns expressed mark this constitution as a social contract of the twentieth century?
2. How do you think John Locke (Source 5.1), Edmund Burke (Source 6.2), and Karl Marx (Source 8.1) would assess the kind of state that is being designed in this constitution?

10.4 "IT IS PROVED IN THE PAMPHLET THAT THE WAR OF 1914–18 WAS IMPERIALIST." V. I. LENIN, *IMPERIALISM, THE HIGHEST STAGE OF CAPITALISM: A POPULAR OUTLINE*, 1917 AND 1920

Vladimir Ilyich Ulyanov (1870–1924), better known by his alias "Lenin," led the Russian Bolshevik Revolution of October 1917 and was the first head of state of the Soviet Union, serving from 1922 to 1924. Despite the success of the Russian Revolution, Lenin, like others who advocated Marxist revolution, had to explain why the widespread revolution against capitalism, which Marx predicted was imminent in 1848, had not yet occurred. The document excerpted here is part of Lenin's answer. Lenin describes imperialism as "the highest stage of capitalism" because it enabled capitalism to expand beyond the limits Marx envisioned in two ways: first, by expanding beyond the geographical base of a single country to exploit resources and markets abroad; and second, by expanding to include not only industrial capitalism but also finance.

Lenin's writing here is based on the works of the English economist John Hobson, who in 1902 advanced most of these ideas. Lenin updates Hobson by including the effects of World War I, which he considers an illustration of the ambitions and dangers of imperialism and capitalism. The following text has two parts, one published in 1917 and another added as part of the preface to a new edition of the pamphlet, published in 1920.

We have seen that in its economic essence imperialism is monopoly capitalism. This in itself determines its place in history, for monopoly that grows out of the soil of free competition, and precisely out of free competition, is the transition from the capitalist system to a higher socio-economic order. . . .

Firstly, monopoly arose out of the concentration of production at a very high stage. This refers to the monopolist capitalist associations, cartels, syndicates, and trusts. We have seen the important part these play in present-day economic life. At the beginning of the twentieth century, monopolies had acquired complete supremacy in the advanced countries, and although the first steps towards the formation of the cartels were taken by countries enjoying the protection of high tariffs (Germany, America), Great Britain,

Source: *Lenin's Selected Works* (Moscow, 1963). Marxists Internet Archive: www.marxists.org/archive/lenin/works/1916/imp-hsc.

with her system of free trade, revealed the same basic phenomenon, only a little later, namely, the birth of monopoly out of the concentration of production.

Secondly, monopolies have stimulated the seizure of the most important sources of raw materials, especially for the basic and most highly cartelised industries in capitalist society: the coal and iron industries. . . .

Thirdly, monopoly has sprung from the banks. The banks have developed from modest middleman enterprises into the monopolists of finance capital. . . .

Fourthly, monopoly has grown out of colonial policy. To the numerous "old" motives of colonial policy, finance capital has added the struggle for the sources of raw materials, for the export of capital, for spheres of influence, i.e., for spheres for profitable deals, concessions, monopoly profits and so on, economic territory in general. When the colonies of the European powers, for instance, comprised only one-tenth of the territory of Africa (as was the case in 1876), colonial policy was able to develop—by methods other than those of monopoly—by the "free grabbing" of territories, so to speak. But when nine-tenths of Africa had been seized (by 1900), when the whole world had been divided up, there was inevitably ushered in the era of monopoly possession of colonies and, consequently, of particularly intense struggle for the division and the redivision of the world. . . .

On the whole, capitalism is growing far more rapidly than before; but this growth is not only becoming more and more uneven in general, its unevenness also manifests itself, in particular, in the decay of the countries which are richest in capital (Britain). . . .

The receipt of high monopoly profits by the capitalists in one of the numerous branches of industry, in one of the numerous countries, etc., makes it economically possible for them to bribe certain sections of the workers, and for a time a fairly considerable minority of them, and win them to the side of the bourgeoisie of a given industry or given nation against all the others. The intensification of antagonisms between imperialist nations for the division of the world increases this urge. . . .

FROM THE PREFACE OF A NEW EDITION, PUBLISHED IN 1920

It is proved in the pamphlet that the war of 1914–18 was imperialist (that is, an annexationist, predatory,

war of plunder) on the part of both sides; it was a war for the division of the world, for the partition and repartition of colonies and spheres of influence of finance capital, etc. . . .

Private property based on the labour of the small proprietor, free competition, democracy, all the catchwords with which the capitalists and their press deceive the workers and the peasants are things of the distant past. Capitalism has grown into a world system of colonial oppression and of the financial strangulation of the overwhelming majority of the population of the world by a handful of "advanced" countries. And this "booty" is shared between two or three powerful world plunderers armed to the teeth (America, Great Britain, Japan), who are drawing the whole world into their war over the division of their booty.

The Treaty of Brest-Litovsk dictated by monarchist Germany, and the subsequent much more brutal and despicable Treaty of Versailles dictated by the "democratic" republics of America and France and also by "free" Britain, have rendered a most useful service to humanity by exposing both imperialism's hired coolies of the pen and petty-bourgeois reactionaries who, although they call themselves pacifists and socialists, sang praises to "Wilsonism," and insisted that peace and reforms were possible under imperialism.

The tens of millions of dead and maimed left by the war—a war to decide whether the British or German group of financial plunderers is to receive the most booty—and those two "peace treaties," are with unprecedented rapidity opening the eyes of the millions and tens of millions of people who are downtrodden, oppressed, deceived and duped by the bourgeoisie. Thus, out of the universal ruin caused by the war a world-wide revolutionary crisis is arising which, however prolonged and arduous its stages may be, cannot end otherwise than in a proletarian revolution and in its victory. . . .

It is precisely the parasitism and decay of capitalism, characteristic of its highest historical stage of development, i.e., imperialism. As this pamphlet shows, capitalism has now singled out a handful (less than one-tenth of the inhabitants of the globe; less than one-fifth at a most "generous" and liberal calculation) of exceptionally rich and powerful states which plunder the whole world simply by "clipping coupons." Capital exports yield an income of eight to ten thousand million francs per annum, at pre-war prices and according to pre-war bourgeois statistics. Now, of course, they yield much more.

Obviously, out of such enormous superprofits (since they are obtained over and above the profits which capitalists squeeze out of the workers of their "own" country) it is possible to bribe the labour leaders and the upper stratum of the labour aristocracy. And that is just what the capitalists of the "advanced" countries are doing: they are bribing them in a thousand different ways, direct and indirect, overt and covert. . . .

Unless the economic roots of this phenomenon are understood and its political and social significance is appreciated, not a step can be taken toward the solution of the practical problem of the communist movement and of the impending social revolution.

Imperialism is the eve of the social revolution of the proletariat. This has been confirmed since 1917 on a world-wide scale.

QUESTIONS TO CONSIDER

1. How do you assess Lenin's analysis of the causes of World War I? What other factors, if any, do you think are necessary to explain the war?
2. Compare this document with other documents addressing globalization (Source 13.5, for instance). What similarities and differences do you see? How do you think Lenin might change his analysis if he were writing today?

10.5 "THROUGHOUT HISTORY ONE OF THE CONSTANT FEATURES OF SOCIAL STRUGGLE HAS BEEN THE ATTEMPT TO CHANGE RELATIONSHIPS BETWEEN THE SEXES." ALEXANDRA KOLLONTAI, *SEXUAL RELATIONS AND THE CLASS STRUGGLE*, 1921

Alexandra Kollontai (1872–1952), born Alexandra Domontovich, was a Russian revolutionary, joining Lenin's Bolsheviks in 1915 and becoming a diplomat, eventually serving as Ambassador to Norway, Mexico, and Sweden. She became best known for her radical views on marriage, sex, and social relations between men and women. Whereas most communists focused solely on equality between classes, Kollontai insisted that the most fundamental inequality in society was that between men and women. On that basis, she criticized traditional marriage as depriving women of rights and property. Although she is often associated with ideas of "free love," she argued that until women had rights equal to those of men, casual sexual encounters were likely to exploit women. Instead, she advocated long-lasting, stable relationships built on equality between partners. Her writings and speeches called for deep-seated, fundamental change to relations between the sexes.

Source: *Alexandra Kollontai, Selected Writings*, trans. Alix Hold (London: Allison & Busby, 1977).

Among the many problems that demand the consideration and attention of contemporary mankind, sexual problems are undoubtedly some of the most crucial. There isn't a country or a nation, apart from the legendary "islands," where the question of sexual relationships isn't becoming an urgent and burning issue. Mankind today is living through an acute sexual crisis which is far more unhealthy and harmful for being long and drawn-out. Throughout the long journey of human history, you probably won't find a time when the problems of sex have occupied such a central place in the life of society; when the question of relationships between the sexes has been like a conjuror, attracting the attention of millions of troubled people; when sexual dramas have served as such a never-ending source of inspiration for every sort of art.

As the crisis continues and grows more serious, people are getting themselves into an increasingly hopeless situation and are trying desperately by every available means to settle the "insoluble question." But with every new attempt to solve the problem, the confused knot of personal relationships gets more tangled. It's as if we couldn't see the one and only thread that could finally lead us to success in controlling the stubborn tangle. The sexual problem is like a vicious circle, and however frightened people are and however much they run this way and that, they are unable to break out.

The conservatively inclined part of mankind argue that we should return to the happy times of the past, we should re-establish the old foundations of the family and strengthen the well-tried norms of sexual morality. The champions of bourgeois individualism say that we ought to destroy all the hypocritical restrictions of the obsolete code of sexual behaviour. These unnecessary and repressive "rags" ought to be relegated to the archives—only the individual conscience, the individual will of each person can decide such intimate questions. Socialists, on the other hand, assure us that sexual problems will only be settled when the basic reorganisation of the social and economic structure of society has been tackled. Doesn't this "putting off the problem until tomorrow" suggest that we still haven't found that one and only "magic thread"? Shouldn't we find or at least locate this "magic thread" that promises to unravel the tangle? Shouldn't we find

it now, at this very moment? The history of human society, the history of the continual battle between various social groups and classes of opposing aims and interests, gives us the clue to finding this "thread." It isn't the first time that mankind has gone through a sexual crisis. This isn't the first time that the pressure of a rushing tide of new values and ideals has blurred the clear and definite meaning of moral commandments about sexual relationships. The "sexual crisis" was particularly acute at the time of the Renaissance and the Reformation, when a great social advance pushed the proud and patriarchal feudal nobility who were used to absolute command into the background, and cleared the way for the development and establishment of a new social force—the bourgeoisie. The sexual morality of the feudal world had developed out of the depths of the tribal way of life—the collective economy and the tribal authoritarian leadership that stifles the individual will of the individual member. This clashed with the new and strange moral code of the rising bourgeoisie. The sexual morality of the bourgeoisie is founded on principles that are in sharp contradiction to the basic morality of feudalism. Strict individualism and the exclusiveness and isolation of the "nuclear family" replace the emphasis on collective work—that was characteristic of both the local and regional economic structure of patrimonial life. Under capitalism the ethic of competition, the triumphant principles of individualism and exclusive private property, grew and destroyed whatever remained of the idea of the community, which was to some extent common to all types of tribal life. For a whole century, while the complex laboratory of life was turning the old norms into a new formula and achieving the outward harmony of moral ideas, men wandered confusedly between two very different sexual codes and attempted to accommodate themselves to both.

What are the roots of this unforgivable indifference to one of the essential tasks of the working class? How can we explain to ourselves the, hypocritical way in which "sexual problems" are relegated to the realm of "private matters" that are not worth the effort and attention of the collective? Why has the fact been ignored that throughout history one of the constant features of social struggle has been the attempt to change relationships between the sexes, and the type of moral codes that determine these relationships; and that the way personal relationships are organised in a certain social group has had a vital influence on the outcome of the struggle between hostile social classes? . . .

The "inequality" of the sexes—the inequality of their rights, the unequal value of their physical and emotional experience—is the other significant circumstance that distorts the psyche of contemporary man and is a reason for the deepening of the sexual crisis." The "double morality" inherent in both patrimonial and bourgeois society has, over the course of centuries, poisoned the psyche of men and women. These attitudes are so much a part of us that they are more difficult to get rid of than the ideas about possessing people that we have inherited only from bourgeois ideology. The idea that the sexes are unequal, even in the sphere of physical and emotional experience, means that the same action will be regarded differently according to whether it was the action of a man or a woman. Even the most "progressive" member of the bourgeoisie, who has long ago rejected the whole code of current morality, easily catches himself out at this point since he too in judging a man and a woman for the same behaviour will pass different sentences. One simple example is enough. Imagine that a member of the middle-class intelligentsia who is learned, involved in politics and social affairs—who is in short a "personality," even a "public figure"—starts sleeping with his cook (a not uncommon thing to happen) and even becomes legally married to her. Does bourgeois society change its attitude to this man, does the event throw even the tiniest shadow of doubt as to his moral worth? Of course not.

Now imagine another situation. A respected woman of bourgeois society—a social figure, a research student, a doctor, or a writer, it's all the same—becomes friendly with her footman, and to complete the scandal marries him. How does bourgeois society react to the behaviour of the hitherto "respected" woman? They cover her with "scorn," of course! And remember, it's so much the worse for her if her husband, the footman, is good-looking or possesses other "physical qualities." "It's obvious what she's fallen for," will be the sneer of the hypocritical bourgeoisie.

If a woman's choice has anything of an "individual character" about it she won't be forgiven by bourgeois society. This attitude is a kind of throwback to the traditions of tribal times. Society still wants a woman to take into account, when she is making her choice, rank and status and the instructions and interests of her family. Bourgeois society cannot see a woman as an independent person separate from her family unit and outside the isolated circle of domestic obligations and virtues. Contemporary society goes even further than the ancient tribal society in acting as woman's trustee, instructing her not only to marry but to fall in love only with those people who are "worthy" of her.

We are continually meeting men of considerable spiritual and intellectual qualities who have chosen as their friend-for-life a worthless and empty woman, who in no way matches the spiritual worth of the husband. We accept this as something normal and we don't think twice about it. At the most friends might pity Ivan Ivanovich for having landed himself with such an unbearable wife. But if it happens the other way round, we flap our hands and exclaim with concern. "How could such an outstanding woman as Maria Petrovna fall for such a nonentity? I begin to doubt the worth of Maria Petrovna." Where do we get this double criterion from? What is the reason for it? The reason is undoubtedly that the idea of the sexes being of "different value" has become, over the centuries, a part of man's psychological make-up. We are used to evaluating a woman not as a personality with individual qualities and failings irrespective of her physical and emotional experience, but only as an appendage of a man. This man, the husband or the lover, throws the light of his personality over the woman, and it is this reflection and not the woman herself that we consider to be the true definition of her emotional and moral make-up. In the eyes of society the personality of a man can be more easily separated from his actions in the sexual sphere. The personality of a woman is judged almost exclusively in terms of her sexual life. This type of attitude stems from the role that women have played in society over the centuries, and it is only now that a re-evaluation of these attitudes is slowly being achieved, at least in outline. Only a change in the economic role of woman, and her independent involvement in production, can and will bring about the weakening of these mistaken and hypocritical ideas.

The three basic circumstances distorting the modern psyche—extreme egoism, the idea that married partners possess each other, and the acceptance of the inequality of the sexes in terms of physical and emotional experience—must be faced if the sexual problem is to be settled. People will find the "magic key" with which they can break out of their situation only when their psyche has a sufficient store of "feelings of consideration," when their ability to love is greater, when the idea of freedom in personal relationships becomes fact and when the principle of "comradeship" triumphs over the traditional idea of inequality and submission. The sexual problems cannot be solved without this radical re-education of our psyche. . . .

The attempt by the middle-class intelligentsia to replace indissoluble marriage by the freer, more easily broken ties of civil marriage destroys the essential basis of the social stability of the bourgeoisie. It destroys the monogamous, property-orientated family. On the other hand, a greater fluidity in relationships between the sexes coincides with and is even the indirect result of one of the basic tasks of the working class. The rejection of the element of "submission" in marriage is going to destroy the last artificial ties of the bourgeois family. This act of "submission" on the part of one member of the working class to another, in the same way as the sense of possessiveness in relationships, has a harmful effect on the proletarian psyche. It is not in the interests of that revolutionary class to elect only certain members as its independent representatives, whose duty it is to serve the class interests before the interests of the individual, isolated family. Conflicts between the interests of the family and the interests of the class which occur at the time of a strike or during an active struggle, and the moral yardstick with which the proletariat

views such events, are sufficiently clear evidence of the basis of the new proletarian ideology.

Suppose family affairs require a businessman to take his capital out of a firm at a time when the enterprise is in financial difficulties. Bourgeois morality is clear-cut in its estimate of his action:

"The interests of the family come first." We can compare with this the attitude of workers to a strike-breaker who defies his comrades and goes to work during a strike to save his family from being hungry. "The interests of the class come first." Here's another example. The love and loyalty of the middle-class husband to his family are sufficient to divert his wife from all interests outside the home and end up by tying her to the nursery and the kitchen. "The ideal husband can support the ideal family" is the way the bourgeoisie looks at it. But how do workers look upon a "conscious" member of their class who shuts the eyes of his wife or girl-friend to the social struggle? For the sake of individual happiness, for the sake of the family, the morality of the working class will demand that women take part in the life that is unfolding beyond the doorsteps. The "captivity" of women in the home, the way family interests are placed before all else, the widespread exercise of absolute property rights by the husband over the wife—all these things are being broken down by the basic principle of the working-class ideology of "comradely solidarity." The idea that some members are unequal and must submit to other members of one and the same class is in contradiction with the basic proletarian principle of comradeship. This principle of comradeship is basic to the ideology of the working class. It colours and determines the whole developing proletarian morality, a morality which helps to re-educate the personality of man, allowing him to be capable of feeling, capable of freedom instead of being bound by a sense of property, capable of comradeship rather than inequality and submission. . . .

QUESTIONS TO CONSIDER

1. Kollontai points to the deeply entrenched double standards that gave men power over women. What is the fundamental hypocrisy that she sees in both "bourgeois morality" and the "middle-class intelligentsia" when it comes to relations between the sexes?
2. Why does Kollontai believe that "family values" are harmful not only to the members of the family but to society as a whole?

10.6 "THE PEOPLES OF ASIA HAVE CHERISHED THE HOPE OF SHAKING OFF THE YOKE OF EUROPEAN OPPRESSION." SUN YAT-SEN, *SPEECH ON PAN-ASIANISM*, 1924

Resistance to imperialism took many forms and sometimes brought together unlikely allies. One such example is Sun Yat-sen, the founder of China's first Republic, which took power after overthrowing the Qing Dynasty. The Chinese Republic struggled with both internal division and international pressures. Although China did not become a European colony, foreign countries including France, Britain, the United States, Germany, Japan, and Russia gained special, semicolonial privileges throughout China. In the 1920s, Sun was one of the leading advocates of Pan-Asianism as a means of resisting European expansion.

Sun delivered the speech excerpted here in Kobe, Japan in 1924 (just a few months before he died of cancer). In this speech, he tries to make the case that resistance to European (and American) imperialism would unite Asia. An important context for this essay, though, is the imperial ambitions of Japan. Japan had a greater presence in China than any other foreign power, and many saw Japan's support for Pan-Asianism as a means to develop its own empire in the region. Underscoring this assumption, after Japan invaded China and implemented a collaborationist regime, the speech was included in a 1941 volume published by the Chinese government cooperating with Japanese occupiers as "a guide for China's foreign policy by Dr. Sun Yat-sen" to suggest that China should support Japan in dominating Asia.

Thirty years ago, . . . [m]en thought and believed that European civilization was a progressive one—in science, industry, manufacture, and armament—and that Asia had nothing to compare with it. Consequently, they assumed that Asia could never resist Europe, that European oppression could never be shaken off. Such was the idea prevailing thirty years ago. It was a pessimistic idea. Even after Japan abolished the Unequal Treaties and attained the status of an independent country, Asia, with the exception of a few countries situated near Japan, was little influenced. Ten years later, however, the Russo-Japanese war broke out and Russia was defeated by Japan. For the first time in the history of the last several hundred years, an Asiatic country has defeated a European Power. The effect of

this victory immediately spread over the whole Asia, and gave a new hope to all Asiatic peoples. . . .

In former days, the colored races in Asia, suffering from the oppression of the Western peoples, thought that emancipation was impossible. We regarded that Russian defeat by Japan as the defeat of the West by the East. We regarded the Japanese victory as our own victory. It was indeed a happy event. Did not therefore this news of Russia's defeat by Japan affect the peoples of the whole of Asia? Was not its effect tremendous? While it may not have seemed so important and consequently have had only a slight effect on the peoples living in East Asia, it had a great effect on the peoples living in West Asia and in the neighborhood of Europe who were in constant touch with Europeans

Source: Sun Yat-sen, et al. *China and Japan: Natural Friends—Unnatural Enemies: A Guide for China's Foreign Policy.* Ed. T'ang Liang-li. Shanghai: China United Press, 1941, 141-151.

and subject to their oppression daily. The suffering of these Asiatic peoples was naturally greater than that of those living in the further East, and they were therefore more quick to respond to the news of this great victory.

Since the day of Japan's victory over Russia, the peoples of Asia have cherished the hope of shaking off the yoke of European oppression, a hope which has given rise to a series of independence movements—in Egypt, Persia, Turkey, Afghanistan, and finally in India. Therefore, Japan's defeat of Russia gave rise to a great hope for the independence of Asia. From the inception of this hope to the present day only 20 years have elapsed. The Egyptian, Turkish, Persian, Afghan, and Arabian independence movements have already materialized, and even the independence movement in India has, with the passage of time, been gaining ground. Such facts are concrete proofs of the progress of the nationalist idea in Asia. Until this idea reaches its full maturity, no unification or independence movement of the Asiatic peoples as a whole is possible. In East Asia, China and Japan are the two greatest peoples. China and Japan are the driving force of this nationalist movement. What will be the consequences of this driving force still remains to be seen. . . . [T]he Westerners consider themselves as the only ones possessed and worthy of true culture and civilization; other peoples with any culture or independent ideas are considered as Barbarians in revolt against Civilization. When comparing Occidental with Oriental civilization they only consider their own civilization logical and humanitarian. . . .

Which civilization, the rule of Might or the rule of Right, will prove to be beneficial to justice and humanity, to nations and countries? You can give your own answer to this question.

I may cite an example here to illustrate the point. For instance, between 500 and 2000 years ago, there was a period of a thousand years when China was supreme in the world. Her status in the world then was similar to that of Great Britain and America today. What was the situation of the weaker nations toward China then? They respected China as their superior and sent annual tribute to China by their own will, regarding it as an honor to be allowed to do so. They wanted, of

their own free will, to be dependencies of China. Those countries which sent tribute to China were not only situated in Asia but in distant Europe as well. But in what way did China maintain her prestige among so many small and weaker nations. Did she send her army or navy, i.e., use Might, to compel them to send their contributions? Not at all. It was not her rule of Might that forced the weaker nations to send tribute to China. It was the influence of her rule of Right. Once they were influenced by the "Kingly Way" of China they continued to send tribute, not merely once or twice, but the practice was carried on from generation to generation. This influence is felt even at the present moment; there are still traces and evidences of it. . . .

Now, what is the problem that underlies Pan-Asianism, the Principle of Greater Asia, which we are discussing here to-day?

Briefly, it is a cultural problem, a problem of comparison and conflict between the Oriental and Occidental culture and civilization. Oriental civilization is the rule of Right; Occidental civilization is the rule of Might. The rule of Right respects benevolence and virtue, while the rule of Might only respects force and utilitarianism. The rule of Right always influences people with justice and reason, while the rule of Might always oppresses people with brute force and military measures. People who are influenced by justice and virtue will never forget their superior State, even if that country has become weak. So Nepal even now willingly respects China as a superior State. People who are oppressed by force never submit entirely to the oppressor State. The relations of Great Britain with Egypt and India form a typical example. Although under British rule, Egypt and India have always entertained the thought of independence and separation from Great Britain. If Great Britain becomes weaker some day, Egypt and India will overthrow British rule and regain their independence within five years. You should now realize which is the superior civilization, the Oriental or the Occidental?

If we want to realize Pan-Asianism in this new world, what should be its foundation if not our ancient civilization and culture? Benevolence and virtue must be the foundations of Pan-Asianism. With this as a sound foundation we must then learn science from Europe for our industrial development and the improvement of our armaments, not, however, with a view to oppressing or destroying other countries and peoples as the Europeans have done, but purely for our self-defense.

Japan is the first nation in Asia to completely master the military civilization of Europe. Japan's military and naval forces are her own creation, independent of European aid or assistance. Therefore, Japan is the only completely independent country in East Asia. There is another country in Asia who joined with Central Powers during the European War and was partitioned after her final defeat. After the war, however, she was not only able to regain her territory, but to expel all Europeans from that territory. Thus she attained her status of complete independence. This is Turkey. At present Asia has only two independent countries, Japan in the East and Turkey in the West. In other words, Japan and Turkey are the Eastern and Western barricades of Asia. Now Persia, Afghanistan, and Arabia are also following the European example in arming themselves, with the result that the Western peoples dare not look down on them. China at present also possesses considerable armaments, and when her unification is accomplished she too will become a great Power. We advocate Pan-Asianism in order to restore the status of Asia. Only by the unification of all the peoples in Asia on the foundation of benevolence and virtue can they become strong and powerful.

But to rely on benevolence alone to influence the Europeans in Asia to relinquish the privileges they have acquired in China would be an impossible dream. If we want to regain our rights we must resort to force. In the matter of armaments, Japan has already accomplished her aims, while Turkey has recently also completely armed herself. The other Asiatic races, such as the peoples of Persia, Afghanistan, and Arabia, are all war-like peoples. China has a population of four hundred millions, and although she needs to modernize her armament and other equipment, and her people are a peace-loving people, yet when the destiny of their country is at stake the Chinese people will also fight with courage and determination. Should all Asiatic peoples thus unite together and present a united front against the Occidentals, they will win the final victory.

Compare the populations of Europe and Asia: China has a population of four hundred millions, India three hundred and fifty millions, Japan several scores of millions, totaling, together with other peoples, no less than nine hundred millions. The population in Europe is somewhere around four hundred millions. For the four hundred millions to oppress the nine hundred millions is an intolerable injustice, and in the long run the latter will be defeated. What is more, among the four hundred millions some of them have already been influenced by us. Judging from the present tendency of civilization, even in Great Britain and America, there are people who advocate the principles of benevolence and justice. Such an advocacy also exists in some of the barbarian countries. Thus, we realize that the Western civilization of utilitarianism is submitting to the influence of Oriental civilization of benevolence and justice. That is to say the rule of Might gives way to the rule of Right, presaging a bright future for world civilization. . . .

What problem does Pan-Asianism attempt to solve? The problem is how to terminate the sufferings of the Asiatic peoples and how to resist the aggression of the powerful European countries. In a word, Pan-Asianism represents the cause of the oppressed Asiatic peoples. Oppressed peoples are found not only in Asia, but in Europe as well. Those countries that practice the rule of Might do not only oppress the weaker people outside their continent, but also those within their own continent. Pan-Asianism is based on the principle of the rule of Right, and justifies the avenging of the wrongs done to others. An American scholar considers all emancipation movements as revolts against civilization. Therefore now we advocate the avenging of the wrong done to those in revolt against the civilization of the rule of Might, with the aim of seeking a civilization of peace and equality and the emancipation of all races. Japan to-day has become acquainted with the Western civilization of the rule of Might, but retains the characteristics of the Oriental civilization of the rule of Right. Now the question remains whether Japan will be the hawk of the Western civilization of the rule of Might, or the tower of strength of the Orient. This is the choice which lies before the people of Japan.

QUESTIONS TO CONSIDER

1. In the speech, Sun identifies principles of "oriental" and "occidental" civilization. How do these ideas fit with the idea of a "modern world"? Can both be considered "modern"? How does the construction of ideas like civilization, modernity and identity in this speech compare with the way others are using these terms after World War I?

2. What does the use of this speech as Japanese propaganda during World War II say about the idea of Pan-Asianism? Can it be understood independently of Japanese expansion? What other paths might Pan-Asianism have followed?

10.7 "THE FASCIST CONCEPTION OF LIFE STRESSES THE IMPORTANCE OF THE STATE." BENITO MUSSOLINI AND GIOVANNI GENTILE, *THE POLITICAL AND SOCIAL DOCTRINE OF FASCISM*, 1934

Benito Mussolini (1883–1945) was born in northeastern Italy a little more than a decade after Italian unification. Mussolini's early political leanings were toward the left wing of the political spectrum. His father was a blacksmith and a socialist. In 1913, Mussolini became editor of a socialist newspaper called *Avanti (Forward)*. Mussolini experienced a political transformation during World War I; in 1919, he organized a new political movement called the Fasci di Combattimento (Fascist Party). In 1921, thirty-five fascists, including Mussolini, were elected to the Chamber of Deputies. In 1922, the fascists organized a march on Rome to demonstrate their popularity and power. At the same time, King Victor Emmanuel III asked Mussolini to serve as Prime Minister and form a government. Allied with fascists elsewhere in Europe and Asia as one of the Axis powers, Mussolini's Italy entered World War II. Discontent with Mussolini's leadership during the war was widespread. When Allied troops invaded Italy in 1943, the Grand Council of Fascism passed a resolution of no confidence in Mussolini and ordered his arrest. Escaping with the help of the Nazis, Mussolini was propped up as ruler of a Nazi puppet state in territory controlled by the German military in northern Italy. In 1945, Mussolini was captured while attempting to escape from advancing opposition forces. He was summarily executed by a firing squad of Italian communists.

Mussolini was a tireless propagandist for fascism. The following excerpts are from an English translation of his most well-known distillation of the fundamental principles of fascism. Although this entire essay was attributed to Mussolini, the first part was written, at least in part, by Italian philosopher Giovanni Gentile (1875–1944).

Source: Benito Mussolini, *The Political and Social Doctrine of Fascism*, trans. Jane Soames (London: Hogarth Press, 1934), 7–26.

Fascism is now a completely individual thing, not only as a regime but as a doctrine. And this means that today Fascism, exercising its critical sense upon itself and upon others, has formed its own distinct and peculiar point of view, to which it can refer and upon which, therefore, it can act in the face of all problems, practical or intellectual, which confront the world.

And above all, Fascism, the more it considers and observes the future and the development of humanity quite apart from political considerations of the moment, believes neither in the possibility nor the utility of perpetual peace. It thus repudiates the doctrine of Pacifism—born of a renunciation of the struggle and an act of cowardice in the face of sacrifice. War alone brings up to its highest tension all human energy and puts the stamp of nobility upon the peoples who have the courage to meet it. All other trials are substitutes, which never really put men into the position where they have to make the great decision—the alternative of life or death. Thus, a doctrine which is founded upon this harmful postulate of peace is hostile to Fascism.

And thus hostile to the spirit of Fascism, though accepted for what use they can be in dealing with particular political situations, are all the international leagues and societies which, as history will show, can be scattered to the winds when once strong national feeling is aroused by any motive—sentimental, ideal, or practical. . . .

The Fascist loves in actual fact his neighbour, but this "neighbour" is not merely a vague and undefined concept, this love for one's neighbour puts no obstacle in the way of necessary educational severity, and still less to differentiation of status and to physical distance. Fascism repudiates any universal embrace, and in order to live worthily in the community of civilized peoples watches its contemporaries with vigilant eyes, takes good note of their state of mind and, in the changing trend of their interests, does not allow itself to be deceived by temporary and fallacious appearances.

Such a conception of life makes Fascism the complete opposite of that doctrine, the base of so-called scientific and Marxian Socialism, the materialist conception of history; according to which the history of

human civilization can be explained simply through the conflict of interests among the various social groups and by the change and development in the means and instruments of production. That the changes in the economic field—new discoveries of raw materials, new methods of working them, and the inventions of science—have their importance no one can deny; but that these factors are sufficient to explain the history of humanity excluding all others is an absurd delusion. Fascism, now and always, believes in holiness and in heroism; that is to say, in actions influenced by no economic motive, direct or indirect. And if the economic conception of history be denied, according to which theory men are no more than puppets, carried to and fro by the waves of chance, while the real directing forces are quite out of their control, it follows that the existence of an unchangeable and unchanging class-war is also denied—the natural progeny of the economic conception of history. And above all, Fascism denies that class-war can be the preponderant force in the transformation of society. . . .

After Socialism, Fascism combats the whole complex system of democratic ideology, and repudiates it, whether in its theoretical premises or in its practical application. Fascism denies that the majority, by the simple fact that it is a majority, can direct human society; it denies that numbers alone can govern by means of a periodical consultation, and it affirms the immutable, beneficial and fruitful inequality of mankind, which can never be permanently levelled through the mere operation of a mechanical process such as universal suffrage. The democratic regime may be defined as from time to time giving the people the illusion of sovereignty, while the real effective sovereignty lies in the hands of other concealed and irresponsible forces. Democracy is a regime nominally without a king, but it is ruled by many kings—more absolute, tyrannical and ruinous than one sole king, even though a tyrant. This explains why Fascism, having first in 1922 (for reasons of expediency) assumed an attitude tending towards republicanism, renounced this point of view before the march to Rome; being convinced that the question of political form is not to-day of prime importance, and after having studied the examples of monarchies and republics past and present reached the conclusion that monarchy or republicanism are not to be judged, as it were, by an absolute standard; but that they represent forms in which the evolution—political, historical, traditional or psychological—of a particular country has expressed itself. Fascism supersedes the antithesis monarchy or republicanism, while democracy still tarries beneath the domination of this idea, forever pointing out the insufficiency of the first and forever the praising of the second as the perfect regime. To-day, it can be seen that there are republics innately reactionary and absolutist, and also monarchies which incorporate the most ardent social and political hopes of the future. . . .

Fascism has taken up an attitude of complete opposition to the doctrines of Liberalism, both in the political field and the field of economics. There should be no undue exaggeration (simply with the object of immediate success in controversy) of the importance of Liberalism in the last century, nor should what was but one among many theories which appeared in that period be put forward as a religion for humanity for all time, present and to come.

Liberalism only flourished for half a century. . . .

The era of Liberalism, after having accumulated an infinity of Gordian knots, tried to untie them in the slaughter of the World War—and never has any religion demanded of its votaries such a monstrous sacrifice. Perhaps the Liberal Gods were athirst for blood? But now, to-day, the Liberal faith must shut the doors of its deserted temples, deserted because the peoples of the world realize that its worship—agnostic in the field of economics and indifferent in the field of politics and morals—will lead, as it has already led, to certain ruin. . . .

The foundation of Fascism is the conception of the State, its character, its duty, and its aim. Fascism conceives of the State as an absolute, in comparison with which all individuals or groups are relative, only to be conceived of in their relation to the State. . . .

The State, as conceived of and as created by Fascism, is a spiritual and moral fact, since its political, juridical and economic organization of the nation is a concrete thing: and such an organization must be in its origins and development a manifestation of the spirit. The State is the guarantor of security both internal and external, but it is also the custodian and transmitter of the spirit of the people, as it has grown up through the centuries in language, in customs and in faith. And the State is not only a living reality of the present, it is also linked with the past and above all with the future, and thus transcending the brief limits of individual life, it represents the immanent spirit of the nation. The forms in which States express themselves may change, but the necessity for such forms is eternal. It is the State which educates its citizens in civic virtue, gives them a consciousness of their mission and welds them into unity; harmonizing their various interests through justice, and transmitting to future generations the mental conquests of science, of art, of law and the solidarity of humanity. . . .

The Fascist State organizes the nation, but leaves a sufficient margin of liberty to the individual; the latter is deprived of all useless and possibly harmful freedom, but retains what is essential; the deciding power in this question cannot be the individual, but the State alone. . . .

For Fascism, the growth of empire, that is to say the expansion of the nation, is an essential manifestation of vitality, and its opposite a sign of decadence. Peoples which are rising, or rising again after a period of decadence, are always imperialist; and renunciation is a sign of decay and of death. Fascism is the doctrine best adapted to represent the tendencies and the aspirations of a people, like the people of Italy, who are rising again after many centuries of abasement and foreign servitude. But empire demands discipline, the coordination of all forces and a deeply felt sense of duty and sacrifice: this fact explains many aspects of the practical working of the regime, the character of many forces in the State, and the necessarily severe measures which must be taken against those who would oppose this spontaneous and inevitable movement of Italy in the twentieth century, and would oppose it by recalling the outworn ideology of the nineteenth century—repudiated wheresoever there has been the courage to undertake great experiments of social and political transformation; for never before has the nation stood more in need of authority, of direction and order. If every age has its own characteristic doctrine, there are a thousand signs which point to Fascism as the characteristic doctrine of our time. For if a doctrine must be a living thing, this is proved by the fact that Fascism has created a living faith; and that this faith is very powerful in the minds of men is demonstrated by those who have suffered and died for it.

QUESTIONS TO CONSIDER

1. According to the authors, what are the distinguishing features of fascism compared to those of other political ideologies of this era?
2. Fascist movements emerged throughout the world in the 1930s, and fascists came to power in a number of states. How might the rise of fascist movements correlate to the experiences of World War I and the decade following?

CHAPTER 11

THE ONGOING CRISIS OF GLOBAL ORDER, 1919–1948

11.1 "CERTAINLY A GOVERNMENT NEEDS POWER, IT NEEDS STRENGTH." ADOLF HITLER, *MUNICH SPEECH (APRIL 12)*, 1921

Adolf Hitler (1889–1945) led a fascist government in Germany in the 1930s and 1940s that began World War II as well as a program of mass persecution, relocation, and, eventually, murder of Jews and other groups. His political career began in the 1920s, after he was discharged from the Austrian army in World War I. In 1921, he became leader of the National-Socialist German Workers' (Nazi) Party and led an attempted coup in 1923, which failed, before he finally rose to power in 1933.

This speech, one of his first public speeches, contains the themes of populism, antisemitism, and nationalism that Hitler would use to build his constituency.

And the Right has further completely forgotten that democracy is fundamentally not German: it is Jewish. It has completely forgotten that this Jewish democracy with its majority decisions has always been without exception only a means towards the destruction of any existing Aryan leadership. The Right does not understand that directly every small question of profit or loss is regularly put before so-called "public opinion," he who knows how most skillfully to make this "public opinion" serve his own interests becomes forthwith master in the State. And that can be achieved by the man who can lie most artfully, most infamously; and in the last resort he is not the German, he is, in Schopenhauer's words, "the great master in the art of lying"—the Jew *[Arthur Schopenhauer (1788–1860) was an influential philosopher–Ed.]*.

There are only two possibilities in Germany: do not imagine that the people will forever go with the middle party, the party of compromises: one day it will turn to those who have most consistently foretold the coming ruin and have sought to dissociate themselves from it. And that party is either the Left: and then God help us! for it will lead us to complete destruction—to Bolshevism, or else it is a party of

Source: Norman H. Baynes, trans. and ed., *The Speeches of Adolf Hitler*, Vol. 1, April 1922–August 1939 (New York: Howard Fertig, 1969), 13–21.

the Right which at the last, when the people is in utter despair, when it has lost all its spirit and has no longer any faith in anything, is determined for its part ruthlessly to seize the reins of power—that is the beginning of resistance of which I spoke a few minutes ago. Here, too, there can be no compromise: . . . there are only two possibilities: either victory of the Aryan or annihilation of the Aryan and the victory of the Jew.

It is from the recognition of this fact, from recognizing it, I would say, in utter, dead earnestness, that there resulted the formation of our Movement. There are two principles which, when we founded the Movement, we engraved upon our hearts: firstly, to base it on the most sober recognition of the facts and secondly to proclaim these facts with the most ruthless sincerity.

And this recognition of the facts discloses at once a whole series of the most important fundamental principles which must guide this young Movement which, we hope, is destined one day for greatness:

1. "National" and "social" are two identical conceptions. It was only the Jew who succeeded, through falsifying the social idea and turning it into Marxism, not only in divorcing the social idea from the national, but in actually representing them as utterly contradictory. That aim he has in fact achieved. At the founding of this Movement we formed the decision that we would give expression to this idea of ours of the identity of the two conceptions: despite all warnings, on the basis of what we had come to believe, on the basis of the sincerity of our will, we christened it "National Socialist". We said to ourselves that to be "national" means above everything to act with a boundless and all-embracing love for the people and, if necessary, even to die for it. And similarly, to be "social" means so to build up the State and the community of the people that every individual acts in the interest of the community of the people and must be to such an extent convinced of the goodness, of the honourable straightforwardness of this community of the people as to be ready to die for it.

2. And then we said to ourselves: there are no such things as classes: they cannot be. Class means caste and caste means race. If there are castes in India, well and good; there it is possible, for there were formerly Aryans and dark aborigines. So it was in Egypt and in Rome. But with us in Germany where everyone who is a German at all has the same blood, has the same eyes and speaks the same language, here there can be no class, here there can be only a single people and beyond that nothing else. Certainly, we recognize, just as anyone must recognize, that there are different "occupations" and "professions" (Stände)—there is the Stand of the watchmakers, the Stand of the navvies [manual laborers–Ed.], the Stand of the painters or technicians, the Stand of the engineers, officials, &c. Stände there can be. But in the struggles which these Stände have amongst themselves for the equalization of their economic conditions, the conflict and the division must never be so great as to sunder the ties of race.

   And if you say, "But there must after all be a difference between the honest creators and those who do nothing at all"—certainly there must! That is the difference which lies in the performance of the conscientious work of the individual. Work must be the great connecting link, but at the same time the great factor which separates one man from another. The drone is the foe of us all. But the creators—it matters not whether they are brain-workers or workers with the hand—they are the nobility of our State, they are the German people! We understand under the term "work" exclusively that activity which not only profits the individual but in no way harms the community, nay rather which contributes to form the community.

3. And in the third place it was clear to us that this particular view is based on an impulse which springs from our race and from our blood. We said to ourselves that race differs from race and, further, that each race in accordance with its fundamental demands shows externally certain specific tendencies, and these tendencies can

perhaps be most clearly traced in their relation to the conception of work. The Aryan regards work as the foundation for the maintenance of the community of the people amongst its members, the Jew regards work as the means to the exploitation of other peoples. The Jew never works as a productive creator without the great aim of becoming the master. He works unproductively, using and enjoying other people's work. And thus we understand the iron sentence which Mommsen once uttered: "The Jew is the ferment of decomposition in peoples"; that means that the Jew destroys and must destroy because he completely lacks the conception of an activity which builds up the life of the community. *[Theodor Mommsen (1817–1903) was a German historian and archeologist–Ed.].* And therefore, it is beside the point whether the individual Jew is "decent" or not. In himself he carries those characteristics which Nature has given him, and he cannot ever rid himself of those characteristics. And to us he is harmful. Whether he harms us consciously or unconsciously, that is not our affair. We have consciously to concern ourselves for the welfare of our own people.

4. And fourthly we were further persuaded that economic prosperity is inseparable from political freedom and that therefore that house of lies, "Internationalism," must immediately collapse. We recognized that freedom can eternally be only a consequence of power and that the source of power is the will. Consequently, the will to power must be strengthened in a people with passionate ardour.

5. We as National Socialists and members of the German Workers Party . . . must be on principle the most fanatical Nationalists. We realized that the State can be for our people a paradise only if the people can hold sway therein freely as in a paradise: we realized that a Slave-State will never be a paradise, but only always and for all time a hell or a colony.

6. And then sixthly we grasped the fact that power in the last resort is possible only where there is strength, and that strength lies not in the dead weight of numbers but solely in energy. Even the smallest minority can achieve a mighty result if it is inspired by the most fiery, the most passionate will to act. World-history has always been made by minorities. And lastly.

7. If one has realized a truth, that truth is valueless so long as there is lacking the indomitable will to turn this realization into action!

These were the foundations of our Movement, the truths on which it was based and which demonstrated its necessity. . . .

That is the mightiest thing which our Movement must create: for these widespread, seeking, and straying masses a new Faith which will not fail them in this hour of confusion, to which they can pledge themselves, on which they can build so that they may at least find once again a place which may bring calm to their hearts.

QUESTIONS TO CONSIDER

1. What are Hitler's attitudes toward the values of the Enlightenment that we have seen in this book? How does he explain and justify these attitudes?
2. What are the bases of Hitler's criticisms of both "the left" and "the right"? In calling himself a "national-socialist," what elements of nationalism and socialism does he embrace or reject? How does his rhetoric compare to other documents in this sourcebook that address nationalism or social welfare?

11.2 "IT IS INTERNATIONAL MORALITY WHICH IS AT STAKE." HAILE SELASSIE, *SPEECH TO THE LEAGUE OF NATIONS*, 1936

Haile Selassie (1892–1975), the son of an Ethiopian military leader and provincial governor, served as governor himself before rising to the role of regent and crown prince in 1916. He became Emperor upon Empress Zewditu's (1876–1930) death and remained Emperor until he was deposed in a military coup in 1974.

Ethiopia and Italy had a long history of tension. The Italian state had established imperial control over Somaliland (1888) and Eritrea (1880) and looked to expand its advantages in the Horn of Africa at Ethiopia's expense in the 1890s. However, the First Italo-Ethiopian War (1895–1896) ended with Ethiopian victory at the Battle of Adwa, and the subsequent Treaty of Addis Ababa recognized Ethiopia's sovereignty. Under Mussolini's fascist regime, Italian aggression in the Horn of Africa reignited with a dispute over the boundary between Italian Somaliland and Ethiopia. In October 1935, Italian armed forces, without declaring war, invaded Ethiopia, forcing Haile Selassie into exile in 1936. Mussolini annexed Ethiopia, which remained occupied by Italy from 1936 to 1941.

In the months leading up to the Italian invasion, optimists hoped that arbitration of the dispute through the League of Nations could lead to a peaceful resolution. After the invasion began, Emperor Haile Selassie spoke directly to the members of the league. His speech, delivered on June 30, 1936, is excerpted here.

It is my duty to inform the Governments assembled in Geneva, responsible as they are for the lives of millions of men, women and children, of the deadly peril which threatens them, by describing to them the fate which has been suffered by Ethiopia. It is not only upon warriors that the Italian Government has made war. It has above all attacked populations far removed from hostilities, in order to terrorize and exterminate them.

At the beginning, towards the end of 1935, Italian aircraft hurled upon my armies bombs of tear-gas. Their effects were but slight. The soldiers learned to scatter, waiting until the wind had rapidly dispersed the poisonous gases. The Italian aircraft then resorted to mustard gas. Barrels of liquid were hurled upon armed groups. But this means also was not effective; the liquid affected only a few soldiers, and barrels upon the ground were themselves a warning to troops and to the population of the danger.

It was at the time when the operations for the encircling of Makalle [*a city in northern Ethiopia–Ed.*] were taking place that the Italian command, fearing a rout, followed the procedure which it is now my duty to denounce to the world. Special sprayers were installed on board aircraft so that they could vaporize, over vast areas of territory, a fine, death-dealing rain. Groups of nine, fifteen, eighteen aircraft followed one another so that the fog issuing from them formed a continuous sheet. It was thus that, as from the end of January 1936, soldiers, women, children, cattle, rivers, lakes and pastures were drenched continually with this deadly rain. In order to kill off

Source: "Haile Selassie, Appeal to the League of Nations," *African Yearbook of Rhetoric* 2, no. 3 (2011): 9–18.

systematically all living creatures, in order more surely to poison waters and pastures, the Italian command made its aircraft pass over and over again. That was its chief method of warfare.

The very refinement of barbarism consisted in carrying ravage and terror into the most densely populated parts of the territory, the points farthest removed from the scene of hostilities. The object was to scatter fear and death over a great part of the Ethiopian territory. These fearful tactics succeeded. Men and animals succumbed. The deadly rain that fell from the aircraft made all those whom it touched fly shrieking with pain. All those who drank the poisoned water or ate the infected food also succumbed in dreadful suffering. In tens of thousands, the victims of the Italian mustard gas fell. It is in order to denounce to the civilized world the tortures inflicted upon the Ethiopian people that I resolved to come to Geneva. None other than myself and my brave companions in arms could bring the League of Nations the undeniable proof. The appeals of my delegates addressed to the League of Nations had remained without any answer; my delegates had not been witnesses. That is why I decided to come myself to bear witness against the crime perpetrated against my people and give Europe a warning of the doom that awaits it, if it should bow before the accomplished fact.

Is it necessary to remind the Assembly of the various stages of the Ethiopian drama? For 20 years past, either as Heir Apparent, Regent of the Empire, or as Emperor, I have never ceased to use all my efforts to bring my country the benefits of civilization, and in particular to establish relations of good neighbourliness with adjacent powers. In particular I succeeded in concluding with Italy the Treaty of Friendship of 1928, which absolutely prohibited the resort, under any pretext whatsoever, to force of arms, substituting for force and pressure the conciliation and arbitration on which civilized nations have based international order. . . .

In October 1935, the 52 nations who are listening to me today gave me an assurance that the aggressor would not triumph, that the resources of the Covenant would be employed in order to ensure the reign of right and the failure of violence.

I ask the fifty-two nations not to forget today the policy upon which they embarked eight months ago, and on faith of which I directed the resistance of my people against the aggressor whom they had denounced to the world. Despite the inferiority of my weapons, the complete lack of aircraft, artillery, munitions, hospital services, my confidence in the League was absolute. I thought it to be impossible that fifty-two nations, including the most powerful in the world, should be successfully opposed by a single aggressor. Counting on the faith due to treaties, I had made no preparation for war, and that is the case with certain small countries in Europe.

When the danger became more urgent, being aware of my responsibilities towards my people, during the first six months of 1935 I tried to acquire armaments. Many Governments proclaimed an embargo to prevent my doing so, whereas the Italian Government through the Suez Canal, was given all facilities for transporting without cessation and without protest, troops, arms, and munitions. . . .

I assert that the problem submitted to the Assembly today is a much wider one. It is not merely a question of the settlement of Italian aggression. It is collective security: it is the very existence of the League of Nations. It is the confidence that each State is to place in international treaties. It is the value of promises made to small States that their integrity and their independence shall be respected and ensured. It is the principle of the equality of States on the one hand, or otherwise the obligation laid upon small Powers to accept the bonds of vassalship. In a word, it is international morality that is at stake. Have the signatures appended to a Treaty value only in so far as the signatory Powers have a personal, direct and immediate interest involved? . . .

I ask the fifty-two nations, who have given the Ethiopian people a promise to help them in their resistance to the aggressor, what are they willing to do for Ethiopia? And the great Powers who have promised the guarantee of collective security to small States on whom weighs the threat that they may one day suffer the fate of Ethiopia, I ask what measures do you intend to take?

Representatives of the World, I have come to Geneva to discharge in your midst the most painful of the duties of the head of a State. What reply shall I have to take back to my people?

QUESTIONS TO CONSIDER

1. What have been the primary military actions, targets, and goals of the Italian army in Ethiopia? On what principles does Haile Selassie object to the Italian invasion?
2. Why was it imperative for the League of Nations to act at this time in defense of Ethiopia against Italy? What were the implications of inaction?

11.3 "THEY WILL SWEEP ALL THE IMPERIALISTS, WARLORDS, CORRUPT OFFICIALS, LOCAL TYRANTS AND EVIL GENTRY INTO THEIR GRAVES." MAO ZEDONG, *REPORT OF AN INVESTIGATION INTO THE PEASANT MOVEMENT IN HUNAN*, 1927

Mao Zedong (1893–1976), who would go on to found the People's Republic of China in 1949 and lead it until his death in 1976, was born to a peasant family of modest means. He became one of the founding members of the Chinese Communist Party (CCP) in 1921. Mao differed from most other early members of the party in two ways: he had little experience outside China (he left the country only once, in 1949); and he challenged Marxist orthodoxy that believed communist revolution could only arise from an industrialized economy.

The document presented here includes one of Mao's most famous lines: "Revolution is not a dinner party." This quip accompanies Mao's analysis of a peasant uprising in rural Hunan. In the spring of 1927, the party had sent him to study whether this uprising, or similar peasant rebellions, could be understood as Marxist revolutions. Mao's assertions that peasant uprisings were essential parts of a communist revolution in China were met with skepticism by the CCP leadership. However, as Mao was writing this document, Chiang Kai-shek's Nationalists betrayed the CCP in the spring of 1927 and murdered most of the CCP leadership. As a result, Mao's views soon became party policy.

IMPORTANCE OF THE PEASANT PROBLEM

During my recent visit to Hunan *[one of several rural provinces with peasant uprisings at the time–Ed.]* I made a firsthand investigation of conditions in the five counties of Hsiangtan, Hsianghsiang, Hengshan, Liling and Changsha. In the thirty-two days from January 4 to February 5, I called together fact-finding conferences in villages and county towns, which were attended by

Source: "Report of an Investigation into the Peasant Movement in Hunan," in Mao Tse-Tung, *Selected Works, Vol. 1, 1926–1936* (New York: International Publishers, 1954), 21–61.

experienced peasants and by comrades working in the peasant movement, and I listened attentively to their reports and collected a great deal of material. Many of the hows and whys of the peasant movement were the exact opposite of what the gentry in Hankow and Changsha are saying. I saw and heard of many strange things of which I had hitherto been unaware. I believe the same is true of many other places, too. All talk directed against the peasant movement must be speedily set right. All the wrong measures taken by the revolutionary authorities concerning the peasant movement must be speedily changed. Only thus can the future of the revolution be benefited. For the present upsurge of the peasant movement is a colossal event. In a very short time, in China's central, southern and northern provinces, several hundred million peasants will rise like a mighty storm, like a hurricane, a force so swift and violent that no power, however great, will be able to hold it back. They will smash all the trammels that bind them and rush forward along the road to liberation. They will sweep all the imperialists, warlords, corrupt officials, local tyrants and evil gentry into their graves. Every revolutionary party and every revolutionary comrade will be put to the test, to be accepted or rejected as they decide. There are three alternatives. To march at their head and lead them? To trail behind them, gesticulating and criticizing? Or to stand in their way and oppose them? Every Chinese is free to choose, but events will force you to make the choice quickly. . . .

THE QUESTION OF "GOING TOO FAR"

. . . . [A] revolution is not a dinner party, or writing an essay, or painting a picture, or doing embroidery; it cannot be so refined, so leisurely and gentle, so temperate, kind, courteous, restrained and magnanimous. A revolution is an insurrection, an act of violence by which one class overthrows another. A rural revolution is a revolution by which the peasantry overthrows the power of the feudal landlord class. Without using the greatest force, the peasants cannot possibly overthrow the deep-rooted authority of the landlords which has lasted for thousands of years. The rural areas need a mighty revolutionary upsurge, for it alone can rouse the people in their millions to become a powerful force. All the actions mentioned

here which have been labeled as "going too far" flow from the power of the peasants, which has been called forth by the mighty revolutionary upsurge in the countryside. It was highly necessary for such things to be done in the second period of the peasant movement, the period of revolutionary action. In this period it was necessary to establish the absolute authority of the peasants. It was necessary to forbid malicious criticism of the peasant associations. It was necessary to overthrow the whole authority of the gentry, to strike them to the ground and keep them there. There is revolutionary significance in all the actions which were labeled as "going too far" in this period. To put it bluntly, it is necessary to create terror for a while in every rural area, or otherwise it would be impossible to suppress the activities of the counter-revolutionaries in the countryside or overthrow the authority of the gentry. Proper limits have to be exceeded in order to right a wrong, or else the wrong cannot be righted. Those who talk about the peasants "going too far" seem at first sight to be different from those who say "It's terrible!" as mentioned earlier, but in essence they proceed from the same standpoint and likewise voice a landlord theory that upholds the interests of the privileged classes. Since this theory impedes the rise of the peasant movement and so disrupts the revolution, we must firmly oppose it.

OVERTHROWING THE CLAN AUTHORITY OF THE ANCESTRAL TEMPLES AND CLAN ELDERS, THE RELIGIOUS AUTHORITY OF TOWN AND VILLAGE GODS, AND THE MASCULINE AUTHORITY OF HUSBANDS

A man in China is usually subjected to the domination of three systems of authority: (1) the state system (political authority), ranging from the national, provincial and county government down to that of the township; (2) the den system (clan authority), ranging from the central ancestral temple and its branch temples down to the head of the household; and (3) the supernatural system (religious authority), ranging from the King of Hell down to the town and village gods belonging to the nether world, and from the Emperor of Heaven down to all the various gods and spirits belonging to the celestial world. As for women, in addition to being dominated by these three systems of authority, they are also dominated by the men (the authority of the husband). These four authorities—political, clan, religious and masculine—are the embodiment of the whole feudal-patriarchal system and ideology, and are the four thick ropes binding the Chinese people, particularly the peasants. How the peasants have overthrown the political authority of the landlords in the countryside has been described above. The political authority of the landlords is the backbone of all the other systems of authority. With that overturned, the clan authority, the religious authority and the authority of the husband all begin to totter. Where the peasant association is powerful, the den elders and administrators of temple funds no longer dare oppress those lower in the clan hierarchy or embezzle clan funds. The worst clan elders and administrators, being local tyrants, have been thrown out. No one any longer dares to practice the cruel corporal and capital punishments that used to be inflicted in the ancestral temples, such as flogging, drowning and burying alive. The old rule barring women and poor people from the banquets in the ancestral temples has also been broken. The women of Paikno in Hengshan County gathered in force and swarmed into their ancestral temple, firmly planted their backsides in the seats and joined in the eating and drinking, while the venerable den bigwigs had willy-nilly to let them do as they pleased. At another place, where poor peasants had been excluded from temple banquets, a group of them flocked in and ate and drank their fill, while the local tyrants and evil gentry and other long-gowned gentlemen all took to their heels in fright. Everywhere religious authority totters as the peasant movement develops. In many places the peasant associations have taken over the temples of the gods as their offices. Everywhere they advocate the appropriation of temple property in order to start peasant schools and to defray the expenses of the associations, calling it "public revenue from superstition." In Liling County, prohibiting superstitious practices and smashing idols have become quite the vogue. In its northern districts the peasants have prohibited the incense-burning processions to propitiate the god of pestilence. There were many idols in the Taoist temple at Fupoling in Lukou, but when extra room was needed for the

district headquarters of the Kuomintang, they were all piled up in a corner, big and small together, and no peasant raised any objection. Since then, sacrifices to the gods, the performance of religious rites and the offering of sacred lamps have rarely been practised when a death occurs in a family. Because the initiative in this matter was taken by the chairman of the peasant association, Sun Hsiao-shan, he is hated by the local Taoist priests. In the Lungfeng Nunnery in the North Third District, the peasants and primary school teachers chopped up the wooden idols and actually used the wood to cook meat. More than thirty idols in the Tungfu Monastery in the Southern District were burned by the students and peasants together, and only two small images of Lord Pao [an official of the Northern Song Dynasty (960–1127 CE–Ed.] were snatched up by an old peasant who said, "Don't commit a sin!" In places where the power of the peasants is predominant, only the older peasants and the women still believe in the gods, the younger peasants no longer doing so. Since the latter control the associations, the overthrow of religious authority and the eradication of superstition are going on everywhere. As to the authority of the husband, this has always been weaker among the poor peasants because, out of economic necessity, their womenfolk have to do more manual labour than the women of the richer classes and therefore have more say and greater power of decision in family matters. With the increasing bankruptcy of the rural economy in recent years, the basis for men's domination over women has already been weakened. With the rise of the peasant movement, the women in many places have now begun to organize rural women's associations; the opportunity has come for them to lift up their heads, and the authority of the husband is getting shakier every day. In a word, the whole feudal-patriarchal system and ideology is tottering with the growth of the peasants' power. At the present time, however, the peasants are concentrating on destroying the landlords' political authority. Wherever it has been wholly destroyed, they are beginning to press their attack in the three other spheres of the clan, the gods and male domination. But such attacks have only just begun, and there can be no thorough overthrow of all three until the peasants have won complete victory in the economic struggle. Therefore, our present task is to lead the peasants to put their greatest efforts into the political struggle, so that the landlords' authority is entirely overthrown. The economic struggle should follow immediately, so that the land problem and the other economic problems of the poor peasants may be fundamentally solved. As for the den system, superstition, and inequality between men and women, their abolition will follow as a natural consequence of victory in the political and economic struggles. If too much of an effort is made, arbitrarily and prematurely, to abolish these things, the local tyrants and evil gentry will seize the pretext to put about such counter-revolutionary propaganda as "the peasant association has no piety towards ancestors," "the peasant association is blasphemous and is destroying religion" and "the peasant association stands for the communization of wives," all for the purpose of undermining the peasant movement. . . .

While I was in the countryside, I did some propaganda against superstition among the peasants. I said:

. . . "The gods? Worship them by all means. But if you had only Lord Kuan *[the God of War, based on a warrior who lived from 160–219* CE*–Ed.]* and the Goddess of Mercy and no peasant association, could you have overthrown the local tyrants and evil gentry? The gods and goddesses are indeed miserable objects. You have worshipped them for centuries, and they have not overthrown a single one of the local tyrants or evil gentry for you! Now you want to have your rent reduced. Let me ask, how will you go about it? Will you believe in the gods or in the peasant association?"

My words made the peasants roar with laughter.

QUESTIONS TO CONSIDER

1. In Mao's view, how do the peasants fit into plans for a communist revolution in China? How does this differ from Marxist orthodoxy?
2. What does Mao see as the role of violence in revolution? How does he compare to other advocates of social change such as Mohandas Gandhi (Source 9.5)? What do you see as the advantages or disadvantages of these different positions regarding violence?

11.4 "WHEN WILL IT NO LONGER BE NECESSARY TO ATTACH SPECIAL WEIGHT TO THE WORD 'WOMAN'?" DING LING, *THOUGHTS ON MARCH 8 (INTERNATIONAL WOMEN'S DAY)*, 1942

Ding Ling was the pen name of Jiang Bingzhi (1904–1986). She began writing fiction in her teens and went on to become one of China's most prominent authors. After her husband was arrested and executed by the Nationalist government in 1931, she joined the Chinese Communist Party (CCP) and moved to their base at Yan'an (also written as Yenan), in rural northwest China. Mao Zedong (Source 11.3) was their leader.

Source: *New Left Review*, no. 92 (July–August 1975), 102–105.

While at Yan'an, Ding Ling observed that the behavior of male leaders in the Communist Party was often at odds with their stated ideology of equality, especially equality between the sexes. The document excerpted here contains some of her criticisms of CCP leaders. As a result of this and other statements, she was forced to issue a public self-criticism, in which she retracted much of what she said. She would later be purged from the party, spending nearly twenty years in prison and then a labor camp for "rightist" political views. She was released and rehabilitated in 1978.

When will it no longer be necessary to attach special weight to the word "woman" and to raise it specially?

Each year this day comes round. Every year on this day meetings are held all over the world where women muster their forces. Even though things have not been as lively these last two years in Yenan as they were in previous years, it appears that at least a few people are busy at work here. And there will certainly be a congress, speeches, circular telegrams and articles.

Women in Yenan are happier than women elsewhere in China. So much so that many people ask enviously: "How come the women comrades get so rosy and fat on millet?" It doesn't seem to surprise anyone that women make up a big proportion of the staff in the hospitals, sanatoria and clinics, but they are inevitably the subject of conversation, as a fascinating problem, on every conceivable occasion.

Moreover, all kinds of women comrades are often the target of deserved criticism. In my view these reproaches are serious and justifiable.

People are always interested when women comrades get married, but that is not enough for them. It is impossible for women comrades to get onto friendly terms with a man comrade, even more so with more than one. Cartoonists ridicule them: "A departmental head getting married too?" The poets say: "All the leaders in Yenan are horsemen, and none of them are artists. In Yenan it's impossible for an artist to find a pretty sweetheart." But in other situations they are lectured at: "Damn it, you look down on us old cadres and say we're country bumpkins. But if it wasn't for us country bumpkins, you wouldn't be coming to Yenan to eat millet!" But women invariably want to get married. (It's even more of a sin not to be married, and single women are even more of a target for rumours and slanderous gossip.) So they can't afford to be choosy, anyone will do: whether he rides horses or wears straw sandles [sic], whether he's an artist or a supervisor. They inevitably have children. The fate of such children is various. Some are wrapped in soft baby wool and patterned felt and looked after by governesses. Others are wrapped in soiled cloth and left crying in their parents' beds, while their parents consume much of the child['s] allowance. But for this allowance (25 yuan a month, or just over three pounds of pork), many of them would probably never get a taste of meat. Whoever they marry, the fact is that those women who are compelled to bear children will probably be publicly derided as "Noras who have returned home" [*This is a reference to the heroine of Henrik Ibsen's* A Doll's House, *who left home to achieve her freedom–Ed.*]. Those women comrades in a position to employ governesses can go out once a week to a prim get-together and dance. Behind their backs there would also be the most incredible gossip and whispering campaigns, but as soon as they go somewhere they cause a great stir and all eyes are glued to them. This has nothing to do with our theories, our doctrines and the speeches we make at meetings. We all know this to be a fact, a fact that is right before our eyes, but it is never mentioned.

It is the same with divorce. In general there are three conditions to pay attention to when getting married. (1) Political purity; (2) both parties should be more or less the same age and comparable in looks; (3) mutual help. Even though everyone is said to fulfil these conditions—as for (1), there are no open traitors in Yenan; as for (3), you can call anything "mutual help," including darning socks, patching shoes and even feminine comfort—everyone nevertheless makes a great show of giving thought-ful attention to them. And yet, the pretext for divorce is invariably the wife's political backwardness. I am the first to admit that it is a shame when a man's wife is not progressive and retards his progress. But let us consider to what degree they are backward. Before marrying, they were inspired by the desire to soar in the heavenly heights and lead a life of bitter struggle. They got married partly due to physiologi-cal necessity and partly as a response to sweet talk about "mutual help." Thereupon they are forced to toil away and become "Noras returned home." Afraid of being thought "backward," those who are a bit more daring rush around begging nurseries to take their children. They ask for abortions, and risk punishment and even death by secretly swallowing potions to produce abortions. But the answer comes back: "Isn't giving birth to children also work? You're just after an easy life, you want to be in the limelight. After all, what indispensable political work have you performed? Since you are so frightened of having children, and are not willing to take responsibility once you have had them, why did you get married in the first place? No-one forced you to." Under these conditions it is impossible for women to escape this destiny of "backwardness." When women capable of working sacrifice their careers for the joys of mother-hood, people always sing their praises. But after ten years or so, they have no way of escaping the tragedy of "backwardness" (i.e., divorce). Even from my point of view, as a woman, there is nothing attractive about such "backward" elements. Their skin is beginning to wrinkle, their hair is growing thin and fatigue is robbing them of their last traces of attractiveness. It should be self-evident that they are in a tragic situa-tion. But whereas in the old society they would prob-ably have been pitied and considered unfortunate, nowadays their tragedy is seen as something self-inflicted, as their just deserts. Is it not so that there is a discussion going on in legal circles as to whether divorce should be granted simply on the petition of one party or on the basis of mutual agreement? In the great majority of cases it is the husband who peti-tions for divorce. For the wife to do so, she must be leading an immoral life; then of course she deserves to be cursed!

I myself am a woman, and I therefore understand the failings of women better than others. But I also have a deeper understanding of what they suffer. Women are incapable of transcending the age they live in, of being perfect, or of being hard as steel. They are incapable of resisting all the temptations of society or all the silent oppression they suffer here in Yenan. They each have their own past writ-ten in blood and tears, they have experienced great emotions—in elation as in depression, whether engaged in the lone battle of life or drawn into the humdrum stream of life. This is even truer of the women comrades who come to Yenan, and I therefore have much sympathy for those fallen and classed as criminals. What is more, I hope that men, especially those in top positions, and women themselves will consider the mistakes women commit in their social context. It would be better if there were less empty theorizing and more talk about real problems, so that theory and practice are not divorced, and if each Communist Party member were more responsible for his own moral conduct.

But we must also hope for a little more from our women comrades, especially those in Yenan. We must urge ourselves on and develop our comradely feeling.

People without ability have never been in a pos-ition to seize everything. Therefore, if women want equality, they must first strengthen themselves. There is no need to stress this point, since we all understand it. Today there are certain to be people who make fine speeches bragging about the need to first acquire pol-itical power. I would simply mention a few things that any frontliner, whether a proletarian, a fighter in the war of resistance or a woman, should pay atten-tion to in his or her everyday life:

1. Don't allow yourself to fall ill. A wild life can at times appear romantic, poetic and attractive, but in today's conditions it is inappropriate. You are the best keeper of your life. There is nothing more unfortunate nowadays than to lose your health. It is closest to your heart. The only thing to do is keep a close watch on it, pay careful attention to it and cherish it.

2. Make sure you are happy. Only when you are happy can you be youthful, active, fulfilled in your life and steadfast in the face of all difficulties; only then will you see a future ahead of you and know how to enjoy yourself. This sort of happiness is not a life of contentment, but a life of struggle and of advance. Therefore we should all do some meaningful work each day and some reading, so that each of us is in a position to give something to others. Loafing about simply encourages the feeling that life is hollow, feeble and in decay.

3. Use your brain, and make a habit of doing so. Correct any tendency not to think and ponder, or to swim with the current. Before you say or do anything, think whether what you are saying is right, whether that is the most suitable way of dealing with the problem, whether it goes against your own principles, whether you feel you can take responsibility for it. Then you will have no cause to regret your actions later. This is what is known as acting rationally. It is the best way of avoiding the pitfalls of sweet words and honeyed phrases, of being sidetracked by petty gains, of wasting our emotions and wasting our lives.

4. Resolution in hardship, perseverance to the end. Aware, modern women should identify and cast off all their rosy, compliant illusions. Happiness is to take up the struggle in the midst of the raging storm and not to pluck the lute in the moonlight or recite poetry among the blossoms. In the absence of the greatest resolution, it is very easy to falter in mid-path. Not to suffer is to become degenerate. The strength to carry on should be nurtured through the quality of "perseverance." People without great aims and ambitions rarely have the firmness of purpose that does not covet petty advantages or seek a comfortable existence. But only those who have aims and ambitions for the benefit not of the individual but of mankind as a whole can persevere to the end.

DAWN, 3 AUGUST

Postscript. On re-reading this article, it seems to me that there is much room for improvement in the passage on what we should expect from women, but because I have to meet a date-line with the manuscript, I have no time to revise it. But I also feel that there are some things which, if said by a leader before a big audience, would probably evoke satisfaction. But when they are written by a woman, they are more than likely to be demolished. But since I have written it, I offer it as I always intended, for the perusal of those people who have similar views.

QUESTIONS TO CONSIDER

1. How does Ding Ling describe what she finds in Yan'an? What are her biggest disappointments and criticisms? Why do you think CCP leaders forced Ding Ling to retract these statements?

2. What similarities and differences do you see in the way gender and other elements of identity interact in Ding Ling's writing, compared to other documents in this sourcebook (e.g., Sources 5.1, 6.3, 8.3, 8.4, 9.3, 10.5, and/or 11.3)?

11.5 "WHO IS TO BLAME FOR THE CONDITION OF CHINA?" HIROSI SAITO, *THE CONFLICT IN THE FAR EAST*, 1939

In July 1937, years of tension between China and Japan turned into armed conflict. Chinese and Japanese troops exchanged fire in the suburbs of Beijing (often called Beiping at the time), and soon thereafter Japan launched a large-scale invasion of coastal China. By most accounts, this was the beginning of World War II in Asia.

For the next 4½ years, Japan presented a case for its presence in China using numerous arguments designed to win European and American support for Japanese goals (or at least to avoid their intervention in the conflict). The document presented here was originally published in the journal *World Affairs* in December 1937, the same month that Japanese troops carried out the brutal atrocities of the "Rape of Nanking." In this document, Japan's Ambassador to the United States, Hirosi (also anglicized as Hiroshi) Saito (1886–1939) laid out a series of justifications for Japan's presence in China. Saito had a long history with the United States, having been stationed in Washington previously (1911–1918). During his earlier service as a diplomat in the United States, he had befriended then-Secretary of the Navy Franklin D. Roosevelt (1882–1945), who would serve as US President from 1933 to 1945.

Saito died of tuberculosis in 1939, at the age of 46. Illustrating the speed with which international relations can change, Saito was honored in October 1940 with a monument to his memory at the US Naval Academy in Annapolis, Maryland. Fourteen months later, Japan attacked the American naval base at Pearl Harbor, Hawai'i, and brought the United States into another world war. Protests for the removal of the monument occurred during the war, but the memorial remains on the campus of the Naval Academy.

The conflict in the Far East is by no means as simple in origin as some Europeans and Americans seem to think. The trouble did not begin last July. It is a result of the condition of China, which has caused the invasion of foreign armies for more than a century and is the reason for the presence there today of British, French, Italian, Dutch and American troops.

If China's house were in order there would be no need for the presence of these foreign forces or of Japan's present action. In fact, if law and order were maintained in China, if China were a unified and stabilized nation, it would be able to "drive all foreigners into the sea"—which has been the objective of many of its anti-foreign movements.

Who is to blame for the condition of China? Is it Great Britain, which sought for decades to help successive Chinese governments to organize their two principal sources of revenue, the Maritime Customs and the Salt Gabelle [*tax–Ed.*], and administer them without corruption? Is it France, which organized and directed a postal service for the Chinese? Is it the United States, which has sent more missionaries and teachers to them than to all other backward nations combined? Is it Japan, which staked almost her existence in a war with Russia to prevent "the break-up of

Source: Hirosi Saito, "The Conflict in the Far East," *World Affairs* 100, no. 4 (December 1937): 216–220.

China"—a disaster expected throughout the world at the time of the Boxer Rising in 1900? It is difficult for many Japanese to understand how so many people of the West can fail to see that the trouble is not of foreign but of Chinese making.

China was "opened" by Western Powers long before Japan, and while many of the invaders were seeking only selfish interests many were also seeking only to enlighten and assist the Chinese. China was "opened" half a century before Japan but is still today in turmoil and disorder, while Japan, "opened" by the American Commodore Perry in 1854, is a modern nation, free of extraterritoriality and other foreign infringements of its integrity because the people reorganized their government, established law and order, developed schools, promoted industry and looked to their own defences. China refused the advice and assistance of the many good friends who warned and pled with her. She held the West and Japan in contempt and continued her corruptions in politics, resulting in internecine warfare, leaving drought and flood, which bring perennial famine, to continue their devastations. . . .

In my opinion, if the Powers of the West should heed now the appeal of the Chinese, and, through the League of Nations or the Nine-Power Treaty group, go to the aid of China in the present conflict, they would be doing the sorely-afflicted Chinese people infinite harm. They would throw them back upon the mercy of their War Lords, who have slain and plundered them for more than a score of years, ever since the so-called Republic was proclaimed in 1912. . . .

The present trouble with Japan was born in Sianfu, in Shensi Province, less than a year ago, when there was being held a meeting of the so-called "anti-Japanese Popular Front." For nearly ten years Generalissimo Chiang had been an active opponent of the Communists, sending his armies hither and thither across the country to "exterminate" them. But, unknown to him, his ally in Shensi, Marshal Chang Hsuehliang, came to an understanding with the enemy forces in the Northwest, and when the Generalissimo appeared on the scene his personal bodyguard were suddenly attacked and slain and he himself made prisoner. His American-educated wife went in an American airplane to his relief and

arranged the terms of his release, which included a cessation of his warfare against Communists and a union with them with the purpose of fighting Japan. Chiang Kai-shek had been wary of the Movement since its organization, in 1935, but now acceded to it; and the fat was then in the fire, for Japan could not accept being driven out of China.

Had any country with rights in China withdrawn in the face of the Boxer Uprising in 1900? Had any done so in the face of the Communist attacks in 1927? British and American forces, like Japanese, had participated in the defence of foreign rights on both those occasions. Now that the anti-foreignism was directed specifically against Japanese our Government warned that of Nanking and those of other sections of China emphatically and repeatedly against the movement, pointing out its dangers to the highest Chinese officials. But the warnings were not heeded-nor did the League of Nations pay attention to the seriousness of the developing situation. . . .

The present conflict has been forced upon Japan, and Japan wants to end it as quickly as possible. But she is determined to end it in a way so decisive that a situation like the present can never recur. Our objective, therefore, is a genuine change-of-heart on the part of those in power at Nanking. We insist that the organized campaign to stir up hate against Japan be discontinued and that the Central Government renounce the union with Communism. . . .

This underlying accord of our peoples prompts in me high hope that when the leaders of the Nanking regime and the Chinese Nationalist Party adopt a reasonable policy toward Japan, it will not take long to spin close ties of friendship and harmony of incalculable benefit to both China and Japan, and of much also to the rest of the world. With permanent peace between Japan and China, progress will be made in the East of Asia that will redound to the benefit of others in a spread of the feeling of security and an expansion of general and profitable trade and cultural relations. The progress of Japan has brought an enormous increase of trade to Western Countries, particularly the United States, and the peace of China cannot fail to bring progress to the industrious and well-meaning masses of her people.

QUESTIONS TO CONSIDER

1. How does Saito justify Japan's actions in China? What problems does he see in China? What does he describe as the causes, and possible solutions, of the problems? Does knowing the course of events after the publication of this article—including Japan's attack on Pearl Harbor—affect your interpretation of Saito's argument?
2. How does Saito's description of Japan's role in China compare to other descriptions or justifications of imperialism (e.g., Sources 9.1 and/or 9.2)?

11.6 "THE WORK OF OPERATING THE GAS CHAMBERS WAS CARRIED OUT BY A SPECIAL COMMANDO." PRIMO LEVI WITH LEONARDO DE BENEDETTI, *AUSCHWITZ REPORT*, 1946

Primo Levi (1919–1987) was born in Turin, Italy. Trained as a chemist, Levi faced many challenges as a Jew navigating the increasing restrictions of fascist Italy. Trying to join the resistance movement in 1943, he was arrested by fascist militia and placed in an internment camp that was subsequently taken over by the Nazis. In February 1944, Levi was deported to Monowitz, part of the Auschwitz complex in Poland. He survived the war and went on to a career as an author, known best for his short stories, novels, and memoirs, including *Survival in Auschwitz* (1947), perhaps his most well-known work.

Leonardo de Benedetti (1898–1983) was a physician, from a generation older than Levi's, but also an Italian Jew from Turin; he was rounded up and sent from Fossoli to Auschwitz in 1944. Of the 650 people transported on the same train with Levi and de Benedetti, only 24 would survive the war.

When the Auschwitz camps were liberated by the Soviet army in 1945, both Levi and de Benedetti were still alive. They remained for several months in a Russian holding camp for "displaced persons," with de Benedetti providing health care and Levi working as his assistant. Toward the end of their time at Katowice, they co-authored a report on their experience of Monowitz-Auschwitz as part of the investigation that would form the basis for prosecuting Nazi war criminals. We provide brief excerpts from that report here.

The influx of patients was always very great, far in excess of the capacity of the various wards, so to make room for the new arrivals a certain number of patients would be discharged every day, even if not completely recovered and still in a state of serious general debility, despite which they would have to start work again the following day. But those suffering from chronic diseases, or whose stay in hospital

Source: Primo Levi with Leonardo De Benedetti, *Auschwitz Report* (London: Verso, 2006), 71–77.

had lasted longer than a period of about two months, or who were readmitted too often due to relapses of their illness, were sent—as we have already reported in the case of those with tuberculosis, syphilis or malaria—to Birkenau and there eliminated in the gas chambers. The same fate was suffered by those too depleted to be able to work. Every so often—about once a month—the so-called "selection of the Muslims" (this picturesque term denoted precisely these extremely emaciated individuals) took place in the various wards of the hospital, with the most physically broken down being singled out to be dispatched to the gas chambers. These selections were conducted with great rapidity and were carried out by the doctor in charge of medical services, in front of whom all the patients filed naked, while he judged the general condition of each one with a superficial glance, instantly deciding their fate. A few days later, those selected underwent a second examination by a medical captain in the SS *["Schutzstaffel," the Nazi elite "Protective Echelon"–Ed.]* who was the director general of medical services in all the camps subsidiary to Auschwitz. It has to be admitted that this inspection was more thorough than the previous one, with each case being weighed up and discussed; at all events, it was only a lucky few who were removed from the list and readmitted to hospital for further treatment or sent to some Commando where the work was regarded as light; the majority were condemned to death. One of us was included in the list of "Muslims" no fewer than four times, and escaped each time from a fatal outcome, thanks simply to the fact of being a doctor; since—we do not know whether as a general rule or through an initiative on the part of the administration of the Monowitz Camp—doctors were spared from such a fate.

In October 1944, the selection, instead of being restricted to the wards of the hospital, was extended to all the "blocks"; but this was the last one, since after that date this kind of exercise was discontinued and the gas chambers at Birkenau were demolished. Nevertheless, 850 victims were selected during that tragic day, among them eight Jews of Italian nationality.

The work of operating the gas chambers and the adjacent crematorium was carried out by a special Commando which worked day and night, in two shifts. The members of this Commando lived in isolation, carefully segregated from any contact with other prisoners or with the outside world. Their clothes gave off a sickening stench, they were always filthy, and they had an utterly savage appearance, just like wild animals. They were picked from amongst the worst criminals, convicted of serious and bloody crimes.

It appears that in February 1943 a new crematorium oven and gas chamber were inaugurated at Birkenau, more functional than those which had been in operation up to that month. These consisted of three areas: the waiting room, the "shower room," and the ovens. At the centre of the ovens rose a tall chimney, around which were nine ovens with four openings each, all of them allowing the passage of three corpses at a time. The capacity of each oven was two thousand corpses a day. The victims would be ushered into the first room and ordered to undress completely, because—they were told—they had got to take a shower. To make the foul deception more credible, they were handed a piece of soap and a towel, after which they were made to enter the "shower room." This was a very large room equipped with fake shower fittings, and with conspicuous signs on the walls saying things like, "Wash thoroughly, because cleanliness is health," "Don 't economize on soap," "Remember not to leave your towel here!", so as to make the place look just like a large public bath-house. In the flat ceiling of the room there was a large aperture, hermetically closed by three big metal plates that opened with a valve. A set of rails traversed the whole breadth of the chamber, leading from it to the ovens. When everyone had entered the gas chamber, the doors would be locked (they were airtight) and a chemical preparation in the form of a coarse powder, blue-grey in colour, would be dropped through the valve in the ceiling. It was in metal containers whose labels read: "Zyklon B—For the destruction of all kinds of vermin," and carried the trade mark of a factory in Hamburg. In fact, it was a preparation of cyanide which evaporated at a certain temperature. In the course of a few minutes, all those locked into the gas chamber would die; and then the doors and windows would be flung open, and the members of the Special Commando, equipped with gas masks, would enter in order to take the corpses to the crematorium ovens.

Before putting the bodies into the ovens, a specially designated squad would cut off the hair from those who still had it, that is, from the corpses of those who, as soon as they arrived with their transports, were immediately taken to be slaughtered without entering the camps; and they also extracted the gold teeth from those who had them. The ashes, it is well known, were then scattered in fields and vegetable gardens as a fertilizer for the soil.

Towards the end of 1944, orders reached the Monowitz Camp that all doctors present in the Camp were to be released from working in the Commandos and employed in the various sections of the hospital, as doctors or, in the absence of available posts, as nurses. Before being assigned to their new duties, they had to spend a month gaining experience in the various clinical and surgical departments, following a certain rota, and at the same time they had to take a theoretical training course on the medical organization of the concentration camps and how they were run, the characteristic pathology of the camps and the treatments to be practised on the patients. These orders were duly carried out and the course began in early January 1945; but towards the middle of the same month it was broken off due to the overwhelming Russian offensive in the Krakow–Katowice–Wroclaw direction, in the face of which the German forces gave themselves up to headlong flight. The Monowitz Camp was evacuated, along with all the others in the region of Auschwitz, and the Germans dragged about 11,000 prisoners along with them, who, according to information received later from someone who made a miraculous escape, were almost all slaughtered by bursts of machine-gun fire a few days later, when the soldiers escorting them realized that they were completely surrounded by the Red Army and so no longer had any way open to retreat. They had already travelled some seventy kilometres on foot, almost without stopping and with no food, since the provisions they received before leaving the Camp had consisted only of a kilogram of bread, 75 grams of margarine, 90 grams of sausage and 45 of sugar. Later they had been loaded onto various trains which, though taking various different directions, were unable to reach any destination. The massacre then took place of the survivors of such superhuman exertions; many—perhaps three or four thousand—who had stopped on the road, overcome by fatigue, had already been butchered on the spot by pistol shots or by the gun-butts of the soldiers escorting them.

QUESTIONS TO CONSIDER

1. As described in this document, what are the key features of daily life in a Nazi concentration camp?
2. What do the events described in this excerpt reveal about the challenges facing the global community at the time Levi and Benedetti were writing their account (1945–1946)?

11.7 "OUR FORCES DARE TAKE THEIR POSITION BESIDE ANY FORCE IN THE WORLD." GENERAL AUNG SAN, *ADDRESS TO THE EAST WEST ASSOCIATION*, 1945

Aung San (1915–1947) is often regarded as "the father of modern Burma" (known today as Myanmar) for his role in securing Burmese independence from Great Britain. His is a complicated political legacy. He was an activist student leader at Rangoon University in the 1930s before entering national politics to oppose British rule. He later left Burma and helped found the Burmese Communist Party, but he demonstrated a willingness to cooperate with any group that would help him oppose British rule, seeking support in China and then Japan.

Aung San returned to Burma in 1941 and became a decorated army officer, first working on behalf of the Japanese, who expelled the British from Burma, then reversing himself and allying with British forces when he decided that Japan was an even more dangerous imperialist threat. After the defeat of Japan, Aung San became premier of British-controlled Burma and signed an agreement with Britain that granted Burma full independence. Before independence was achieved, however, Aung San was assassinated. His daughter, Aung San Suu Kyi (1945–), was awarded the Nobel Peace Prize in 1991 for her resistance to the Burmese military regime and is today a leading figure in politics in Myanmar.

The document presented here illustrates the complex relationship between colonialism, imperialism, and nationalism in Aung San's thinking and in many Asian colonies.

Until the beginning of 1942, Burma remained under British Rule for so many decades. When Britain and France declared war against Germany in 1939, Burma also was declared to be a belligerent country by the Governor without consulting the Burma Legislature at all. Mr. Chamberlain declared then to the world that Britain was fighting for democracy and freedom or words to that effect. You will remember perhaps then that the Indian National Congress asked for the clarification of the British war aims—whether those aims applied to India at all. Burma also did similarly.

After taking stock of the situation in our country and the world, we finally decided to form a Freedom Bloc of all parties desiring to strive for the emancipation of our country and for democratic freedom. I had also to act as Secretary of this Freedom Bloc for some time. This Freedom Bloc also declared its aim to be democratic freedom for which Britain was said to be fighting. We declared to the British Government—I am speaking from memory of course— that it would be consistent and proper for us to join the war for democratic freedom, only if we would likewise be assured that democratic freedom in theory as well as in practice. So we asked that beginning with the declaration of war, principles of democratic freedom should be applied in our case too.

But our voice went unheeded. To us then the war in Europe was plainly a war between two sets of

Source: Aung San, "The Resistance Movement," *The Political Legacy of Aung San*, Revised Edition, ed. Josef Silverstein (Ithaca, NY: Cornell University Southeast Asian Program Series, No. 11, 1993), 77–93.

imperialists and could have no appeal of any kind. We therefore finally resorted to an anti-imperialist, antiwar campaign. . . .

Several of our members were clapped in jail, some after trial and others without trail. In fact all important leaders of the party to which I belonged and who with me together formed sort of the only left forces in Burma genuinely anti-fascist, . . . all these important leaders were arrested. I was also to be arrested. But as you all know perhaps, I went underground. Then almost accidentally we were informed by Dr. Ba Maw and Dr. Thein Maung who were in the Freedom Bloc at that time that we could, if we desired, get Japanese help. The question of whether we should accept Japanese help was discussed. It was then felt by many that at least international propaganda was necessary for our cause and if any international help might be further secured, it might be better. And we all agreed that to attempt to get such things was impossible inside Burma. Some of us must go either to China or Siam *[Thailand–Ed.]* or Japan for that matter. We chose China first because we had some contacts there. But then the China–Burma Road had to be closed for three months after the fall of France in 1940 according to the demand of the Japanese Government. Personally though I felt that international propaganda and assistance of our cause was necessary, the main work, I thought, must be done in Burma which must be the mobilisation of the masses for the national struggle. I had a rough plan of my own—a country-wide mass resistance movement against British imperialism on a progressive scale, so to speak, co-extensive with international and national developments in the form of series of local and partial strikes of industrial and rural workers leading to general and rent strike finally, also all forms of militant propaganda such as mass demonstrations and people's marches leading finally to mass civil disobedience, also economic campaign against British imperialism in the form of boycott of British goods leading to the mass non-payment of taxes, to be supported by developing guerilla action against military and civil and police outposts, lines of communication, etc., leading finally to the complete paralysis of the British administration in Burma when we should be able along with developing world situation to make the final and ultimate bid for the capture

of power. And I counted then upon the coming over the troops belonging to the British Government to our side—particularly the non-British sections. In this plan I also visualised the possibility of *[a Japanese–Ed.]* invasion of Burma—but here I had no clear vision. (all of us at the time had no clear view in this respect, though some might now try to show themselves, after all the events, to have been wiser than others: in fact you might remember it was a time when I might say the Left forces outside China and the USSR. were in confusion almost everywhere.) As I have said, I couldn't think out clearly. I just said in my plan, we would try to forestall *[the Japanese–Ed.]* invasion, set up our own independent State and would try to negotiate with Japan before it came into Burma; only when we could not stop Japan's coming into Burma, then we should be prepared to resist Japan.

[In the next paragraphs, Aung San asserts that his colleagues vetoed this plan and turned to Japan for support "not by any pro-fascist leanings but by our naive blunders and petit-bourgeois timidity." Then, he details events during the Japanese occupation of Burma under the Ba Maw government and the uprising against Japan which he led. He concludes his talk with an appeal for postwar action–Ed.]

Anyway the war is now over, and it has been won—and won, as we see it, by the peoples of the world. Since 1931, the world had witnessed bloody struggles in one or other part of the globe till all these combined into a world conflagration in the West and the East. Now at long last, peace has come, and I wish to God that the peace that the United Nations should build would be a living, creative peace, creative of freedom, progress and prosperity in all parts of the world, and that it would not all events become a peace of the graveyard. So far as we in Burma are concerned the immediate thing before us is the question of forming a sufficient nucleus of the Burma Defence Force, so that by the time in the next, say two or three years, Burma becomes a Dominion equal in status with the rest of the British Commonwealth of Nations, there will have been built a defence structure sufficient for the minimum defence of our country. . . .

If, however, any measure taken by the authorities concerned in this regard is done without proper understanding of the conditions, the sentiments, and aspirations of our forces and our people, in that case, to say the least, neither Britain nor Burma will achieve their mutual aim with the result that the same frustration of hopes and aspirations fostered by our people and the people in Britain before the war will continue to exist. I hope that this will not be the case now, and that the war just ended has also closed this era of frustration. Let us therefore join hands, Britons, Burmans and all nations alike, to build up an abiding fruitful peace over the foundations of the hard-won victory that all of us desiring progressive direction in our own affairs and in the world at large, have at long last snatched firmly and completely from the grabbing hands of Fascist barbarians, a peace, as I have said, not of the graveyard, but creative of freedom, progress and prosperity in the world.

QUESTIONS TO CONSIDER

1. How does Aung San assess Burma's situation at the outset of World War II? In what specific ways did being a British colony affect Burma, for better or worse? What led Aung San to make the decisions that he did during the war?
2. How does Aung San's description of his experiences compare to Sun Yat-sen's statement on Pan-Asianism (Source 10.6)?

CHAPTER 12

HOT WARS, COLD WARS, AND DECOLONIZATION 1942–1975

12.1 "AN IRON CURTAIN HAS DESCENDED ACROSS THE CONTINENT." WINSTON CHURCHILL, *ADDRESS AT WESTMINSTER COLLEGE* (FULTON, MISSOURI), 1946

Winston Churchill (1874–1965) had a long career in British politics. He first served in Parliament in 1900 and held various cabinet positions, such as First Lord of the Admiralty and Chancellor of the Exchequer. He was Prime Minister from 1940 to 1945, leading the British government and people through most of World War II, and then again from 1951 to 1955. Churchill was known as a powerful and persuasive orator and writer. He was awarded the Nobel Prize in Literature in 1953.

Out of public office after his party's electoral defeat in summer 1945, Churchill began to write and travel, deciding to go on a lecture tour of the United States. In March 1946, he delivered a speech at Westminster College in Fulton, Missouri, which is often referred to as "the Iron Curtain Speech." Churchill was not the first to use this phrase, but he became the person most closely associated with its use. The speech in which he used it, excerpted here, became one of the most influential expressions of concern over Soviet ambitions in the early postwar era.

The United States stands at this time at the pinnacle of world power. It is a solemn moment for the American Democracy. For with primacy in power is also joined an awe-inspiring accountability to the future. If you look around you, you must feel not only the sense of duty done but also you must feel anxiety lest you fall below the level of achievement.

Opportunity is here now, clear and shining for both our countries. To reject it or ignore it or fritter it away will bring upon us all the long reproaches of the after-time. It is necessary that constancy of mind, persistency of purpose, and the grand simplicity of decision shall guide and rule the conduct of the English-speaking peoples in peace as they did in

Source: Winston Churchill, *"Address at Westminster College,"* National Churchill Museum, www.nationalchurchillmuseum.org/sinews-of-peace-iron-curtain-speech.html.

war. We must, and I believe we shall, prove ourselves equal to this severe requirement. . . .

When I stand here this quiet afternoon I shudder to visualise what is actually happening to millions now and what is going to happen in this period when famine stalks the earth. None can compute what has been called "the unestimated sum of human pain." Our supreme task and duty is to guard the homes of the common people from the horrors and miseries of another war. We are all agreed on that. . . .

A world organisation has already been erected for the prime purpose of preventing war; UNO, the successor of the League of Nations, with the decisive addition of the United States and all that that means, is already at work. We must make sure that its work is fruitful, that it is a reality and not a sham, that it is a force for action, and not merely a frothing of words, that it is a true temple of peace in which the shields of many nations can some day be hung up, and not merely a cockpit in a Tower of Babel. Before we cast away the solid assurances of national armaments for self-preservation we must be certain that our temple is built, not upon shifting sands or quagmires, but upon the rock. Anyone can see with his eyes open that our path will be difficult and also long, but if we persevere together as we did in the two world wars—though not, alas, in the interval between them—I cannot doubt that we shall achieve our common purpose in the end. . . .

It would nevertheless be wrong and imprudent to entrust the secret knowledge or experience of the atomic bomb, which the United States, Great Britain, and Canada now share, to the world organisation, while it is still in its infancy. It would be criminal madness to cast it adrift in this still agitated and un-united world. No one in any country has slept less well in their beds because this knowledge and the method and the raw materials to apply it, are at present largely retained in American hands. I do not believe we should all have slept so soundly had the positions been reversed and if some Communist or neo-Fascist State monopolised for the time being these dread agencies. The fear of them alone might easily have been used to enforce totalitarian systems upon the free democratic world, with consequences appalling to human imagination. God has willed

that this shall not be and we have at least a breathing space to set our house in order before this peril has to be encountered: and even then, if no effort is spared, we should still possess so formidable a superiority as to impose effective deterrents upon its employment, or threat of employment, by others. . . .

A shadow has fallen upon the scenes so lately lighted by the Allied victory. Nobody knows what Soviet Russia and its Communist international organisation intends to do in the immediate future, or what are the limits, if any, to their expansive and proselytising tendencies. I have a strong admiration and regard for the valiant Russian people and for my wartime comrade, Marshal Stalin. There is deep sympathy and goodwill in Britain—and I doubt not here also—towards the peoples of all the Russias and a resolve to persevere through many differences and rebuffs in establishing lasting friendships. We understand the Russian need to be secure on her western frontiers by the removal of all possibility of German aggression. We welcome Russia to her rightful place among the leading nations of the world. We welcome her flag upon the seas. Above all, we welcome constant, frequent and growing contacts between the Russian people and our own people on both sides of the Atlantic. It is my duty however, for I am sure you would wish me to state the facts as I see them to you, to place before you certain facts about the present position in Europe.

From Stettin in the Baltic to Trieste in the Adriatic, an iron curtain has descended across the Continent. Behind that line lie all the capitals of the ancient states of Central and Eastern Europe. Warsaw, Berlin, Prague, Vienna, Budapest, Belgrade, Bucharest and Sofia, all these famous cities and the populations around them lie in what I must call the Soviet sphere, and all are subject in one form or another, not only to Soviet influence but to a very high and, in many cases, increasing measure of control from Moscow. Athens alone—Greece with its immortal glories—is free to decide its future at an election under British, American and French observation. The Russian-dominated Polish Government has been encouraged to make enormous and wrongful inroads upon Germany, and mass expulsions of millions of Germans on a scale grievous and undreamed-of are now taking place. The Communist parties, which were very small in all these Eastern States of Europe, have been raised to pre-eminence and power far beyond their numbers and are seeking everywhere to obtain totalitarian control. Police governments are prevailing in nearly every case, and so far, except in Czechoslovakia, there is no true democracy. . . .

I have felt bound to portray the shadow which, alike in the west and in the east, falls upon the world. I was a high minister at the time of the Versailles Treaty and a close friend of Mr. Lloyd-George, who was the head of the British delegation at Versailles. I did not myself agree with many things that were done, but I have a very strong impression in my mind of that situation, and I find it painful to contrast it with that which prevails now. In those days there were high hopes and unbounded confidence that the wars were over, and that the League of Nations would become all-powerful. I do not see or feel that same confidence or even the same hopes in the haggard world at the present time. . . .

From what I have seen of our Russian friends and Allies during the war, I am convinced that there is nothing they admire so much as strength, and there is nothing for which they have less respect than for weakness, especially military weakness. For that reason the old doctrine of a balance of power is unsound. We cannot afford, if we can help it, to work on narrow margins, offering temptations to a trial of strength. If the Western Democracies stand together in strict adherence to the principles of the United Nations Charter, their influence for furthering those principles will be immense and no one is likely to molest them. If, however, they become divided or falter in their duty and if these all-important years are allowed to slip away then indeed catastrophe may overwhelm us all.

QUESTIONS TO CONSIDER

1. According to Churchill, what is the "Iron Curtain"? Where does it come from? What should be done about it?
2. What advice does Churchill provide to his US audience about the role he thinks the United States should play in the post-World War II era? On what does he base this advice?

12.2 "MR. CHURCHILL AND HIS FRIENDS BEAR A STRIKING RESEMBLANCE TO HITLER." *JOSEPH STALIN INTERVIEW, 1946*

Joseph Stalin (1879–1953) succeeded Lenin as leader of the Soviet Union and head of the Communist Party in the mid-1920s. Stalin rapidly expanded Soviet territory and accelerated industrialization but at a very high human cost. Dissent was brutally repressed. In the late 1930s, Stalin reached a nonaggression agreement with Adolf Hitler, but when Hitler violated its terms, the Soviet Union joined the anti-fascist coalition, including England and the United States, that defeated the Axis powers.

Source: "The Meaning of Churchill's Call for War Against the Soviet Union," in Joseph V. Stalin and V. M. Molotov, *The Soviet Union and World Peace* (New York: New Century Publisher, 1946), 20–26. Memorial University of Newfoundland Digital Archives Initiative: http://collections.mun.ca/PDFs/radical/TheSovietUnionandWorldPeace.pdf.

Strains among the Allied powers were evident even before the end of World War II. Conflicts erupted in a series of meetings to determine tactics to end the war and build the peace in 1944 and 1945. By the war's end, Allied leaders were already planning ways to check each other's ambitions in the postwar world. Winston Churchill's distrust of Stalin and the Soviet Union is encapsulated in his "Iron Curtain Speech" (Source 12.1). Stalin's response to Churchill was expressed in a series of interviews given to journalists during the same time frame. In the following, we provide excerpts from the text of an interview published in *Pravda*, the official newspaper of the Soviet Communist Party, on March 13, 1946. In the context of the propaganda struggle of the early Cold War era, it is interesting to note that this text appeared as part of a much longer English-language pamphlet entitled *The Soviet Union and World Peace*.

I appraise *[Winston Churchill's recent speeches–Ed.]* as a dangerous act, calculated to sow the seeds of dissension among the Allied States and impede their collaboration. . . .

As a matter of fact, Mr. Churchill now takes the stand of the warmongers, and in this Mr. Churchill is not alone. He has friends not only in Britain but in the United States of America as well.

A point to be noted is that in this respect Mr. Churchill and his friends bear a striking resemblance to Hitler and his friends. Hitler began his work of unleashing war by proclaiming a race theory, declaring that only German-speaking people constituted a superior nation. Mr. Churchill sets out to unleash war with a race theory, asserting that only English-speaking nations are superior nations, who are called upon to decide the destinies of the entire world. The German race theory led Hitler and his friends to the conclusion that the Germans, as the only superior nation, should rule over other nations. The English race theory leads Mr. Churchill and his friends to the conclusion that the English-speaking nations, as the only superior nations, should rule over the rest of the nations of the world.

Actually, Mr. Churchill, and his friends in Britain and the United States, present to the non-English speaking nations something in the nature of an ultimatum: "Accept our rule voluntarily, and then all will be well; otherwise war is inevitable."

But the nations shed their blood in the course of five years' fierce war for the sake of the liberty and independence of their countries, and not in order to exchange the domination of the Hitlers for the domination of the Churchills. It is quite probable, accordingly, that the non-English-speaking nations, which constitute the vast majority of the population of the world, will not agree to submit to a new slavery.

It is Mr. Churchill's tragedy that, inveterate Tory that he is, he does not understand this simple and obvious truth. . . .

. . . It needs no particular effort to show that . . . Mr. Churchill grossly and unceremoniously slanders both Moscow, and the . . . States bordering on the USSR.

The following circumstance should not be forgotten. The Germans made their invasion of the USSR through Finland, Poland, Rumania, Bulgaria and Hungary. The Germans were able to make their invasion through these countries because, at the time, governments hostile to the Soviet Union existed in these countries. As a result of the German invasion the Soviet Union has lost irretrievably in the fighting against the Germans, and also through the German occupation and the deportation of Soviet citizens to German servitude, a total of about seven million people. In other words, the Soviet Union's loss of life has been several times greater than that of Britain and the United States of America put together. Possibly in some quarters an inclination is felt to forget about these colossal sacrifices of the Soviet people which secured the liberation of Europe from the Hitlerite yoke. But the Soviet Union cannot forget about them. And so, what can there be surprising about the fact that the Soviet Union, anxious for its future safety, is trying to see to it that governments loyal in their attitude to the Soviet Union should exist in these countries? How can anyone, who has not taken leave of his wits, describe these peaceful aspirations of the Soviet Union as expansionist tendencies on the part of our State?. . . .

Mr. Churchill comes somewhere near the truth when he speaks of the increasing influence of the Communist Parties in Eastern Europe. It must be remarked, however, that he is not quite accurate. The influence of the Communist Parties has grown not only in Eastern Europe, but in nearly all the countries of Europe which were previously under Fascist rule—Italy, Germany, Hungary, Bulgaria, Rumania, and Finland—or which experienced German, Italian or Hungarian occupation—France, Belgium, Holland, Norway, Denmark, Poland, Czechoslovakia, Yugoslavia, Greece, the Soviet Union and so on.

The increased influence of the Communists cannot be considered fortuitous. It is a perfectly logical thing. The influence of the Communists has grown because, in the years of the rule of Fascism in Europe, the Communists showed themselves trusty, fearless, self-sacrificing fighters against the Fascist regime for the liberty of the peoples. Mr. Churchill in his speeches sometimes recalls the plain people from little homes, slapping them patronisingly on the back and parading as their friend. But these people are not so simple as may at first sight appear. These plain people have views of their own, a policy of their own, and they know how to stand up for themselves. It was they, the millions of these plain people, that defeated Mr. Churchill and his party in Britain by casting their votes for the Labourites. It was they, the millions of these "plain people," who isolated the reactionaries and advocates of collaboration with Fascism in Europe, and gave their preference to the Left democratic parties. It was they, the millions of these "plain people," who after testing the Communists in the fires of struggle and resistance to Fascism, came to the conclusion that the Communists were fully deserving of the people's confidence. That was how the influence of the Communists grew in Europe.

Of course, Mr. Churchill does not like this course of development and he sounds the alarm and appeals to force. But neither did he like the birth of the Soviet regime in Russia after the First World War. At that time, too, he sounded the alarm and organised an armed campaign of 14 States against Russia setting himself the goal of turning back the wheel of history. But history proved stronger than the Churchill intervention, and Mr. Churchill's quixotry led to his unmitigated defeat at that time. I don't know whether Mr. Churchill and his friends will succeed in organising a new armed campaign against Eastern Europe after the Second World War; but if they do succeed—which is not very probable because millions of plain people stand guard over the cause of peace—it may confidently be said that they will be thrashed, just as they were thrashed once before, 26 years ago.

QUESTIONS TO CONSIDER

1. What does Stalin offer as reasons for the growth of communist movements in Eastern Europe in the aftermath of World War II?
2. According to Stalin, what were the primary causes of the growing rift between the Soviet Union and its World War II allies?

12.3 "VIETNAM HAS THE RIGHT TO BE A FREE AND INDEPENDENT COUNTRY." *VIETNAMESE DECLARATION OF INDEPENDENCE, 1945*

This is the second time a document associated with Ho Chi Minh (1890–1969) appears in this sourcebook (see Source 10.2). After his advocacy for Vietnamese "national self-determination" was frustrated at the 1919 Versailles Peace Conference, Ho studied in Moscow during the 1920s and worked for the Soviet Communist International. During World War II, he founded an anti-Axis guerrilla group called the Viet Minh (Vietnamese League for Independence). During the war, Ho worked with the United States, helping to rescue pilots shot down behind Japanese lines. Within weeks of the Japanese surrender in 1945, Ho Chi Minh and his colleagues proclaimed the Democratic Republic of Vietnam and issued a Declaration of Independence, excerpted here. France rejected this assertion of independence and attempted to reclaim its colonial territories, including those in Indochina (today's Vietnam, Cambodia, and Laos). Decades of warfare in Southeast Asia ensued.

"All men are created equal. They are endowed by their Creator with certain inalienable rights; among these are Life, Liberty, and the pursuit of Happiness." This immortal statement was made in the Declaration of Independence of the United States of America in 1776. In a broader sense, this means: All the peoples on the earth are equal from birth, all the peoples have a right to live, to be happy and free. The Declaration of the French Revolution made in 1791 on the Rights of Man and the Citizen also states: "All men are born free and with equal rights, and must always remain free and have equal rights."

Those are undeniable truths.

Nevertheless, for more than eighty years, the French imperialists, abusing the standard of Liberty, Equality, and Fraternity, have violated our Fatherland and oppressed our fellow citizens. They have acted contrary to the ideals of humanity and justice.

In the field of politics, they have deprived our people of every democratic liberty.

They have enforced inhuman laws; they have set up three distinct political regimes in the North, the Center, and the South of Vietnam in order to wreck our national unity and prevent our people from being united.

They have built more prisons than schools. They have mercilessly slain our patriots; they have drowned our uprisings in rivers of blood.

They have fettered public opinion; they have practised obscurantism against our people.

To weaken our race they have forced us to use opium and alcohol.

In the field of economics, they have fleeced us to the backbone, impoverished our people, and devastated our land.

They have robbed us of our rice fields, our mines, our forests, and our raw materials. They have monopolized the issuing of banknotes and the export trade.

They have invented numerous unjustifiable taxes and reduced our people, especially our peasantry, to a state of extreme poverty.

They have hampered the prospering of our national bourgeoisie; they have mercilessly exploited our workers.

Source: Ho Chi Minh, "Declaration of Independence of the Democratic Republic of Vietnam," *Selected Writings* (Hanoi: Foreign Languages Publishing House, 1960–1962), 17–21.

In the autumn of 1940, when the Japanese Fascists violated Indochina's territory to establish new bases in their fight against the Allies, the French imperialists went down on their bended knees and handed over our country to them.

Thus, from that date, our people were subjected to the double yoke of the French and the Japanese. Their sufferings and miseries increased. The result was that from the end of last year to the beginning of this year, from Quang Tri province to the North of Vietnam, more than two million of our fellow citizens died from starvation. On March 9, the French troops were disarmed by the Japanese. The French colonialists either fled or surrendered showing that not only were they incapable of "protecting" us, but that, in the span of five years, they had twice sold our country to the Japanese.

On several occasions before March 9, the Vietminh League urged the French to ally themselves with it against the Japanese. Instead of agreeing to this proposal, the French colonialists so intensified their terrorist activities against the Vietminh members that before fleeing they massacred a great number of our political prisoners detained at Yen Bay and Caobang.

Notwithstanding all this, our fellow citizens have always manifested toward the French a tolerant and humane attitude. Even after the Japanese putsch of March 1945, the Vietminh League helped many Frenchmen to cross the frontier, rescued some of them from Japanese jails, and protected French lives and property.

From the autumn of 1940, our country had in fact ceased to be a French colony and had become a Japanese possession.

After the Japanese had surrendered to the Allies, our whole people rose to regain our national sovereignty and to found the Democratic Republic of Vietnam.

The truth is that we have wrested our independence from the Japanese and not from the French.

The French have fled, the Japanese have capitulated, Emperor Bao Dai has abdicated. Our people have broken the chains which for nearly a century have fettered them and have won independence for the Fatherland. Our people at the same time have overthrown the monarchic regime that has reigned supreme for dozens of centuries. In its place has been established the present Democratic Republic.

For these reasons, we, members of the Provisional Government, representing the whole Vietnamese people, declare that from now on we break off all relations of a colonial character with France; we repeal all the international obligation that France has so far subscribed to on behalf of Vietnam and we abolish all the special rights the French have unlawfully acquired in our Fatherland.

The whole Vietnamese people, animated by a common purpose, are determined to fight to the bitter end against any attempt by the French colonialists to reconquer their country.

We are convinced that the Allied nations, which at Tehran and San Francisco have acknowledged the principles of self-determination and equality of nations, will not refuse to acknowledge the independence of Vietnam.

A people who have courageously opposed French domination for more than eighty years, a people who have fought side by side with the Allies against the Fascists during these last years, such a people must be free and independent.

For these reasons, we, members of the Provisional Government of the Democratic Republic of Vietnam, solemnly declare to the world that Vietnam has the right to be a free and independent country—and in fact is so already. The entire Vietnamese people are determined to mobilize all their physical and mental strength, to sacrifice their lives and property in order to safeguard their independence and liberty.

QUESTIONS TO CONSIDER

1. Ho Chi Minh's Declaration of Independence incorporates references to and language from the US War of Independence and the French Revolution. What purpose do these references serve in this document? How might one account for the apparent contradiction in which the

French and US governments opposed an independence movement built on American and French ideals?

2. What important differences exist between the US Declaration of Independence (Source 6.1) and the Vietnamese Declaration? What can these differences tell us about changes in political ideologies, the material world, and global relationships between the late eighteenth and mid-twentieth centuries?

12.4 "THE EQUAL AND INALIENABLE RIGHTS OF ALL MEMBERS OF THE HUMAN FAMILY." UNITED NATIONS, *UNIVERSAL DECLARATION OF HUMAN RIGHTS*, 1948

Established in 1945—at the end of World War II—the United Nations attempted to make good on the promise of the failed League of Nations: an international body that would establish and enforce international law and promote goodwill among nations. Central to this mission was the concept of human rights, which had influenced numerous documents and doctrines but had not been codified in a single set of standards. Identifying and promoting certain rights as common to all people was one of the UN's first objectives.

The Universal Declaration of Human Rights was adopted by the United Nations General Assembly in Paris in December 1948.

PREAMBLE

Whereas recognition of the inherent dignity and of the equal and inalienable rights of all members of the human family is the foundation of freedom, justice and peace in the world,

Whereas disregard and contempt for human rights have resulted in barbarous acts which have outraged the conscience of mankind, and the advent of a world in which human beings shall enjoy freedom of speech and belief and freedom from fear and want has been proclaimed as the highest aspiration of the common people,

Whereas it is essential, if man is not to be compelled to have recourse, as a last resort, to rebellion against tyranny and oppression, that human rights should be protected by the rule of law,

Whereas it is essential to promote the development of friendly relations between nations,

Whereas the peoples of the United Nations have in the Charter reaffirmed their faith in fundamental human rights, in the dignity and worth of the human person and in the equal rights of men and women and have determined to promote social progress and better standards of life in larger freedom,

Source: United Nations Documents, www.ohchr.org/EN/UDHR/Documents/UDHR_Translations/eng.pdf.

Whereas Member States have pledged themselves to achieve, in cooperation with the United Nations, the promotion of universal respect for and observance of human rights and fundamental freedoms,

Whereas a common understanding of these rights and freedoms is of the greatest importance for the full realization of this pledge,

Now, therefore,

The General Assembly,

Proclaims this Universal Declaration of Human Rights as a common standard of achievement for all peoples and all nations, to the end that every individual and every organ of society, keeping this Declaration constantly in mind, shall strive by teaching and education to promote respect for these rights and freedoms and by progressive measures, national and international, to secure their universal and effective recognition and observance, both among the peoples of Member States themselves and among the peoples of territories under their jurisdiction.

ARTICLE 1

All human beings are born free and equal in dignity and rights. They are endowed with reason and conscience and should act towards one another in a spirit of brotherhood.

ARTICLE 2

Everyone is entitled to all the rights and freedoms set forth in this Declaration, without distinction of any kind, such as race, colour, sex, language, religion, political or other opinion, national or social origin, property, birth or other status. Furthermore, no distinction shall be made on the basis of the political, jurisdictional or international status of the country or territory to which a person belongs, whether it be independent, trust, non-self-governing or under any other limitation of sovereignty.

ARTICLE 3

Everyone has the right to life, liberty and security of person.

ARTICLE 4

No one shall be held in slavery or servitude; slavery and the slave trade shall be prohibited in all their forms.

ARTICLE 5

No one shall be subjected to torture or to cruel, inhuman or degrading treatment or punishment.

ARTICLE 6

Everyone has the right to recognition everywhere as a person before the law.

ARTICLE 7

All are equal before the law and are entitled without any discrimination to equal protection of the law. All are entitled to equal protection against any discrimination in violation of this Declaration and against any incitement to such discrimination.

ARTICLE 8

Everyone has the right to an effective remedy by the competent national tribunals for acts violating the fundamental rights granted him by the constitution or by law.

ARTICLE 9

No one shall be subjected to arbitrary arrest, detention or exile.

ARTICLE 10

Everyone is entitled in full equality to a fair and public hearing by an independent and impartial tribunal, in the determination of his rights and obligations and of any criminal charge against him.

ARTICLE 11

1. Everyone charged with a penal offence has the right to be presumed innocent until proved guilty according to law in a public trial at which he has had all the guarantees necessary for his defence.

2. No one shall be held guilty of any penal offence on account of any act or omission which did not constitute a penal offence, under national or international law, at the time when it was committed. Nor shall a heavier penalty be imposed than the one that was applicable at the time the penal offence was committed.

ARTICLE 12

No one shall be subjected to arbitrary interference with his privacy, family, home or correspondence, nor to attacks upon his honour and reputation. Everyone has the right to the protection of the law against such interference or attacks.

ARTICLE 13

1. Everyone has the right to freedom of movement and residence within the borders of each State.
2. Everyone has the right to leave any country, including his own, and to return to his country.

ARTICLE 14

1. Everyone has the right to seek and to enjoy in other countries asylum from persecution.
2. This right may not be invoked in the case of prosecutions genuinely arising from non-political crimes or from acts contrary to the purposes and principles of the United Nations.

ARTICLE 15

1. Everyone has the right to a nationality.
2. No one shall be arbitrarily deprived of his nationality nor denied the right to change his nationality.

ARTICLE 16

1. Men and women of full age, without any limitation due to race, nationality or religion, have the right to marry and to found a family. They are entitled to equal rights as to marriage, during marriage and at its dissolution.
2. Marriage shall be entered into only with the free and full consent of the intending spouses.

3. The family is the natural and fundamental group unit of society and is entitled to protection by society and the State.

ARTICLE 17

1. Everyone has the right to own property alone as well as in association with others.
2. No one shall be arbitrarily deprived of his property.

ARTICLE 18

Everyone has the right to freedom of thought, conscience and religion; this right includes freedom to change his religion or belief, and freedom, either alone or in community with others and in public or private, to manifest his religion or belief in teaching, practice, worship and observance.

ARTICLE 19

Everyone has the right to freedom of opinion and expression; this right includes freedom to hold opinions without interference and to seek, receive and impart information and ideas through any media and regardless of frontiers.

ARTICLE 20

1. Everyone has the right to freedom of peaceful assembly and association.
2. No one may be compelled to belong to an association.

ARTICLE 21

1. Everyone has the right to take part in the government of his country, directly or through freely chosen representatives.
2. Everyone has the right to equal access to public service in his country.
3. The will of the people shall be the basis of the authority of government; this will shall be expressed in periodic and genuine elections which shall be by universal and equal suffrage and shall be held by secret vote or by equivalent free voting procedures.

ARTICLE 22

Everyone, as a member of society, has the right to social security and is entitled to realization , through national effort and international co-operation and in accordance with the organization and resources of each State, of the economic, social and cultural rights indispensable for his dignity and the free development of his personality.

ARTICLE 23

1. Everyone has the right to work, to free choice of employment, to just and favourable conditions of work and to protection against unemployment.
2. Everyone, without any discrimination, has the right to equal pay for equal work.
3. Everyone who works has the right to just and favourable remuneration ensuring for himself and his family an existence worthy of human dignity, and supplemented, if necessary, by other means of social protection.
4. Everyone has the right to form and to join trade unions for the protection of his interests.

ARTICLE 24

Everyone has the right to rest and leisure, including reasonable limitation of working hours and periodic holidays with pay.

ARTICLE 25

1. Everyone has the right to a standard of living adequate for the health and well-being of himself and of his family, including food, clothing, housing and medical care and necessary social services, and the right to security in the event of unemployment, sickness, disability, widowhood, old age or other lack of livelihood in circumstances beyond his control.
2. Motherhood and childhood are entitled to special care and assistance. All children, whether born in or out of wedlock, shall enjoy the same social protection.

ARTICLE 26

1. Everyone has the right to education. Education shall be free, at least in the elementary and fundamental stages. Elementary education shall be compulsory. Technical and professional education shall be made generally available and higher education shall be equally accessible to all on the basis of merit.
2. Education shall be directed to the full development of the human personality and to the strengthening of respect for human rights and fundamental freedoms. It shall promote understanding, tolerance and friendship among all nations, racial or religious groups, and shall further the activities of the United Nations for the maintenance of peace.
3. Parents have a prior right to choose the kind of education that shall be given to their children.

ARTICLE 27

1. Everyone has the right freely to participate in the cultural life of the community, to enjoy the arts and to share in scientific advancement and its benefits.
2. Everyone has the right to the protection of the moral and material interests resulting from any scientific, literary or artistic production of which he is the author.

ARTICLE 28

Everyone is entitled to a social and international order in which the rights and freedoms set forth in this Declaration can be fully realized.

ARTICLE 29

1. Everyone has duties to the community in which alone the free and full development of his personality is possible.
2. In the exercise of his rights and freedoms, everyone shall be subject only to such limitations as are determined by law solely for the purpose of securing due recognition and respect for the rights and freedoms of others and of meeting the just requirements of morality, public order and the general welfare in a democratic society.
3. These rights and freedoms may in no case be exercised contrary to the purposes and principles of the United Nations.

ARTICLE 30

Nothing in this Declaration may be interpreted as implying for any State, group or person any right to engage in any activity or to perform any act aimed at the destruction of any of the rights and freedoms set forth herein.

QUESTIONS TO CONSIDER

1. What do you think the rights listed in this document have in common with one another? How and why do you think they were chosen?
2. What rights would you consider adding to this list? Are there rights you think should be removed? If this list were created today, how do you think it might be different?
3. Where and when do you think the ideas behind these rights originated? Does your answer to this question affect how these rights might be viewed in different parts of the world?

12.5 "WE CANNOT AFFORD EVEN TO THINK OF FAILURE." *KWAME NKRUMAH SPEECHES,* 1957 AND 1962

Kwame Nkrumah (1909–1972) was born in what is now Ghana, then the British colony of the Gold Coast. He came to the United States in 1935 to attend University, earning degrees from Lincoln University and the University of Pennsylvania, both in Philadelphia. He developed an interest in anti-colonial activism while living in Philadelphia and New York, and then after moving to London in 1945. When World War II ended, he returned to the Gold Coast and took a leadership role in the colony's move toward independence. Shortly after his arrival, he was involved in the protests leading to violent confrontation with colonial authorities and spent time in jail, which raised his profile and popularity.

Nkrumah went on to become the first Prime Minister of Ghana—the first British colony in Africa to win independence—in 1957. He left a complex political legacy. He was a founder of the African Union and the Non-aligned Movement. He also endorsed elements of Marxism that earned him the Soviet Union's Lenin Prize, but at the same time he rejected the overtures of most African socialist leaders. Having led Ghana to independence, he turned the country into a single-party dictatorship and arranged for his own election as President for Life in 1964. A military coup overthrew Nkrumah while he was on a state visit to China. He lived the rest of his life in exile.

These two short documents are speeches from the early days of Ghanaian independence. The first was delivered on the day Ghana became independent: March 6, 1957. The second is from a radio address presented in May 1962.

Sources: Excerpt 1: www.bbc.co.uk/worldservice/focusonafrica/news/story/2007/02/070129_ghana50_independence_speech.shtml; Excerpt 2: www.nkrumah.net/gov-pubs/gp-a1474-61-62/gen.php?index=0.

EXCERPT 1: INAUGURATION SPEECH

At long last, the battle has ended!

And thus Ghana, your beloved country is free forever.

And yet again I want to take the opportunity to thank the chiefs and people of this country, the youth, the farmers, the women who have so nobly fought and won this battle.

Also I want to thank the valiant ex-service men who have so co-operated with me in this mighty task of freeing our country from foreign rule and imperialism.

And as I pointed out . . . I made it quite clear that from now on—today—we must change our attitudes, our minds, we must realise that from now on, we are no more a colonial but a free and independent people.

But also, as I pointed out, that also entails hard work.

Reshaping Ghana's destiny

I am depending upon the millions of the country, and the chiefs and people, to help me to reshape the destiny of this country.

We are prepared to pick it up and make it a nation that will be respected by every nation in the world.

We know we are going to have difficult beginnings, but again, I'm relying upon your support, I'm relying upon your hard work.

Seeing you in this . . . it doesn't matter how far my eye goes, I can see that you are here in your millions and my last warning to you is that you are to stand firm behind us so that we can prove to the world that when the African is given a chance he can show the world that he is somebody!

We have awakened. We will not sleep anymore. Today, from now on, there is a new African in the world!

That new African is ready to fight his own battles and show that after all, the black man is capable of managing his own affairs.

We are going to demonstrate to the world, to the other nations, that we are prepared to lay our own foundation.

Our own African identity

As I said in the assembly just minutes ago, I made a point that we are going to create our own African personality and identity. It's the only way that we can show the world that we are ready for our own battles.

But today, may I call upon you all—that on this great day, let us all remember that nothing in the world can be done unless it's had the purport and support of God.

We have won the battle and we again re-dedicate ourselves. . . . Our independence is meaningless unless it is linked up with the total liberation of Africa.

Let us now fellow Ghanaians, let us now ask for God's blessing and for only two seconds in your thousands and millions, I want to ask you to pause only for one minute and give thanks to almighty God for having led us through our difficulties, imprisonments, hardships and suffering to have brought us to the end of our trouble today.

One minute silence.

Ghana is free forever and here I will ask the band to play the Ghana national anthem.

EXCERPT 2: RADIO ADDRESS

At the present moment, all over Africa, dark clouds of neo-colonialism are fast gathering. African States are becoming debtor-nations, and client States day in and day out, owing to their adoption of unreal attitudes to world problems, saying "no" when they should have said "yes" and "yes" when they should have said "no." They are seeking economic shelter under colonialist wings, instead of accepting the truth—that their survival lies in the political unification of Africa.

Countrymen, we must draw up a programme of action and later plan details of this programme for the benefit of the whole people. Such a programme is the one that the Party now brings to you, the people of Ghana, in the hope that you will approve it critically and help to make it a success.

We have a rich heritage. Our natural resources are abundant and varied. We have mineral and agricultural wealth and above all, we have the will to find the means whereby these possessions can be put to the greatest use and advantage. . . .

We cannot afford to fail. We cannot afford even to think of failure. But if there is one thing we in this great

Party have learnt, it is that nothing has been achieved or will ever be achieved without unstinted effort and the determination to succeed. Nothing succeeds like success. So, all of us must tighten our belts and plunge head first into the fight for the urgent socialist reconstruction about which we have talked so much. . . .

. . . . An emergent country which attempts to follow a policy of socialism at home and a policy abroad of positive non-alignment, is challenging many vested interests. It would have been most criminal folly for us not to take note of the lessons of contemporary history.

QUESTIONS TO CONSIDER

1. How does Kwame Nkrumah's rhetoric compare with other proclamations and documents in this sourcebook asserting national independence or renewal (for instance, Sources 6.1, 10.3, 12.3)? What do the ideas of independence and sovereignty mean to Nkrumah?
2. To what degree does Nkrumah's rhetoric reflect, defy, or take sides in the global Cold War? How does his rhetoric change between 1957 and 1962?

12.6 "WE WANT TO ADVANCE IN THE TECHNOLOGICAL SPHERE AND THE SCIENTIFIC SPHERE RAPIDLY." JAWAHARLAL NEHRU, *CONVOCATION ADDRESS, INDIAN INSTITUTE OF TECHNOLOGY*, 1956

Jawaharlal Nehru (1889–1964) was born in British India and trained as a lawyer in England. He became a supporter of Mohandas Gandhi and a fierce advocate for Indian self-rule, rising to a leadership role in the Indian National Congress. Nehru later served as independent India's first Prime Minister, from 1947 to 1964. He became a leading voice among the heads of state of the nonaligned, or "third world" movement, and was one of the most important political leaders of the twentieth century. He also was part of one of the most important families in Indian politics: his daughter Indira (Source 12.7) and grandson Rajiv both served as Indian Prime Minister (and both were assassinated).

The institution that became the Indian Institute of Technology (IIT) at Kharagpur was established in 1950 as the Eastern Higher Technical Institute (EHTI) to train scientists and engineers. An Act of the Indian Congress reorganized the college as the IIT, the first of a number of IIT campuses throughout the country. Prime Minister Nehru came to the campus to deliver a convocation address to celebrate the institute's new status.

Source: Jawaharlal Nehru, "Convocation Address, Indian Institute of Technology," *The Scholars' Avenue: The Campus Newspaper of IIT Kharagpur*, August 20, 2011. www.scholarsavenue.org/news/convocation-address-by-shri-jawaharlal-nehru-at-the-first-annual-convocation-held-on-21st-april-1956.

When I look at the young men and the new graduates I have a feeling which is slightly akin to envy. Perhaps envy is not the right word, but I can think of no other, because I see them launching out not only on their life's career which is an exciting business for every young man and young woman at this time of life, but launching out on it at a time of peculiar significance to this country and to them.

I suppose that I am partial to India in my thinking. I cannot help it because India is in my blood and bone and everywhere and in my thoughts. But I try to think, nevertheless, objectively, in so far as one can and to see this India in the larger context of the world today, in the larger context of history, and looking at it in this way it seems to me that at the present moment there is no more exciting place to live in than India. Mind you, I use the word exciting. I did not use the word comfortable or any other soothing word, because India is going to be a hard place to live in. Let there be no mistake about it; there is no room for soft living in India, not much room for leisure, although leisure, occasional leisure is good. But there is any amount of room in India for living the hard, exciting, creative adventure of life. It is, therefore, that I said I rather envy the young men and young women who, having acquired a certain training, launch out on this adventure at this particular juncture of India's history.

I have no reason to complain, because people of my generation have also lived rather exciting lives and have had our full measure of adventure. We have also seen many things happening. There was a time and the time is not past when we indulged in all kinds of dreams, and it was exciting to work for those dreams and to see those dreams come true. There is no greater joy in life than to work for a great purpose and gradually to see the realisation of that purpose and so, people of my generation in India, we joined ourselves to this great purpose of freeing India. Because we allied ourselves to a mighty purpose, something of the greatness of that task fell on us also. Because the higher you act, the higher you think, the nobler your enterprise, something of that nobility comes to you. If you indulge in small activities, in small thinking then you remain small. But if you dare and go in for the really big things of life

then, even in your endeavour to realise them, you become big in the process. So, I have no reason to complain of our lives because we had had adventures and even fulfilment in full measure.

Nevertheless, the great part of our lives was spent not in building directly, although there was plenty of building in a sense, but rather in breaking up political and economic and other structures which had grown up and which confined India and prevented it from developing. It is true that during the last eight or nine years, we have had a chance of constructive, creative, building effort and we have taken advantage of it to the best of our ability and this process no doubt will continue. . . .

It is well that it should be so because no generation should impose itself upon another. The world would soon be in a bad way if there was too much imposition of one generation over other. There is always a tendency to do that. As we grow older, we tend to impose ourselves upon the younger people. We tend to bully them a lot by good advice and the like. Well, good advice is often needed, I suppose, but ultimately the good develops in us not by the advice and the sermons that we hear but by other factors. If you have been trained here in this Institute in the proper way, leaving it to you to develop your personality, your thinking, then you are developing along right lines and whenever difficulties face you, you will be able to overcome them. So, I am not here to offer you good advice—be good, do this or that. We are up against far too great and tremendous problems for us to solve them by some cheap advice to each other. . . .

In India today, uncommon things are necessary—uncommon efforts are necessary, uncommon application to work, creativeness and the like, because remember that in India to-day we are attempting a task which in its own way is rather unique. As a matter of fact, every country has a unique task. I did not mean that India is superior to other countries "and in that sense" our task is unique. Do not fall into that error of a narrow nationalism, thinking that your country is somehow superior to others. The people of every country often think in that way and take pride in the fact that somehow or other they are superior to others. That is not a wise approach.

Every country has its good points and bad points. Every country has to make good through its own efforts and, therefore, for every country it is an exciting adventure. That is true. Nevertheless, I said that India is going through a rather unique period of her existence; and even from the world point of view, there are very unusual and unique features about our present endeavours to go ahead. Other countries are far ahead of us in many ways, in this very matter which you are learning here, in technology and science, in the applications of science and in the wealth that those applications have produced, far ahead of us. There are again countries in Asia which are behind us, we are ahead of them. But, broadly speaking, we still are classified as an underdeveloped country in this respect, and rightly so. We are underdeveloped. The developed countries have gone through that process for 150/170 years or more and gradually adapted themselves more and more or more or less to these changing circumstances. Some countries like the Soviet Union and others have bustled and hastened through those processes in a particular way and certainly arrived at a certain goal of technological efficiency and progress. There is no doubt about it, having paid a very heavy price for it and having adopted a system, which I am not here to criticise or to praise, but which is different from the system that we endeavour to follow here.

Now, therefore, we wish to solve our problems in India, that is to say, we want to advance in the technological sphere and the scientific sphere rapidly. And yet we want to adhere to certain methods which, normally speaking, do not help rapid advance. That is the problem before us. Well, only the future in history will show how far we have succeeded, all I can say, that even in the present and even with the brief experience of the last 7/8 years one can look upon this problem with a measure of optimism. We have done well, I think, in spite of any number of difficulties and obstructions. Difficulties and obstructions coming from where? Not from anybody outside us, not from any other country, or any other people. Difficulties and obstructions arising out of our own failings. It is because of our own failings and weaknesses that we stumble and fall and sometimes are pulled back. At no time have I ever had the slightest sensation of fear or apprehension from any external quarters. I am not afraid of what any country big or small can do to India. Of course, other countries can do good to India or do ill to India. They can make a difference to India, to our problems, I do not deny that but what I said was that I have no sensation of fear from any country—and that is saying a very big thing for me—because there is plenty of fear in the world today, one country fearing another. Fortunately, among the many lessons that it was my privilege to learn working under Gandhi-ji [*Mohandas Gandhi–Ed.*]—there was this lesson—not to be afraid of anything and, so I am not afraid of any external thing happening to us, but I shall be quite frank with you. Doubts and apprehensions arise in my mind about our own internal weaknesses and failings not things external to us. If we function rightly, if we, in India, function with unity and co-operate with each other and go in the right direction, more or less, then there is nothing in the wide world that can come in our way.

QUESTIONS TO CONSIDER

1. According to Nehru, why are this moment, and this institution, so important for India?
2. What insights about the "third world" movement can you derive from this address?

12.7 "SOME GOVERNMENTS STILL REST ON THE THEORY OF RACIST SUPERIORITY." INDIRA GANDHI, *PRESENTATION OF THE JAWAHARLAL NEHRU AWARD FOR INTERNATIONAL UNDERSTANDING TO MARTIN LUTHER KING, 1969*

Indira Gandhi (1917–1984) was the third Prime Minister of independent India and to date the only woman to hold that office. She was the daughter of Jawaharlal Nehru (Source 12.6), India's first Prime Minister. Gandhi (not related to Mohandas Gandhi) served two terms as Prime Minister, from 1966 to 1977 and again from 1980 to 1984. Her time in office was controversial: she oversaw the creation of India's nuclear program and testing of an atomic bomb. She also supported East Pakistan in its independence struggle that led to the creation of Bangladesh. Domestically, she is associated with centralization of political power, including two years of Emergency Rule that enabled her to bypass Parliament. She is credited, however, with making India self-sufficient in terms of food and other economic and agricultural reforms, and also for uniquely navigating the Cold War politics of the United States and USSR (frustrating both sides at times). She was assassinated in 1984.

The following excerpt is taken from a speech delivered to Martin Luther King's widow, Coretta Scott King, at her presentation with the Jahawarlal Nehru Prize for International Understanding. The award recipient, Dr. Martin Luther King, Jr., was assassinated on April 4, 1968. King's receipt of this award is noteworthy in part because it demonstrates the extent of the international influence of King, Mohandas Gandhi, and other nonviolent activists. It also points out the global importance of race and racism, the legacies of colonialism, and the interplay of these forces with Cold War conflict.

This is a poignant moment for all of us. We remember vividly your last visit to our country. We had hoped that on this occasion, Dr. King and you would be standing side by side on this platform. That was not to be. He is not with us but we feel his spirit. We admired Dr. King. We felt his loss as our own. The tragedy rekindled memories of the great martyrs of all time who gave their lives so that men might live and grow. We thought of the great men in your own country who fell to the assassin's bullet and of Mahatma Gandhi's martyrdom here in this city, this very month, twenty-one years ago. Such events remain as wounds in the human consciousness, reminding us of battles, yet to be fought and tasks still to be accomplished. We should not mourn for men of high ideals. Rather we should rejoice that we had the privilege of having had them with us, to inspire us by their radiant personalities. So today we are gathered not to offer you grief, but to salute a man who achieved so much in so short a time. It is befitting,

Madam, that you whom he called the "courage by my side," you who gave him strength and encouragement in his historic mission, should be with us to receive this award.

You and your husband both had foreseen that death might come to him violently. It was perhaps inherent in the situation. Dr. King chose death for the theme of a sermon, remarking that he would like to be remembered as a drum major for justice, for peace and for righteousness. When you were once asked what you would do if your husband were assassinated, you were courage personified, replying that you might weep but the work would go on. Your face of sorrow, so beautiful in its dignity coupled with infinite compassion, will forever be engraved in our hearts.

Mahatma Gandhi also had foreseen his end and had prepared himself for it. Just as training for violence included learning to kill, the training for non-violence, he said, included learning how to die. The true badge of the satyagrahi *[one who practices non-violence–Ed.]* is to be unafraid.

As if he too had envisaged the martyrdoms of Mahatma Gandhi and Martin Luther King, Rabindranath Tagore once sang:

In anger we slew him,
With love let us embrace him now,
For in death he lives again amongst us,
The mighty conqueror of death.

This award, Madam, is the highest tribute our nation can bestow on work for understanding and brotherhood among men. It is named after a man who himself was a peace-maker and who all his life laboured passionately for freedom, justice and peace in India and throughout the world. Dr. Martin Luther King's struggle was for these same values. He paid for his ideals with his blood, forging a new bond among the brave and the conscientious of all races and all nations.

Dr. King's dream embraced the poor and the oppressed of all lands. His work ennobled us. He spoke of the right of man to survive and recognized three threats to the survival of man—racial injustice, poverty and war. He realised that even under the lamp of affluence which was held aloft by science, lay the shadow of poverty, compelling two-thirds of the peoples of the world to exist in hunger and want. He proclaimed that mankind could be saved from war only if we cared enough for peace to sacrifice for it.

Dr. Martin Luther King drew his inspiration from Christ, and his method of action from Mahatma Gandhi. Only through truth can untruth be vanquished. Only through love can hatred be quenched. This is the path of the Buddha and of Christ, and in our own times, that of Mahatma Gandhi and of Martin Luther King.

They believed in the equality of all men. No more false doctrine has been spread than that of the superiority of one race over another. It is ironical that there should still be people in this world who judge men not by their moral worth and intellectual merit but by the pigment of their skin or other physical characteristics.

Some governments still rest on the theory of racist superiority—such as the governments of South Africa and the lawless regime in Rhodesia. Unregenerate groups in other countries consider one colour superior to another. Our own battle is not yet over. Caste and other prejudices still survive, but most of us are ashamed of them and recognise them as evils to be combated. We are trying hard to eradicate them.

While there is bondage anywhere, we ourselves cannot be fully free. While there is oppression anywhere, we ourselves cannot soar high. Martin Luther King was convinced that one day the misguided people who believed in racial superiority would realise the error of their ways. His dream was that white and black, brown and yellow would live and grow together as flowers in a garden with their faces turned towards the sun. As you yourself said, "All of us who believe in what Martin Luther King stood for, must see to it that his spirit never dies." That spirit can never die. There may be setbacks in our fight for the equality of all men. There may be moments of gloom. But victory must and will be ours. Let us not rest until the equality of all races and religions becomes a living fact. That is the most effective and lasting tribute that we can pay to Dr. King.

QUESTIONS TO CONSIDER

1. What comparison does Gandhi imply between African Americans and Indians? What does this comparison suggest about the nature of colonialism in different contexts?
2. How does the context of the Cold War fit into Gandhi's speech, particularly in her comments about Rhodesia and South Africa? What insight can these comments give us about Cold War politics in other countries?

CHAPTER 13

THE MANY WORLDS OF THE TWENTY-FIRST CENTURY, 1972–2012

13.1 "WE SHALL CONFRONT THE WORLD WITH OUR IDEOLOGY." *AYATOLLAH RUHOLLAH KHOMEINI SPEECH*, 1980

Ruhollah Khomeini (1908–1989) was born in Khomeyn, Persia. As a young man, he trained as an Islamic cleric at a renowned Shi'a theological school, where he later taught. From about 1930, Khomeini was addressed with the title Ayatollah (the word signifies "religious leader"). When Khomeini was a young man, a new family dynasty seized power in Persia. Reza Khan crowned himself Shah in 1925. Looking for inspiration and lessons in the experience of Turkey, Reza Shah and, later, his son (Mohammad Reza Pahlavi) set out to build with their allies what they saw as a "modern" nation-state, now known as Iran. The Ayatollah Khomeini became an outspoken critic of the new state, inspiring protests. He was forced into exile in 1963, but he continued to criticize the regime.

The modern Iranian state developed as a secular nation-state with authoritarian tendencies. In the 1970s, protests against the government of the Shah of Iran mounted from many sides. Liberal critics assailed the regime's disregard for the rule of law embodied in Iran's constitution. Though banned by law, Marxist groups operated as well, hoping to redirect Iran toward a communist future. The Ayatollah's supporters condemned the current regime and aspired to establish a nation based on the Ayatollah's interpretations of Islamic law. Amidst mounting unrest, the Shah and his family fled Iran in January 1979. The Ayatollah returned soon thereafter. Within months, a new political framework created the Islamic Republic of Iran, and the Ayatollah was given the title Supreme Leader, which he held until his death in 1989. The following excerpt is taken from a radio address the Ayatollah delivered on March 21, 1980.

Source: Middle East Research and Information Project published in *MERIP Reports*, Volume 10 (May/June 1980), www.merip.org/mer/mer88/khomeini-we-shall-confront-world-our-ideology.

In the name of God, the compassionate, the merciful, let me congratulate all oppressed people and the noble Iranian nation on the occasion of the new year, whose present is the consolidation of the foundation of the Islamic Republic. The will of almighty God, may He be praised, decreed the release of this oppressed nation from the yoke of the tyranny and crimes of the satanical regime and from the yoke of the domination of oppressive powers, especially the government of the world-devouring America, and to unfurl the banner of Islamic justice over our beloved country. It is our duty to stand up to the superpowers and we have the ability to stand up against them, provided that our intellectuals give up their fascination with Westernization or Easternization and follow the straight path of Islam and nationalism.

We are fighting against international communism to the same degree that we are fighting against the Western world—devourers led by America, Israel and Zionism. My dear friends, you should know that the danger from the communist powers is not less than America and the danger of America is such that if we show the slightest negligence we shall be destroyed. Both superpowers have risen for the obliteration of the oppressed nations and we should support the oppressed people of the world. . . .

My dear youth, who are the object of my attention, take the Koran in one hand and the weapon in the other and so defend your dignity and honor that you can deprive them of the power of thinking and plotting against you.

Be so merciful to your friends that you do not cease from bestowing upon them all that you possess. Be aware that today's world is the world of oppressed people and that, sooner or later, theirs is the victory! The oppressed are the ones who shall inherit the earth and shall govern by God's decree. . . .

. . . . The noble nation should know that the entire victory was achieved through the will of almighty God and by means of transformation which came about throughout the country, and through the spirit of faith and a spirit of self-sacrifice, which was manifested in the decisive majority of the nation. Turning toward God and the unity of expression was the basis of our victory. If we forget the secret of victory and we turn away from great Islam and its holy teachings and

if we follow the path of disunity and dissension, there is the danger that the bounty of God almighty may cease and the path may be laid open for the oppressors, and that the deceits and plots of the satanical powers may put our beloved nation in bondage and waste the pure blood which has been shed on the path of independence and freedom and spoil the hardships which our dear young and old have endured, and that our Islamic country may forever endure that which passed during the satanical regime, and that those who were defeated as a result of the Islamic revolution may do to us that which they did and continue to do to the deprived and oppressed people of the world.

Therefore, being conscious of my divine and religious duty, I remind you of certain points. . . .

—This year is a year in which security should return to Iran and the noble people live in utmost comfort. Once again, I announce my support for the noble Iranian armed forces. However, the armed forces of the Islamic Republic should fully observe all laws and regulations. His excellency, the president, who has been appointed commander in chief of the armed forces on my behalf, is duty-bound to severely punish anyone, regardless of his position and grade, who wishes to create disruption in the army or organize strikes or indulge in slowdowns or violate army discipline and regulations or rebel against army regulations.

—The police and the gendarmerie of the country should observe order. As I have been informed, there are a great number of slowdowns at police stations. Those who do not have good records should strive to show greater harmony with the people in order to establish order throughout Iran. They should regard themselves as part of the nation. I hope that in the future a fundamental reorganization be carried out in the gendarmerie and the police. The security forces should regard themselves as belonging to Islam and the Muslims. . . .

—Revolution Courts throughout the country should be perfect examples of the implementation of God's religion. They should try not to be diverted from the teachings of God almighty, even by one step. . . .

—The government is duty-bound to provide the means of labor and production for workers, farmers and laborers. However, they too should know that strikes and slowdowns will not only strengthen the superpowers, but also cause the hope of the oppressed people in the Islamic and non-Islamic countries who have risen to be turned into despair. . . .My dear workers, you should know that those who every day create tumult in a corner of the country and who basically come to the field with the logic of force are your headstrong enemies and wish to turn you away from the path of the revolution. . . .

—In government departments, all government employees must obey the government elected by the people; otherwise, harsh actions are needed. Anybody who wishes to disrupt a government department should be expelled immediately and should be made known to the nation. I am amazed at how the responsible officials are not making use of the strength of the people. The people themselves will settle their accounts with the counter-revolutionaries and expose them. . .

—Revolution should come about in all the universities throughout Iran, so that the professors who are in contact with the East or the West will be purged, and so that the universities may become healthy places for the study of higher Islamic teachings. The false teachings of the former regime should be abruptly stopped in universities throughout Iran because all the misery of the Iranian society during the reign of this father and son was due to these false teachings. If we had a proper set-up in our universities, we would have never had a university-educated intelligentsia who during Iran's most critical period are engaged in conflict and schism among themselves and are cut off from the people and are so negligent of what happens to the people, as though they do not live in Iran. All of our backwardness is due to the lack of proper understanding by most of the university intellectuals of the Islamic society of Iran. Unfortunately, the same thing is still true. Most of the deadly blows which have been delivered to this society have been due to the majority of these university-educated intellectuals who have always regarded—and still regard—themselves as being great and have always said things—and still continue to say things—which only their other intellectual friends can understand, regardless of whether the people understand them or not. Because the public is of no significance to them and all that is important to them is themselves. This is due to the fact that false university education during the reign of the Shah so

trained university-educated intellectuals that they attached no value whatsoever to the oppressed masses. Unfortunately, even now it is the same.

Committed and responsible intellectuals, you should set aside dissension and schism and should think of the people and you should free yourselves from the evil of the "isms" and "ists" of the East or the West, for the sake of the salvation of the people, who have given martyrs. You should stand on your own feet and should refrain from relying on foreigners. The students of religious teaching and university students should carefully study Islamic principles and should set aside the slogans of deviant groups and should replace all deviationist thinking with beloved and genuine Islam. Religion students and university students should know that Islam is itself a rich school, which is never in need of grafting any other ideologies to it. All you should know that mixed thinking is a betrayal of Islam and the Muslims and the bitter results of such thinking will become apparent in future years.

Most regrettably, at times it can be seen that due to the lack of the proper and precise understanding of Islamic issues, some people have mixed Islamic ideas with Marxist ideas and have created a concoction which is in no way in accordance with the progressive teachings of Islam. Dear students, do not follow the wrong path of the uncommitted university intellectuals and do not separate yourselves from the people.

—Another issue is the press and the mass media. Once again, I ask all the press throughout Iran to come and join hands and freely write about the issues, but not to engage in plots. I have repeatedly said that the press should be independent and free.

But unfortunately, and with great amazement I have seen a number of them engaged in implementing the evil designs of the right or the left, most unjustly, in Iran; and they are still doing it. In every country the press plays an essential role in the creation of a healthy or unhealthy atmosphere. I hope that they will engage in service to God and the people. Also, radio and television should be independent and free and should broadcast every kind of criticism with complete impartiality, so that once again we will not see the radio and television from the time of the deposed Shah. Radio and television should be purged of its pro-Shah or deviant elements.

QUESTIONS TO CONSIDER

1. According to the Ayatollah, what were the major reasons for victory over the regime of the Shah of Iran?
2. What kind of political system does the Ayatollah propose for the new Iranian state? What are the major steps that need to be taken to build that state? What are the major threats to the consolidation of the new state?

13.2 "COMRADE GORBACHEV RECOMMENDED NOT TO BE DETERRED." *MEMORANDA OF CONVERSATION BETWEEN EGON KRENZ AND MIKHAIL S. GORBACHEV, 1989*

After forty years of single-party rule, communist parties across Central and Eastern Europe began to fall in 1989. The election of a noncommunist government in Poland was the first clear indication of this trend, but just as important was the fact that the Soviet Union did not send troops to suppress protest as had occurred in earlier demonstrations against communist rule.

On November 1, the newly installed leader of communist East Germany, Egon Krenz (who succeeded Erich Honecker, who had resisted Gorbachev-style reforms), met with Soviet head of state Mikhail Gorbachev to discuss the protests in Germany and across the region as well as prospects for reform.

The excerpts presented here are two different accounts of the same conversation between Krenz and Gorbachev. One is the East German record of the event; the other is the Soviet one. They give insights into the events of 1989 but are especially useful for how they illustrate the challenges of working with primary sources.

EAST GERMAN RECORD

Comrade Gorbachev recommended not to be deterred by the complicated problems. From his own experience he knew that comrades were at times depressed because even after several years of *perestroika [restructuring–Ed.]* in the Soviet Union there were still such great problems to resolve. He then always told them that the Party itself had wanted perestroika. It had involved the mass of people in politics. If now some processes were not running as expected, if there were stormy and emotionally charged arguments, then one would had [sic–Ed.] to

Source: Egon Krenz, "Memorandum of Conversation Between Egon Krenz, Secretary General of the Socialist Unity Party and Mikhail S. Gorbachev," *Making the History of 1989*, Item #435, http://chnm.gmu.edu/1989/items/show/435 and Mikhail Gorbachev, "Soviet Record of Conversation between Mikhail Gorbachev and Egon Krenz," *Making the History of 1989*, Item #436, http://chnm.gmu.edu/1989/items/show/436 (accessed October 23, 2017).

cope with that, too, and not become afraid of one's own people.

He did not mean to say that perestroika had been fully achieved in the Soviet Union. The horse was saddled but the ride was not over. One could still be thrown off. On the other hand, much experience had already been gained, which had great significance. Now the phase of intensified work for the continuation of perestroika was beginning in the Soviet Union. . . .

The population, however, resented the Party for having the mass media in particular create a world of illusion that did not coincide with the practical experience of the people and their everyday life. That caused a break of confidence between Party and people. This was actually the worst thing that could happen to a party.

Some say that the cause for this is to be found in the fact that the party leadership misjudged the domestic political situation in the last three months. It proved to be speechless when so many people left the GDR *[German Democratic Republic: communist East Germany–Ed.].* This was a tough accusation. In addition, besides political mistakes, important psychological mistakes were also made in this difficult situation: In the newspapers it was stated that we did not weep any tears after these people left. This deeply hurt the feelings of many mothers and fathers, relatives, friends and comrades of these people whose leaving caused them great pains.

Despite these facts the Politburo of the CC *[Central Committee–Ed.]* of the SED *[Socialist Unity Party, the governing communist party of the German Democratic Republic–Ed.]* agreed that the political crisis in which the GDR currently found itself had not just begun this summer. Many problems had been accumulating for a long time. . . .

Comrade Krenz stated that they in the GDR had unfortunately left many questions regarding perestroika in the Soviet Union to the judgment of the enemy and failed to have a dialogue with the people about it. This happened despite the fact that Comrade Gorbachev had advised Comrade Erich Honecker *[General Secretary of the East German Socialist Unity Party, 1971–1989–Ed.]* until at one of their first meetings to deal with the opinions which had appeared in Soviet publications and with which he disagreed.

Comrade Krenz pointed out that the prohibition of [the Soviet magazine] *Sputnik* in the GDR had led to a situation in which the enemy could raise questions about the GDR citizens' right of access to information. The comrades and citizens outside the Party who complained about it were not primarily concerned about the contents of Sputnik. The problem was that the GDR leadership on the one hand was watching as the population was receiving broadcasts from the Western TV stations every evening for many hours, but, on the other hand, prohibited the reading of a Soviet newspaper. This was an important turning-point in the political thinking of GDR citizens. After the 9th Plenum of the CC of the SED [on 18 October 1989], one of the first steps to be ordered therefore was the return of Sputnik onto the list of permitted newspapers. . . .

On the subject of the still on-going demonstrations, Comrade Krenz stated that the situation was not easy. The composition of the demonstrators was diverse. Some real enemies were working among them. A large part were dissatisfied [citizens] or fellow travelers. The SED leadership was determined to resolve political problems by political means. The demonstrations would be legalized, and there would be no police action against them. The situation, however, was developing according to its own dynamics. For the weekend, a large demonstration with possibly half a million participants was planned in Berlin. It had been initiated by artists and some of their associations. . . .

Comrade Gorbachev explained that it was now necessary to revive creative Marxism, socialism in a Leninist way, the humanistic and democratic socialism in which man really felt that this was his society and not an elite society. This process was not easy to implement. Of this he had become aware during his visit to Cuba. There had been a tense atmosphere initially. He himself, however, had explained that perestroika resulted from the development of the Soviet Union, and was necessary for the solution of Soviet problems. The question of whether socialism in the Soviet Union would succeed or fail was of importance for the entire world, including Cuba. . . .

SOVIET RECORD

. . .

GORBACHEV: The Soviet people are very interested in everything that is going on now in the GDR.

We hope to get the most recent information from you, although, of course, we know a lot. The situation in the GDR, judging by everything we see, is moving at an increasing speed. Is there a danger of getting left behind the reforms? Remember, we said in Berlin that to be behind is always to lose. We know that from our own experience. . . .

KRENZ: We have already taken a number of steps. First of all, we gave orders to the border troops not to use weapons at the border, except in the cases of direct attacks on the soldiers. Secondly, we adopted a draft of Law on Foreign Travel at the Politburo. We will present it for a public discussion, and we plan to pass it in the Volkskammer even before Christmas. . . .

GORBACHEV: Kohl *[Helmut Kohl (1930–2017), Chancellor of West Germany–Ed.]* was visibly worried when I mentioned the perverse interpretation of some of our agreements with the FRG *[Federal Republic of Germany: West Germany–Ed.]* in my 8 October speech in Berlin. He immediately gave me a telephone call regarding that.

KRENZ: Yes, he is worried; I noticed it in my conversation with him. He was even forgetting to finish phrases.

GORBACHEV: Kohl, it seems, is not a big intellectual, but he enjoys [a] certain popularity in his country, especially among the petit-bourgeois public.

QUESTIONS TO CONSIDER

1. What are the most important concerns being discussed in this encounter? In what ways do they reflect new circumstances in global or national affairs? In what ways are they the enduring concerns of any heads of state in the modern world?
2. How does knowing the sources of the documents (i.e., that one is Soviet and the other East German) influence the way you analyze and interpret them? How does reading two accounts of the same meeting enhance or challenge your understanding of the dynamics and content of the encounter?

13.3 "AN AXIS OF EVIL." GEORGE W. BUSH, *STATE OF THE UNION ADDRESS*, 2002 AND HUGO CHÁVEZ, *ADDRESS TO THE UNITED NATIONS GENERAL ASSEMBLY*, 2008

George W. Bush (1946–) was the 43rd president of the United States, serving from 2001 to 2009. The son of US President George H.W. Bush (1924–), and grandson of US Senator Prescott Bush (1895–1972), George W. Bush also served as Governor of Texas from 1995 to 2000. Eight months into Bush's presidency, the terrorist attacks of September 11, 2001, occurred. In response, the

Source: The White House Archived Web Pages of President George W. Bush, https://georgewbush-whitehouse.archives.gov/news/releases/2002/01/20020129-11.html; American Rhetoric Online Speech Bank, http://www.americanrhetoric.com/speeches/hugochavezunitednations.htm.

Bush administration declared a "war on terror" that led to deploying US troops to Afghanistan and Iraq. The administration also named other countries as potentially hostile forces in this war.

Hugo Chávez (1954–2013) served as president of Venezuela from 1999 to 2013. A career military officer, he joined an unsuccessful coup attempt in the 1980s, for which he was imprisoned. Emerging from jail, he burst onto the national political scene, denouncing Venezuela's traditional political parties. Running for president outside of the political party structures, Chávez tapped into widespread anger and disaffection among sectors of Venezuelan society and won the presidential election in 1998. Declaring that he would carry out a revolution inspired by Venezuela's first president, Simón Bolívar (see Source 6.5), Chávez nationalized key industries, wrote a new constitution, and advocated for a new international coalition to resist US imperialism. Increasingly, the United States government under President Bush began to place Venezuela in the category of hostile regimes. Chávez remained in power until his death in 2013.

Two speeches are excerpted here. The first is President Bush's 2002 State of the Union address, in which he articulates the ways in which his administration plans to respond to changed global realities. The second is a speech delivered to the UN General Assembly by President Chávez in 2008.

EXCERPT 1: GEORGE W. BUSH SPEECH

My hope is that all nations will heed our call, and eliminate the terrorist parasites who threaten their countries and our own. Many nations are acting forcefully. . . .

But some governments will be timid in the face of terror. And make no mistake about it: If they do not act, America will.

Our second goal is to prevent regimes that sponsor terror from threatening America or our friends and allies with weapons of mass destruction. Some of these regimes have been pretty quiet since September the 11th. But we know their true nature. North Korea is a regime arming with missiles and weapons of mass destruction, while starving its citizens.

Iran aggressively pursues these weapons and exports terror, while an unelected few repress the Iranian people's hope for freedom.

Iraq continues to flaunt its hostility toward America and to support terror. The Iraqi regime has plotted to develop anthrax, and nerve gas, and nuclear weapons for over a decade. This is a regime that has already used poison gas to murder thousands of its own citizens—leaving the bodies of mothers huddled over their dead children. This is a regime that agreed to international inspections—then kicked out the inspectors. This is a regime that has something to hide from the civilized world.

States like these, and their terrorist allies, constitute an axis of evil, arming to threaten the peace of the world. By seeking weapons of mass destruction, these regimes pose a grave and growing danger. They could provide these arms to terrorists, giving them the means to match their hatred. They could attack our allies or attempt to blackmail the United States. In any of these cases, the price of indifference would be catastrophic.

We will work closely with our coalition to deny terrorists and their state sponsors the materials, technology, and expertise to make and deliver weapons of mass destruction. We will develop and deploy effective missile defenses to protect America and our allies from sudden attack. And all nations should know: America will do what is necessary to ensure our nation's security.

We'll be deliberate, yet time is not on our side. I will not wait on events, while dangers gather. I will not stand by, as peril draws closer and closer. The United States of America will not permit the world's most dangerous regimes to threaten us with the world's most destructive weapons.

Our war on terror is well begun, but it is only begun. This campaign may not be finished on our watch—yet it must be, and it will be waged on our watch. . . .

In this moment of opportunity, a common danger is erasing old rivalries. America is working with

Russia and China and India, in ways we have never before, to achieve peace and prosperity. In every region, free markets and free trade and free societies are proving their power to lift lives. Together with friends and allies from Europe to Asia, and Africa to Latin America, we will demonstrate that the forces of terror cannot stop the momentum of freedom.

EXCERPT 2: HUGO CHÁVEZ SPEECH

The devil came here yesterday. Yesterday, the Devil was here in this very place. This rostrum still smells like sulfur. Yesterday, ladies and gentlemen, from this podium, the President of the United States, whom I refer to as the Devil, came here talking as if he owned the world. It would take a psychiatrist to analyze the speech he delivered yesterday.

As the spokesperson for imperialism, he came to give us his recipes for maintaining the current scheme of domination, exploitation and pillage over the peoples of the world. . . .

We cannot allow this to happen. We cannot allow a world dictatorship to be installed or consolidated.

The statement by the tyrannical president of the world was full of cynicism and hypocrisy. Basically, it is with imperial hypocrisy that he attempts to control everything. They want to impose upon us the democratic model they devised, the false democracy of elites. And, moreover, a very original democratic model, imposed with explosions, bombings, invasions and bullets. What a democracy! In light of this, Aristotle's and those theories made by the first Greek thinkers who spoke about democracy shall be reviewed, so as to analyze what kind of democracy that is, one which imposes itself through marines, invasions, aggressions and bombs. . . .

The President of the United States addressed the peoples of Afghanistan, the people of Lebanon and the people of Iran. Well, one has to wonder, when listening to the US President speak to those people: if those people could talk to him, what would they say?

I am going to answer on behalf of the peoples because I know their soul well, the soul of the peoples of the South, the downtrodden peoples would say: Yankee imperialist, go home! That would be the shout springing up everywhere, if the peoples of the world could speak in unison to the United States' Empire.

Therefore, Madam President, colleagues, and friends, last year we came to this same Hall, as every year over the last eight, and we said something that has been completely confirmed today. I believe that almost no one in this room would dare to stand up and defend the United Nations system, let us admit this with honesty: the United Nations system that emerged after World War II has collapsed, shattered, it does not work anymore. . . .

Despite all this, Madam President, I believe that there are many reasons to be optimistic. Hopelessly optimistic, as a poet may say, because beyond the threats, bombs, wars, aggressions, preventive war, destruction of entire peoples, one can see that a new era is dawning, as Silvio Rodríguez *[a Cuban folk singer (1946–)–Ed.]* says in his song: "this era is giving birth to a heart." Streams, alternative thoughts and movements, youths with different ideas are arising. In barely a decade, it has been demonstrated that the theory of the End of History was totally false, as totally false were also the theory of the founding of the American Empire, the American peace, the establishment of the capitalist and neo-liberal model that generates misery and poverty. This theory is totally false, and it has fallen down. Now it is time to define the future of the world. There is a new dawning on this Planet that can be seen everywhere: in Latin America, Asia, Africa, Europe, and Oceania. I would like to highlight this vision of optimism to strengthen our conscience and our willingness to fight in favor of the world's salvation and for the construction of a new, a better world.

QUESTIONS TO CONSIDER

1. According to each leader, what are the biggest threats facing the global community in the twenty-first century? Where do these threats come from?
2. How does each leader try to define and encourage the formation of new alliances emerging in the twentieth-first century? Who should belong to these alliances? What common goals should bind the members of these alliances together?

13.4 "THE BACKWARD GLANCE LEADING TO SELF-KNOWLEDGE." MARY ROBINSON, *KEYNOTE ADDRESS*, INTERNATIONAL CONFERENCE ON HUNGER, 1995

The Columbian Exchange introduced new food sources to Europe that helped reduce hunger on the continent. Tragically, it also indirectly contributed to one of the worst famines in modern history. So successful and widespread was potato production after it was introduced in the seventeenth century that it became the most important source of domestic food in Ireland. Land distribution and British imperial policy contributed to this skew toward potato dependency. When a disease destroyed the potato crop in the 1840s, approximately one million people fled Ireland, and another million starved in what became known as the Irish Potato Famine. On the 150th anniversary of that famine, Mary Robinson (1944–) delivered a keynote address for an international conference on hunger in New York. Robinson, the first woman to be elected President of Ireland and also the first woman to be appointed United Nations High Commissioner on Refugees, sought to apply lessons from the Irish famine to illustrate links among hunger, poverty, international politics, and migration at the end of the twentieth century.

Let me give you, right away, an example of the fact of hunger and its companion circumstance which is poverty. And let me put that against the idea of it. In 1993, we are informed, more than twelve million children under the age of five died in the developing world. This in itself is a terrible fact. What is almost as terrible is that that figure could, according to the World Health Organisation report, have been cut to 350,000—almost one thirty-fourth—if those children had the same access to health care and nutrition as the modern Irish child does. Now how did the idea of hunger so fail the fact of it, that a vast waste of human life occurred in the midst of our knowledge, our understanding and our resources and yet was not prevented?

Hunger and poverty need to become realities. They became a reality to me when in Somalia I sat beside women whose children were dying—children whose mothers were dying. As a mother I felt the sheer horror of that. But as the Head of State of a country which was once devastated by famine I also felt the terrible and helpless irony that this could actually be happening again. And quite frankly I felt then, and I have never lost, a profound sense of anger and outrage and, indeed, self-accusation that we are all participants in that re-enactment.

And yet having begun like this, I want to make clear that I believe that ideas about hunger and poverty in themselves are both valuable and essential. It is only our capacity to relate the ideas to the reality that is in question. I am particularly aware of their value because this year has seen the start of the one hundred and fiftieth anniversary of the Irish famine. . . .

And yet that past still contains questions and secrets and puzzles which we need to decipher. When we decipher them, we will have gone some way to closing that gap between fact and idea. At the conclusion of a book which I have read with enormous interest, written by the main organiser here—[*The End of Hidden*

Source: Gifts of Speech: Women's Speeches from Around the World, http://gos.sbc.edu/r/robinson.html.

Ireland (Oxford University Press, 1995)–Ed.] by *[New York University Professor–Ed.]* Robert Scally—there is a striking and moving sentence. Describing the emigrants who set out on the desolate journey from Ireland to America he writes: "Peering from the stern rather than the bow of the emigrant ship, that backward glance at the incongruous palms and gaily painted houses along the shore near Skibbereen was not only their last sight of Ireland but the first sight of themselves."

It is the backward glance leading to self-knowledge which in this sentence is so striking. Let me take it here as the pointer to a further question. What if those helpless and defenseless emigrants, who stared out at the shore of Skibbereen, had not been able to take those ships? Terrible as those ships were they were vehicles of an economic migration which, for those fortunate enough to survive the rigours of a voyage that claimed countless thousands of lives, provided escape from something still more terrible. And with the people who escaped went the story. A story of devastation, yes. But also of survival and courage and endurance. . . .

Poverty, as I have said, is the companion of hunger. But so is silence. Breaking that silence allows us to see the past, not only in its suffering, but in its complexity. And allows us to ask such questions as that one I just posed about the coffin ships. Let me return to it again and now in an international, as well as a national, context. Ironically the economic migration on which the Irish embarked in their hundreds of thousands, was not only a painful necessity, it represented a vital freedom, a second chance of survival. But would a people today, enduring the devastation of famine, and needing exactly that refuge from it, to the same places, under the same circumstances, be able to avail of it? The answer must be no. The door which was open for the Irish, through which they entered into the cities and circumstances of a new life—and I am not minimising the hardship of that entry—is now closed.

It is closed, I should say, in the West. It is closed in the very places which have the resources to make the entry through that door sustaining. But in much poorer places—where the cost of opening those doors is huge—they stand open. Why is it that the neighbours who are themselves hard-pressed, who have so little to give, give it more freely than those who have more and will not part with it? Is it simply that they retain that empathy that comes from recent experience? And, if so, we need to ask what it is that makes us lose that human empathy? . . .

We need to reflect carefully on the purpose of commemorating an event such as the famine. The terrible realities of our past hunger present themselves to us as nightmare images. The bailiff. The famine wall. The eviction. The workhouse. And yet how willing are we to negotiate those past images into the facts of present-day hunger? How ready are we to realise that what happened to us may have shaped our national identity, but is not an experience confined to us as a people? How ready are we to see that the bailiff and the workhouse and the coffin ship have equally terrible equivalents in other countries for other peoples at this very moment?

For every lesson our children learn about the Famine Relief of 1847 they should learn an equal one about the debt burden of 1995. For every piece of economic knowledge they gain about the crops exported from Ireland during the famine years, let them come to understand the harsh realities of today's markets, which reinforce the poverty and helplessness of those who already experience hunger. As they learn with pride how we as a people clung to education, the folklore of the hedge schools, how we held on to poetry and story-telling in the midst of dire poverty, let them become acquainted with the declining literacy rates of the most vulnerable countries in our modern world. . . .

I began by noting the gap between the idea of hunger and the reality of it. I recognise the difficulty of finding a language to close that gap. But if we are to account for the sheer horror of the disparity between twelve million children who died in one year and the few hundred thousand it could have been if the world's resources were better distributed, then we will need to send young people into the world who have been prepared, through the challenges of education on this topic, to close that gap between the idea of hunger and the fact of it. We need to help them to face the future with the understanding that famine is not something which can be understood only through history. It must be understood with every fibre of our moral being.

QUESTIONS TO CONSIDER

1. Robinson points out the similarities and differences facing economic refugees in the 1840s and the 1990s. How had things changed over those 150 years? What do those changes suggest about the idea of "progress" in human history?
2. Robinson suggests that history can act as "a backward glance leading to self-knowledge." Can you think of examples of history working in this way? In your own life? On a national or global scale?

13.5 "THE DEEPEST ROOTS OF MOST OF THE PROBLEMS OF CONTEMPORARY CIVILIZATION LIE IN THE SPHERE OF THE HUMAN SPIRIT." VÁCLAV HAVEL, *MAHATMA GANDHI AWARD ACCEPTANCE SPEECH*, 2004 AND NIGEL FARAGE, *ADDRESS TO THE UKIP CONFERENCE*, 2013

These two short speeches illustrate the ways that commonly accepted political preconceptions can obscure patterns and complicate attempts to understand the modern world. Václav Havel (1936–2011) was a dissident and playwright in Czechoslovakia until the sudden collapse of the communist government brought him abruptly to the presidency of that country (and subsequently of the Czech Republic) in 1989. His defiance of an authoritarian regime—while retaining his humanism and sense of humor—earned him admiration and respect across the political spectrum. The document reproduced here is his speech on the occasion of being awarded the 2003 Mahatma Gandhi Peace Prize by the Government of India. As President of the Czech Republic, Havel initiated the process for his country's inclusion in the European Union, which was completed in 2004, the year Havel gave the speech excerpted here.

Whereas Havel is typically associated with the political left, Nigel Farage (1964–) is on the right wing of British politics, a founding member of the UK Independence Party (UKIP). The speech reproduced here, his address to the UKIP in 2013, lays out his basic reasons for opposition to the European Union. In a national referendum in 2016, a majority of the United Kingdom's electorate voted to leave the European Union.

Despite the obvious political differences between these two individuals and the disparate occasions on which they delivered their remarks—one a far-right political party conference and

---

"Vaclav Havel's address on receiving The Mahatma Gandhi Peace Prize," Delhi, India (2004): www.vaclavhavel.cz/showtrans.php?cat=projevy&val=907_aj_projevy.html&typ=HTML; "Nigel Farage's Speech at the UKIP Conference–full text and audio." *The Spectator Online*, September 20, 2013, https://blogs.spectator.co.uk/2013/09/nigel-farages-speech-full-text-and-audio.

the other an awards ceremony honoring a pacifist organizer against British imperialism—the views expressed in these two documents are worth considering side by side, particularly as they relate to the issue of globalization.

EXCERPT 1: VÁCLAV HAVEL SPEECH

We all know how irreversibly our civilization is destroying the climate, how it is derailing the entire planet from the path that has been in the making for hundreds of thousands of years. We know how recklessly it is plundering natural resources and how, in a kind of free fall, it is deepening—without wanting or having to—the enormous social gaps between its different spheres. We know how thoughtlessly it imposes a uniformity on the life of nations and cultures, offering them, quite subtly, the same tempting and, at the same time destructive, way of life.

At the same time, the world is becoming wonderfully interconnected, although this is happening in a strange, and I would even say, highly ambiguous way. Nowadays, for instance, it is quite usual for people to call themselves entrepreneurs, and no one is really interested to know what line of business this involves. The times when people were innkeepers, mine owners, landowners or car manufacturers seem to be slowly receding into the past. Ownership and specific human labour are drifting apart and the biggest owners have almost stopped managing the specific production of tangible goods; instead, they manage billions of dollars' worth of assets that circulate in digital form around the world. At present, the world economy seems to profit by it, at least that is what the measurable factors indicate. Yet in the long-term perspective, this growing gap between the generation of profits and the generation of values cannot be beneficial.

Let me repeat: I am not against human inventions, against telephones, lorries, nuclear power stations, or computers. I am impressed with them all, and as a matter of fact, the less I understand them, the more I am impressed with them. What I'm talking about is the fact that global civilization can't seem to cope responsibly with its own products. Despite the thousands of intelligent books on the subject, nothing changes. We know what dangers confront us, yet though we know,

we continue to exert the least possible effort to confront those challenges or to avoid them.

By now you have certainly realized why I am talking of this. I have been thinking about Mahatma Gandhi, of course, and what he would say were he faced with today's so-called globalization.

I daresay I know, or can imagine, what he would say. He would warn us, as he warned India about the Manchester textile mills or about the railways. Without a shadow of doubt, he would sound the alarm, his voice filled with compelling urgency.

What is perhaps less obvious and worth emphasizing, is the message that Gandhi often repeated to his fellow citizens, as he reminded them of their responsibility for everything that was plaguing them. He certainly did not see colonial rule and the material exploitation of India as an unavoidable catastrophe, something that had come down from the sky like an enormous meteorite. Instead, he saw it as something everyone, including the Indians themselves, allowed to happen, a process in which everybody participated in one way or another and thus helped to perpetuate and develop.

I believe this is exactly how things are today, too. I am convinced that it is absurd for us to rant against a particular company for flooding the world with disgusting fast food thick, mouth-wrenching and constantly disintegrating sandwiches which we continue to eat without qualms. Yes, such food is probably less expensive, but the question is: how high is the price we will all have to pay one day for this cheapness? Big transnational corporations are often branded the main culprits, responsible for all the bad things in the current state of civilization. But isn't blaming them simply a red herring that turns them into substitute culprits whose indictment relieves us of taking responsibility for our own lives? Aren't we ultimately all responsible for the noxious aspects of their activities, because by our behaviour we make such activities possible? Actually, Gandhi's passive resistance alone can successfully confront such activities! Of course, it is also true that such a course of action is anything but easy.

Indeed, how can we complain that car manufacturers the world over are flooding the earth with more and more automobiles, heedless of the deplorable consequences of such an action, including the congestion of most large cities in the world? How can we be upset with companies that have petrol stations behind every tree all around the world, and yet be incapable of imagining life without being able to move around in anything other than a car of our own of the latest model even though we may be the only person sitting in the car for hours as in the vast majority of all other cars, too?

Let me put this in other words, returning to a theme I have been trying to put across for a long time. It is this: that the deepest roots of most of the problems of contemporary civilization lie in the sphere of the human spirit. It is up to us alone, those of us living today, whether we, or those who come after us, will be swallowed up by our own civilization. Humanity's ability to brave the dangers that confront it today hinges entirely on our attitude to eternity, to life and its gifts, to death, and on the degree to which we accept responsibility for ourselves and the world.

So, each and every one of us must look within ourselves, and however insignificant our influence on the general march of events may seem to be, strive to contend with both seen and unseen threats to the world. This, it seems to me, is the eternally fresh message of Mahatma's lifelong work and activity.

EXCERPT 2: NIGEL FARAGE SPEECH

I always believed since 1999 that Britain was a square peg in the round hole I've come to realize something bigger than that. The union is not just contrary to our interests but contrary to the interests of Europe itself. The Commission has hijacked the institutions of Europe by adopting a flag, an anthem, a president, and through their mad euro project *[the creation of a common European currency, the Euro–Ed.]* they have driven tens of millions into poverty. Their climate change obsession has destroyed industry across Europe, and their refusal to listen to the people will lead to the very extreme nationalisms the project was supposed to stop. We are the true Europeans. We want to live and work and breathe and trade in a Europe of democratic nations. But in the last ten or fifteen years this country has seen astonishing change. There has been a phenomenal collapse in national self-confidence. When we signed up to government from the Continent, most Britons didn't know what they were letting themselves in for. Our laws have come from Brussels—and what laws. What directives. What a list of instructions. How this shall be done. How that shall be regulated. Process and compliance and inspection and regulation are taking over from production and leadership and enterprise. . . .

No one knows for sure exactly how much of our law comes from Brussels. Could be 70 or 80 per cent. We have given up our concept of civil rights. Magna Carta, 800th anniversary the year after next, at the general election. Habeas corpus. Rights of inheritance. And not just for the aristocracy, as time went by. Our civil rights grew and kept pace with the times and expanded through the Common Law into the modern world—Europe has supplanted it with their Human Rights charter. . . .

How did they do that to us? They lied to us. They had to. We'd never have agreed to it if they told us the truth and asked for our agreement. And it's created a complete charade in our national life.

QUESTIONS TO CONSIDER

1. Both Havel and Farage raise concerns about some of the interconnectedness of the contemporary world. What are their concerns? How are they similar, and where do they diverge?
2. Both men make a call to action based on appeals to identity. What are the important identities and senses of belonging to which each individual appeals? How do their constructions of identity conform to or deviate from your own understanding of modern political identity and belonging?

13.6 "PEOPLE HAVE NOT BECOME MORE OPEN-MINDED." SRI MULYANI INDRAWATI, *COMMENCEMENT ADDRESS AT THE UNIVERSITY OF VIRGINIA, 2016*

Sri Mulyani Indrawati (1962–) was born in Indonesia, on the island of Sumatra. Trained as an economist, she earned an undergraduate degree from the Universitas Indonesia and her Ph.D. from the University of Illinois at Urbana-Champaign in 1992. Over the course of her career she has worked at international economic organizations like the International Monetary Fund and the World Bank, both of which have their roots in the 1944 Bretton Woods Conference on the future of the global economy, held in the latter stages of World War II. Dr. Indrawati has also served as the Finance Minister of Indonesia.

The following excerpts are from an address delivered by Dr. Indrawati to students receiving their degrees from the School of Leadership and Public Policy at the University of Virginia commencement in May 2016.

Given the current environment, we at the World Bank worry a lot about the global economy, and how low commodity prices and slow trade are affecting the poor. How can we promote equality for girls and women to give everyone a chance to fulfill their potential? How can we prevent conflict and ease the lives of refugees? And how can we generate economic growth while stopping climate change? . . .

One thing you should always remember is that the most important word in "public policy" is "public." In other words, it is the people you will affect through your work and the choices you make. . . .

When I graduated, public policy was all about government, but today you will enter a world full of many more options. You can work for NGOs, for civil society organizations, for the media. Or you can join the private sector or development institutions like ours.

But it is important to keep in mind that whatever you do as a public policymaker, it is going to affect the wellbeing of many people.

But who is the public? And what are the issues they care about?

Every generation has policy issues based on their concerns and the context they live in. My generation, the so-called Generation X, was very concerned about the possibility of war against the backdrop of a nuclear arms race. Economically, we dealt with stagnation and inflation, causing the scarcity of goods and high unemployment. Globalization was still in its very early stages. China only started to develop and Ethiopia experienced frequent famines. Telecommunication was limited and very expensive. —I remember when I did my PhD in Illinois, I was very homesick. I used more than half of my stipend, so I could call my family in Indonesia only once a month. . . .

But China is now the second largest economy in the world and Ethiopia is one of the fastest growing in Africa. You have to handle abundance and figure out how to create meaningful livelihoods in a post-industrial world, where technology creates unlimited

Source: Sri Mulyani Indrawati, Commencement Address at the University of Virginia, 2016, http://www.worldbank.org/en/news/speech/2016/05/21/commencement-speech-uva-world-bank-managing-director-coo-sri-mulyani-indrawati.

possibilities and communication is fast, cheap or even for free.

You are the first generation to feel the impact of climate change and your security concerns are different from ours. They are asymmetrical, unpredictable, and a lot more complex. You face small violent groups that are creating havoc and cause human suffering and defy the normal definition of state.

But regardless of whether you are generation X, Y, or Z: people—or the public—across generations want the same things: they want prosperity and dignity, they want equality of opportunity, and they want justice and security.

The only thing that changes is their context.

So, what is different for your generation?

In this multi-polar world, we are all connected. Globalization has made the world a lot smaller. In this global village, people, businesses, capital, technology, information and knowledge are spreading regardless of time zones and boundaries.

Today, all of us have access to instant information from a smartphone. With data practically at everyone's fingertip. No country is no longer [sic] truly isolated—no matter how much some governments want to insulate themselves from the global public.

In fact, you are the generation that is living through the democratization of knowledge.

But the irony is that with more access to more information than ever, people have not become more open-minded. Your generation's challenge is not the availability and accessibility of information, but the choices you make when you seek it out. It has become a lot easier to confirm one's own assumptions and stereotypes by blending out the other side. It now takes more effort to reach across the lines of division and understand the people one doesn't agree with.

This plays into the hands of populists who shout louder, who see all problems as black and white, who exploit fears and offer magic solutions to complex issues. This is making your job as policymakers so much more challenging.

For you as future policy makers and future leaders this means that your "public" is more impatient and people get angry quickly, because expectations are high, and they want delivery as fast as an instant message.

So, what does it take to become a good policy maker?

First, technical competence is non-negotiable for you to take informed decisions. Together with good judgment, it helps you understand the trade-off, the merit and demerit of your decisions. But, most importantly, it allows you to identify winners and losers and how to address their issues.

Even if you are convinced of the quality of your policy, not everyone will benefit immediately. This is true for every country whether rich, middle-income or low-income. It affects people's lives in very real ways.

And just because your policy makes sense and the numbers add up, it doesn't mean it works. In fact, you will see that rarely in life you can choose between the best and the second-best option. Sometimes even the third best option is out of reach.

When I was a finance minister, Indonesia like many other countries was affected by the global financial crisis. Commodity prices dropped, and as an oil producer and open economy, we were close to economic collapse. There were corrupt officials and powerful interest groups who benefited from the status quo and tried to undermine every effort to reform our country and rebuild confidence.

Not every problem may have this proportion, but when crisis stares you in the face, the least bad option may be all you have. Because reality is actually very different from what you find in text books. It is full of people who have emotions, expectations, attitudes and competing interests. . . .

QUESTIONS TO CONSIDER

1. According to Dr. Indrawati, what are the major global realities that distinguish 2016 from the era when she was in graduate school three decades earlier?
2. What characteristics distinguish this assessment of the challenges of the contemporary world from those provided in the speeches of Václav Havel and Nigel Farage, excerpted in Source 13.5? Is there any common ground among the three sources?

CREDITS

CHAPTER 1

1.1 Pages 340–342 from Nehemiah Levtzion & J. F. P. Hopkins, *Corpus of Early Arabic Sources for West African History*. © Nehemiah Levtzion and J. F. P. Hopkins 1981, published by Cambridge University Press.

1.3 George Vernadsky, ed. *A Source Book for Russian History from Early Times to 1917, Vol. 1, Early Times to the Late 17th Century*. New Haven and London: Yale University Press, 1972. pp. 76–77. Copyright © Yale University Press. Reprinted with permission.

1.4 Pages 269–273 from Nehemiah Levtzion & J. F. P. Hopkins, *Corpus of Early Arabic Sources for West African History*. © Nehemiah Levtzion and J. F. P. Hopkins 1981, published by Cambridge University Press.

CHAPTER 2

2.2 Hernán Cortés, *Letters from Mexico*. Translated, edited and with new introduction by Anthony Pagden; With an Introductory essay by J. H. Elliott (Yale University Press, 1986): 48, 57–61. Copyright © Yale University Press. Reprinted with permission.

2.4 Pages 185–194 from James Lockhart, Enrique Otte (eds), *Letters and People of the Spanish Indies – Sixteenth Century*. © Cambridge University Press 1976.

2.6 Reprinted with permission of M. E. Sharpe, from *Japan: A Documentary History: The Dawn of History to the Late Tokugawa Period*. Edited by David J. Lu (Armonk, New York: M. E. Sharpe, 1997); permission conveyed through Copyright Clearance Center, Inc.

CHAPTER 3

3.1 Reprinted with permission of Hackett Publishing Company, Inc. All rights reserved.

3.3 Pages 231–238 from "The Twelve Articles of the Upper Swabian Peasants" in Michael G. Baylor, *The Radical Reformation*. © Cambridge University Press 1991.

3.4 Reprinted with permission of Hackett Publishing Company, Inc. All rights reserved.

3.5 Reprinted, with permission, from *The Baburnama: Memoirs of Babur, Prince and Emperor*, trans. Wheeler M. Thackston, pp. 320–30, 422–25. Copyright 1996, Freer Gallery of Art and Arthur M. Sackler Gallery, Smithsonian Institution.

3.6 Reprinted with permission of Columbia University Press, from *Sources of the Chinese Tradition, Vol. 2*. Second Edition. Compiled by W. T. de Bary and R. Lufrano. New York: Columbia University Press, 2000; permission conveyed through Copyright Clearance Center, Inc.

CHAPTER 4

4.1 Reprinted by permission of Eland Publishing Ltd. Translation and commentary © Robert Dankoff & Sooyong Kim.

4.3 Selections from *Natural and Moral History of the Indies*, José de Acosta; Jane E. Mangan, Ed., pp. 176–178, 182–183. Copyright, 2002, Duke University Press. All rights reserved. Republished by permission of the copyright holder. www.dukeupress.edu.

CHAPTER 5

5.3 Reprinted with permission of Columbia University Press, from *Sources of the Chinese Tradition,*

Vol. 2. Second Edition. Compiled by W. T. de Bary and R. Lufrano. New York: Columbia University Press, 2000; permission conveyed through Copyright Clearance Center, Inc.

5.5 Reprinted with permission of University of Oklahoma Press, from Jorge Juan and Antonio Ulloa, *Discourse and Political Reflections on the Kingdom of Peru.* Edited by John J. TePaske. University of Oklahoma Press, 1978; permission conveyed through Copyright Clearance Center, Inc.

CHAPTER 6

6.7 From Darline Gay Levy, Harriet Branson Applewhite, and Mary Durham Johnson, eds., *Women in Revolutionary Paris, 1789–1795* (Urbana, University of Illinois Press, 1980), pp. 87–96. © 1979 by the Board of Trustees of the University of Illinois. Reprinted with permission.

CHAPTER 8

8.3 Republished with permission of Indiana University Press, from Doris Beik et al. *Flora Tristan: Utopian Feminist,* (Indiana University Press, Bloomington 1993): 104–123; permission conveyed through Copyright Clearance Center, Inc.

8.4 Reprinted with permission of M. E. Sharpe, from *Japan: A Documentary History: The Dawn of History to the Late Tokugawa Period.* Edited by David J. Lu (Armonk, New York: M. E. Sharpe, 1997); permission conveyed through Copyright Clearance Center, Inc.

8.5 Reprinted with permission of Columbia University Press, from *Sources of the Chinese Tradition, Vol. 2.* Second Edition. Compiled by W. T. de Bary and R. Lufrano. New York: Columbia University Press, 2000; permission conveyed through Copyright Clearance Center, Inc.

8.6 Reprinted with permission of University of California Press, from *Land Without Ghosts: Chinese Impressions of America from the Mid-Nineteenth Century to the Present.* Trans. and ed. by R. David Arkush and Leo O. Lee. Berkeley: University of California Press, 1989; permission conveyed through Copyright Clearance Center, Inc.

CHAPTER 9

9.2 Fredrich Fabri, *Does Germany Need Colonies?,* Translated, edited and introduced by E. C. M. Bruening and M. E. Chamberlain. Lewiston: Edwin Mellen Press, 1998. Reprinted with permission of Edwin Mellen Press. All rights reserved.

9.3 Reprinted with permission of M. E. Sharpe, from *Japan: A Documentary History: The Dawn of History to the Late Tokugawa Period.* Edited by David J. Lu (Armonk, New York: M. E. Sharpe, 1997); permission conveyed through Copyright Clearance Center, Inc.

CHAPTER 10

10.2 © Mark Bostridge and Rebecca Williams, literary executors for the Vera Brittain Estate 1970.

CHAPTER 11

11.1 *The Speeches of Adolf Hitler, April 1922–August 1939.* Trans. and ed. By Norman H. Baynes. (Oxford: Oxford University Press, 1942). Copyright © 1942. Published under the auspices of The Royal Institute of International Affairs. Reproduced with permission of the Licensor through PLSclear.

11.5 Primo Levi with Leonardo De Benedetti. *Auschwitz Report.* Translation by Judith Woolf. pp. 71–77. Reprinted with permission of Verso Book UK.

11.6 Reprinted from *The Political Legacy of Aung San, Revised Edition,* edited by Josef Silverstein. Copyright © 1993 by Cornell University. Used by permission of the publisher, Cornell University Press.

11.7 Ting Ling, "Thoughts on March 8." *New Left Review,* no. 92, July–August 1975. Reprinted with permission of New Left Review.

CHAPTER 12

12.1 Reproduced with permission of Curtis Brown, London, on behalf of The Estate of Winston S. Churchill. © The Estate of Winston S. Churchill.

12.7 From Indira Gandhi, *Selected Speeches of Indira Gandhi: January 1966–August 1969,* (New Delhi: Publications Division, Ministry of Information and Broadcasting, Govt. of India, 1984), pp. 312–313; Copyright © Publications Division, Ministry of Information and Broadcasting, Govt. of India, 1984.

CHAPTER 13

13.5 Reprinted with permission of Václav Havel's estate.